Systems
Management

Systems Management

J. Stanley Baumgartner

The Bureau of National Affairs, Inc.
Washington, D.C.

Library of Congress Cataloging in Publication Data
Systems management.
   1. Industrial project management—Addresses,
essays, lectures. 2. United States—Armed forces—
Procurement—Addresses, essays, lectures.
I. Baumgartner, John Stanley.
HD69.P75S96   658.4'04   79-11634
ISBN 0-87179-297-4

International Standard Book Number: O-87179-297-4
Printed in the United States of America

For S. S. and R.
And M., the ultimate systems manager

Foreword

This book is about jobs that are too tough, too complex for ordinary management approaches. It is about getting results. It concerns the who and how in accomplishing difficult tasks that have well-defined time and cost limitations.

"I defy anyone to write a book on how to manage one of these things!" the director of a well-known, project-oriented organization has said. He may have been correct about any one person writing this kind of book. After all, who has the experience, at multiple levels, in multidisciplines, in a broad spectrum of government and industrial programs, to write a "how to" volume?

The problem though with learning by experience is that it is so costly, in terms of both project results and career effect. Project costs range from several thousand dollars to more than a million dollars *per day*. With costs like these, what major organization can afford *not* to have effective people in systems management, people who have the necessary education and experience? "Good management is cheap," observes one senior executive, "because mismanagement costs a helluva lot more." As regards the individual, the education of a student of management is not complete without knowledge of the problems, the means of approaching them, and the environment of systems or project environment. Nor will he or she be as well prepared for top management responsibilities without this background.

This book is an assembly of material presented for the first time as well as selected recent articles, with the objective that tough lessons learned in the past may not have to be relearned through costly experience. Much of the wisdom and insight gained in systems management appear fleetingly in current periodicals. With the next issue these flashes of truth are often then lost from view. The writings presented here have been chosen from more than a thousand on the basis of their significance, interest, staying power, and timeliness. Most have been written within the past several years. The original material includes discussions with recognized experts in diverse fields of systems management.

Many of the selections are defense oriented, because many problems and their solutions are first encountered on the services' programs, and because of the number and magnitude of defense systems. Nondefense systems, however, often are no less challenging. The scope of nondefense projects covered here includes the Apollo program, an oil recovery project, Kelly Johnson's Skunk Works, facilities design and development, unmanned space programs, and the annual automobile line changeover. The achievements in meeting reliability requirements and technical and organizational challenges attest to the skill with which these nondefense program managers (PMs) have met their objectives.

The terms "system management," "project management," and "program management" as used in this book are generally interchangeable. "System management" may connote greater emphasis on systems engineering, and programs are sometimes considered to be of greater magnitude than projects. But in the writings presented here the terms are in most cases used interchangeably.

Certain themes recur throughout the 70 selections, regardless of the type of system produced. Clear focus on objectives is basic to all successful system managers. Particularly important is a keen grasp of the balance among technical, cost, and schedule parameters, and trade-offs between technical performance factors. Getting good people and using them effectively are key factors. Good communication is a necessity.

Systems management is a generalist's skill. It is not surprising that systems management is viewed in industry and in defense as valuable experience in selecting generalists, whether general managers or general officers. It requires a scope of experience, knowledge, judgment, and perspective that sets the PM apart, just as a band or orchestra director's skills are distinct from those of a versatile instrumentalist. Perhaps the key attribute of the system manager is his ability to put specific parts in perspective, the tangibles and intangibles, relative to the overall system or program.

Systems management is a dynamic and growing field. The reason is, simply, that it gets results. It addresses the complex job, and how to get these jobs done effectively and efficiently. The need for people who can accomplish these difficult tasks and be comfortable operating on diagonal, horizontal, and vertical lines is therefore growing. In a world of increasingly complex problems, systems management gets results that other forms of management cannot achieve. Who can imagine successful achievement of the Apollo program, for instance, on the basis of business as usual? Curiously, the approach by most government agencies responsible for meeting the increasingly difficult challenges of social programs in public administration has been one of more intense application of the hierarchical organization and traditional plans and controls. The resulting nonresponsiveness to problems, the inertia, and the vast expenditures incurred are not surprising. With various levels of government costing about 40 percent of the gross national product, here is a ripe field for the application of systems management.

Many of the writings presented here have been condensed, but it is believed that they retain the thrust and language of the original articles. In most of the selections the author's title or position is given as of the time the article was published.

Section 1, The Systems Management Task, provides the rationale for project management, the nature of the PM's task, and the kind of results sought and achieved. This provides an essential grasp of the system manager's challenge and why his job differs from that of other managers. The viewpoints include those of higher levels, the PM himself, and members of the program office.

A highlight of the book is a discussion with the Director of the Apollo Program, the most remarkable achievement in a remarkable century. The guts required of a system manager comes through in this discussion with Gen. Sam Phillips. Apollo 6, an unmanned flight, had several major problems, and the next one was scheduled to be the first manned flight out to the lunar distance. The risk to life was obvious. But so was the program objective: land a man on the moon and bring him safely back before the end of the 1960s. Here was a classic case of technical risks versus risk to the other program objectives. No program has had higher visibility. Gen. Phillips made the decision: go, on schedule, with Apollo 8, knowing that probably his career and reputation were on the line. Few individuals outside NASA and Apollo are aware of this and other crises requiring the high moral courage displayed by the Apollo program director.

Section 2 is a look at the systems manager and how he goes about his task. It is interesting to note the similarity in management patterns among PMs in defense, defense industry, and nondefense endeavors.

Section 3 concerns the project organization, the structure, people, and administrative practices that form the core of the system management team. Building this team is probably the PM's most important task.

The basis for most programs is a contract, although the development of proprietary products is one type of exception. Contracting, discussed in Section 4, is a distinct and complex field. The contributors, and William W. Thybony particularly, cover a great deal of the scope of contracting and contracts administration.

Throughout the text are writings that address more than one aspect of systems management. Thus the divisions between Sections 5, 6, and 7 on system plans and controls may reflect differences in emphasis rather than differences in subject matter, since results sought and resources available are so closely interwoven. Actual versus planned costs, for example, is not a particularly significant measure compared to progress for the money spent.

Section 5 relates to overall system planning, while Section 6 pertains to time management, and Section 7 concerns cost and fiscal control. Section 8 is on technical performance management, developing the solution to a requirement.

Industry's involvement is presented in Section 9. This section includes a comparison of commercial versus defense systems management in industry and an inside look at Lockheed's Skunk Works. It also gives perspective on industrial involvement in the oft-maligned military-industrial complex.

Section 10 is a look at higher levels' guidance and expectations, including those of Congress and the Joint Logistics Commanders. It concludes with the role of the PM as an advocate and offers suggestions for him in his frequent encounters with the "outside" environment.

Finally, the purpose of the Glossary is to decipher the jargon used in defense systems acquisition. It may be a consolation to readers not involved in these systems to know that those who are familiar with them occasionally have to decipher the jargon too.

Contents

Section 1—

THE SYSTEMS MANAGEMENT TASK

1

Why Project Management?*

J. S. Baumgartner

As recently as 21 years ago, project management in defense systems acquisition was almost non-existent. Except for a rare, huge undertaking like WW II's Manhattan Project, there was no need for a project manager or a project organization. Aircraft, ships, and tanks were developed and produced as part of the normal, ongoing function of factories, shipyards, and arsenals. A government contracting officer was the key individual in DOD-industry relations.

Even as late as two years ago a crusty 2-star combat commander, serving on a promotion board, said, "Project management seems to be in vogue now, but like other concepts with temporary appeal, it will be superseded by some other management concept."

The number of projects in each of the services argues otherwise. At the present time the Army has 31 project managers, the Navy 57, and the Air Force 56 system program directors. In addition there are many smaller projects where at least one individual is fully dedicated to achieving his project's objectives. Clearly the services believe there are advantages to be gained by "projectizing"—establishing a project manager (PM) and project organization and holding the PM accountable for achieving the required technical, cost, and schedule results.

However, the reasons for adopting project management (by whatever name—program/system/project management) are not universally understood, particularly in view of widely publicized cost overruns incurred on Defense programs in the past. If project management is so good what does it do that wasn't being done

*National Defense, September-October 1975, pp. 112–115.

before? What are the disadvantages, and how does defense project management compare with this form of enterprise in other areas of endeavor?

Project management in defense systems acquisition is like task force command in an operational mission, and these special forms of organization are adopted for the same reason—some tasks are just too difficult to accomplish in a routine way. That is why a team of military and civilian managers and engineers began to assemble in a schoolhouse in Inglewood, California in mid-1954. Their chief, then-Brig. Gen. Bernard A. Schriever, had the responsibility for developing the free world's first ICBM, an immensely complex technical task. And he was expected to do this in half the dozen years' time normally required to develop an operational system. Atlas was the beginning of modern project management, and the success achieved has had a major influence on management in defense and industry.

The factors that determine whether projectizing is appropriate are similar to those for a task force:

- Stringent time, cost, and technical performance requirements exist.
- The undertaking is of greater complexity or scope than normal.
- Significant contribution is required by two or more functional organizations.
- The rewards of success or penalties for failure are particularly high.

There are three basic goals in every defense project. The foremost is technical performance (as distinct from management performance). The technical expertise of many organizations must be brought together as perfectly as the hardware they are charged with designing and developing. The chances of system success are greatly enhanced when these contributing teams are directed by an individual who is held accountable for results, particularly in view of the high level of sophistication of modern systems.

The second reason for project management is the value of time. This relates not only to whether or not a system is available for operational readiness. It relates also to costs. Inflation obviously increases costs according to project duration. Less obvious is the fact that stretching out the development and production of a system usually reduces its potential operational life.

Concurrency, now frowned upon, was a "good" word in times of crash scheduling such as on Atlas and Polaris. There may again come a situation like that following the launching of Sputnik I in

October 1957 when the requirement was, "Never mind the cost—get it out the door!" No other form of management is so responsive to change and the value of time as project management.

The third basic reason for project management is lower system acquisition costs. There is no question as to functional organizations' greater efficiency in performing normal tasks, compared with project organizations. But in dealing with new and different requirements, functional organizations have several weaknesses, all resulting in cost growth so that emphasis on the project is lost.

Functional organizations often are uncooperative. Too many decisions involving more than one functional organization have to be made at the top, slowing down or stopping decision making. The purpose of a project—the solution to a particular operational requirement—may become distorted, so the system may only partially meet its intended purpose.

It should be noted here, though, that occasionally in the past operational "requirements" have been "nice-to-have" capabilities —for which a tremendous premium sometimes has been paid.

The history of project management since the beginning of Atlas has hardly been one of unbroken successes, as any casual reader of events knows. Many of the control, performance, and organizational problems existed before adoption of the project concept, of course, but were never clearly defined because no one in functional organizations was specifically responsible for getting results. These problems and their cost impact "surfaced" with the designation of a focal point charged with meeting cost, schedule, and performance goals.

The cost elements of a B-29 system, for example, were fragmented among various government agencies and industrial organizations. True system costs were not available. Costs clearly are lower when responsibility is centralized; nevertheless, greater visibility as to costs renders projects an inviting target for critics.

The foremost problem in the late 1950's and early 1960's was how to make "matrix management" work, particularly in defense contractor organizations. As a result of the successes of Atlas and Polaris, the services "desired" that their industrial counterparts establish project offices. Naturally, they did.

But "fully projectizing," as on the Manhattan project and the pyramids where the PM has full line authority over project personnel, is generally too expensive for the benefits obtained. Project personnel therefore generally remain assigned to their parent organizations but are on temporary duty to a project. The result is a matrix where project organizations ("horizontal") are superimposed on vertical functional organizations.

The problem then confronting an engineer, for example, is "Who is my boss—my engineering manager or the project manager?" Not surprisingly, many functional managers in the early 1960's looked upon systems or project management as a threat.

Several years' experience in developing working relationships was required before these growing pains began to subside. An Air Force Institute of Technology study documents the strides made in the aerospace industry between 1965 and 1970: there were much greater managerial control and visibility and lower program costs, while complexity of internal operations and inconsistency in application of company policy were markedly reduced. The same study found that 28 per cent of the companies surveyed showed higher profit margins from projectizing, while none reported lower profit ("Perceptions on the Usefulness of Project Management," by Arnold A. Tesch, unpublished master's thesis, Air Force Institute of Technology, September 1970, pp. 55–57).

The pioneering pangs of the aerospace industry and the results obtained were instrumental in causing adoption of project management throughout the defense industry. Paralleling this development has been increasing use of project management (by whatever name: product management, new ventures management, program development) in commercial and industrial use.

The job of the project manager is one of the most complex, demanding, and rewarding tasks in government or industry. A new kind of leader—well-rounded, skilled in many facets, and highly dedicated to achieving specific future results—is required to cope with the very difficult problems that arise during the course of a project (there wouldn't be a need to projectize if the problems were easy ones).

A key difficulty in the past has been the lack of a pool of officers and civilians with the necessary project management skills. As in operational fields, there is no substitute for experience and knowledge. Recognizing the magnitude of resources entrusted to project managers, each of the services has therefore established a career field to develop individuals with the broad skills required. The Defense Systems Management School, established at Fort Belvoir, Va. in 1971, provides an educational background in project management for individuals in this career field.

Another major problem has been to develop plans and controls that provide adequate visibility. The usual time-phased budget, with corresponding actual expenditures, merely tells the PM whether he is spending money as fast as planned. What he needs to know is whether, particularly during development, he is getting adequate progress or value for the money spent.

Only within the past few years have techniques been developed for giving the project manager this vital information. Tools are now available whereby he can determine, with considerable accuracy and to as low a level as he needs, cost status, trends, and the cost impact of problem areas.

Related to this is a fundamental problem in work definition formerly prevalent and still a source of headaches—the work breakdown structure. The "what" of a project often has been confused by intermingling the "who"—individuals and organizations responsible for particular work. Where this occurs there invariably is a reduction in cost visibility.

Most of these problem areas have been or are being resolved. The greatest problem at this time, however, is outside the control of the project manager—inflation, which has been running almost twice the average consumer rate.

Costs initially were not a major reason for adopting project management, as evidenced by early widespread use of cost-type contracts in which all or most of the cost risk is borne by the government. But the importance of costs has risen greatly in recent years to the point that costs are now equated to technical performance in importance.

Recognizing that stories of cost overruns have been sensationalized, whereas underruns and superbly managed programs, such as the Marines' LVTP-7 landing vehicle, have received little or no recognition, it is nevertheless fair to ask how project management in defense stacks up against project management in other spheres of activity. Civil agency projects provide one comparison.

Little attention has been given to civil agency programs until recently. On February 25th of this year the Government Accounting Office released a report on Federal construction projects. Cost overruns, averaging a 75 per cent increase for the 269 projects reviewed, total a whopping $57 billion. Independent estimates indicate the cost overrun on Washington's Metro rapid transit system alone will be twice the highly publicized overrun of the C-5A cargo aircraft.

The reasons for these overruns sound like a repeat of DOD's earlier experience: engineering changes, changes in estimate calculations, and increases in size. Interestingly, Federal agencies attributed only 3.5 per cent of their cost increases to inflation, although GAO believes inflation must have been a much more important factor. Inflation accounts for all but a small portion of the $17 billion, 12 per cent cost growth on the 49 largest defense programs, according to a February 5th GAO report.

There is no satisfaction of course in these results for defense-related individuals, whose taxes pay for civil as well as for military projects. The report provides a rough comparison, however, on how DOD projects are being managed.

Another comparison is industry's batting average in developing commercial and industrial products versus the defense average. In terms of the cost to produce successfully deployed products (i.e., operational defense products compared with profitable industrial/ commercial products), the defense batting average is about four times as good (.800 vs. .200) in spite of generally greater sophistication of defense items and the fact the defense planner's crystal ball may require a system having a 20- to 30-year useful life (like the B-52 or F-4 aircraft) versus only a few years' life average for non-defense products. These industrial figures are based on an American Management Association report of 200 large, well-managed companies. In DOD, during a 25-year period from 1943 to 1968, less than 20 percent of the RDT&E budget went into canceled programs such as MOL and the B-70. And such subsystems as the Navajo missile's guidance and control and propulsion were subsequently used on other programs.

The best yardstick of achievement of defense programs, however, is a comparison of each program's status versus the plan for that particular project. And while past and on-going efforts to improve project management show great improvement in meeting cost goals particularly, "target cost," rather than something between target and ceiling, is the goal sought on each major program.

In a little over two decades, project management has grown into an accepted, effective, and efficient way to bring defense systems into being and into operational use. Along the way, new management techniques have been tried; some have been rejected (like PERT-cost), and others have been refined, until project management is emerging as a rapidly maturing field of management. Many of the techniques now in general use were developed on defense programs.

The outlook for project management in defense is probably one of no great changes, either in application or in principles and techniques. There will, of course, be refinements in techniques and more attention to specific areas, such as subcontracts management and overhead costs. There will continue to be overruns, however, if for no other reason than that no one has 20–20 foresight in advancing into systems development.

The greatest change probably will derive from defense rather than concern it directly, as civil agencies at Federal, state and local levels adopt techniques developed in DOD to their major programs.

The taxpayer has a right to expect a full measure of results for his tax dollar. Project management gets results.

2

Eight Basic Tasks for Successful Program Management*

Grant L. Hansen

What is the process of successful program management? What does one do to "get the job done right?" The following is my own eight-point formula for success in program management. Every program that I have ever seen in real trouble has failed to accomplish one or more of these eight basic tasks.

Formula for Successful Program Management

Task 1—Establish and maintain a teamwork relationship of mutual trust and confidence between government and contractor program management.

Many times there is more of an adversary relationship. Some contractual arrangements have fostered a distant relationship. Sometimes personalities clash. I sincerely believe that a good team relationship is extremely important to program success. Industry needs government management and vice versa. Mutual trust and confidence may be difficult to develop, but if each recognizes and respects the role of the other, it is a major step toward working effectively together. There must be a lot of emphasis on *what* is right rather than *who* is right. Relationships must be built at various levels and in various specialties. Good teamwork at the top only will not be sufficient. Neither the government people nor the industry peo-

*Extract from *Manage,* National Management Association, March-April 1974, pp. 14, 15.

ple can be successful if the other fails, or look good if the other looks bad. When buyer and seller publicly point fingers at each other, both lose.

Task 2—*Really* understand the program objectives.

To properly make trade-offs, the requirements and program objectives must be considered as possible variables to trade with other program elements. To be properly analyzed for trades, they must be thoroughly understood. Contractors should understand government program objectives and government managers should understand contractor objectives for the program. Each stated user requirement should be tested to know how much of a hard point it is for the program. In the past, many service program managers have considered the operational capability requirements to be sacred and uncontestable, regardless of difficulty or cost. While the SPO Director cannot change the requirements or objectives of the program unilaterally, it is his primary responsibility to identify and recommend proper revisions and attempt to sell them to the proper authorities.

Program objectives are *really* fundamental. How can you tell if you're on course if you don't know where you're going? How can you tell if you're finished if you don't really understand what you're trying to do?

Task 3—Have program plans which are well prepared and highly visible.

This rule sounds like motherhood, but is too often not accomplished. Inadequate planning can result in costly inefficiencies. Visibility of plans is vital. It is not enough that certain people have good plans in their heads. Master plans and detailed plans must be displayed in such a way that all contributors can mesh-in properly. Visible charting of plans constitutes a map by which all concerned can know how they are expected to meet intermediate and final objectives.

Task 4—Get accurate and timely information concerning actual progress on the planned work.

This is another motherhood-sounding rule that has been very badly violated. Some years ago, former Army Secretary Frank Pace, then Chairman of the Board of General Dynamics, told me that the financial disaster on the Convair 880–990 program was due in significant part to the lack of proper status information available to senior management.

A friend of mine joined a shipyard and quickly identified tens of millions of additional cost to complete which hadn't previously surfaced to management. How did he do it? Simply by going into the yard to look at the state of completion instead of merely accepting the status claimed in the production report.

How can one get accurate and timely information on actual progress? It isn't easy. Seeing for yourself in the shop is one good way. Knowing who *really* knows and talking with him is another way. Spot checks and audits may be needed. Remember that a report at 95 percent completion may be a best guess, but it doesn't assure that 5 percent more effort will achieve completion. A fatigue life objective isn't necessarily half met when half the test hours have been successfully run.

Getting timely and good information is one of the most difficult things for a program manager to do. It is a fertile area for his ingenuity and personal skill. Much judgment is involved and there is never enough time available to do the thorough job one would like to be able to do. When I was in Washington I liked a sign in the office of my Navy counterpart, Secretary Frosch, which said, "Don't brief me—tell me what the briefing says."

Task 5—Promptly note and evaluate all deviations between plans and actuals.

With visible plans and good actuals, it becomes a simple matter to display these together and note deviations. Understanding the cause of the deviation and its probable effects is more difficult. There is a tendency to let the deviation continue a little longer to determine its trend. This can be very deadly. Strive to detect and understand, in minimum time, any deviation between the plan and what really happens. There is a special version of Murphy's law that says if you think the problem will go away without your doing anything, you've probably just discovered tomorrow's headlines.

Task 6—Determine and implement corrective action based upon trade-off judgments.

Proper corrective action may be simply to adjust the plan to agree with the way things are going, but most likely it is to shift resources, change emphasis, or alter objectives. Because the program is not proceeding as expected, some of the planning "facts" were probably wrong. These same "facts" or assumptions were used in making the original balance of program factors. As better data becomes available, a new analysis should be made of the balance of cost, schedule, performance, and other relevant factors to determine if objectives and/or plans should be changed.

Task 7—Follow up to ensure that the corrective actions selected are producing the desired corrections.

This seems obvious enough, but is frequently not done in a timely manner or at all. Even a President of the United States soon finds out that his ordering it may not make it so according to his visualization. The process of plan, measure, compare, correct and evaluate must be constantly reiterated until the program objectives are met. Every planned program solution should be checklisted to include a verification that it succeeded in solving the problem.

Task 8—Make friends, not enemies, for the program.

Sooner or later, every program gets into some trouble, despite our best efforts to prevent any. Friends help, or at least look the other way. Enemies magnify every problem. Friends are needed among competitors, in the administration and Congress, in the press, in the universities and any place else you can think of. How to make friends properly is beyond the scope of this article. However, the following are almost sure bets to make nonfriends:

- Blame others for your shortcomings.
- Make no contact until you are in deep, desperate trouble.
- Build walls around your program and post them with "no trespassing" signs.
- Ignore advice.
- Don't bother to answer the mail.
- Fail to recognize contributions and achievements.
- Brag a lot.

I believe so strongly in the fundamental importance of these eight basic tasks of program management that I repeat them now for emphasis:

1. Establish and maintain a teamwork relationship of mutual trust and confidence between government and contractor program management.

2. *Really* understand the program objectives.

3. Have program plans which are well prepared and highly visible.

4. Get accurate and timely information concerning actual progress on the planned work.

5. Promptly note and evaluate all deviations between plans and actuals.

6. Determine and implement corrective action based upon tradeoff judgments.

7. Follow up to ensure that the corrective actions selected are producing the desired corrections.

8. Make friends, not enemies, for the program. A defense system or industry program office demands outstanding management talent and dedication.

3

A Discussion With the Apollo Program Director, General Sam Phillips

J. S. Baumgartner

> I believe this nation should commit itself to achieving the goal, before this decade is out, of landing a man on the moon and returning him safely to earth. No single space project in this period will be more impressive to mankind, or more important for the long range exploration of space; and none will be so difficult or expensive to accomplish.

President Kennedy spoke these words in May 1961.

On July 20, 1969, Astronaut Neil Armstrong stepped from the Apollo lunar excursion module onto the surface of the moon.

The individual who held the responsibility for translating the goal into reality was Gen. Samuel C. Phillips, Director of the Apollo Program. Gen. Phillips, who previously had headed the Air Force's Minuteman program, was on loan to NASA for six years for this purpose.

My Job Was, Simply, to Land a Man on the Moon . . . and Bring Him Back

Gen. Phillips, how did you organize the Apollo effort?

When I joined NASA late in 1963, I found that the Apollo program had been organized on a projectized, hardware basis;

different groups were responsible for the LEM (lunar excursion module), the Command and Service Module, Saturn S-1B engine, and so forth. This introduced a number of problems, it seemed to me, particularly in view of the wide geographical spread of Apollo activities. So I changed the organization to a functional basis with five elements: system engineering, checkout and test, operations, reliability and quality assurance, and program control. The Apollo Program Office in Washington and the Apollo office at each center were organized with the same five functional elements. Contractors' organizations were also organized in this way.

My job was, simply, to land a man on the moon with necessary equipment and bring him back, within a certain time.

Would you have organized this way if you did not have the problem of geographical spread?

Yes, because it gives continuity throughout a major program like Apollo. We had found on Minuteman that this works very well on large development programs.

What was the relation between the Apollo Program Office and NASA's functional organization?

Apollo was one of several major program offices reporting to the Office of Manned Space Flight, headed by Dr. George Mueller, my boss, who in turn reported to the NASA Administrator and Associate Administrator. The Gemini and Mercury programs, and other manned programs, also reported to George Mueller; and so did three NASA centers: the Manned Spacecraft Center in Houston, the Marshall Space Flight Center in Huntsville, Alabama, and the Kennedy Space Center at Cape Kennedy. Each center has regular on-going functional directorates.

How many people were involved in the program at its largest point?

Three hundred thousand or more. Our own office at NASA headquarters was relatively small, however.

How many people were in your headquarters office?

One hundred twenty-one.

That's amazingly small!

Yes; I wanted a small organization but one in which everyone was very capable. We made maximum use of delegation; we delegated authority, responsibility, and a word we use too rarely, *accountability.* In turn, the Apollo program managers did pretty much the same thing.

How do you get loyalty and dedication to a program so that these qualities permeate the whole 300,000-man organization?

Two things are particularly important: you have to have a people-to-people basis—organizations have to work closely together, just as the hardware they produce must work exactly together. And there has to be a framework of systems or procedures or practices—call them whatever you want—established by the Program Directorate. Also of course there must be competence at each level, up and down.

Doing What You Said You Were Going to Do

What were your plan and controls for meeting the Apollo schedule, cost and performance objectives?

The plan for doing the job turned out to be a document about two inches thick. When this was approved by Dr. George Mueller and others, this was the guiding document for the program. This is what we said we were going to do; the doing then followed. *Program management basically is simply doing what you said you were going to do.* The job included the spacecraft itself, the Saturn rockets, system tests, and then receipt, assembly, and checkout at Cape Kennedy.

I kept about 400 to 500 key milestones at my level for control. We called this level one. There were four levels; level two was the Apollo program manager at each of the NASA centers; level three was the stage manager at Marshall (stages I, II, and III and the Instrument Unit), and the CSM (command and service module) and LEM at Houston. Level four was the contractor level, such as North American Aviation on the CSM and Grumman on the LEM.

This breaking the job into four levels was the basis for our controls and for determining who was going to do what. Initially performance and design specs were adequate for defining the tasks; but later we got more detailed as the program proceeded. There were tens of thousands of activities that had to be performed and coordinated.

To control changes we used configuration management; there was a CCB (configuration control board) at each level. This CCB was responsible for evaluating all aspects of a change—technical, interface, logistics, cost, and schedule impact. The result of every engineering change proposal was kept on file; and when it was approved, it was formalized by a directive.

How did you keep from getting bogged down in paper work?

Periodically we reviewed and analyzed the amount of paper work involved to see if we could reduce it. But on a large, complex program it's necessary to document, for communication and control purposes.

General, what were your primary tools for management control?

Program directives were one. In five and a half years the total number of program directives was only about 40; but they were directives that beyond any question were to be complied with. I needed something that wasn't going to be issued unless by God it was going to be followed. I wanted to establish at the outset that we weren't going to write a directive and I wasn't going to sign it unless I meant it. That was a key factor in keeping the directives down to a small number. In that series of 40, one that I particularly remember was number 4; that was the top authoritative document regarding schedules, control milestones, and authorized pieces of equipment—number of spacecraft, launch vehicles, and other equipment.

What was the size of these program directives?

Some were two or three pages; the thickest, Directive 4, was about 20 pages.

What was the general concept of the directives?

Numbers 6 through 9, for example, established the minimum essential pattern of actions in managing a development program such as the spacecraft, and which set the requirement for the different sequences of design reviews and the reviews for accepting equipment and so on. This was intended to require that throughout the program the same basic process would be followed in carrying out the development of all major assemblies. One directive in that series prescribed the process for determining flight readiness, for example, and required the discipline to follow through on failure reports. Another established the requirement and the process for certifying the design as flight-worthy and safe for manned operations. We called that the design certification review. So it was principally through these program directives that patterns were established by which people were expected to organize and pursue their work at all levels. Our next level of managers picked up the same theme and issued corresponding directives, as necessary. George Low, for instance, issued Spacecraft Program Directives.

The Action Center

One other management tool I might mention is what we called the action center, located at our headquarters in Washington. This was a control room, a very important working tool in controlling the program. It had sliding panels and wall displays showing key essential information on the entire program. We had similar control rooms at each of the centers, and data were continuously exchanged and coordinated between headquarters and these centers. Each of the program managers used his control room rather extensively. And I might add that a control room or action center is only as useful as the boss makes it. I've seen places where a lot of time and money went into a control room but was wasted because the boss didn't use it. Where it is used, a control center can be quite productive.

In my observation this kind of center may be used for one of three purposes: to impress visitors; for information displays, for active use by people involved in the program; or for making decisions. It sounds as though you made operational use, including decision making, of your action center.

Very definitely. For example, we used it for what might be called telephone conferences. Often the four centers had to meet on a variety of problems; these meetings would have involved a great deal of time and cost for travel. But in 1967 we ran across the "LDX" system. This was a set of equipment that could be leased and over which we could transmit view graphs; it took only six seconds per view graph for transmittal over this equipment. We developed a technique of LDX conferences; with a prearranged agenda and set of charts, we held conferences in which the only missing element was the eyeball-to-eyeball contact. Each of the key participants had a microphone, and there was an overhead speaker in each control room so that everyone could hear. Since everyone was well-acquainted with everyone else, the voice contact was almost as good as holding conferences in person. We conducted a great deal of our conference-type business by this technique.

How many people would assemble for one of these conferences?

It varied; sometimes only four or five; at other times maybe as many as a hundred at a location.

I remember after the Apollo 6 flight, the second flight of Saturn V, unmanned, we had several problems—two engines failed on the flight, we had a structural difficulty and substantial longitudinal oscillation—and over a period of several months we had a number of these LDX conferences to identify the problems and determine and validate the "fixes." During this series of conferences each center had three or four displays showing work to be done, and each had a record of what it and the other centers were going to be doing. One of the advantages of the action center was our ability to refer to a standing portrayal of an integrated schedule.

We Had the Most Effective Financial Management System I've Seen

Gen. Phillips, turning to cost and schedules control, a lot of people may believe that a fundamental reason for Apollo's success was an open checkbook, unlimited funds. I believe this is not a correct impression; the program started at an estimated $20 billion and wound up costing $21.35 billion; so the cost was close to the original estimate, in spite of the effects of inflation and the fact that much of the hardware developed is usable in subsequent landings and in other programs. How did you control Apollo expenditures?

We had the most effective finacial management system I've seen. It was a combination of several things. First, we had what NASA called the run-out costs of the program, which we projected every quarter and looked at quite critically. The financial management system was based on a document called the Program Operating Plan, or POP, which was updated and issued each quarter. Then, on a monthly basis, we looked at the actual expenditures, commitments, and obligations. Within seven or eight days after the end of a month, I had an accounting of figures from all the contractors which were sort of quick readouts from their accounting systems. These figures were subject to a final computation which might come along 30 to 60 days later, but the preliminary figures were always quite accurate. We projected what the costs should be, by contractor, all the way through the program. Then, on a monthly basis, we observed his actual expenditures; if these departed from the plan line in a significant way, we found out why and did something about it.

I think we developed one of the simplest techniques for portraying the summary financial situation. It was a clear and simple matrix, with months portrayed across the top, for two fiscal years; and at the left a listing of contractors. For each contractor we showed, month by month, both cumulative and monthly expenditures. If there were deviations where costs were above planned expenditures, that box was colored red, so that it would stand out. We also had a monthly review, in more detail, for each contractor. It consisted of a view-graph presentation of each contractor's financial plan and actual financial situation.

These financial controls provided a graphic picture of how the program was going financially. They were consistent with the job to be done, and with the plans and commitments for expenditures versus time, and for total commitments.

On a quarterly basis we always looked very critically at the run-out figure as I mentioned. The figure I tracked over a period of years was $17 something; $17 billion plus. The difference between this and the $21-billion figure is due to the fact that I was not responsible for some programs—Gemini, for instance—which provided support to Apollo and other manned space programs.

So the $17-billion figure was constant over a period of some years?

Yes. But it didn't remain constant easily. It was a combination of a number of things. In the latter part of 1966 we began to see that the current monthly spending rates would run us out of money before the fiscal year was over the following June. So we prescribed actions to cut out some things that may have increased risks—for instance, cutting out some backup efforts—but which were necessary because of costs. I instructed the contractors at a meeting to figure how we could bring their costs down. That meeting was followed by a lot of staff work and a follow-up meeting a few months later; and they all responded by action within their own plans to scrub down costs one way or another. As a result, we managed to come through that fiscal year with a small amount of reserve.

That kind of assessment—the trade-off between risk and costs—is one that probably no one other than the program director is in a position to make.

Right. That's one of the jobs of the program manager—to decide whether to take a chance you can squeeze down in some area in order to keep costs down, in the interests of total program objectives, or whether to incur the lashes of asking for more money.

I would guess that you tried to retain a contingency or reserve, however, for unexpected expenses. Is this in fact what happened?

Yes. I believe that on a sizeable development program, with a lot of unknowns involved, a range of 20 percent to 10 percent for a reserve is reasonable; early in the program it might be 20 percent, and range down to 10 percent later in development. But we never had as much as 20 percent on Apollo; it was more like 10 percent. Later, when a program goes into production or is beyond development, this range goes down, from as much as 5 percent to about zero.

How did you maintain the Apollo schedule? In view of the slippage that resulted from the fire in 1967, you must also have had a time buffer. Is this correct?

The initial schedule called for a manned moon flight possibly as early as the Fall of 1968. In spite of the loss of time following the fire in January 1967, which cost almost a year's time, we were able to launch the Apollo 11 mission, which sent Armstrong, Aldrin, and Collins to the moon and back, in July 1969. We encountered a number of problems of course.

The Biggest Problem Was the Fire

What were some of the biggest problems you encountered?

As far as technical problems are concerned, the biggest was the Apollo fire, in January 1967.[1] That disaster set the program back about a year; it was the result of technical oversight or failing to fully appreciate and follow through, in proper detail, on the flamability and spacecraft atmosphere of oxygen under high pressure. That was the biggest technical problem.

The biggest management problem we ran into was also due to the aftermath of the fire. There was a feeling among a number of key people of great personal loss and responsibility for what had happened; this had a great demoralizing effect. Up through June 1967 there was what I would call a national inquisition, in the nature of congressional hearings and proceedings. Most of the program management and all the key people spent a great deal of time dealing with these hearings and inquiries. So the management problems were a combination of dealing with a demoralized organization and having to spend a great deal of time and effort with the investigations and hearings that were being held during that period.

How did this affect the time "mix" of the program director?

A program director normally has to spend a substantial part of his time dealing with the "outside world"—with people outside his program organization.

What percentage, would you estimate?

It varies, from program to program and during different phases of a program. When I was Minuteman director for five years before Apollo, I used to devote half or more of my time to the outside world—the lateral and upward structure within the Air Force, with Congress, and to some degree with the public. In Apollo the percentage differed with time, but probably averaged 50 percent. In the period from January to July 1967, these outside activities required 70 or 75 percent of my time. I had to steal time to make necessary trips to California, Houston, Huntsville, and Florida, to work out details for the plans ahead.

So in most cases, regardless of the nature of the project, a PM must spend at least 25 percent of his time on these outside activities?

That would be a reasonable figure. In the case of an industrial project manager, he would have to spend a considerable part of his time with customers or potential customers.

Incidentally, how many hours a week did you work on Apollo?

[1]The fire which claimed the lives of three astronauts during a system check.

I think 70 or 80 might be a reasonable average. Some weeks it was a lot more, and some weeks less.

The Importance as Viewed From the Top Never Did Dim

We were identifying some technical and management problems. Perhaps the second greatest technical problem was that that developed on Apollo 6—the oscillation, engine failures, and structural failures in the shroud structure that I mentioned. That particular set of problems and the actions taken over several months are kind of a classic case study. It involved determining how the problems arose; what was done to deal with them; and how this flight affected subsequent decisions. Apollo 6 was the second flight of the Saturn vehicle and was unmanned. The next flight of the Saturn V vehicle was scheduled for Apollo 8; that was a manned flight— Borman's flight out to lunar orbit, the first flight away from earth. So the actions that took place between the Saturn V flight that bordered on being a disaster and the next that took man away from the earth are quite a story. There was a period of a year and three fourths between the two events.

And part of this period was during the demoralizing effect of the fire. How does a program director bring an organization back from something like that?

I don't know that there's any simple answer. Part of it is just hard work on something that's important. We worked on Apollo 7 during this period; and we were heavily involved in redesigning the spacecraft.

In addition, after Apollo 6 had its troubles the launch area, including the people at Marshall and their contractors, had to face up to the same kind of problem—identifying in detail what the problems were, and the engineering, design, and testing work that were necessary to get all those things fixed. So getting people back to working hard, toward an important objective, I think was one of the answers to getting the organization working again. And it was very important that recognition of the importance of the Apollo program was always reasonably well maintained during the whole program; the importance as viewed from the White House and the top of the government in carrying out the initial lunar landing never did dim, and that's very important in motivating an organization to carry out all the hard work that's necessary to get the program done.

The events leading to flying Apollo 8 involved an interesting set of problems that were converted into success, in terms of steps toward carrying out the lunar landing. Briefly, I faced a decision whether to fly Apollo 8 testing the Saturn V engine in earth orbit;

or to risk that it would be properly shaken down and ready to test a manned mission out to lunar distance, short of a landing. You see, if we stayed with an earth-orbit mission, we probably couldn't have made a lunar landing in 1969. On the other hand, a manned lunar mission was the first time that it could take as long as three days to get the spacecraft back to earth; before Apollo 8, it was a matter of minutes, or at the most an hour, of being able to get a man back to earth. This involved a very involved set of management decisions and actions. To make a long story short, we decided to drop the LEM from the Apollo 8 mission and test the system out to lunar distance.

How much ahead of time did you make that decision?

The decision was made rather late; the mission was flown in December 1968, and the decision was made in November. But problems began to surface earlier, in July; and the actions that committed the configuration were taken and decided in August. We didn't have one very vital piece of information, however, until October: the results of the first manned flight (Apollo 7).

This series of decisions and options from mid-1968 to the flight in December —this maintaining progress and having an option of at least two choices at each decision point along the way—must in itself be quite an art.

It's an interesting challenge. I might add that that period is one of the best documented and most interesting sequences of the Apollo program; I felt it was absolutely essential to have extensive documentation during this period.

There were other technical problems that I am reminded of: getting proper payload performance out of the Saturn V, for instance, and the fact that the lunar module turned out to be a more difficult design job than we had originally expected.

How did you keep track of technical achievement?

One of the practices I have adopted over a period of years is to establish a small number of key technical areas where I attempt to establish meaningful requirements and track our progress. On Apollo, weight and performance were two of these; we had a monthly meeting on the performance capability of the launch vehicle, and similarly on the weight status of the payloads. It became apparent that for fuel safety margins and contingencies we had to have a greater payload capacity than our planned 85,000 pounds. Another key indicator as to whether things are going right or not is electrical power. Another is heat dissipation. Computer capacity, the on-board computer capacity in digital words, is also a key technical control area.

I Didn't Have a Statement of Authority, and I Didn't Ask for One . . .

General, I'd like to touch on what is perhaps the ultimate problem, the matter of the program manager's authority. How does he gain the authority necessary to carry out his mission?

Probably the most important way is his taking the necessary authority. The program director is responsible for accomplishing whatever his objectives are. I've observed far too many people who want to be told exactly what their job is and exactly how to do it, or exactly what their authority is, when they'd be far better off to operate on the basis of good judgment and determining what's required to get something done, and then do it. So I think the most important aspect of the program director's authority is that which he considers necessary himself to get his job done, and he assumes it and uses it. I think that people of good judgment normally can operate pretty effectively that way. It's far better to have superiors put reins on somebody or restrain him from assuming too much authority, than to have to fire him for not getting the job done because he's waiting to be told what to do. The other source of authority may be rules or laws or regulations; and in this regard the upper levels of government or upper levels of a corporation have the important job of establishing the proper environment and rules within which the PM can get his job done.

Did you on Apollo have any statement of your authority, or anything other than a statement of the Apollo mission?

No, and I didn't ask for one, either. A philosophy that I think is important is that if a PM has to be told what his authorities are, he's the wrong man for the job.

So part of selecting the right individual is that he should be an individual who will take whatever authority is required to get the job done.

Right.

In the selection, training, and development of PMs, what are the main qualifications this individual should have? In view of your own background in electrical engineering, should he have a technical background, for instance?

I don't believe there's any stereotyped pattern. But I am convinced that if the program has a high technical content, the PM should have a technical background, because the program he's running succeeds or fails according to the technical content—whether the thing does what it's supposed to do.

And I believe that the director of a big, active program has to be in reasonably good health and condition, and able to stand a pretty grueling existence for the period of years he's responsible for the program.

What do you do to keep in shape?

In terms of exercise, my principal exercise is running or jogging and walking. I've done this for a number of years. Various of the Apollo program managers spent a fair amount of time in the gyms available at each center.

Attributes of the Program Manager

As to the other attributes of the PM—I think he has to be a leader. This is a bit hard to define; but what that means to me is a person who can get a large number of other people to do a job. Leadership is the best word I can think of. I think a program director also has to be able to associate effectively in the outside world, with whoever is his boss, in contacts with the public, and so forth. It's a combination of personableness, ability to communicate, and the ability to establish and maintain confidence. This matter of confidence is very important. Some people can establish confidence and maintain a feeling of credibility and dependability; others can't. Of course, in the final analysis, that person has to produce. But there's usually a long period of time in which it's important to have established the feeling of confidence that will enable you to get your job done.

On Apollo, did you have the freedom of action you needed to get the job done?

Yes; I did have this freedom, and this is important.

Is there any way, Gen. Phillips, to develop this kind of program manager, or does he just happen to be in an organization by chance?

I think that principally the way to get program director caliber people is to develop them. Over the years that's what the Air Force has done, and I believe it has done this the best. It's a matter of bringing people up through a program-oriented system, from junior positions and ranks on up through higher and higher positions. In parallel with that as a general pattern, there's the conduct of formalized training. Also, one very desirable element of experience is that the individual have experience in the particular field that he'll be developing equipment for; a person who'll develop a strategic bomber, for example, ought to have had some experience in the Strategic Air Command, and preferably in bombers.

So it's a matter of experience, the right characteristics, and education to develop project managers.

Yes. The only way I know of other than bringing people up

through a program-oriented system is to get people who are highly motivated and have the right characteristics, even without previous experience in program management; but only one out of 15 or 20 program directors might come up this way. And usually key people under him must have had program experience.

Is there any other major point from Apollo that might benefit project managers in other fields?

Yes; one item that's important is attention to detail, careful and rigorous attention to the proper detail. That may sound inconsistent with the idea of managers getting away from detail; but in a program with high technological content there may be thousands or even millions of elements that, if they fail or don't work properly, may negate the whole mission. So that in an organized and structured sense, it is necessary for people all the way to the top to have enough information to be satisfied that proper attention to detail is being given to all those pieces. And secondly, it is important that the conclusions and decisions reached in the progression of design reviews, and the failures that occur in test programs, be identified and tracked to management's satisfaction that they have been properly dealt with. That's what I mean by attention to detail.

In case after case on the Apollo program, I think that success of the program can be attributed to upper managers' having been properly equipped and willing to take the time and the effort, and their having the energy required, to sort out some of these details and work them through personally. There are a great number of case examples of this. For instance, George Low, the spacecraft manager, worked out stress corrosion of the spacecraft himself, in detail. Without this, we might have encountered a flight or preflight situation that would have caused a failure. Attention to detail requires highlighting; so obviously a program has to be properly organized and have sufficient flow of information so that managers can, on the right occasions, satisfy themselves as to details and get involved personally. It is important to have the information and visibility with which to do the job.

A Lot of People Haven't Yet Focused on Objectives

Incidentally, the establishment of objectives—what is it you're trying to achieve—is one of the most important elements of project management. A lot of people, I feel, haven't yet focused on that simple, clear thing: What are you trying to get done.

4

Management of Major Weapon Systems Acquisition*

Honorable Barry J. Shillito

In today's environment, much criticism has been levied against the Defense Department. A sizeable portion of such criticism has been directed at the way in which DOD has in the past managed the acquisition of major weapon systems.

My purpose in this article is neither to defend nor to condemn such criticism, but rather to raise the general level of understanding of the nature of the management problems involved in bringing into our operational inventory a major weapon system for our national defense. Additionally, I shall describe some of the changes in our methods and procedures, which our extensive review of this process has shown to be necessary, if we are to effect the improvements all of us desire.

At the outset it is important to recognize that in dealing with these complicated weapon systems of the future requiring such substantial outlays of public funds, we are faced with the problem of managing the weapon system acquisition process in an environment that is constantly changing. With change come risks of varying size and composition which management must face. How DOD management deals with these categories of risks becomes a central issue in understanding the major weapon system acquisition process.

First, let me identify and briefly discuss the nature of these

*Defense Industry Bulletin, January 1970, pp. 1–4.

risks which we expect to some degree in every weapon system, and to a larger degree in every major weapon system.

Management Risks

The first category of risks involves the time it takes to acquire a weapon system.

A major weapon system acquisition has a time span of five to seven years, and sometimes longer. It is comprised of hundreds of subsystems, tens of thousands of parts, and hundreds of thousands of connections and lesser components. The interfaces and linkages on which the system's successful performance depends can run into the millions. Dealing as we are so far in the future, DOD managers must effectively deal with the risks of making cost projections over this time span, and stand accountable for decisions made.

Another category of risks that must be successfully dealt with is caused by the fact that a major weapon system involves nearly every field of technology. Over the past few years, the technologies have had a growth rate unparalleled with any similar prior time period. In any single weapon system, a significant number of these expanding technologies are often interdependently tied together. In looking downstream, DOD managers must resolve the nature and amount of forecasted growth in an array of technologies that can, optimally, be counted on for inclusion in a major weapon system to be operational so far in the future. There are substantial risks in doing this.

The ever-changing levels of capability of our current or potential adversaries present another form of risk that must be effectively dealt with. The weapon system must also be designed to meet a forecasted threat derived from such variables as support of our international commitments, obsolescence of our current weapon systems, an unsolvable strategic or tactical problem, changing threats, greater weapon systems effectiveness, or a combination of any or all of these. In undertaking the development and production of a major weapon system, our management process must be responsive to the needs of effectively resolving the risks presented by this facet of this dynamic environment.

Another category of risk that our weapon system acquisition management must face is that, in developing and producing a weapon system that has not existed before, provision must be made for the proper identification and timely resolution of the many uncertainties our past experience tells us attend such an effort—the "unknowns" as one study described them. Even more important, when these foreseeable uncertainties, in turn, surface unforeseeable "unknowns," our management process must be able to prevent or minimize degradation to cost, schedule, or performance of the weapon system that has occurred in the past.

Finally, the contracting effort in support of the weapon system acquisition process must provide the degree of flexibility necessary to deal effectively with the kinds of risks peculiar to the weapon system in question. The contracting process must be responsive to the range of risks, balancing the opportunities for economic gain to the contractor with quality and timeliness of his performance in developing or producing the weapon system.

Development Concept Paper*

As mentioned before, a major weapon system acquisition program involves the expenditure of very large amounts of public funds over a five-to-seven year period. It is important to provide a means by which the Secretary of Defense and his principal advisors can make a comprehensive review and decision on a major program, before heavy financial resources are committed to its development. The continuously improving management process which provides such a mechanism is the Development Concept Paper (DCP).

The officer who has the primary responsibility for DCP's in DOD is the Director of Defense Research and Engineering. It is his responsibility to ensure the initiation of a DCP at the appropriate time in the life cycle of an important system. Important systems are those which are anticipated to require at least $75 million of research, development, test, and evaluation funds or $300 million of production funds, or both; are high priority or are otherwise important, e.g., because of unusual organizational complexity or technological advancement. The most common point at which DCP's have been introduced has been when a sponsoring military service is ready to go from concept formulation into contract definition.

The broad objectives of this management system are to improve decision making and implementation on important development programs by increased assurance that:

- Full military and economic consequences and risks of these programs are explored before they are initiated or continued.
- Information and recommendations on these programs are prepared collaboratively or coordinated with all interested parties, prior to review and decision by the Secretary of Defense.

*Now called the Decision Coordinating Paper.

- Premises and essential details of his decision on these programs are regularly recorded, and made known to all those responsible for their implementation.
- Opportunity for review is provided to the Secretary of Defense if any of the information or premises, on which his decision was based, change substantially.

The contents of a typical Development Concept Paper are:

Issues for Decision. Management issue or issues involved.

Program Purposes. Threat which the system is designed to meet or exceed; in short, the reason for the system.

Alternative Solutions. Are there different ways of meeting the threat or fulfilling the military mission?

Proposed Cost of the System. Expected effectiveness of the system in meeting the threat, and the planned schedule on which the system would be developed and put into production.

Pros and Cons. Is the system, in fact, needed? Would it be cheaper, for example, not to have such a system at all, but to take certain recognized losses that we might face in combat if we did not have this system?

Threshold Page. A most important part, because it is the gross management tool which the Secretary of Defense will use thereafter to ensure that the system is remaining on track throughout its life. In the case of an aircraft, the threshold sheet would contain figures on technical and operational performance, such as the maximum weight growth which would be allowed before the entire development program is reopened for review by the Office of the Secretary of Defense. Similarly, other thresholds, having to do with cost and with schedule, are established in this portion of the DCP. For example, if the estimated cost of a system in development is $100 million, a threshold of say $110 million might be established. Within these bounds, the sponsoring military service is fully responsible for the entire management of the program. If, however, a system runs over or threatens to run over the $110 million threshold figure, then the system is fully examined, not only by the sponsoring service, but by the Office of the Secretary of Defense. A new DCP may be written, and a new decision may be made.

Management Plan. How does the service plan to manage the program? What is the composition of the System Program Office?

Matter of Security. What has to be classified about the development? What can be unclassified? This is very important with respect to industrial considerations.

Conditions for Revisions. As previously indicated, a DCP is supposed to be a living document which can be referred to throughout the life of the system and found to be accurate at any time. The DCP will normally be updated at the end of contract definition so that it contains more accurate figures on the system, its performance, its schedule, and its cost. Similarly, the DCP is updated at the time the production decision is made. This updated DCP is to ensure that we go forward into production with a valid and current understanding of the major features of and surrounding the system, including the threat which it is intended to meet, the performance parameters, and the cost and schedule features.

Decision Options or Alternatives. The Secretary of Defense is presented various alternatives from which he may choose, such as to allow the candidate system to go into contract definition. Another alternative might be not to go ahead with contract definition, but either to perform further advanced development or simply not to develop this system in favor of developing another one, or making another do to meet the mission requirement.

Signatures. A DCP contains the signatures of the Director of Defense Research and Engineering, the sponsoring Service Secretary, certain Assistant Secretaries of Defense, and then the signature of the Secretary of Defense or the Deputy Secretary indicating his decision.

Defense Systems Acquisition Review Council

As a means of providing management overview for timely decision making, the Secretary of Defense has established the Defense Systems Acquisition Review Council. The mission of the council is to review major and important weapon system acquisition programs at appropriate milestone points in their life cycle. These reviews are to permit coordinated evaluation and deliberation among senior managers, to assure that the advice given the Secretary of Defense is as complete and objective as possible prior to a decision to proceed to the next step of the system's life cycle. The operation and evaluation of this council serves to complement the Development Concept Paper system.

The Defense System Acquisition Review Council is composed of the Director for Defense Research and Engineering and the Assistant Secretaries of Defense for Installations and Logistics, Systems Analysis, and Comptroller. While the council can meet as the need dictates, or at the request of an individual service, the council will generally review and evaluate the status of each appropriate program at three basic milestone points:

- When initiation of contract definition (or equivalent effort) is proposed.
- When transition from contract definition to full-scale development is proposed.
- When transition from the development phase into production for service deployment is proposed.

The council is chaired by the Director of Defense Research and Engineering for consideration of entry into contract definition, and for entry into full-scale development. For the transition from development to production, chairmanship of the council shifts to the Assistant Secretary of Defense (Installations and Logistics). For additional reviews, the council will be chaired by either of these two officials, as appropriate. Thus, it can be seen that before a major system can move to the next important step in its life cycle, it must pass the scrutiny of senior DOD managers. They determine that satisfactory progress has been made and is expected to continue, in accordance with the finite original and updated plans for accomplishing the acquisition of the system. The council is then in a position to make recommendations for decision to the Secretary of Defense or the Deputy Secretary of Defense.

Continuing Study of Acquisition Process

As mentioned at the outset, we have been subjecting the entire weapon system acquisition process to intensive study. There are areas which are subject to improvement. We are looking at them in order to determine how best to proceed.

One such area is the source selection process and decision making attendant to it. This involves the whole matter of concept formulation and contract definition:

- How we narrow down to and, finally, select one contractor.
- How and when we make the various decisions relative to development and readiness for production.
- How we select the type of contracting which is best fitted to a particular program.

We are generally convinced that over the years management changes have been made basically in the right direction. Problems were identified in the mid- and late 1950's with respect to improving the disciplines of weapon system management. Since that period, there has been a continuum of improvements in this area. However, contracting methods, as well as concept formulation and contract definition policies and regulations, may have moved so far that we have deprived ourselves of appropriate flexibility to allow the most effective acquisition to take place.

There have been many criticisms in the past few years by industry that it has been forced by the government, or by the prevailing environment, into making over-optimistic estimates of the cost and schedule of the development and production of a system, in order to allow themselves any real chance of winning the competition. DOD does not want industry to be overoptimistic. We want to be informed what industry considers to be an accurate appraisal of the development risks ahead in a program. The government is prepared to pay a fair price for a system, provided we are assured that the system is needed and we can make an estimate ahead of time of what it is going to cost, so we can evaluate its military utility *versus* its cost. It is not the desire of DOD to put a contractor in a position where he must take an overly optimistic view of the risks ahead, in order to give himself any opportunity to be successful in the competition.

On the other hand, we must know what we may encounter in the way of costs and development problems. We feel we cannot shift to the other end of the scale, where we would do business completely on a cost-plus basis without regard to evaluation of the risks ahead. In this connection, we are convinced at the present time that we would be well advised to attempt to do more design validation and more prototyping rather than to depend, as much as we have, on paper estimates and paper analyses of what risks lie ahead of us. Quite desirable, of course, would be to have competitive prototypes for every system or every component that we develop. This, as we all recognize, is not practical.

It is feasible, however, to conduct prototype competitions of certain major subsystems, such as engines, avionics, radars, or even aircraft missile systems. Such competitions might logically be conducted with a prime contractor's subcontractors, depending upon the circumstances. We believe that we may have been making our decisions to produce too early in the life of a system. We may be well advised, in many cases, to attempt to carry competition farther along than we have, until we are assured that more of the risks involving unknowns are behind us—until we, indeed, have purely engineering ahead rather than experimental development, and until contractors can make more accurate estimates of what the remaining development and production of a system will entail. All these things are involved in the source selection and decision making. We are looking at them carefully, and expect to make changes indicated by our studies as soon as we have convinced ourselves that we are moving in the right direction.

Milestone Contracting Concept

We are presently attempting to structure into the weapon system contract, at the time of initial award, a discrete number of significant milestones which permit objective evaluation of the contractor's actual accomplishment, as against the planned accomplishment. Included in both the development phase and in the initial production phase, the attainment, or lack of attainment, of such milestones will give enhanced visibility to the technical progress of the program.

The milestones chosen will be meaningful and measurable points of technical accomplishment and useful alike to both contractor and government management, for the orderly direction of a program's progress. Further, by contractually tying successful accomplishment of milestones in the development contract to release of funds for long-lead time production items, as well as the exercise of production options, demonstration of technical accomplishment will ensure that the program commitment is increased at a pace that is commensurate with the reduction in program risks. Finally, by placing the development/production effort within a contracting envelope that properly recognizes the risk/reward balance, and under the stimulation of appropriate incentives, we aim to avoid many problems that have in the past occurred in acquiring major weapon systems, wherein commitments to production have been made that were inconsistent with the technical risks then remaining in the program.

Excessive Documentation

A continuing problem area is in the matter of documentation. This takes two forms:

- Technical documentation which the contractor is required to provide to the government in responding to a request for proposal.
- Documentation pertaining to the management of the program by the contractor, if he wins the contract for the development. This includes not only the type of management, but the depth of management detail called for.

There is a growing feeling with respect to the former that not only has the government been asking for too much depth of detail in the technical documentation, but the contractors frequently have overdone technical documentation on their own initiative, to convince the government that their depth of knowledge of the system is such that they should be given the contract. We are going to try to stem this tendency toward excess technical documentation.

On the balance, management of our major programs is being accomplished by capable, well educated, highly motivated individuals. The magnitude of these programs, however, causes us not to be fully satisfied with our program management policies and organization. We believe that we probably need better and more extensive training for our program managers, a longer tenure in their jobs for both program managers and other key people in the System Program Offices. Further, a program manager frequently does not have authority to match his responsibility. In some cases he needs clearer delineation as to what his responsibilities are. In his work he frequently is subjected to such a volume of directives that he cannot possibly be fully familiar and comply with them all. We need high quality, well trained and experienced program managers, with good teams working for them, in a framework of management which permits them to carry out their jobs with a minimum of impediments and extraneous requirements.

In summary, the thrust of our ongoing efforts in the field of defense weapon system acquisition management is this:

> The management of defense weapon system acquisition is a titanic task involving the spending of billions of dollars a year covering many programs of a widely divergent nature. It is impossible to find one single policy or method of management which best fits all.

We have tried many methods to get the most defense for each dollar expended. We have made some improvements in the past. More improvements in the future are necessary and planned. We may have overreacted in our handling of some problems. This we would like to avoid in the future. We want to correct and improve the management of our defense weapons system acquisition and do it as prudently as we can, after we are sure we have correctly identified a problem and developed an appropriate solution.

✷ ✷ ✷ ✷ ✷

Acquisition of major systems by the government constitutes one of the most crucial and expensive activities performed to meet national needs.

—OMB Circular A-109

5

A Discussion With L. B. Curtis of Continental Oil Company

J. S. Baumgartner

Oil was discovered in commercial quantities in 1966 in the Gulf of Arabia, 60 miles off the Shiekdom of Dubai. A feasibility study was made by Continental Oil Company for the five-company ownership of the concession, and a unique concept was developed to build a completely self-contained producing, storage, and loading system at the offshore site. Today a huge bottle, the size of a football field and 20 stories high, submerged in 150 feet of water, stores the oil pumped from the Fateh Oil Field. Even more remarkable than this award-winning breakthrough, however, is the broad range of management skills required to meet the combined challenges of owner companies from five countries, workers from many nations "like Custer's last stand," a climate with 130-degree temperatures and 90 percent humidity, an outflow of $50,000 per day, soil like styrofoam, a highly variable rate of production, and the need for great diplomacy in working with a host government. These were some, but not all, of the problems that confronted Continental's L. B. "Buck" Curtis.

With the high costs, many unknowns, and obvious problems in coordination and communications, how do you go about handling a project like this?

First of course there's the exploration activity, which is a separate field in itself. Active oil exploration started in 1963, but we weren't successful until the summer of 1966 when we drilled a well 58 miles off the coast of Dubai. The well looked good, but there were a lot of unknowns to be evaluated before committing the large sums necessary to develop the field.

We attacked the problem in three phases:

1. Evaluation, to determine the size of the oil reserve. We were under considerable time pressure, both because of the host government's continual pressing for action as soon as possible and because the more time and money you put into the feasibility stage, the longer the period before income is generated.

2. Design of a system and components to handle an output estimated at somewhere between 100,000 and 400,000 barrels per day (B/D). This included production platforms, pumps, storage vessels, pipelines, off-loading buoys, and support activities. As you can see, the range of the expected output posed quite a design challenge.

3. Programming and execution. This included procurement, on a worldwide basis, of the equipment required; preparing specifications; selection of contractors to execute the job; and then carrying out the work.

During the evaluation phase, how did you determine whether the reserve would be big enough to go ahead with the project?

The discovery well was the beginning. We had tapped a reservoir but a single well is insufficient, so we drilled two more wells two miles on either side of the discovery well. With this, we assessed the reserve picture as being capable of producing 100,000 barrels per day or more. So that became the minimum design figure.

How deep were the wells?

About 7,500 to 8,500 feet, which is a moderate depth. The water depth ranged from 110 to 180 feet.

A Submerged Tank Was a Possibility

In the second phase, how did you design for such a wide range of outputs?

The basic concept was to plan for economical development with the objective of placing the field on production as soon as possible and to allow for expansion if our initial estimate was on the low side. The storage problem—where to store the crude until it's shipped to market—was the key to the system. We had a choice of going two ways: building storage facilities at Dubai, which meant building an expensive pipeline 60 miles long from the oil field to Dubai, and then building another pipeline 10 miles out to sea because of the shallow water depth in this part of the Gulf; or storing the oil at sea near the field. If we decided to go the second route—

and the more we looked at it, the more this seemed the obvious thing to do—we could use floating tankers. But having experience with the maintenance and problems of tankers, we thought we'd really like to use some other method. A submerged tank was a possibility; but this was a brand new idea and never proven, other than on a limited scale. But we grew confident that we could do this. CB&I (Chicago Bridge and Iron Company) had an underwater storage idea on the drawing boards and had done some of the engineering. We started working with them and kept at it until we had the final product.

This was a key decision then, where logic pointed to going with a breakthrough concept. But you could have been a real villain if the submerged tank idea didn't work.

Yes, I suppose so. But it was carefully thought out. It turned out to be a top engineering feat. CB&I won a Professional Engineering Society award for it.

It Looks Like a Huge Champagne Glass

What's this storage tank made of? What does it look like?

It's made of steel and concrete. It looks like a huge champagne glass turned upside down. It's 270 feet in diameter at the bottom and has a "stem" that rises to a height of 205 feet; this is all underwater, except for the top 46 feet of the stem, which is above sea level. There are tremendous forces on the tank—horizontal forces as well as up and down loads. The boundary design parameters included a study of the 100-year period of storms, with the tank completely filled with oil, 500,000 barrels. We made an extensive analysis of all the factors involved, including how it would be pinned to the sea floor. We built it on the coast of Dubai, floated it out to the site, pulled by two tugs, and sank it.

To continue with the design phase, we established the goal of making our design sound and complete such as to avoid on-site changes, or at least minimize them. We paid a lot of attention to detail. And we also ran an independent system analysis before construction. These—the detail and independent analysis—revealed several changes which saved on-site alterations. All in all there were few major changes, considering the scope of the job.

How did you design for the range of possible production, this 100,000 B/D to 400,000 B/D?

If we had done more evaluation to define the total reserve and maximum production capacity, we could have designed single units for handling the ultimate capacity. But, because of economies and timing we approached the problem on a modular basis. This is easier said than done, however; for example, how do you modularly construct undersea pipelines, which are very costly, from wells to storage areas? Thus, we decided to use a modular approach starting with a 100,000 B/D production, and retain all facilities at the field site.

How did you plan the execution phase?

After the design we started programming, which basically includes procurement, preparation of specifications, and selecting contractors to carry out the job.

We selected a single prime contractor to do the on-site work, "single" for administrative reasons, and a contractor because he's generally better staffed and qualified in the construction field. We have found that within an operating company, such as ours, it's a problem to find enough qualified construction personnel who are interested in an overseas assignment, so we use our own manpower for coordination and supervision.

Procurement Is Always a Problem

Procurement on a job of this size is always a problem, particularly when material is purchased from all over the world. We don't have any magic solution to procurement problems; we use our "in house" purchasing expertise and keep tight control on scheduling, shipping, expediting, and receiving. Our success was good, but we did have to airfreight some items into Dubai, and also had to do some makeshift procurement in the Arabian Gulf area after the main effort started.

Equipment components were let for bid to qualified suppliers, including prepackaging. We issued minimum specifications for equipment and identified all parts subject to abnormal usage or environment. For quality control we had on-site inspection of all major units. We also staged a mock-up of the entire production handling unit at a marshaling yard near Houston to check the operability of all equipment pieces.

Expert teams were also sent to each construction site in the United States and Europe to run a final check on the equipment before acceptance and shipment to either Dubai or the marshaling yard.

You must have had a pretty good fabrication capability at the site, however.

We built it from scratch. But it was probably one of the most modern fabrication yards in the world.

Was this on a barge?

No, it was a shore installation. We had to do some of the fabrication work inside Dubai for two reasons: One, the platforms are extremely bulky and, with high shipping costs, we found it was better to ship the steel to Dubai and fabricate them on site; we had all pieces labeled and they were checked as part of the receiving process, the same as you'd do on any project. The second reason for fabricating there was in response to a Government request, and logically so, to do as much work within Dubai as possible to boost the Dubai economy.

What does it cost per day to run an operation of this kind?

We were running a rig operation that costs in the neighborhood of $10,000 per day; a fabrication system that costs $5,000 to $6,000, just for labor; and the barge system that costs about $28,000 per day. This includes a 500-ton derrick barge, some cargo barges, a 100-ton barge, four tugs and some crew boats, plus a helicopter service. All of these were running concurrently for part of the time. Costs of course have risen considerably since then.

With costs like that, there's obviously a tremendous premium on planning and logistics and other backup support.

Yes, the execution effort says how well the previous parts of the job were done. We did run into one major problem we hadn't foreseen, at least to the extent it turned out to be. This was the subsoil condition for supporting the submerged tank and structures. We'd made soil tests, of course; but we unexpectedly came upon a zone we thought was firm but turned out to be like styrofoam. When we hit this zone we had to do some fast analytical work, because the cost of standby operations is prohibitive. We did the analysis and design alteration here in the United States, but needed information from Dubai. Needless to say, communication on a problem like this is very poor. But after many cables and several computer runs we obtained a satisfactory solution. This took about 10 days. It turned out that the "styrofoam" zone was shell fragments, cemented together but with 40- to 60-percent void space. Our solution was to cut through this layer to firmer soil and insert "pin" piles for rigidity. This was our biggest problem; it could have meant the whole design was bad, but fortunately we were able to solve it by modifying the substructure.

Like Custer's Last Stand

Where did the workers come from in carrying out the execution phase?

It was like Custer's last stand; they came from all over—Pakistan, India, Iran, Dubai, and the other Arab states. The population of Dubai is only 35,000, so they had to come from all over.

How do you control a group like that, with different languages, customs, experience, and training levels?

Well, we used a careful selection procedure. We set up tests to weed out the unqualified. Occasionally we managed to obtain a man who had worked on a project like this before; we considered him a real prime candidate, as a little bit of experience goes a long way. And, of course, you try to have supervisors who can speak their language, as well as English and French in some cases . . . it takes a lot of repetition of communication.

When the word gets around about hiring, all kinds of people come in and the labor supply exceeds the demand; and naturally the host government will make sure its own people are placed preferentially. But if you get in a situation where a lot of different nationalities come in, it can create morale problems. These are often one-shot deals; and when cleared up, they're gone.

Did you have to set up training programs for these people?

Occasionally we'd get a skilled craftsman, but mostly they weren't and it took a while to teach and qualify them. Needless to say, our quality control inspections turned up much that was unacceptable and had to be redone. This kind of problem has to be expected.

Incidentally, with so many people thrown together in a small country, it puts a burden on such things as facilities, supplies, labor wages, housing, etc. We think the Government of Dubai did a remarkable job in meeting these problems. Also I give great credit to the Dubai leadership for their foresight in seeing that the offshore storage system was in their best interests and would benefit them economically.

One other problem related to execution was the environment. We tried to program the onshore fabrication work during the cooler months of the year, but it was impossible to avoid working in some of the extremely hot weather. From May through October the temperature ranged from 90 to 130 degrees F., and the humidity was rarely under 90 percent. The best we could do was start the work day early in the morning and stop about noon.

Turning to the ownership and management of the facility, what was the relation of the companies involved?

Initially, ownership of the concession was shared by Continental Oil Company, British Petroleum, Compagnie Francaise des Petroles, Deutsche Erdol-Aktengeselischaft, and Sun Oil Company. The British Petroleum interest was later sold to the French company and to Hispanoil, a Spanish firm. We're the operators, Continental Oil Company, through the Dubai Petroleum Company, a wholly owned subsidiary.

We Used Extreme Care in Planning

How do you get agreement and an okay for action from such a diverse group of companies?

The biggest thing we did was to use extreme care in planning the operation—when a system was unfolded before the group, it was logical and tied together in all respects. You do it in such a way that you give them the choices and costs, all of which can be explained. A primary objective is to reduce the risk down to a minimum. When you do this and measure the economic gain, the answer comes out. Our projection of the gain to be realized in this case was such that it was worth taking a specific risk.

Did you have regular periodic meetings?

Yes, sometimes we had them every two or three months, early in the game; and during one period the meetings were every two or three weeks. Toward the end, I'd say we met every five or six months. There wasn't a fixed pattern. When we reached certain points, as controlled by the system or progress of the job, we'd get together.

Whose idea was it to use the submerged tank concept?

It seemed clear that we'd have to handle the storage problem at the site some way or other. So we ran a survey of available storage, and the more we looked at the CB&I unit, the more convinced we became that this was the thing to do.

Looking at logistics—having all the required items on hand when they're needed—how do you develop a system that foresees all the requirements, that doesn't have any flukes?

It's difficult, and we didn't succeed in foreseeing all the things, but fortunately they were minor. The answer is just attention and care of details. We ran an independent system analysis after the design was set, as I mentioned; this was done by someone that hadn't been involved in the job. Also we had an independent materials check; and each time we had a shipment, we checked it against what was required, as well as on delivery. If something was missing, we responded accordingly. Even so, you miss bushings or a valve piece here and there; or you have to modify a valve because it doesn't do what you want it to do.

The Results Are Excellent

I've observed that people in the oil industry have a tremendous sense of dedication to getting the job done. Are there ways of developing this spirit?

Most of them are objective, which helps tremendously. And, of course, you have to have good people integrated into the effort at a very early stage. I don't know what techniques I used personally; nothing specifically different . . . but people respond. Everybody has a job to do, and they can feel it.

Where project management differs particularly (from functional controls) is in evaluating performance against time, and progress against costs incurred, collectively. The ability to evaluate performance versus time versus money on each part of his program is one of the requirements and special skills that distinguishes the project manager from all other managers.

—John Stanley Baumgartner

In doing a job, an individual reaches successive "plateaus" of learning where no improvement in his skill can be detected for a time. There is no advance warning when the individual is able to move to the next higher plateau in his skill. No mathematical models show what to expect from an individual. One never knows when the highest plateau has been reached. Consider the blind poet Milton; the deaf musician Beethoven; the once tongue-tied orator Demosthenes; the once crippled boy, later holder of the world record for the mile run, Glenn Cunningham.

—Wiley F. Patton

6

Faith Restored—The F-15 Program*

Major Gilbert B. Guarino
Major Relva L. Lilly
Major James J. Lindenfelser

With the initiation of full-scale development on 1 January 1970, the F-15 System Program Office (SPO) was charged by Deputy Secretary of Defense David Packard to develop the world's best air superiority fighter aircraft and, at the same time, restore Congress' and the public's faith in the ability of DOD to manage weapon system programs successfully.

The concepts and techniques used on the F-15 were not all new. Many had existed for quite some time. The significant fact was that the F-15 represented the first instance where all appropriate management concepts were successfully integrated and implemented. In short, the F-15 served as the model and test program for what was to become Secretary Packard's documented philosophy, as provided in DOD Directive 5000.1: "Acquisition of Major Defense Systems."

This brief introduction sets the stage for a discussion of the F-15 weapon system acquisition concepts implemented in response to the demand for effective and efficient program management.

*Air University Review, January-February 1976, pp. 63–77.

Personnel

The single most critical factor in the successful acquisition of a weapon system is the personnel responsible for program accomplishment. Above all else, the program must be directed by an individual with proven management ability. He must possess a complete understanding of the weapon system acquisition process and its inherent problems. Furthermore, he must be given full responsibility and authority for the success or failure of the program.

The selection of the F-15 System Program Director (SPD), Major General Benjamin N. Bellis (then a B/G selectee), in mid-1969 reflected these considerations. Having acquired extensive program experience during previous assignments, he was given full responsibility and authority for the direction of the F-15 program. To complement his position, the SPD was allowed to operate under the "Blueline Management Concept," which streamlined the chain of command. This concept gave the SPD immediate access to top USAF and OSD decision-makers. Blueline management proved to be extremely valuable during the course of the F-15 program and resulted in timely and effective decisions on critical program issues.

Just as the selection of the SPD is critical to the success of a program, so is the selection of all key subordinate personnel. The F-15 SPD was given complete authority to handpick all personnel. Consequently, each person assigned to the F-15 SPO was carefully screened and selected on the basis of proven performance. SPO personnel were given tremendous responsibility and authority to carry out their assigned tasks.

Continuity of key military personnel, usually a problem on most programs, was maintained by a personnel freeze for a period of five years. Reassignment prior to five years was at the option of the individual and the SPD. Consequently, it was rare when a key manager was transferred at an inopportune time.

Another important aspect of personnel management was the phased manning concept used to staff the SPO. Personnel who normally are not assigned to a SPO until the development or production phases were assigned to the F-15 during the conceptual and validation phases. This allowed experts in test, production, logistics, as well as other functional disciplines, to be involved during the basic program planning, thereby reducing the possibility of problems and misunderstandings.

Organization

The F-15 organization was based on a matrix that integrated two types of traditional organizations: project and functional. A project manager was designated for each major program development area, including airframe, engine, avionics, armament, TEWS, AGE, training, and support.

The project organization was overlaid onto a functional organization, consisting of Engineering, Configuration Management, Test and Deployment, Integrated Logistics Support, Production and Procurement, and Program Control Directorates. Each directorate was charged with specific functional tasks across all project areas. Both project and functional personnel performed their tasks in accordance with the overall program plan. Project managers were focal points for specific program areas, reporting directly to the SPD. For problems and tasks not detailed in the program plan, project managers were responsible for resolution and implementation. In short, each project manager was a mini-SPD for his area of responsibility.

The strength of this type of organization rested on two separate and internal SPO interfaces. The first was the daily interface between the project and functional managers, which facilitated early problem identification and resolution. The second was the interface between the project managers and the functional managers with the SPD. This latter interface was extremely successful in assuring that problems would surface before permanent impacts could result.

Command Interface

Early involvement of using and supporting command personnel greatly contributed to the success of the F-15 program. From early in the conceptual phase, TAC, AFLC, and ATC personnel were involved during requirements formulation and Request for Proposal (RFP) preparation. Colocated in the SPO, these personnel were an integral part of the F-15 team. Reporting directly to the top levels of their respective commands, they could handle problems and misunderstandings in a timely and effective manner. Further, specific individuals within the respective command headquarters were designated as focal points, which facilitated rapid and effective communications.

The Integrated Logistics Support (ILS) Directorate was staffed with both AFLC and AFSC personnel. The director of this organization reported both to the SPD and through the AFLC chain of command. This individual would ultimately become the AFLC System Manager (SM) for the F-15. The ILS Directorate was vitally concerned with weapon system supportability, and they, along with the Engineering Directorate, had a tremendous effect on reducing projected F-15 operations and maintenance costs.

The three elements just presented (personnel, organization, and command interface) provided the framework upon which the success of all other management concepts rests. As the remaining concepts are discussed, these elements should be kept in mind.

Planning

The F-15 SPO placed maximum emphasis on early and definitized planning in an effort to stabilize and control the program in terms of cost, schedule, and technical performance. The primary objectives of this extensive planning were to identify potential problems early enough to allow timely corrective action, minimize misunderstandings between the SPO and the contractors, and above all else, optimize the F-15 weapon system cost-of-ownership.

In support of this latter objective, the F-15 weapon system design emphasized simplicity, complete subsystem integration and testing, and designed-in reliability and maintainability. The early involvement of using and supporting commands facilitated planning and enabled early stabilization of program requirements.

Comprehensive plans and specifications, which documented program requirements and time-phased cost objectives for all program segments, were completed well in advance of contract award. This effort was not limited to just the air vehicle. It also provided for air vehicle support: training, spares, technical data, and facility requirements. This total planning approach proved to be an immeasurable asset in the success of the F-15 program.

System Definition and Design

The most important result of F-15 planning was realistic system definition. Unrealistic performance requirements, which are either unnecessary or push the state of the art to an unreasonable limit, often result in significant cost growth and/or schedule delays. Indiscriminate application of military standards and specifications can further impact the accomplishment of program objectives.

F-15 planners within OSD, Hq USAF, Hq TAC, Hq AFSC, and the SPO recognized these dangers. Consequently, the F-15 weapon system was designed primarily for a single mission requirement—air superiority. The design philosophy stressed utilization of existing state-of-the-art equipment and the discriminate application and tailoring of military standards and specifications.

Test Philosophy

The basic test philosophy of the F-15 program emphasized early and complete subsystem and system ground testing well in advance of flight testing. Complete ground subsystems functional, static, and fatigue tests were accomplished before significant hardware was committed to test aircraft fabrication. This philosophy, coupled with the extensive planning effort, minimized the possibility of surprises during the flight-test program and consequent costly and time-consuming modifications.

F-15 testing utilized the "test-before-fly" and "fly-before-buy" concepts wherever possible. During the validation phase, two prototype development contracts were awarded for each of three critical subsystems: the engine, the fire control radar, and the advanced 25-mm gun. Competitive development of these three systems significantly reduced the degree of risk to an acceptable level before full-scale development was undertaken by a single source.

Although highly desirable, "fly-before-buy" cannot always be applied in the full prototype sense, because of the prohibitive costs and time associated with large complex systems such as the F-15. However, extensive wind-tunnel testing, simulation, and subsystem prototype testing and analysis can be quite effective when total system prototyping is not feasible. This approach was used on the F-15 program and effectively minimized unnecessary risks prior to contract award and flight-testing. The "test-before-fly" and "fly-before-buy" philosophy resulted in a highly successful, on-schedule flight-test program with an excellent safety record.

Additionally, early participation of Air Force flight-test and support personnel from AFSC, TAC, AFLC, and ATC in what was then called the Contractor Development, Test and Evaluation Program (CDT&E) was a key element of the F-15 test plan. Past programs have demonstrated the need for early identification of weapon system deficiencies in order to minimize retrofit liability, ensure early production effectivity of flight-test changes, and minimize multiple operational configurations.

Supportability

Integrated Logistics Support was another key concept effectively employed in the F-15 program. Integrated plans and schedules for all support activities, including hardware and software, were prepared well in advance of contract award and were integral elements of both the RFP and contract specifications. Supportability is usually the last consideration on most acquisition programs, and it often results in enormous support costs and maintenance problems. Not so for the F-15. Supportability considerations were as much a part of the F-15 program planning as was the basic aircraft design. The ultimate benefit of this approach will be reduced O&M costs for an F-15 squadron.

Traditionally, weapon system managers design-the-support and support-the-design, but rarely do they design-for-support in terms of incorporating supportability considerations into the basic system design. In the case of the F-15, maximum emphasis was placed on this latter activity in an attempt to achieve one of the major program goals: minimum cost of ownership.

F-15 planning also placed early emphasis on determining the optimum level of repair for all F-15 hardware and identifying those items that would be best repaired at the organizational, intermediate or depot levels. The importance of AGE, spares, technical data, facilities, and training requirements was recognized, and they were planned and developed concurrently with the air vehicle. This effort helped ensure that adequate support would be available at the time of initial operations. In spite of this excellent support planning, initial support of F-15 operations was not without its problems. Had supportability considerations not been given such a high priority early in the development program, weapon system support would have been impacted even more. Hopefully, the lessons learned in this critical area of weapon system acquisition can be transfused to new acquisitions to provide an improved initial support posture.

Suffice it to say that supportability considerations were given a high priority along with the performance of the air vehicle. As a result, the forecasted F-15 O&M costs are almost 35 per cent less than those for the F-4 when the F-15 reaches maturity.

Contracting Methodology

The F-15 contracting approach enabled the program to capitalize on the strong points of current acquisition philosophies and concepts. The contract on any program is undoubtedly a major factor in determining the success or failure of that program. The contract, its specifications, plans, and data requirements must be specifically defined to clearly delineate contractor and government responsibilities. At the same time, the contract must provide the flexibility demanded by the dynamic weapon system acquisition environment. In particular, Congressional actions and program changes must be handled without breaking the contract, if at all possible. With these points as guides, F-15 contracts were written to reflect the degree of risk involved in the development and production programs.

To provide the control and flexibility required, the F-15 contracts contained many innovative management clauses. One of the most successful is the Total System Performance Responsibility (TSPR) clause. This clause clearly charged the air vehicle prime contractor (McDonnell Aircraft Company—McAIR) with responsibility for total system integration, performance and support. This provision covered all components of the F-15, whether built by the TSPR contractor, subcontracted by him, or provided to him in the form of government-furnished equipment (GFE). This clause shifted a great deal of responsibility and risk from the government to the TSPR contractor.

A second unique contract clause provided funding stability to the F-15 program. The Limitation of Government Obligation (LOGO) requires the contractor to identify any changes in negotiated fiscal year (FY) funding requirements 17 months prior to the start of the FY. If appropriate notification was not received, any additional funding required during a given FY would have to be funded by the contractor until the SPO could obtain the additional funding during the next budget cycle. Interest on any loan or lost interest from investment was not reimbursable. The incentive, therefore, to forecast funding requirements accurately was considerable.

A third clause, Correction of Deficiency (COD), defined the contractor's responsibility for correcting defective equipment once accepted by the government. This clause protected the government from long-range defects that could not be identified at the time of acceptance.

These three contract provisions serve as examples of the type of well-planned and innovative approaches that the F-15 SPO took in formulating its contracts to ensure control of the program. During the course of the program, the F-15 contracts proved to be a cornerstone for effective program management.

SPO/Contractor Interface

The interface between F-15 SPO personnel and the contractors was critical to the execution of the contract and the attainment of program goals. All levels of SPO management were totally involved in the day-to-day problems facing the prime contractors as well as many of their primary subcontractors and vendors. This total management engagement philosophy was implemented in order to prevent, or at least minimize, surprises at the contract level. This is not to say that resolution of problems immediately became a joint effort. On the contrary, it was the contractor's responsibility to develop solutions, submit them for approval (when required), and implement them to satisfy contract requirements. Early SPO awareness, however, ensures timely contractor action and SPO/higher-headquarters decisions (when required) and minimizes the risk of a serious impact to program cost, schedule, or technical objectives.

To operate effectively under this total engagement philosophy, temporary duty (TDY) was an essential element of the F-15 program approach. To fully engage the contractor and his key vendors (with prime contractor coordination) and obtain full visibility, personnel from the SPO and the contractors traveled extensively. Daily interfaces, problem-solving sessions, and in-plant reviews at all working levels were essential to ensure problem identification and prompt corrective action. A successful SPD must look at his TDY budget as a cost-effective tool in terms of the rate of return obtained from total engagement.

Cost and Schedule Control

Establishment of a reasonable time-phased initial program cost estimate is the key to achieving financial stability and credibility with Congress. After clearly defining program requirements, solid cost estimates for the F-15 were developed and time-phased with the program schedule plan. Anticipated scope and schedule changes were appropriately considered. Stabilized requirements, rigorous change control, and early identification of problems enabled F-15 financial managers to forecast budget requirements accurately. For more than four years, the F-15 program budget remained unchanged. Only unforeseen double-digit inflation and the withdrawal of the Navy from the joint engine program impacted the initial program budget as prepared in 1969. This was a singular accomplishment.

From a performance measurement standpoint, the F-15 implemented the Cost/Schedule Control System Criteria (C/SCSC). This management approach required all F-15 prime contractors and the McAIR radar subcontractor to design, develop, and implement management control systems (MCS's), which provided timely and valid cost and schedule status. These MCS's were based on existing contractor business practices and management techniques but were appropriately modified to meet the broad guidelines of C/SCSC. The most important benefit derived from C/SCSC application was the disciplined, detailed planning required early in the program.

Control of program costs and schedules directly relates to many of the technical management concepts discussed previously. However, to control these parameters, it is essential to know the program's status and potential problem areas. The cost/schedule control techniques employed on the F-15 proved to be extremely valuable in this regard.

Production and Quality Assurance

The production and quality assurance management philosophy also contributed significantly to the success of the F-15 program.

Preparation of the F-15 production and quality plans involved SPO, contractor, and government plant representative personnel. This joint effort, conducted prior to development contract award, ensured mutual understanding of procedures and techniques to be used by both the contractor and the government. Production and quality requirements were levied on all prime contractors, with the stipulation that they require all their subcontractors and vendors to comply with the same type of contractual provisions. The F-15 program excelled in this area because of the degree to which these requirements were implemented, practiced, and monitored. Production and quality assurance discipline helped to ensure minimum rework and acceptable performance, thereby assisting in the control of program costs.

Configuration Management

Configuration management, or change control discipline, was one more key to the successful management of the F-15 development program. Changing requirements and the resultant rework are expensive and time consuming. To maintain change control, the SPD established stringent criteria for the evaluation of changes. Prior to the submittal of any change to the SPO, a coordinated SPO/contractor analysis was accomplished to justify formal submittal of the change. There had to be a sound technical basis for the change or else it was not considered. Furthermore, proposed changes had to be justified and related to standard practice, development testing, or operational experience.

Unforeseen changes to any program, no matter how well planned and defined, are inevitable. Therefore, an effective means of handling them is essential. Change administration on the F-15 program had to meet one major constraint. No changes would be authorized without completing negotiations, including cost, schedule, and technical modifications.

All proposed changes, regardless of their source, were challenged for need. Proposals were thoroughly reviewed by all SPO activities, contractors, and the using and supporting commands. After a complete review the proposed change was submitted to the SPO Configuration Control Board (CCB). The CCB, consisting of a representative of each SPO directorate, TAC, AFLC, ATC, and the Judge Advocate's office, discussed each change and then recommended approval or disapproval. Integral to this entire process was the relationship between cost, contractual, and technical disciplines. If the change was determined to be essential, the funds had to be available and authorized for use before the change could be negotiated and contractually authorized. Rigorous adherence to change control procedures by all contractor and SPO personnel maintained program stability and facilitated cost and schedule control.

Considerable credit for the success of the F-15 program must go to the advanced and forward-looking policies of the DOD that were just being established at the time the F-15 program was being initiated. Most of the credit, however, must go to the F-15 team, which implemented those policies and invented new ones along the way.

The ultimate purpose of this article is to highlight many successful techniques and concepts used to acquire a complex weapon system. It was not by magic that the F-15 acquisition was as relatively trouble-free as it was. Comprehensive, detailed, and exhaustive effort toward one common goal—to build the best, on time, and within the budget—contributed to the F-15 success.

If DOD is to succeed in providing for the nation's continued security, weapon system managers must learn from the successes and failures of past programs. The F-15's lessons learned can provide considerable help to ensure future acquisition successes. Specifically, many of the techniques and concepts applied to the F-15 program are as applicable in today's environment as they were at the height of F-15 development. Each new program, however, must be evaluated individually and appropriate concepts selected and tailored for successful application in the ever-changing weapon system acquisition environment.

7

A Program Manager Looks at Program Management*

Captain M. H. Sappington, USN
Captain W. E. Meyer, USN

Program management requires a central coordinator and decision-maker throughout the entire life cycle of a major weapon system. The manager is the point of authority and commitment for his program, both technically and fiscally. The emphasis placed by Mr. Packard on the manager's role has focused attention on his function, relationship to OSD, and his responsibility.

Program management is influenced by organizational tradition, the size, importance and urgency of the program and a multitude of other factors, not excluding the strength and will of the manager himself. It is profitable to look at specific examples to identify some of the problems experienced in evolving program management techniques, and thereby to help guide the applications of this dynamic concept in the future.

AEGIS is an excellent case study since the requirements and technical approach were defined in 1963, the time that project definition (now called contract definition) was being born. AEGIS has had a program manager from its inception. The program has experienced several changes and mutations in weapon system acquisition procedures as they have evolved—concept formulation, contract definition, the OSD management review, the DSARC, the DCP, and the SAR to name some of the most prominent steps. The

*Defense Management Journal, Fall 1971, pp. 42–45.

AEGIS program has had the benefits, the growing pains, and the problems resulting from the management evolution of the last decade.

The AEGIS is a medium range, surface-to-air, all weather system for first line Navy escorts providing defense against attack aircraft, air-to-surface and surface-to-surface missiles, and surface targets. It will provide the surface fleet with a modern air defense capability to meet future threats as these evolve. The development project involves the typical challenges of the times in respect to great cost, technical complexity, interfaces with other programs, and a scope requiring coordination of many normally more independent agencies and fields of activity.

The program was generated by the classic evolutionary process of identifying the problem, cataloging and evaluating possible solutions, and selecting the most suitable set of answers. This process was iterated over a longer period of time than is often the case. Approximately $30 million were spent up through contract definition. These funds were devoted to laying out a detailed system performance specification and in conducting technical experiments to verify that the program objectives could be achieved within the state of the art. This magnitude of effort had two major impacts. First, it generated an extremely knowledgeable Navywide team with close-knit cooperation and group spirit. Second, it led to a system specification that was orders of magnitude more completely defined than any preceding specification for a Navy weapons system, firmly based on demonstrated technology.

The AEGIS program is now in the midst of engineering development, guided by a program manager who is filling exactly the role intended. Such management is essential and is proving successful by all conventional yardsticks. However, without challenging the general concept of program management, a number of difficulties are becoming evident which it will be instructive to examine.

The first two problem areas arise from the extensive buildup of Navy capability and knowledge and the articulation of the detailed specifications which, of course, are basically of great benefit to the whole program. In the long contract definition evolution for AEGIS, the Navy technical groups supported by the Applied Physics Laboratory of John Hopkins University worked through many alternate system concepts, ran experiments on components and simulations of systems, and studied the consequences of many potential courses of development. As a result, many key design features were, to a degree, imposed on the competing contractors rather than evolved by the competition itself. The winning contractor, however, was expected to assume full responsibility for performance of the system and for executing the program. The complete transfer of responsibility to an initially less-informed group, who had had rather little opportunity to influence the approach to be taken, and even many of the details, has led to a rather lengthy period of adjustment and learning. Thus, the ideal continuity of effort, and the desired prompt vigorous start on the contract development, was not supported by the way the experience had been built up.

As a consequence of the very detailed specification provided by the government, the contractor responses during the competitive phase were also very detailed. This led to what is now recognized as an excessive amount of material submitted for review in the selection process. Just the processing of all this material, both on the part of the contractors and the government, was a large burden, probably not all productive. More importantly, however, the detailed and structured requirements, especially in a competitive atmosphere, may have tended to foster conformity rather than creativity, and thereby some potential benefits of competition and industry know-how may have been lost. Even if this did not occur, there was an inevitable tendency for the contractors to freeze their approaches at this very early stage in a rigid program to respond to the very definitive specification. There is a delicate balance required in such contracting between, on the one hand, the government deciding precisely what it wants in order to control the effort and, on the other hand, leaving freedom to incorporate the good ideas that can be provided by industry and that may grow as the program proceeds. The best of both benefits has not yet been assured.

A program development is, quite properly, carried out in an environment of many standard regulations, military specifications, engineering requirements, and contract policies. In a large complex system, however, combinations of those constraints can sometimes cascade into impractical or unrealistic requirements, not originally intended. The program manager must frequently review the consequences of these more or less routine requirements, to adapt them to his needs. The normal procedures do not assure bringing to bear the wisdom of the past in an acceptable manner, without new initiative.

People are the manager's most important resource. Mr. Packard has stressed the need to retain the program managers for longer tours and to relieve them only at carefully selected times relative to project milestones. Possibly as much attention should also be paid to the team that works with the manager. The individual experts are dedicated, skilled, and cooperative. Problems arise, however, because of the organizational ties of the staff. Program management is fundamentally a vertical organization function. The staffing and support is normally supplied to the program by a number of more permanent parent activities with horizontally aligned organizations. The manager does not have complete control over staff assignments, tenure, number of people, or priorities of work. Effective working relations with the parent organizations are, of course, vital to the program. Experience suggests, however, that a greater degree of program office autonomy in personnel, possibly made visible by explicit program budgeting for support of the staff, would help the manager in applying his total resources effectively.

The responsibility of the manager to assign priorities and exercise his authority through the control of funds is fundamental to his operation. The manager controls a larger budget than is represented by his prime contract, in order to support government furnished equipment and tests, backup or alternate approaches in risk areas, growth studies, and of course, the management itself, which is considerable. The focus of reviews of budget or program performance tends to be on the prime contract because of its size and prominence in setting up the work under competition. Moreover, the prime contract tends to be most tightly funded, because of the competitive bidding. The program manager, however, must allocate and adjust his total budget as events unfold. Circumstances outside the prime contractor's activities may nevertheless affect his support. The reviews could well reflect this broader view.

In view of large program costs, there tend to be frequent and persistent reviews of the value and priorities of the development. There are recurring proposals for different schedules, different technical characteristics, and different applications or goals. The manager must be responsive to genuine and necessary changes in objectives, support, or technology, but he is required in practice also to divert much effort to justifications and debate that do not arise from fundamentally new circumstances. Programs are increasingly having to struggle to maintain stability of approved plans and support within the military department. Every re-examination of a past decision, if not really necessary, detracts efforts from development progress. A better balance between program stability and proper responsiveness to changing circumstances within the Department of Defense would significantly contribute to timely program accomplishment. The number of offices in Navy, DOD, Bureau of Budget and various advisory and review boards which can (and do) institute an examination of a program already underway is alarming, in spite of their competence and constructive purpose.

There is a formal review agency (DSARC) for measuring the project performance relative to a formal standard (DCP). This is helpful to the manager in defining his job clearly and provides for re-examination of the plans as found appropriate. However, the manager is not in control of some actions directly affecting the success or progress of the project, such as imposed by the contracting regulations (e.g., consequence of a strike), or by the higher budget officers (e.g., rescheduling of funds). The manager has responsibility but not exactly matching authority.

AEGIS, like any large project, is intimately related to others under separate control. Two examples of AEGIS are the new ship construction which will provide the seagoing platform for the new weapon system and the whole ship command and control complex derived from the Navy tactical data system (NTDS). When these other projects change, as they frequently do, in respect to budgets, priorities, schedules, or technical approaches, there is a significant potential impact on the AEGIS program itself. There is no adequate mechanism for keeping all these efforts mutually in tune. The respective managers try, on their personal initiative, to keep informed and to keep their separate programs adaptive. Some of the interactions are too large to handle on this basis and, of necessity, are pushed upward for resolution or decision.

The project is constrained to rigid goals, schedules and costs, by contracts and by higher management (e.g., DSARC). On the other hand, there are major pressures for change, due to new goals (such as installing AEGIS on a smaller ship), technology evolution (such as electronic switching of transmitters between antennas), or development obstacles or delays (such as problems in implementing ECCM). The formalities stress control; the changing circumstances favor flexibility. The manager wants the protection of the controls, but the freedom of action implied by the flexibility. He has not found a good way to have both and must accommodate to realities, using his judgment based on best advice available.

In large projects, there have developed strong external pressures to make the product cheaper or simpler without loss in essential performance. This approach is variously attributed to an impression that initial designs tend to be unnecessarily "gold plated," or that "real effort" brought about by applied pressure can surely disclose some better approaches. These in some instances can focus on a particular technical or management feature where alternate views are held by the reviewer. Constructive review should always be encouraged. However, a blanket presumption that any carefully considered plan must be further improved may be a very artificial discipline. It is the program manager's responsibility to promote economy and simplicity in keeping with the overall program objectives. A procedure for encouraging and capitalizing on favorable trade-offs or new approaches as development proceeds will generally be more productive than economy by fiat before development starts.

Our final problem area is the most timely and sensitive of all. Cost growth and schedule slippage are treated as indications of incompetence, at least, or even crimes in the eyes of the more vociferous critics. These two potential difficulties hang over the manager as almost inevitable. Accurate prediction of costs and schedules cannot realistically be expected at the beginning of a long complex development. Although there are bureaucratic pressures against including safety margins and to keep costs low when making the initial estimates, such figures would not be any more "honest" or useful. The plain fact is that any large undertaking extending well into the future, especially involving new development, cannot be accurately forecast in advance. An attempt to freeze all subsequent operations to fit a particular forecast will impose rigidity and not necessarily permit the best product to be achieved. Finally, loss of planned and budgeted funds in the middle of a long development program dictates stretchout with ensuing cost growth.

The manager should be expected to produce the best product at the least price, with suitable periodic external reviews (e.g., DSARC) of the adequacy of product and acceptability of price—but not to follow exactly a map drawn up before anyone has entered the new territory. The solution is not to draw a better map, but to adopt an approach that finds the best path.

Many of the difficulties and problems sketched above reflect in one way or another the conflict between providing tight and complete control of a program and providing flexibility to adapt to external circumstances or internally generated new options as the program proceeds. The program manager seeks both, but the major program acquisition process has yet to evolve a final solution to this challenge.

The critical or problem-seeking tone of this discussion should not obscure the great advances that have been achieved in program management. Program management has a new and mature look, and there is evidence that it can meet the challenge of today's incredibly complex undertakings such as AEGIS. Our task is to build on the foundation of responsibility, authority, and accountability that is now established, in order to perfect this important tool.

8

Getting Weapons That Do the Job*

Lieutenant General Bryce Poe, II

I am delighted to be here this evening. I have always been a fan of the American Defense Preparedness Association and my respect for your organization has grown still more since I've taken over my present job as commander, Air Force Acquisition Logistics Division (AFALD). For example, I particularly appreciate the part the association has played in sponsoring software life cycle system management courses. That is exactly what we need to improve our performance in that critical and different area.

What We Do

For the next few minutes, let's talk about the Air Force Acquisition Logistics Division, why we were formed, what we're trying to do. Our mission in your Air Force is to deter war or, that failing, fight war. Too often, however, instead of being ready to deliver weapons like this (F-111), the aircraft are spread all over the depot floor; instead of F-4's being lined up for takeoff, all too many are lined up at Ogden or Casa Getafe.

Make no mistake, I'm proud of the Air Force. We do things very well—much better than any other air force I know—but we're big, and there's a long distance, physically and psychologically,

*Extract from a speech to The American Defense Preparedness Association, February 23, 1977

between factory or depot and flight line. Sometimes this is compounded by money problems—for example, when we see a chance to save money in the long run but it costs so much now that the additional requirement for funds may literally kill the program; the question then is, "Do you want the system, faults and all, or don't you want it?"

We also have many circumstances when we're faced with a sudden reduction or stretchout of program funds—as by the Congress. When such an unprogrammed cut hits us, the support area almost always takes the brunt.

Problems Self-Induced

Many of our problems are, however, self-induced. Due to ignorance, indifference, or just lack of attention to detail, we not only make mistakes—understandable—but repeat them—unforgivable.

Let's begin with my favorite example—removal of the ejection seat in the F-4. This is the most common maintenance task in the Air Force, consistently one of the top-ranking logistic support costs worldwide.

We spend one-quarter million dollars a month (over 58,000 manhours) in logistics support costs to remove those seats. There's nothing wrong with the seat—we have to take it out to get at a radio whose cost of repair is so low it doesn't even appear in the top-20 ranked logistics support cost items.

In the GBU-15 we went to great lengths to build intermediate level support equipment designed to provide fault isolation of guidance module failures to the individual circuit card. However, access to that card requires a "clean room," neither authorized nor available at that level.

A new 1,000-dollar fuse mechanical unit was developed as a sealed, nonreparable, discard-at-failure item. It included a $50 battery with a 90-day service life.

We have persisted in using heavy castings, such as T-6 aluminum, on landing gear, even with a history of stress corrosion cracks.

Some of our tech data compounds the problem. Example from the APN-185 Doppler radar alignment tech data: "Turn simulator power off. This is accomplished by removing 16 cross-recessed screws from the front panel." There are 19 screws in the panel, none of which will turn off the power.

I've started with these examples because now and again I meet people who say that the only real problems we have supporting weapons are money problems. We have those, of course, but in many cases I feel they're in the minority. So, it's our job in AFALD to improve reliability, maintainability, and supportability of weapon systems. The key to this is getting into the acquisition process early.

Weapons Acquisition

Let's review the system for weapons acquisition. Traditionally, program managers have made their decisions on the interaction between technical performance, schedule, and costs. Under a free enterprise system, market conditions determine the give-and-take between these parameters. However, military program managers have normally operated on the leading edge of technology. In seeking to give our fighting men the best possible weapon systems, military program managers have tended to make technical performance a fixed goal. Schedule and acquisition cost then become variables which were adjusted to account for the risk associated with extending technology to achieve that performance goal.

That management approach, together with inflation, led to the cost overruns with which we are all too familiar. Recognizing the problem, Deputy Secretary of Defense Packard in the early '60s issued DOD instructions which decentralized program management in the acquisition of major defense systems; and formally introduced integrated logistics support considerations into the acquisition cycle.

As a result of these two policy changes, program managers were directed to make their decisions on the basis of four coequal parameters: technical performance, schedule, acquisition cost, and operating and support (O&S) costs. Formal consideration of logistics supportability as a "design-to" requirement meant treating O&S costs coequally with technical performance, schedule, and acquisition cost. This significantly expanded the system program director's workload. To assist him in the integrated logistics support area, a deputy program manager for logistics was added.

Now we all realize that trades between these four coequal parameters must be made carefully—cheap and ineffective weapons won't deter our enemy or win in war. So we began to work the problem. We bought tires by the cost per landing instead of the cost per tire, we pooled resources with our sister services, and we began to learn how to do cost analyses over the entire life of a system.

Increased Costs

Nevertheless, by 1968 the costs of supporting a weapon system increased past the combined cost of development and acquisition; and the trend didn't stop there, but continued on until O&S began to significantly reduce the dollars available for development of new systems. Why? There were many reasons. The pay of the Air Force flightline mechanic was finally raised to a proper level. Even more significant was that the increasing threat caused us to demand still more and more performance, so we were directing the contractors to build even more complex equipment—difficult to support, expensive to operate.

The nation had also reordered its priorities. Since 1960 defense's percentage of the Federal budget has decreased from 46 percent to 26 percent, from more than eight percent of the gross national product to less than six percent.

During that same period we've seen priority shift to social programs—the dollars applied to those areas are up 186 percent in the past five years; 15 percent in the year before that. Altogether, they are now two and one-half times that allocated to defense.

I'm certain those areas can profitably use all that money and more, but the change in emphasis had to impact on the cost of operating weapons. For one thing, we kept systems much longer than programmed. Parts wore out that we never anticipated. (For example, who would have guessed at the B-52 rollout in 1952 that the aircraft would still be on alert 25 years later—in 1977—and scheduled to continue on into the 1980's?) With less money available for ever more expensive parts, we found it necessary to remove, *repair,* and replace items that we had planned merely to remove and replace.

Whatever the reasons, the result was clear. Cut operating and support costs or forget about development and acquisition of the new weapons required to meet an ever more serious threat.

Expansion of Role

The whole Air Force worked the problem. In AFLC, a Deputy Chief of Staff for Acquisition Logistics was established and made significant progress in reducing costs. That success prompted the Air Force Chief of Staff, General Jones, to direct an expansion of the AFLC role in acquisition management. On May 6, 1976, he approved establishment of the Air Force Acquisition Logistics Division and charged us to:

- reduce system life cycle costs
- strengthen the AFLC role in the acquisition process
- expand early support planning
- improve AFLC/AFSC operating command/contractor interface
- improve quality and expertise of logisticians
- feed back lessons learned from operational units.

On May 25, 1976, General Rogers, AFLC commander, issued the AFALD activation orders, effective July 1, 1976. His ground rules were:

- Headquarters AFLC retains most policy
- AFALD is not a "DCS"—it's an operational field organization
- Initial procurement tasks: business strategy, procurement planning
- look for joint AFLC/AFSC initiatives
- seek interservice maintenance and standardized opportunities
- phased buildup, functions, and manpower
- not revolutionary—but evolutionary
- not to "take over"—but to help "fill gaps."

That's where I came in—I have been told that my selection was not so much because of my experience as an AFLC center commander and logistician, but for the many more years experience I have in the operational area. I consider myself the "ombudsman" for the flight-line mechanic and his wing commander. Our job is to influence the design of new systems, so that the new system is:

- *available* to that wing commander's mission
- *maintainable* to that flight-line mechanic
- *reliable* to that aircrew that flies the system
- and above all, that the system is *affordable* to the Air Force.

Now, how do we get there from here? We intend to:

- challenge operational requirements
- seek to use technology to improve reliability as often as performance
- feed back problems and successes
- standardize and share when it makes sense
- go "off the shelf" when it makes sense not to re-invent the wheel
- tie product quality (i.e., reliability, maintainability, and availability) to the contractor's profit and loss statement

- go anywhere, look at anything, steal anyone's ideas to get the job done.

In the final analysis, as I mentioned at the outset, what we are most concerned with is the *availability* of weapon systems.

Reliability and Maintainability

Availability of equipment has to do mainly with that equipment's reliability and maintainability. Lack of either greatly increases cost. So, that's really what we're talking about when we say life cycle costs. The cost of designing in reliability, versus the cost of making it work if we don't. In the words of the commercial, "pay me now or pay me later," the presumption is that it is a great deal cheaper to design in reliability than to make it work later if we don't.

What are some of the tools or techniques that we can use to cause our systems to be more reliable? There are many—and several more are still evolving. But first, let me emphasize one very important point: the most effective tool we can have is the attitude of the people who are working the problem—and I mean *all* the people who are working the problem—especially the program managers, the DPML's and the contractors.

It would be difficult to overstate the importance of attitude. All of our tools are essentially designed to motivate the contractors to provide us with field reliable equipment. We think that with varying degrees of success, they do just that.

Where Do We Stand?

So where do we stand?

We have learned some important lessons. First, get into the program as early as possible, and get the contractors to sign up to support cost commitments while they're still in competition.

We've also beefed up our ability to analyze life cycle cost. We've put analysts into our field directorates at the AFSC product divisions, and we've assigned them to the integrated logistics support offices of the larger programs. We have worked with the Air Force Institute of Technology to develop a short course in LCC analysis, and the Air Staff has sponsored a series of seminars on LCC/DTC/RIW.

We're working very hard at feed-back, so that we never make the same mistake twice. We're learning from everyone: experts at the contractors' plants, the product divisions, the air logistics centers, and the mechanics on the flight-line.

At a higher policy level, we're beginning to see program management directives (PMD's) carrying much stronger words on the treatment of LCC. From just a couple years ago, when PMD's were usually totally silent on LCC, they went to at least a nod in the right direction by saying that "life cycle costing will be considered," to the more recent language along the line, "life cycle costs will be estimated and methods for using reliability improvement warranties and support cost guarantees will be investigated." It can't be stressed enough that the contractor is a key participant and a full partner in driving down the cost of ownership. After all, it's through his efforts in designing supportability into his products that we actually reap the benefits of LCC.

Defense industry is clearly getting more interested and involved. Professional articles and seminars, which include LCC and related topics, are appearing more frequently. I mentioned your software course. The National Security Industrial Association has established a separate committee on life cycle costing application and furnished some valuable recommendations to the DOD.

Other Activities

There are a couple of other activities which you ought to be aware of. One is a DOD task group on increasing the visibility of support costs by weapon systems. While we have hundreds of data and cost systems in DOD, nearly all are oriented toward some function, such as provisioning, transportation, procurement, and so forth—and none allows us to add up all the operating and support costs of a single weapon system. The job of the task group is to find a way to accumulate the operating and support costs for a given system. Their initial progress is good.

Another action is the organization of a tri-service working group to study reliability and support incentives. This group includes experts from the R&D, materiel acquisition, and maintenance communities of the three Services and has been in existence for almost a year. One of the specific tasks, for which the Air Force is leading the effort, is the establishment of a tri-service RIW data center to give visibility to lessons learned in this area.

One Key Point

That's all the time I have. Rather than summarize, I'd like to make one key point. If I get only one message across here today, it must be that we in the Air Force mean business when we say we intend to improve the reliability and maintainability—and thereby reduce the cost of operating—our weapons. And, as one who has spent most of his thirty-plus years on the line charged with keeping aircraft and missiles ready to go to war, I say "Three cheers—it's about time!"

Thank you very much for your time and attention.

Some lessons we learned from earlier programs are: go with a really competent project team; get a really capable contractor; recognize the need for flexibility. This is how we laid out the F-15.

—Hon. Robert C. Seamans,
Secretary of the Air Force

The system view is also needed to control engineering optimism. It seems to be a law of nature that as the development progresses, the system will get bigger and never smaller, heavier and never lighter—no matter how conscientious the planning and system design. System trade-offs will be essential, and the system view can be obtained only if you stand apart from subsystem partisanship.

—LMI Introduction to
Military Program Management

If we were to fail to protect our own interests, we would find that there is no one else in the world who could, or would, do it for us.

To my amazement, there are some—even in the Congress—who profess to be unalarmed at the notion of this nation's slipping to second-rank. I can only assume that they have ignored the lessons of history and some obvious hard facts about the world today. Are we so accustomed to having power and being secure that—as with good health—we sometimes fail to recognize where we would be without them? Were the United States to lose the ability to influence events, we could not assume that our own well-being would be untouched. We would suffer economically and politically as our status declined, even before our security was threatened.

—Donald H. Rumsfeld, Secretary of Defense

Section 2—

THE SYSTEM MANAGER

Introduction

Much of the general literature on project management theory is concerned with the PM's authority: formal versus informal, the need for higher level support, and problems of authority versus responsibility. In practice, however, the PM simply *takes* whatever authority he needs. Either the problems disappear, therefore, or the PM does. Asked whether he had a statement on his authority as Apollo Director, Gen. Sam Phillips shot back, "No, and I didn't ask for one, either. If a PM has to be told what his authorities are, he's the wrong man for the job." Another PM says, "Authority is like a balloon. It rises unless the PM has a strong grasp on it."

One element the PM does need, however, is freedom to make decisions and to exercise his ingenuity. "The front office," commented the late Vince Lombardi, "is the worst place to get a run-or-pass decision when it's fourth down and goal to go." Unfortunately, the defense program manager is gradually losing this freedom, due to numerous reviews and approval requirements. His counterpart in industry has considerably more latitude in carrying out his assigned mission. The environment today is different from that when Col. Battle developed his salty code for the system program office.

This section is concerned with the system manager: what kind of individual he is and how he operates. The traits of the PM in industry and in defense are remarkably similar, as the discussion with Robert K. Duke brings out. Related to these characteristics is the ability to instill confidence in a program's sponsors, because there is usually a long period during which they have to rely on faith that the program manager is guiding his program satisfactorily toward their objectives. This higher level concern is related, of course, to the degree of freedom allowed the system manager.

The PM's job is a highly satisfying one though. It offers a keen challenge; a chance to use his full horsepower and the total range of his capabilities; an opportunity to run a "company within a company," even within the services; and visibility. He may also be an explorer, like the F-16 program director, in blazing a trail through multinational production and economics. In his words, "The potential pitfalls and complications are mind-boggling." But his program may well prove to be a model for future international ventures.

Recognition is often the PM's reward. The route to promotion is usually broader and straighter, in both industry and in defense, than in other types of responsibilities. And there's satisfaction in having done a difficult, unique job, like the mountain-climber's challenge: "because it's there, dammit!"

It is not the critic who counts; not the man who points out how the strong men stumbled or where the doer of deeds could have done them better.

The credit belongs to the man who is actually in the arena; whose face is marred by dust and sweat and blood; who strives valiantly; who errs and comes short again and again; who knows the great enthusiasms, the devotions, and spends himself in a worthy cause.

Who, at the best, knows the triumph of high achievement; and who, at the worst, if he fails, at least fails while daring greatly, so that his place shall never be with those cold and timid souls who knew neither victory nor defeat.

—Theodore Roosevelt

9

Marks of a Mature Manager*

Charles C. Gibbons†

A mature manager can best be described in terms of his characteristic behavior patterns. Although no one consistently behaves in a mature manner, mature behavior patterns are more characteristic of some individuals than of others. The mature manager is, first of all, a mature person, and this maturity is reflected in his relationships with subordinates, peers, and superiors.

Goals

The mature manager has well-defined goals and is willing to make the efforts necessary to accomplish them. While goals should be high enough to encourage excellence, they should not be so high as to be unattainable. A goal does not motivate behavior unless it requires effort to be attained. The mature manager knows he must pay the price for what he wants to accomplish; he does not expect to get something for nothing. Resources of money, manpower, time and effort must be allocated according to carefully considered priorities. Since a manager's resources are always limited, they must be allocated according to *his* priorities.

*Business Horizons, Volume 18, No. 5, pp. 54–56. Copyright 1975 by the Foundation for the School of Business at Indiana University. Reprinted by permission.
†Administrative Consultant, The Upjohn Company.

Responsibility

The mature manager is able to accept responsibility for making decisions and taking action. He resists the temptation to postpone difficult decisions or to ask his superior to make them. He knows from experience that he often cannot wait for all the facts he would like to have before deciding. Circumstances often require the manager to make decisions on the basis of insufficient information. If there were enough facts available on which to base each decision, the experience and judgment of the manager would not be needed. A mature manager is confident and secure enough not to be paralyzed by the fear of making a mistake in the decisions he makes and the actions he takes. Undue fear of making a mistake can lead to indecisiveness and procrastination which in themselves can lead to serious problems. A mature manager is willing to compromise on the best possible solution available under the circumstances. He is not a perfectionist holding out rigidly for what he regards as the perfect solution, which is in many cases unattainable.

Help From Others

Because he feels secure, the mature manager is able to accept help from others. Since by definition a manager is a person who gets things done through other people, the effectiveness of a manager depends on his ability and willingness to get help from his subordinates.

Delegation can be defined as entrusting responsibility and authority to others, who then become accountable for results. Books on management agree that managers should delegate but many managers find it difficult to do so. Many managers are afraid to delegate for fear the work will not be done properly unless they do it themselves. A mature manager is able to accept help from his subordinates because he is humble enough to know he doesn't have all the answers himself, and confident enough to know he can correct any mistakes his subordinates make. The mature manager expresses appreciation to others for the help they provide.

Motivation and Control

The mature manager is able to motivate and control himself. It is a mark of maturity to be able to keep one's efforts directed towards the accomplishment of certain goals. Occasionally it is necessary to do things that are difficult or unpleasant. Whereas children are often praised for their good work, adults must learn to get along on less praise than they think they deserve. Most of an adult's activities are internally motivated. A great challenge to many managers is to control their tempers. A childish display of temper often leads to irrational actions and ruptured personal relationships. A manager who is prone to outbursts of temper should regard the mastery of his temper as his first step towards maturity.

Use of Time

The mature manager knows that, since time is a strictly limited resource, he must allocate it carefully to the important projects which he wishes to complete. It takes real maturity to choose to spend one's time on certain activities with the full knowledge that other things will not get done. Peter Drucker has pointed out that it is not so important to do things right as to do the right thing, and the best way to save time is by not doing what does not need to be done. In choosing which matters deserve one's attention it is important to distinguish between the important and the urgent because urgent things are not always important, and important things are not always urgent.

The manager should do those things which only he can do—planning, organizing, directing, communicating, and controlling the operations under his authority. The performance of other activities should be delegated to his subordinates. The mature manager will not waste time making excuses, participating in needless controversy, and scrutinizing the work of his subordinates. He will not use the shortage of time as an alibi, for he knows that he, like everyone else, has twenty-four hours every day and that he does the things he really wants to do.

Good Relations With Others

The mature manager is able to establish and maintain good relations with others. These good relations are based on his accepting other people as they are and on his ability to understand and work harmoniously with them even though he may not like some of them personally. Much depends on his ability to put himself in the other person's shoes and to see a problem from the other person's point of view.

The mature manager must be able to deal effectively with feelings as well as with ideas. First, he must be able to understand, accept, and express his own feelings. No matter how hard he tries to overcome his biases and prejudices, he still has them. It is helpful to acknowledge these residual biases and to make allowance for them in decisions which are made.

The mature manager will be aware of the feelings other people are experiencing and expressing. He will listen for feelings as well as for ideas. It is a difficult, but important, skill to be able to acknowledge and reflect the feelings of others. It is not necessary to agree with the other person but only to let him know that his feelings are understood.

Emotional Maturity

The mature manager has resources within himself for coping with frustration, disappointment, and stress. It is inevitable that every person will face serious problems from time to time. How he handles these problems is a measure of his emotional maturity. A mature manager's equanimity is somewhat *independent* of external circumstances such as his health, good luck, the moods of others and the weather. He has an internal gyroscope that keeps him on an even keel.

Emphasizing the Present

The mature manager approaches relationships and problems in terms of the present rather than the past or the future. Although he uses his knowledge of past events as a guide, he does not follow precedents slavishly and is not borne down by the weight of past mistakes; nor does he fill his days with fanciful daydreams or dreadful fears regarding the future. He knows that the present is the only time he can deal with effectively. He has learned the wisdom of living life in day-tight compartments.

Self-Appraisal and Development

The mature manager is able to appraise himself and his performance objectively. He knows no one is perfect and that there is always room for improvement. Only a mature person can admit being wrong, can admit a weakness, but such an admission is the starting point for all growth and improvement. A part of maturity is being able to forgive oneself for past mistakes. The potential for growth is hampered by self-recrimination and self-doubt. The mature manager expects to keep on growing, to improve his performance as an individual and as a manager. To this end he will develop a tailor-made program for his own development. This program will be aimed at making the most of his strengths and at helping to overcome any weaknesses.

And that, in a one word summary, is the basis on which the SPD performance will be judged: *results.*

> —*Gen. James Ferguson,*
> *USAF, AFSC Commander*

Suggestions for the Program Manager. Following are several suggestions which the PM and his program control staff should consider. Because of variation in program complexity, PO organization, contract, and so forth, not all of these will apply to your office:

a. Document the assumptions upon which the cost estimates are made.

b. Make sure that program additions are submitted promptly for approval.

c. Take your financial manager with you and personally participate in financial reviews, presentations, and so forth.

d. Ensure that your hardware engineers are cost conscious.

e. Be fully knowledgeable of all GFE procurements to avoid duplication.

f. Participate personally in reviews and decisions concerning additions and deletions to the program and ensure that the financial manager participates so he can keep track of changes to programs and advise of the possible effect on program dollars.

g. Ensure that your financial manager establishes through contract action (with the contractor) a format for regular and prompt submittal of dollar and manpower information, progress versus plan, and that the plan or forecast is not changed without your knowledge or approval. The ACO can help in this area. . . .

h. You and the contractor should each have the same information in the agreed upon format on which to base presentations, recommendation for changes, or problem solutions. *This doesn't mean he should know what you have budgeted; he should not.* The contractor should be working to his budget for the package of work he has contracted to provide. . . .

i. A complete annual actual versus planned program progress review is essential to establish a base of departure for the contractor cost study.

j. Have regular meetings with the contractor to review technical progress (quality as well as quantity), schedules, and cost performance.

> —*Air Force Systems Command Pamphlet 800-3*

10

The Military Program Manager*

William F. Finant†

Recently a panel of military program managers examining their role in the weapon system acquisition process likened it to that of the general manager of a small company. If the comparison is apt —and I am sure it is—a story told in the context of commercial project management is equally applicable in describing the situation of the military program manager.

> A project manager and a marketing representative were on a hunting trip. One morning the marketeer woke up early and went into the brush to get a lead on a tiger which was reported to be in the vicinity of their camp. The project manager was about to join his companion when he heard two shots and a blood-chilling roar, and heard his friend run toward the tent yelling, "Open the flap! Open the flap!" Just as the project manager ripped open the flap the marketing representative ran into the tent, chased by a huge, snarling tiger not 20 yards behind him. As the marketeer ran through the tent and out the rear flap, he shouted, "You take care of this one while I bring in another one!"[1]

The Role of the Program Manager

The concept of program management is to provide centralized management authority over all the technical and business aspects of a program. The program manager's role, then, is to tie together, to

*Defense Management Journal, Fall 1971, pp. 37–41.
†President, Logistics Management Institute.
[1]John Stanley Baumgartner, Project Management, Richard D. Irwin, Inc., 1963, p. v.

manage, to direct the development and production of a system meeting performance, schedule, and cost objectives which are defined by his service and approved by the Secretary of Defense. The essence of the program manager's role is to be the agent of the service in the management of the system acquisition process, to focus the authority and responsibility of the service for running the program. He has the vantage of a large perspective of the program and the interrelationships among its elements. He must be the major motive force for propelling the system through its evolution.

The analogy likening the role of the military program manager to that of the general manager of a small company is instructive. It would be impossible to write a meaningful position description for the job of a general manager. It is equally impossible to write one for the program manager's job. What the general manager does is whatever is needed to move the affairs of the business. He does one thing at one time and another thing at another time—whatever is most needed at the moment to achieve his objectives. A general manager is not a "doer" of any job—there are other managers charged with the doing. But the general manager sees to it that what he wants is done, and what he wants is a harmony of things done so that his objectives are achieved. The role implies reliance on others to do the work; but it also implies controlling and coordinating the work so that no one aspect dominates others to the detriment of the whole.

This touches upon what is likely to be the most important function of the program manager: getting people to communicate with each other to achieve a common understanding of the needs of the program and their places in the total program effort.

Judgment and Flexibility

The concept of program management evolved because the ordinary way of doing things was not adequate for the task of managing the acquisition of complex weapon systems. Extraordinary management—program oriented management—was essential if all of the aspects of the program were to be handled correctly and expeditiously.

To achieve this extraordinary management, there is an OSD policy which complements the policy requiring program management: military program managers should be free to exercise judgment and flexibility. Although the program manager is the agent of his service, he should operate in an environment in which he selects and tailors to the specific needs of his program those management systems and formal techniques that will help his program. He should operate in an environment conducive to the exercise of judgment. There is no pet formula a program manager can adopt. He must decide for himself what methods, techniques, and systems he will use. If the program manager is responsible for planning, directing, and controlling a program, he must have the authority to get the job done.

Stated another way, the program manager is encouraged to adapt standard techniques to the peculiar requirements of his program. In turn, he has a right to expect that those in the services who are going to approve his management plans and techniques will exercise properly their own power of approval. That is to say, his plans and techniques will be accepted as satisfactory if they comply with basic policy directives. He has a right to expect that his plans will not be judged by the standard of meticulous compliance with innumerable details hidden away in regulations, directives, instructions, handbooks, manuals, standards, specifications, or similar documents.

What the program manager has a right to expect and what in fact he will be offered are often quite different. Experienced program managers would remind the new program manager that often one must struggle to obtain the management flexibility he is supposed to be given. Higher authorities, and especially their staff organizations, tend to standardize their requirements and to insist on the use of familiar techniques and methods. Their initial disposition is to avoid changes and exceptions to the general rule. Requests for deviations are rarely conceded without being pushed and sold.

Functional Support

The use of judgment and the exercise of flexibility are difficult to achieve in the environment of military program management. The most significant reason for this is that the operation of program management envisions two organizational elements. In some few cases the program office is staffed with all or most of the capability to perform the functional activities. In those cases the program office is largely self-sufficient and does not have to rely on much support from functional activities outside of the line authority of the program manager. Coordination is simplified, but the problems associated with organizing and staffing the program office are magnified. Usually, however, there is a small, centralized management authority consisting of the program manager and his program office. The program office is served by functional organizations which support the centralized authority and which are responsible to it for the execution of assigned tasks. That environment, where the resources for doing the work are largely outside of the line authority of the program manager, is a natural source of conflict.

The practical fact is that there are usually several programs competing for the limited resources of the same functional organizations. Those functional elements are also supporting the normal activities of their parent organizations—the day-to-day, nonprogram activities. When personnel are not available to support all of the demands, the program manager finds less responsiveness than he desires from the functional elements. His situation is made even more difficult because the functional elements were there long before his program started and they plan to be there long after his program ends.

Another aspect of this problem is the tendency of functional specialists to see their discipline as the central core of a successful program. Their commitment to their specialty leads them to try to dictate to the program what will or must be done—as distinguished from advising what should be done. Further, there is no lack of regulations with which they can bolster their claim. One of the most difficult concepts to put across to functional specialists is that the program manager is responsible for determining what will be done. The functional specialist is responsible for how it is done—the how being his area of expertise.

> There is a natural tendency for the functional managers to standardize their operations or efforts, to perform to standards, or to build a standard model. A project manager must, through his influence, force his functional areas to depart from a standard and build something that fits in with the other parts of the project. Someone has to force these people to take action when these actions increase a functional manager's risk or use his resources at a greater rate than he would otherwise. The project manager's role is to balance this risk over all portions of the project. Therefore, he must have authority to move quickly to balance his risk.[2]

Problems with functional specialists are not something new:

> The expert, in fact, simply by reason of his immersion in a routine, tends to lack flexibility of mind once he approaches the margins of his special theme. He is incapable of rapid adaption to novel situations. He unduly discounts experience which does not tally with his own. He is hostile to views which are not set out in terms he has been accustomed to handle. No man is so adept at realizing difficulties within the field that he knows; but, also, few are so incapable of

[2]George A. Steiner and William G. Ryan, *Industrial Project Management,* the Macmillan Company, 1968, p. 29.

meeting situations outside that field. Specialism seems to breed a horror of unwonted experiment, a weakness in achieving adaptability, both of which make the expert of dubious value when he is in supreme command of a situation.[3]

The environment of program management therefore places an extraordinary premium on talent for leadership as distinguished from command, on persuasion as distinguished from direction. The environment requires an emphasis on informal authority, *de facto* authority, or influence as distinct from power. One student of program management has described this authority as derived in part from the program manager's "persuasive ability, his rapport with extra-organizational units, and his reputation in resolving opposing viewpoints within the parent unit and between the external organizations."[4]

Persuasion is not the only way to get things done. One military program manager said that on many occasions he overcame the opposition of functional specialists by "working harder than they did." This program manager found that he could so overwhelm a specialist with facts, figures, and analysis that it became too much of an effort for the specialist to refute the program manager's position.

The comments of this program manager highlighted a point made by several others that there is a need for a strong analytical capability in the program office to coordinate a program whose parts were organizationally and geographically widely dispersed. A talent for analysis and ability to work with people were the key criteria in their selection of program office personnel.

Engagement and Disengagement

In common with the way a general manager must operate, the program manager relies on others to do the work. But he cannot escape the responsibility for the result. If he is responsible, he must be satisfied that what is done in his program makes sense to him and is consistent with his plans. If he cannot be persuaded that it is right for his program, he must direct it to be done the way he wants.

Much has been written about the role of industry and the relationship that should obtain between the defense program man-

[3]Harold J. Laski, "The Limitations of the Expert," *Harper's Magazine*, December 1930. Quoted in *Specialists and Generalists*, a selection of readings by the Committee on Government Operations, U.S. Senate, 90th Cong., 2d Sess., 1968, p. 53.
[4]David I. Cleland, "Project Management," *Air University Review*, Vol. XVI, No. 2, January-February 1965. Reprinted in a book of readings compiled by David I. Cleland and William R. King, *Systems, Organizations, Analysis, Management*, McGraw-Hill Book Company, 1969.

ager and his industry counterpart. Much has been said about "disengagement"—getting out of industry's hair and letting them do the job they have contracted to do. The goal is laudable and, the way it is stated, the idea is entirely consistent with good management concepts. But the ultimate responsibility for a successful program rests squarely on the service and on the military program manager as its agent. The program manager cannot disengage in any literal sense. He must manage contracted work in just the same sense as he manages all other parts of his program. More precisely, in this case he manages contractor management of his program. It is not a question of *whether* he manages; it is only a question of *how* he manages—or mismanages.

Industry project managers and government program managers are agreed on this point:

> It seems clear that the government program manager must exercise rather tight control until such time as he is assured that the industrial project manager has the technical and managerial competence to perform as required.[5]

The obverse is equally true, however: Once the government program manager has obtained the assurance he needs, he should relax his control and concede to his contractors a measure of freedom to exercise judgment and flexibility similar to that which he seeks for himself.

The Soft Sell

Newly appointed program managers may be dismayed to discover that there is less than complete and enthusiastic support for their programs within their service and OSD. Every weapon competes with all the others for limited resources, and competition is especially fierce in periods of tight budgets. At every level in the hierarchy, commanders and staff personnel are confronted by demands from program and functional managers for far more money than is available or can reasonably be obtained. Budget recommendations and decisions must be made that will inevitably favor some programs over others.

The program manager who has done his homework and has kept key people informed about his system's problems and progress will improve the odds that funds for his program will not be reduced. We are not suggesting that a program manager affect a hard-sell stance or that he patrol corridors to buttonhole unwary staff

[5]Steiner and Ryan, *op. cit.*, p. 125.

people. What we are suggesting is that a program manager should be attuned to the information needs and biases of the people who influence budget decisions. This implies a kind of low-key salesmanship—of the soft-sell, helpful variety.

> One of the project manager's greatest sources of authority involves the manner in which he builds alliances in his environment—with his peers, associates, superiors, subordinates, and other interested parties. The building of alliances supplements his legal authority; it is the process through which the project manager can translate disagreement and conflict into authority (or influence power) to make his decisions stand. Sometimes the power and control of the project manager represents a subtle departure from his legal authority.[6]

The program manager must keep in touch with what is going on above him. He has to be aware of what is expected of him by higher authority—both in his service and at the OSD level. He should know the typical questions being asked at major program review points, and he should be aware that these requirements for information by higher authority are constantly changing.

Program managers speak at length on the need to instill confidence in superiors. This confidence is a foundation of rapport with superiors which, in turn, is one of the main sources of the program manager's authority. When it is obvious to functional managers supporting the program that the program manager has this rapport with his superiors, he will not need to rely as much on formal authority. One of the ways this confidence can be instilled is by demonstrating a knowledge of the program in the widest context. Knowledge of the program must embrace the threat, the direction in which the threat is evolving, other systems in the inventory which address the threat, program schedules, costs, technology—in short, everything important about the program.

Effectiveness

Peter F. Drucker says that the job of the executive is to be effective, and effectiveness is getting the right things done.[7] Ineffectiveness is not synonymous with laziness. On the contrary, ineffectiveness is often characterized by a frenzy of busywork, a childlike fascination with, and concentration on, what is interesting, what is familiar, what one is good at doing—and a corresponding avoidance of what needs to be done. The hardest thing a manager has to do

---

[6]David I. Cleland and William R. King, *Systems Analysis and Project Management,* McGraw-Hill Book Company, 1968, p. 239.

[7]Peter F. Drucker, *The Effective Executive,* Harper and Row, 1966.

is to wean himself away from what he likes to do and become adjusted to a diet of different activities.

Among the techniques of effective management, two items—managing the little time he can control and focusing on his particular contribution—have special relevance for military program managers. The items are related: The program manager has little time he can control because briefings, reporting, and budget presentations take so much of his time; but these are also the occasions for a special contribution only he can make. That contribution is the creation and maintenance of the program's image to the world outside the program office.

Inside the program office, nothing dampens spirit faster than a system where everything stops at the program manager's desk waiting for his return from somewhere. If he is not careful, the boss can become the chief clerk and proofreader in the office—the one who checks everything to make sure it is right. Weighing the risks on both sides, there is a consensus among program managers that there is only one way to go. That way is to select the best people you can get, give them a free rein, and rely on being able to fix their mistakes without too much damage being done.

There is another consensus that weekly staff meetings are both a must and an adequate backstop to catch the really significant mistakes. If weekly meetings are not an adequate backstop, the problem is not organization but ineffective subordinates. The solution is not centralization of decision-making but replacement of personnel. This is just another aspect of being effective as a manager, which is the job of a military program manager.

The problem of managing the little time he can control has led some program managers to try a shortcut: managing by information system. A program manager observed recently that it was amazing how little information he really needed and used to help him manage his program. At the same time, he also observed how easy it was for the program office to be carried away with information display —what he called "an artist's view of managing a program." A management information center is a wonderful piece of public relations —especially captivating for those who have never managed programs. One thing is certain, however: every program manager regrets any idea he may have had that he could really manage his program in the comfort of the big swivel chair in the information center.

> In looking back at my experiences in development, including watching a number of Navy developments over the past few years, it seems quite clear that in most cases where a system gets into trouble a

competent manager knows all about the problem and is well on the way to fixing it before his management systems ever indicate that it is about to happen. This happens if for no other reason than because the competent manager is watching what is going on in great detail and perceives it long before it flows through the paper system. That is to say personal contact is faster than form filling and the U.S. mails. (A project manager who spends his time in his Management Information Center instead of roving through the places where the work is being done is always headed for catastrophe.) The Management Information Center can be an assist to the people who are involved in the project toward learning of after-the-fact problems, but that is roughly all that it can do, and its value even for this purpose is frequently questionable.[8]

[8]Robert A. Frosch, "The Emerging Shape of Policies for the Acquisition of Major Systems," *Naval Engineers Journal,* August 1969, pp. 20–21.

11

F-16—Nato's Military and Economic Cornerstone*

Brigadier General James A. Abrahamson†

The F-16 consortium program is a partnership in the deepest sense of the word. The importance of the objectives and the complex dynamics of the program can be seen from a brief examination of the program history, the F-16 itself, the coproduction effort and the depth and significance of F-16 standardization.

The F-16 consortium program was born on both sides of the Atlantic. In the United States, a prototype demonstration program was underway to evaluate the application of advanced technology to a new generation of lightweight, low cost, highly-maneuverable fighter aircraft. Two aircraft companies, General Dynamics (the YF-16 aircraft) and Northrop Aircraft (the YF-17 aircraft), were selected to design and build two lightweight fighter (LWF) prototypes. When the USAF determined that such a concept was feasible and functional, the LWF Prototype Program was accelerated and competitive flyoff conducted. Based on this flyoff and mission and cost considerations, the US decided to develop and produce the F-16. Plans to implement a "full-scale" development program were initiated.

At the time the USAF was pursuing its lightweight fighter prototype efforts, the Belgian, Danish, Netherlands and Norwegian governments were evaluating the need to modernize their tactical air forces by replacing aircraft such as the F-100 and F-104 which

*_Defense Systems Management Review,_ Summer 1977, Vol. I, No. 3, pp. 18–23.
†F-16 System Program Director.

were rapidly approaching obsolescence. Far-sighted individuals in these European nations concluded that the most practical method of approaching the problem was to integrate activities such that a common replacement aircraft, meeting common requirements, could be procured for the respective Air Forces.

The Consortium

A four nation consortium was constructed to pursue selection of a replacement aircraft on a multinational basis. Considerations of economics, balance of payments, technology transfer, and industrial stability were of major concern to the European nations. In addition to the operational aspects of a replacement aircraft, it was decided that selection would also be based on a requirement that the aircraft would be coproduced within the consortium nations to offset aircraft and support equipment investment.

The European governments selected three candidate aircraft for evaluation: the French F-1E Super-Mirage, the Swedish AJ-37 Viggen, and the winner of the U.S. lightweight fighter competition, the YF-16. After an arduous series of evaluations and negotiations, the European governments selected the F-16. This selection was made because the F-16 provided a combination of demonstrated capability and significant advancement in technology and performance while providing a system that was not overly complex. The F-16 offered the potential for lower cost, and improved reliability and maintenance capability. The selection was made on the basis of the commitment that coproduction would take place in each of the four countries such that at least 58 percent of the acquisition cost of a 348 European aircraft program would be offset.

Negotiations for the F-16 Multinational Fighter Program (MNFP) were concluded on 10 June 1975 by the signing of a five-nation Memorandum of Understanding that provides the basis for the current F-16 five-country development program. The participants were the United States, Belgium, Denmark, Norway, and the Netherlands.

In addition to numerous operational features and technological advancements, the F-16 provides innovative and unique economic features that deserve attention.

The F-16 program is a joint business effort to produce the F-16 in the United States and in Europe. As a result management of the program is complex. The ultimate goal of the program is to place certain F-16 production business in Europe to offset 100 percent of the cost of the Europeans' initial buy of 348 aircraft. The 100 percent offset is to be completed with the sale of 2,000 aircraft. This buy represents about $2–3 billion, measured in 1975 dollars. The offset goal is to be achieved in phases based upon the total number of aircraft produced, e.g., 58 percent of the Europeans' outlay is to be offset during the production of the first 998 F-16 aircraft (650 U.S., 348 European) and the target of 100 percent offset should occur when 2,000 aircraft have been produced.

The coproduction of the F-16 consists of the fabrication and assembly of major structural components by both the U.S. and European industries, interchange of these components among the industries, and assembly of the F-16 in the United States and at two locations in Europe. European industrial production will result in 348 aircraft rolling off the assembly lines in Belgium and the Netherlands. Norway and Denmark will be involved primarily with producing avionics and equipment subsystems. Industries in Europe will also support deliveries of the F-16 from the production line at Fort Worth, Texas.

Aircraft and engines manufactured in Europe will be made to U.S. engineering specifications. The U.S. drawings will be provided to the coproducing companies. In most cases, these drawings will be converted to metric and translated to the national language. The drawings will then be used to generate the "factory paper" of the European participants, i.e., shop instructions, blueprints, process sheets, etc. Inspection and acceptance will be to the original U.S. drawings and specifications—in the English language and in non-metric measurement. More than thirty European companies will be involved in this coproduction program. Three experienced aircraft companies (Fokker, Fairey and Sabca) will manufacture airframe components, and assemble and deliver the F-16 to the Air Forces of the European participating governments. The other 27 plus companies in Europe will be involved with avionics items and equipment subsystems. Four countries are participating in fabrication and assembly of the engine. Forty such items are being coproduced with some companies being involved with more than one item. The list reads like a "Who's Who in European Business." All are respected firms.

The coproduction program is not without danger. The U.S. Air Force program management must be sensitive to the complexities of doing business in Europe. The amount and timing of holidays, the use of overtime or multishift operations, risk-taking philosophy and European manufacturing span times are some of the areas that might affect the integrity of schedules. For example, U.S. leadtime for F-16 manufacture and delivery is 24 months, while it is normally 36 months in Europe. Certain management initiatives will be required on the part of the U.S. over the next six years, if the entire program is to be kept on schedule. The task is not easy. The potential pitfalls and complications of delivering high performance aircraft from three assembly lines, each located in a different country, using a base of 4,000 U.S. sub-contractors and suppliers and more than thirty coproducers in Europe, are mind-boggling. Chart A illustrates some program benefits, each of which carries a corollary complexity.

CHART A

Program Benefit	Corollary Complexity
Transfer of technology in areas such as landing gear, engine and assembly line techniques.	Requires relocation of experienced personnel from five countries with subsequent dilution of corporate capabilities.
More jobs and business through "Cascade" effect of increased production.	Careful planning and more lead time are required because of differences in socio-economic systems (i.e., overtime, shifts, wages).
Five countries share cost of development.	Exchange rates, currency commonality, and "fair-shares" must be established.
Interchangeability of parts resulting in inventory reduction and increased supportability, operability, maintenance capability.	Increased emphasis on quality control and data transfer, requirements, and procedures.
Configuration inputs from all countries get into development early.	Changes result in potential cost and time loss.

Among the most difficult of the challenges is configuration management. Problems from "user" inputs have been dealt with in past programs, but the impact of changes on the five-nation coproduction is unusually severe. The related fields of production control, international contracting and financing play an important role in configuration decisions. A Multinational Configuration Control Board decides on the acceptability of changes proposed by the contractors and using Air Forces. The Board is comprised of representatives of the five nations.

The benefits of coproduction, enjoyed on both sides of the Atlantic, constitute the overriding consideration. The increase in jobs in the greater Fort Worth, Texas, area, where the F-16 is produced by General Dynamics, is significant. A little less obvious is the great number of jobs being created throughout the United States at the subcontract level. It is conservatively estimated that 40,000 Americans will be employed in the manufacture of the F-16 when full production is achieved. In Europe, about 6,000 people will owe their livelihood to the F-16 Multinational Fighter Program.

The technical transfer aspects of the program are almost as important as the economic benefits. United States aerospace companies are working closely with various and diverse European industries. In some cases, the relation is one of peers working together to produce a common item. In other cases, the U.S. partner in coproduction has taken the role of mentor and is developing a capability within the European partner that did not previously exist. From a people-to-people standpoint, the F-16 Multinational Fighter Program is a tremendous success and may be a model for future international ventures. Each day brings a closer mutual understanding of viewpoints among the people of the five participating nations. Americans have been placed in Europe to work closely with Belgian, Danish, Dutch and Norwegian industrial or military people on a daily basis. Europeans have been sent to the United States to assist in program management.

The following is a summation of some of the key lessons learned in the F-16 coproduction program. These lessons include considerations of currency exchange, the Buy American Act and the cultural differences of the various countries.

Currency Exchange

The coproduction effort flowing from the F-16 Multinational Fighter Program has grown to encompass more than 30 European companies and in excess of 50 subcontractors. The multifaceted transactions among these European companies, the U.S. subcontractors, and the F-16 primary airframe and engine contractors, require continuous currency transactions. The participating governments of Norway, Denmark, Belgium, the Netherlands and United States agreed, in the Government to Government Memorandum of Understanding signed in June 1975, to the principle that companies participating in the program should be insulated from the inherent risks of open market currency fluctuations. Thus, all F-16 Multinational Fighter Program contracts have been issued using the fixed exchange rates that were established by the five participating countries.

This unique arrangement created a complex problem of implementation for the program office. The resulting procedures, which are still in the process of being finalized, require the combined efforts and talents of the Department of the Treasury, Department of State, Headquarters, United States Air Force, Headquarters, Air Force Systems Command, Air Force Accounting and Finance Center, Air Force Contract Management Division and the international banking community.

The resultant procedures will utilize an Air Force Accounting and Finance Center controlled currency clearing house which will be associated with resident banks in the participating countries.

Currency forecasts will be required from all participating subcontractors to permit allocation of the appropriate mix of funds to the currency clearing house. All contractors then will be required to use the currency clearing house for all transactions requiring currency exchange.

Buy American Act

The Buy American Act restricts Department of Defense procurement of certain non-U.S. products. Where such procurements are necessary, the procuring agency must fully substantiate the requirement on the basis of cost, availability or related factors that justify procurement of a non-U.S. item. Such procurements are normally handled on a case-by-case basis. Depending on the nature of the procurement, authorizations to waive provisions of the Buy American Act are granted at the local level for low value items or at the Service Headquarters or DOD level for large procurements.

Coproduction aspects of the F-16 program, requiring that European industry produce hardware items equivalent in value to ten percent of the procurement value of the USAF acquisition of 650 aircraft, required issuance of an exemption to the Buy American Act. This exemption is reaccomplished annually and applies to those items procured from European industry that count toward achievement of the U.S. offset commitment. The exemption was issued by Headquarters, United States Air Force, Deputy Chief of Staff, Systems and Logistics (AF/LG) with approval of the Office of the Secretary of Defense, Defense Security Assistance Agency (OSD/DSAA).

Exemptions of this nature will be required for all cooperative development/acquisition programs through which the Department of Defense obtains military hardware manufactured outside the U.S.

Cultural Differences

Coproduction planning accomplished by U.S. prime contractors (General Dynamics and Pratt and Whitney Aircraft) was done on the basis of assumptions that did not anticipate cultural differences between U.S. and European industry. In fact, there is a substantial difference between ways of doing business in the U.S. and in Europe.

European Wages. Based on a more socialistic society, European wages include higher amounts for health, social security, retirement and other fringe benefits than do U.S. wages.

European Personnel Income Taxes. European personnel income taxes are substantially higher than U.S. personnel income taxes. These European taxes are based on a more progressive rate structure that results in strict adherence to the basic work week. Much of European industry prohibits the use of overtime, limits operations to a 5-day work week, and works only one shift per day to avoid forcing employees into high income tax brackets.

Vacation Privileges. European society is more conscious of vacation privileges. Where U.S. vacation periods are normally taken at random and there is little or no effect on production rates, European vacations are more structured; industry often shuts down for specific periods of time, and production may come to a complete halt for those periods.

Production Rates. The U.S. industry is oriented toward high rates of production and with little regard for economic or work force stability. European industry is very conscious of these factors and works toward achieving long term stability in both the work force and in production rates, profit, and capital investment.

Schedules. Schedules are directly affected by wages, taxes, worker privileges and production rates. Where an F-16 aircraft can be produced in the U.S. in 24 months, an F-16 aircraft produced in Europe may take as many as 36 months to produce and will be more expensive.

Capital. European industry is under capitalized in comparison with U.S. industry. There is also a substantial portion of European industry which is partially or wholly government owned. As a result, there is a cash-flow problem that results in the use of advance funding and/or application of partial payments at the 90 or 100 percent level rather than at the 80 percent level which is typical in U.S. contracts.

Accounting Practices and Other Problems. There are also differences in accounting practices, audit procedures, solicitation and bidding procedures, procurement regulations and procedures, and contractual procedures and minor differences in quality control standards and procedures. European industry also uses the metric system of weights and measurements while U.S. industry, though slowly changing, is still standardized on the inch/pound system.

All of the factors stated have influenced the way in which F-16 coproduction will be accomplished in Europe and the manner in which program agreements and contracts have been negotiated and implemented.

In all aspects where differences have been encountered the governments and/or the contractors have been required to negotiate a solution. The U.S. cannot impose its procedures or standards on European industry. The result is normally a compromise in which both sides must alter their normal approach or treatment to some degree.

Multinational agreements have been negotiated concerning application of the Armed Services Procurement Regulation (ASPR), cost accounting standards, quality assurance standards, contractual and technical audit procedures, exemption of national taxes and duties, application of the specialty metals clause, liability for patent infringements, liability for ground/flight damage, currency exchange, economic price adjustment, configuration management, and a multitude of other F-16 program aspects of multinational concern.

Terms and conditions of contracts between the USAF and U.S. industry must be passed on to European industry. Negotiation of these terms and conditions was accomplished, but with considerable difficulty. In many instances these negotiations were successfully completed only after reaching agreement at the Government-to-Government level on general principles or policy.

A significant difference, related to but apart from the above, concerns international business experience. Most European firms have been involved in international business and production for many years. United States firms have been involved to a significantly lesser degree and, at that, have dealt with foreign subsidiaries of the parent U.S. corporation or have worked only under a license arrangement with a foreign firm who would manufacture a U.S. developed product for use by their government or for sale in the international market. The F-16 prime and subcontractors had little experience in international industrial cooperation and coproduction. Initial contracts with European industry suffered owing to this lack of experience and the "not invented here" approach taken in dealing with European industry leaders. United States government agencies suffered from this same lack of international experience— the lack of sensitivity to European concerns and issues, and a tendency to deal with the European Air Forces/Governments on the basis that the U.S. way was the only way. Change in this attitude, which is not yet complete, has been a difficult process.

A large number of European business people have spent considerable periods of time in American factories receiving technical training. At the same time, these persons learned about the American way of life. United States personnel assigned to Europe are gaining an appreciation of the quality of life in Europe. The goal of "bringing people together" is being achieved. Every member of the team must go about daily tasks considering the "big picture" and not any single, national point of view.

Thus, we have dealt with the military and economic complexities of the F-16 Multinational Program—a complex program that demonstrates the necessity for partnership management by what may be, perhaps, unexampled cooperation and mutual consultation. The complexities of this pioneering management process often seem staggering but the experience to date has been positive. Progress has been keen. Beyond the routine debate that often characterized NATO common efforts in the past, the F-16 multinational team is hammering out vital decisions, and implementing far-reaching actions for the benefit of all.

At the root of this progress has been a strong, unprecedented spirit of cooperation and trust. Curiously, the bond has been strengthened by common constraints among the participating nations. Each of the five nations has been strongly motivated by the *need* to modernize its tactical air force by the most economical means —and get the most for its money. The F-16 fulfills this need. Each of the countries has been keenly interested in standardizing those weapons systems that are frequently in concurrent use in neighboring Allied Forces. Here the F-16 is a giant step forward. All nations, in the face of shrinking defense budgets, want to recoup expenditures by sharing in the benefits that accrue from sales. The F-16 provides such a solution. Although not a panacea to the problems of procuring economically suitable and credible military hardware, the F-16 carries with it an unusually large and varied number of attributes. These attributes provide high motivation to participating nations—incentives to work hard at solving the inherent management complexities.

The purely military benefits of NATO standardization and tactical modernization are so evident and necessary that the question of objective does not arise. The fundamental decision forum shifts to the economic and political constraints.

As five sovereign nations go about the detailed analysis of tactical doctrines, mission usage, and resultant F-16 equipment selection to meet particular requirements, it might be expected that different equipage and configuration will occur. This has been true in the past, when economic and political factors were applied to potential common programs. This is not the case with the F-16. The five nations began with 21 country-by-country peculiar F-16 configuration requirements. These requirements have devolved to five minor items. Because of early economic and political harmonization, mutual common interests rather than differences are driving the program. In addition to the production economics and operating advantages of a universal F-16, the benefit in having similar support equipment, training equipment, and maintenance and training philosophy can be applied. These benefits yield a broader market for support equipment and allow the quantity increase so necessary for economical coproduction. Further, a pooling of spares and joint usage of depots provides large potential cost savings over the program lifetime.

The ability to operate during wartime situations using the bases, support equipment, armament, maintenance teams, and communications of allies is a tremendous benefit of commonality. Proposed war plans of the five nations are beginning to reflect the increased flexibility that equipment commonality provides.

Just as the American colonies, fortified by a common European heritage, banded together to create an entity stronger than the sum of the parts, the F-16 provides NATO with a dynamic economic, political and military program—a program that provides tangible benefits to all participants in both peace and war. In essence, the F-16 can be described as a major cornerstone expected to put teeth in the NATO Alliance and provide a better defense for all. This then is the real value of the F-16.

✯ ✯ ✯ ✯ ✯

First law of war: The course and outcome of war waged with an unlimited employment of all means of conflict are determined primarily by the correlation of strictly military forces available to the combatants at the beginning of the war, especially in nuclear weapons and means for their delivery.

—*The Basic Principles of*
Operational Art and Tactics
(A Soviet View)

12

A Discussion With Robert K. Duke of Fluor Corporation

J. S. Baumgartner

Bob Duke is an executive manager with the Fluor Corporation, a leading company in engineering and construction of facilities for the oil, gas, chemical, mining, and power industries. Since 1953 he has managed many projects around the globe, ranging in size from $3 million to more than a billion and including such varied processes as refineries, chemical plants, and a fiberglass textile plant. Duke was a Marine Corps company commander in the South Pacific in World War II.

Bob, what is the scope of the project manager's responsibilities in your field?

A project manager in our field is responsible for the whole job, what we call E, P, and C—engineering, procurement, and construction. If at the end of the job he has achieved the financial objectives, met the required schedule, and has a happy client—then it's a successful project.

How do you organize for a project?

The project usually starts with one person—the project manager. He has to build up a task organization right from scratch; get it operating usually with a tight schedule and firm cost controls; get the project done; and then disband the entire task force organization. It's building and then disbanding a complete organization for just one job.

Do people in engineering, for instance, report to the project manager in a line way, or do they work on his project but actually report to a manager in engineering?

This is the biggest problem of all. Right now I'm not a technical expert in anything, although 28 years ago I came up through structural design. But there are many design disciplines required on a project, and each of these is headed by a department head; he has the responsibility for the quality and performance of his designers. The project manager, however, specifies *what* is to be done and *when* it's to be done, and then coordinates all project activities. The PM does this coordination through project engineers who report directly to him. But the actual design is done by design department personnel temporarily assigned to the task force.

The Main Problem Is Communications

The main problem though isn't the technical difficulty, or the cost, or schedules. It's people. More specifically, it's communications. Communications with the client, with people working on the project, with subcontractors, and with suppliers. Communications is so important that Fluor has a subsidiary, in fact, that gives courses on communications to company personnel and to others outside the company.

What are your channels of communication with the client?

Any written communications have to go through the project manager. This is covered by a project procedure, a written procedure which we prepare at the beginning of the job. But you have to encourage direct talking between specialists; you have to have direct exchanges between an engineer specialist on our team, for instance, and the client's corresponding engineer.

It's the Results That Count

You mentioned that the client will be happy if you meet the cost, schedule, and performance requirements. Doesn't a smooth relationship with him as you go make a difference too?

No. Man, that doesn't mean a damn. If you have conflicts along the way, when it starts up and goes on stream, these problems are all forgotten. It's the results that count; if it works right and the costs are right, you'll have a happy client in the end. There is an optimum number of conflicts and adrenalin that should flow during any project.

What kind of contracts are usually involved—cost type or fixed price?

Because of varying field labor costs and conditions, schedule limitations, and escalation, most now are some form of cost-plus-fee type; but some contracts will be converted over at a midway point. Incidentally the PM often takes part in contract negotiations, because he's got the necessary knowledge of the job and because he'll be responsible for meeting the contract's requirements. There's always competition for a project; so the proposed project plan—how we plan to carry out the work, our schedule, manpower, and cost controls, our experience, and so forth—is extremely important.

What do you use for schedule and cost control techniques?

For scheduling we use FAST—Fluor Analytical Scheduling Technique. It's the best method of project planning and control I've seen. But I don't think it will ever take the place of thinking and foresight based on past experience and mistakes. I always advise young project people to use all of the sophisticated computerized techniques as a supplement to horse sense, rather than a substitute for it.

You Have to Allow for Contingencies

Do you try to allow for contingencies in your schedule?

Yes, there *has* to be some leeway, some time allowed for contingencies. Usually the place it should be inserted is at the end of the schedule. How to do this is one of the project manager's trade secrets. Also he has to know *when to expedite;* to do this, he must relate the schedule to costs, because it's usually cheaper to expedite early in the project than later. With the current high rate of interest the schedule gets extremely important. A client company can't afford to tie up its capital because of delays.

As to costs, we relate costs to each activity by a code of accounts; this is one of the first things we get out. Getting people to live within budgets has to be close to the top of the list of major problems. But if you get the doers in the act of planning and budgeting, then you can hold them responsible.

What qualities does your company look for in project managers? What does it take to become a successful project manager?

First, the PM has to merit the respect of those involved in the project—those working on it, and also the client's people. If he creates animosity or if he doesn't know the job well enough, he will probably be replaced by someone else. Like any manager, he must achieve the desired results through people.

He Has to Be Well Rounded

So he needs many of the same leadership qualities found in military officers —knowledge, tact, enthusiasm, judgment, loyalty, and so forth.

Yes. It takes these qualities, among others, to motivate the project organization. The PM isn't too different from other managers, although he may need more drive, more industriousness, and a broader background. We've made up a chart that shows the degree of knowledge and experience the PM should have in a variety of areas, including construction, finance, sales, law, personnel, engineering, procurement, accounting, behavioral sciences, quantitative methods, economics, project control techniques, communications, and so forth. In our business, if he's a really top-flight PM, he has to be responsible for all of these, and more.

As to how he acquires these capabilities, he can get exposure by various ways; one of the best is working under a top-flight PM. But these PMs are always the busiest guys you've got; they don't have a minute to spare. Also, we rotate PM candidates through the various specialty departments. Mainly though they need field experience. They can learn more in the field in two or three years than in an office. It may take 15 years to develop a PM, and a third of that time could well be spent in the field. Outside reading is also necessary to develop the essential background.

The selection of these men comes down to a gut feeling about a potential PM. Maybe 10 percent of the graduate engineers, at the most, would have the traits we're looking for. Some of the most intelligent engineers are the last guys you'd want to go into project work. You certainly want intelligence; but you want people who can communicate and motivate; who are ambitious; who are willing, and whose wives are willing, to move around for a few years; industriousness; and a lot of drive. And if they are "gung-ho" types, this helps.

What's the future of a project manager? What can he expect to become?

There's a lot of pressure to put our best people in project management. After all, that's where the profit or loss is made, as well as future sales to repeat clients. A top-notch PM can expect to move on up into company management. More than half of our vice presidents came up through project management.

13

Why Army Project Managers Are "Princes of the Realm"*

Government Executive

The most trying job in the Army in peacetime for a colonel or lieutenant colonel, says Lt. Gen. George Sammet, Jr., is to be a Project or Product Manager (PM). "They're at war all the time," says the DARCOM (Development and Readiness Command, formerly the Army Materiel Command) Deputy Commanding General for Development.

"They're entrusted with big dollars, fielding critical systems for the next war." And they operate small offices, directing the efforts of major contractors. The one running the XM-1 tank development, for instance, was (until Chrysler won the contract) not only competing Chrysler and General Motors against each other but also stacking them both up against the requirement.

Each competitor can "throw in hundreds of lawyers and marketing people against his (the PM's) handful." Thus, "the caliber of the person must be excellent." The young officers, thinks Sammet, are beginning to realize this is where the challenge is in today's Army. And Army, for some time, has realized how important these people are. "They're princes of the realm," says Sammet. Especially in the last half dozen years or less, a great deal of attention has gone into both how they are selected and how young Army officers are trained for the slots.

Selection. Though Army has had PM's since Army Materiel

*Extract from *Government Executive,* January 1977, pp. 22–24.

Command was created in 1962, their selection in the early stages was largely a matter of "which colonels are due for transfer to a new duty station." If they happened to have good background for a PM job, it was more coincidence than by design.

Today, Department of the Army Selection Boards, which used to pick only unit commanders, now select PM's as well. Moreover, in theory, they have access to and can choose from the "entire personnel assets of the Army"—though in fact they work from a list of 250 top Army colonels whom Personnel has identified as having some background in materiel acquisition.

On the PM selection boards, at least four of the generals must have had some background in materiel acquisition or at least understand the job's requirements. And when there's a conflict between a Board pick and some commander's claim the man is "not available," the case is decided at the top of the Army organization by the Chief of Staff or even the Army Secretary.

Training. Besides that careful screening process, Army has set up a PM Development Program, run for DARCOM by the Personnel people. It was set up because, three years ago when the first PM Selection Board was formed, they had a very small base of personnel to select from and frequently had to waive some of the prerequisites in order to fill a slot.

When they asked for volunteers to enter the development program, 1100 persons either put their names in or were recommended. To date, 600 have been picked by Personnel to go into a program that has identified 1600 different kinds of experience which can contribute to a person's eventually becoming a good PM.

In short, says Sammet, "Where the Air Force once had four to five times as many qualified people" available for project manager posts, "the Army now matches them man for man." Nor is that all. Some time ago, an industry contact told Sammet, "If your (PM) man had asked the right questions, I would have cut our cost estimate another $1 million."

Business OJT. It prompted Sammet to resurrect a Training-in-Industry program that had been dropped when the Technical Services were replaced by Army Materiel Command in 1962. Sammet lined up 24 "young, first-class officers all with masters degrees" after 24 (out of 25) companies he wrote to said they'd be happy to participate. Under the program, the officers are sent out at Army expense for a year to work somewhere in some segment of the company's materiel acquisition business.

Example. Sammet sent one to Sperry Univac (Defense Systems Division). "They played the program real well," says Sammet. "They assigned the man to a Navy program as assistant PM and used him as though he was just an outstanding guy Sperry had hired. Result: he's now back, assigned to the artillery locator program, and doing a first-rate job."

"These people come back (from industry) just loaded with ideas," says Sammet. In general: "They're impressed by industry's integrity, patriotism, energy, desire to do a good job. At the same time, they see that certain corporate aims are just different from Army's—seeing that the bottom line comes out black is what drives industry on a contract." Upshot of the program's success is Sammet has received authorization to increase the program by six spaces.

The Army currently has some 56 PM's at work, nine less than in the early days of Army Materiel Command. But their reporting channels are different than they once were. When all 65 reported to the AMC commanding general, says Sammet, as they once did, "there's just no way he could manage that many."

Organization. Today, the ones who run what the Army calls its "Big Five" programs (Advanced Assault Helicopter, UTTAS utility helicopter development, XM-1 tank, SAM-D surface to air missile now called the "Patriot," and MICV, mechanized infantry combat vehicle) all report directly to Sammet. So do some, such as the Training Aids PM, whose work just doesn't fit neatly in one DARCOM subordinate command. But most, including most of some 20 who report to Sammet's counterpart on the Materiel Readiness side of DARCOM, report to a subordinate single commodity command: the airplane PM's to Aviation Command; the truck PM's to Tank/Automotive Command; communications PM's to Electronics Command, etc.

Those who report directly to Sammet give him a program progress briefing once a quarter; those who report to a commodity commander brief Sammet twice a year. Besides that step to make sure the PM's needs aren't slighted at subordinate levels, Sammet has a colonel on his immediate staff who works full-time "administering to the needs of the PM's" (as does Army Personnel).

Moreover, besides trading ideas through a PM's newsletter, all 56 get together once a year for a two-day meeting to trade information on management techniques that each individually finds working and ones that don't. "We don't let the PM's get hidden away," says Sammet. Just to make absolutely sure of that, he adds succinctly, "The Commodity Commanding general is their rating officer; but I'm the endorsing officer. And I'm also the Commodity Commander's rating officer."

Sammet is as involved in contractor source selections as he is in seeing that the PM's are first-rate.

"Competitive prototyping has paid off for the Army very

well," he says. "It's front-end loaded" (high Research and Development), he points out, "which makes it tough to get funding approval. That *may* (his emphasis) result in greater R&D cost but you get to production earlier and you get two good items to choose from," thus maybe lowering overall costs; and "you reduce the risk and keep a competitive edge."

"I would have loved to have had competitive prototyping on MICV"—although after a great deal of negotiation (with FMC, the contractor) we will come out with a good vehicle, he says, "but it's taking longer than competitive prototyping would have. And I'd give my right arm to have the TT39 digital switch (for communications) on competitive prototyping today."

Competition a Key. Even if the technical approach of two competitors is the same, he contends, the competition means "you're making sure at least one company has solved the engineering problems," the problems of moving to production. "In the meantime, each competitor is driving the cost down."

Besides, he says, the technical approach that starts out differently "is probably always going to end up that way. You just can't change down the line." On the XM-1 tank, for instance, General Motors started out with a diesel engine; the driver on the left; and slaved the gun-sight while stabilizing the gun.

Chrysler put the driver in the center; used a turbine engine; stabilized the sight and slaved the gun to it. In the laboratory, GM's gun is more accurate. But on the battlefield, on rough terrain, the stabilized sight will make for more accuracy. And what each competitor started out with was what he ended up with.

The contract award was held up for 30 days while the Pentagon got assurance that the gun turret could handle both a 105 mm. and a 120 mm. gun and that engines were interchangeable—all to handle a NATO need. Added up, that emphasizes the sometimes mind-stretching awareness demanded of a good PM. He has to know the operational environment where his hardware will be used; be conscious of such things as equipment commonality, training, and interoperability; know the flow of the decision-making process and his project's funding through government—to name just a few things besides the technical details of the project itself.

PM's don't sit on selection boards except as non-voting "secretaries," and they don't decide high level actions that can affect their programs. But, says Sammet, "they can vocalize what those high-level decisions will do to the programs."

And "what he does or can do is also impacted tremendously by budget and Congressional approvals." Just having high-level decisions by Army and Defense Systems Acquisition Review Committees made "more nearly on schedule helps tremendously."

Options Exist. Still the PM's will have some options they can lay out. In a sense, what the PM's can trade off is much like the analysis that goes into picking contractors in the first place. Sammet's personal approach, when he's participated in those kinds of decisions, is to take both the contractor proposals and the source selection board's evaluation of those proposals and ask himself basically two questions:

- How much better than the minimum necessary performance is the proposed solution's performance?
- Is it worth the cost?

Similarly, PM's have a considerable amount of trade-off authority within their programs. On the AAH (Advanced Assault Helicopter) program the PM has only four parameters he can't trade off—cruise speed of the helicopter, vertical rate of climb, endurance and ammunition payload. But other than those minimums, "he can trade off anything else to stay within cost and on schedule."

How well do the PM's do? Higher Army authority, says Sammet, calls him almost regularly with messages that boil down to, "George, we're more and more impressed every day with your PM's." And, he says, Congress routinely would rather talk to the PM's about programs than they would to the brass in the Pentagon.

WHO IS THE PM?

A Career-Oriented Senior Military Officer who is:

- Ambitious,
- Tenacious,
- Fast on his feet with a good soft-shoe routine,
- Flexible in his approach,
- Able to set goals and ruthlessly pursue them,
- Smart enough to know what to demand and gutsy enough to demand it,
- Equipped with an encyclopedic knowledge of the details of his program and the ability to address it in the simplest terms,
- Able to gain and maintain the confidence of OSD, his contractor and his secretary,
- A marketeer.

In Summary, HE IS AN ENTREPRENEUR.

14

A Special Breed of Cat*

Major Lee Lilly

Of all the complaints I have heard in nearly twelve years' service, by far the most common has been lack of real responsibility. However, I did not hear that complaint very many times in the systems acquisition career field. Cost is a convenient measurement of project size and is some indication of the degree of responsibility. Even small projects are measured in hundreds of thousands of dollars, and a minor avionics system can amount to millions in the development phase alone. If you should be so fortunate as to play a major role in an airframe development, the responsibility can be staggering at today's development costs. You do not have to be a general officer to play such a major role, either. For example, the airframe project manager for the F-15 was a lieutenant colonel position.

The real satisfaction, however, is not calibrated according to budget size. It comes from working on an important and difficult management job and from working with professionally dedicated people who accept you as a professional. You work with such people on both the Air Force and the industry side of the defense business. There is something about working on the development of equipment destined to enter the inventory—and which you may use one day in combat—that creates tremendous awareness of its relevance. There is a great incentive to make sure that you do everything in your power to develop the best equipment possible. Much satisfaction is gained as you see the results of your efforts taking form. As a project manager, you would coordinate all activi-

*Extract from *Air University Review,* September-October 1975, pp. 84–88.

ties related to your project. You would require the efforts of people from many disciplines; but you yourself would be responsible for the successful completion of the project. The project manager monitors the progress of the civilian contractor by frequent visits and review of status reports. You will find that the Air Force has many personnel widely recognized as experts in their specialty. You will also find that the Air Force keeps both responsibility and authority vested at a much lower level and in younger personnel than does industry. As an officer directly responsible for a project, you will gain a feeling of accomplishment from working on an equal level with such experts and high-level industry officials.

An educational background suitable to the type of position sought is, of course, desirable. Engineers of many types are needed. Operations experience is applicable to many engineering positions. Training in management or business administration would be helpful in the management positions. It is not necessary to be an expert in systems management techniques, however, unless you wish to work on the program control staff. The management positions most needing operational experience are in project management and in test and deployment management. Attendance at one of the System Program Management Schools en route to the assignment is highly desirable because later attendance is difficult. Lack of formal management education should not be allowed to deter you from seeking a position in systems acquisition management, because experience is the best teacher. You should not be frightened by the lack of experience in systems management but should keep it in mind and realize your need to listen to those around you who have more experience with the unique pitfalls in such work. At first, your primary qualifications will be your operational experience and the innate abilities that you must have if you are to be successful in being selected for AFSC duty. As you become more experienced, you will be more comfortable in your new role.

Not only is it important for operations personnel to seek development assignments but such an assignment can be highly rewarding for the individual in terms of satisfaction and experience for later use as an operational manager or commander. Thus, the Air Force will profit from better weapon systems and better managers, and the individual will be better qualified to manage or command as the result of his opportunity to practice management in a very difficult arena.

15

SPO Code*

Colonel Clarence L. Battle

1. *Keep the SPO small and quick reacting at all cost.*
   a. Exercise extreme care in selecting people, then rely heavily on their personal abilities.
   b. A good program office is oriented to the *technical* side of the problem. Be sure a technical capability exists in every technical field involved. (Don't kid yourself, SPO's are paid off in results—that means the system works.)
   c. Parkinson's law can *kill* you.
2. Be schedule oriented.
   a. If you don't start that way, you will end that way anyhow.
   b. Haste does not make as much waste as foot-dragging in this business.
   c. Make that decision—time is critical to the schedule.
   d. A tight schedule avoids letting *anyone* off the hook.
   e. Early launch testing shortens the time to "fix." (Read it either way—there *is* a double meaning.)
3. *Direct personal involvement* of the Program Director and *all* program office members in the elements of the system is vital.
   a. Program Director must be held personally responsible for all aspects of the program; be held accountable for the consequences of the SPO actions, be the results salutary or punitory. (This is automatically the case—no one else takes his lumps.)

*Based on an Internal Memorandum while Colonel Battle was Director of the DISCOVERER Satellite System, Air Force Space and Missile Systems Organization.

    b. In turn, he holds individuals under him responsible in the same status, etc., etc.

4. Make the *greatest possible* use of SAMSO supporting organizations.

    a. Apply principle *3* to this.

    b. Always make unreasonable demands. (Expect a halfhearted reaction—remember *they* aren't schedule oriented.)

    c. Hold *them* responsible—remember your boss and your boss' boss, etc., etc.—hold *you* responsible.

    d. The details you can force on him (administrative or technical) enable you to live with principle #1. (Read it again.)

5. *Recognize the contractor's role and live with it.*

    a. He is in the driver's seat, technically speaking.

    b. Rely strongly on contractor technical recommendations, (once the program office has performed its function of making sure the contractor has given the problem sufficient effort).

    c. Control the contractor by personal contact. (Each man in the program office has a particular set of contractor contacts—establish them early.)

    d. Hit all checkout and flight failures hard. (A fault uncorrected will come back to haunt you.)

    e. There is *no such thing* as a random failure. (Personnel mistakes are more frequent than engineering design, or established test procedure defects.)

    f. *Repeat:* Hit troubles hard and instantly. (They bite back.)

    g. Good system design and test integration is very important. (Without it you are doomed to failure—it is SPO's responsibility to see that it's done.)

    h. Examine the ties between the home office and field very closely. (Many a program slip has occurred here; technical, schedule, performance, and dollars. Don't let management short-sightedness cause you to fail—this requires imagination.)

6. Relationships with Command elements higher than the SPO should be held to a minimum.

    a. Never *ask* for help to do *your* job—you might get it.

    b. Don't over communicate with higher headquarters. (Comply promptly with all report requirements—in the most abbreviated form that will fulfill their information requirements.)

    c. If you must have guidance or direction—tell them what you want to hear. (They have neither the information nor the system impact analysis ability to give you meaningful guidance.)

    d. If you believe "c" above you have made the first step in doing *your* job effectively. *You* in the SPO are charged with the *total* responsibility. (At this point read principle #3 again.)

7. Financial: Be as dollar conscious as you are schedule oriented.
    a. This is a repeat—if you don't start that way you will end up that way anyhow. (Remember *you* are the manager.)
    b. Dollar consciousness exists only in the program office. (The contractors and other supporting elements all want as big-a-bite as possible from your budget. Only the SPO can balance the bucks vs. the effort.)
    c. You must "live" with the contractor on dollars. (Never let him get behind in keeping you informed on his financial status. This also applies to all other supporting elements that you fund from your budget.)
    d. Incurring an unpredicted over-run is bad; but overrunning without knowing it is disastrous.
    e. Don't make a federal case out of it if your fiscal budget seems too low. (These matters usually take care of themselves. Now read paragraph 7b again and concentrate on the last sentence.)

8. General:
    a. Don't generate paper work. (There are plenty of people willing to do this for you. This is an SPO—not a paper mill.)
    b. Committees are the world's most useless activity. (Avoid the let's-have-a-meeting vogue like poison. They never accomplish anything—there is *always* some individual who has the responsibility for *doing* what the committee thinks it's doing.)
    c. Before you establish a group or call a meeting decide:
        (1) What will its purpose be—what's to be accomplished?
        (2) Who can contribute data pertinent to the accomplishment of its purpose?
        (3) If I were ingenious could I make the decision if the data were made available? (Maybe I don't need the conclave.)
        (4) Regulate attendance so that only those necessary attend.
        (5) Establish the location at a point convenient to the most.
        (6) Tell each participant what is to be accomplished and what is expected of him. (And far enough in advance so that he is ready to contribute.)
        (7) Publish decisions reached post haste.

d. Management surveys are punitive. Recognize it if you are surveyed—and likewise employ them (if ever) accordingly.

9. Insist that all principles herein described apply to *all* contractor and supporting agency activities.

a. Demand more than you expect to get—but expect to get what is necessary to fulfill SPO requirement.

10. Don't look back for the answers to a new problem. (History never repeats itself—if you can find the answer in history you have made the same mistake twice. This is not to say you should not learn from experience; however, your application should be preventative, not corrective.)

We look for a guy who can run the program, whether a Bellis [Maj. Gen. Ben Bellis, F-15 Program Director], who's a helluva good manager, or a Nelson [Maj. Gen. Donald Nelson, B-1 Program Director] with command and operational background. But we start him with a little program.

—Gen. George S. Brown, USAF

The project manager for all his authority and responsibility is a closely-watched fish in a fishbowl.

—Gen. John R. Guthrie, USA

At every crossway—on the road that leads to the future, each progressive spirit is opposed by a thousand men appointed to guard the pass.

—Maurice Maeterlinck

Section 3—

THE PROJECT
ORGANIZATION

Introduction

At a very early stage the system manager must have good people and a viable organization in order to perform the necessary program planning. The team charged with creating the system includes the project office, contractors and their subcontractors, and contributing government agencies such as laboratories and test facilities.

The size of the system office varies greatly. The Navy's F-14 program office had 15 people at a time when the F-15 had 250. The Apollo headquarters office had 121. Admiral Raborn had a basic staff of 50 on the Polaris program, because "I can get more out of one overworked man than out of two underworked men." A Lockheed Skunk Works rule says, "Strong but small project offices must be provided."

Organization development specialists have discussed the various facets of "matrix management" for years. But what appear to them as large, thorny problems have long since been resolved in practice, problems such as where to place the project organization, how it should relate to the parent hierarchical organization, and how it violates principles of the Bible and Henri Fayol about serving only one master. (Douglas McGregor points out, regarding this last point, that there is one organization where individuals have always had two bosses: the family.) Of more timely interest is the two-tier matrix organization, where the program office itself is organized along both functional and work breakdown structure (WBS) lines. General Ben Bellis organized the F-15 program office this way, and this structure may set a trend.

High morale and esprit are earmarks of most project organizations. In his evaluation of two comparable programs, E. H. Kloman says in "Synthesis," "What emerges perhaps most forcefully from a broad retrospective view is the importance of the human aspects of organization and management. . . . the critical nature of human skills, interpersonal relations, compatibility between individual managers and teamwork." The nature of the challenge lends itself to a strong "can do" spirit and development of pride in accomplishment. From another perspective, the authors of "Management of Conflict" note, "the greater the work challenge provided by a [project] manager, the less conflict he experiences with assigned personnel."

Robert Youker portrays an interesting continuum of organizational structures, from functional through completely projectized, and highlights some important "survival techniques" in his article on organizational alternatives.

In "Managing Motivation" James Lowsley presents a concise review of the classic studies and concepts that have evolved from the days of the Hawthorne studies through the theories of Frederick Herzberg and the Blake-Mouton grid.

Left unanswered, and a problem to most PM designees, is the question, "How do I go about getting the people I need?" A partial answer, but only a partial one, is "deserve them." Qualities of leadership developed over the years are not lost on one's supervisors —or the people who will one day decide whether to join his project.

$$\star \quad \star \quad \star \quad \star \quad \star$$

Critical to the success of any organization are the individuals who comprise that organization—the starch that provides the backbone, the character, and ability to define objectives and accomplish the assigned mission. Therefore, it becomes extremely important that the people of the organization understand and identify with characteristics which have a proven track record and high success potential. In my experience, a number of characteristics are both important and measurable. They include integrity, aggressiveness, imagination, industriousness, the ability to work with people, ability to communicate, intelligence, and service orientation. All are essential resources, but only their effective use converts them into results.

—Hon. Gary D. Penisten,
Assistant Secretary of the Navy
(Financial Management)

There is a difference between leadership and management. Leadership is of the spirit, compounded of personality, vision and training. Its practice is an art. Management is a science and of the mind. Managers are necessary; leaders are indispensible.

—Adm. T. H. Moorer, USN, Ret.

16

How to Manage Motivation*

James P. Lowsley, Jr.

How many of us have asked the question, "How can I get my unit to *want* to do what I desire it to do?" Put in other words, "How can I motivate the people in my unit?" or, "What management style will work for me?" Motivation has been a topic of considerable research and theories for a number of years. Many experts attempting to answer these questions have conflicting ideas on the subject.

Various Expert Opinions

Elton Mayo, with F. P. Roethlisberger and W. J. Dickson, conducted studies, known collectively as the Hawthorne Experiment, from 1924 to 1932 in a factory near Chicago. Productivity was measured as working conditions were made better and then again when these improvements were lessened. Strangely, productivity continued to improve even though lighting, rest, lunch periods, and other working conditions were reduced or made less attractive. It was established that the experiment itself was the cause of the increased productivity. In the process of experimenting, attention was lavished on the workers. Quite by accident, human needs (such as feeling respected, important, competent, and growing) were being satisfied as tasks, work processes, and work flows were changed during the experiments. Mayo's Hawthorne Experiment is described in *Management and the Worker* by Roethlisberger and Dickson in which managers were made aware that workers need *two*

*Air Force Engineering and Services Quarterly, February 1977, pp. 13–14.

incomes to do their best. The financial income is not enough—the psychological income must also be provided.

Abraham Maslow's *Hierarchy of Human Needs* is the base upon which most modern motivation theory is built. Man moves up in this hierarchy from a foundation of physical needs to safety (security), a social position (belonging), feeling of esteem (what others think of him), and perhaps finally to some kind of self-actualization (feeling that he is making the most of himself). Once an individual has, in his own eyes, satisfied a need, it is no longer a motivator.

Chris Argyris, in *Integrating the Individual and the Organization* and other books and articles, theorizes that people develop in seven ways: from passive to active; from dependent to independent; from few ways of behaving to many; from shallow interests to deep, strong ones; from a short time perspective to careful consideration of past and future; from a subordinate to an equal or a superior role; and, finally, from being unaware of self to awareness and control of one's self. Argyris believes these developmental channels are blocked in many organizations, thus creating frustrations that result in apathy, absenteeism, and other counterproductive behavior.

Frederick Herzberg's book, *Work and the Nature of Man,* introduced his Motivation-Hygiene Theory in 1966. His research indicates that two different sets of needs are involved in motivation and are directly related to man's tasks. They include challenging work, achievement, recognition, responsibility, and growth.

Douglas M. McGregor wrote *The Human Side of Enterprise,* which is a favorite in both management and academic circles. His theories, summarized in the table below, offer two different assumptions concerning men and work.

David C. McClelland is concerned with achievers or self-motivators. His research indicates that approximately ten percent of the American population can be called achievers. He theorizes that the achievement drive is a "learned motivation" and not something one is born with. It is best learned on a job where one can assume more responsibility, can participate in setting goals, can establish high but not impossible goals, where fast and clear-cut feedback is obtained, and where one gets frank and detailed performance evaluations.

Robert R. Blake and Jane S. Mouton developed and described *The Managerial Grid* in their 1964 book. The grid relates two factors: the leader's concern for production and his concern for people. The horizontal axis of the grid represents increasing levels of concern for production on a scale from 1 to 9. Using the same scale, the vertical axis represents increasing levels of concern for people. A "9-1" manager is production oriented; "1-9" is people oriented; "9-9" is

Theory X	Theory Y
1. Work is inherently distasteful to most people.	1. Work is as natural as play, if the conditions are favorable.
2. Most people are not ambitious, have little desire for responsibilty, and prefer to be directed.	2. Self-control is often indispensable in organizational goals.
3. Most people have little capacity for creativity in solving organizational problems.	3. The capacity for creativity in solving organizational problems is widely distributed in the population.
4. Motivation occurs at the physiological and security levels.	4. Motivation occurs at all levels of Maslow's "Hierarchy of Human Needs."
5. Most people must be closely controlled and often coerced to achieve organizational goals.	5. People can be self-directed and creative if properly motivated.

maximum concern for both people and production (most managers fall into the "5-5" or middle-of-the-road style). The "9-9" manager relates to McGregor's Theory Y assumptions, while both the "9-1" and "1-9" managers relate to McGregor's Theory X assumptions.

Rensis Likert studied five factors: leadership, motivation, decision making, communication, and control. He states that these factors interact to form a continuum of management styles and can be described as systems one through four. System one is much like McGregor's Theory X (low trust), while system four is much like Theory Y, which is based on trust. Likert found that the closer the management style of an organization approaches system four, the more likely it is to have a continuous record of high productivity.

Conclusions

From the foregoing it seems clear that the management style which satisfies both man's physiological and psychological needs will be most successful. It seems that we must be able to stimulate the motivation which comes from within an employee, not that which is generated externally by the manager.

There are several management myths which destroy internal motivation rather than generate it. The first is called the "Paycheck

Myth," or "All they want is the dollar." Money does not have a sustaining effect of motivating a person's performance, although wages prevent job dissatisfaction. However, low dissatisfaction with a job situation represents tolerance and is not the same as job satisfaction or a sense of achievement.

Another myth is the "External Stimulation—Motivation Myth." A manager who depends on this begins with personal favors and personality approaches which soon fail. Therefore, a retrograde movement occurs and an attempt is made on a competitive basis (one unit against another). When all else fails, this manager will threaten and will exercise authority from a stance of power. Fear may bring conformance, but not performance.

The third is the "Accountability Myth." A manager who depends on this approach believes that employees do not want responsibility. Therefore, while he may ask a subordinate to prepare a staff study concerning a particular problem, he also may tell him specifically what facts to consider, what each means, how to write the report, and what conclusions and recommendations are to be made. This manager does not need a staff to advise him—he only needs several secretaries!

There are additional methods used by managers to destroy motivation in employees. The first is to make an assignment lacking usefulness. Another is by not showing job appreciation; another, using humiliation or group embarrassment. Still another is to project a lack of confidence in a person, thinking that this will be an impetus to motivate the employee. (It will, in reverse!) Treating a person as "less than he is" creates a punishment climate and results in apathy. It is better for a manager to continually build and to surround employees with a climate for excellence and a feeling that productive and relevant work is accomplished. Individuals *need* to feel important.

Managers can instill a sense of job and personal importance in an employee by being receptive in permitting the employee to impart influence upward, laterally, and downward. Allowing an employee to influence upward means that the manager is receptive to employee suggestions and innovations. The manager must listen intently, thereby giving a sincere indication of the importance he attributes to the employee as an individual and to his ideas.

The manager permits the employee to exert influence laterally by giving him free rein to deal with other organizations without requiring detailed briefings from him. All that is necessary is for the manager to ask the employee to represent him in solving a problem, to give him the authority to use whatever resources are necessary, and to tell him that he is the judge as to how it should best be handled. Then the employee should be left alone to do what he has been asked to do.

The downward influence a manager should allow employees to exert is to let subordinates make use of their own resources without interference. Not only is this vital to their own supervisory effectiveness and self-importance, but it is also necessary for them to gain respect from their own staff.

Summary

As managers, we should *manage motivation* through the internal sensitivities of employees. We must stimulate the motivation which comes from within an employee, not that which is generated by us. We cannot really motivate employees; it is the need in the hierarchy of needs which motivates them. We must determine what need each employee is attempting to fulfill and tailor our management technique to aid in fulfilling that need.

$$\star \quad \star \quad \star \quad \star \quad \star$$

Raborn operated throughout [the Polaris Program] with a bare-bones staff. . . . He kept his people on the job seven days a week, and when their enthusiasm flagged he gave them what he called the "Raborn rededication treatment." This was a cross between a half-time pep talk and a Fourth of July speech. Said one dazed aide after getting the treatment, "I knew that I was ready to die for someone, but I didn't know whether it was the Admiral, the President, my mother, the head of the Boy Scouts, or who."

—Time, *April 23, 1965, p. 27.*

It's a good outfit where ethical behavior is the rule from top to bottom. A case-in-point involved the commander of an operational wing. One day he got a parking ticket. Instead of ignoring it, he acknowledged his error. When Christmas gifts arrived at the office, he returned them like the reg says. A funny thing happened: When the people in his office got parking tickets, they "paid the price" rather than having them "taken care of." When they got Christmas presents from "politicians," they returned them. *Office standards usually reflect the guy at the top.*

—Capt. Wurster, PGMC, *TIG Brief 2, 1977*

17

The Project Organization*

J. S. Baumgartner

Generally projects involve two or more in-house functional organizations and a number of subcontractors and suppliers who work on project-deliverable items. One can appreciate the challenge confronting the project manager when he realizes that the project manager, in the usual case, depends on these organizations for meeting his project objectives but has no direct authority over them. The project manager must obviously have a high degree of skill in motivating, communicating with, and setting objectives for these elements, which are primarily responsive to someone else.

The following discussion outlines what constitutes the project organization, the relationship between the project manager and these elements, major problem areas and practical solutions to them, and development of the organization into a dynamic, "gung-ho" project team. The project organization considered here is the "partially projectized" type, which is more difficult and much more typical than the "fully projectized" type in which the project manager may be, as he is in some major missile and aircraft projects, a division manager with his own line organization.

It is in specific areas of approval, coordination, primary responsibility, and information that successful interface of the project and functional operations is determined. Figure 5–5 illustrates a simple, effective technique for defining these key relationships.

On large development projects, the practice of retaining systems work within the project office has evolved as a general princi-

*Extract from *Handbook of Business Administration* (New York: McGraw-Hill Book Co., 1967), pp. 5–76 to 5–81.

PROJECT FUNCTIONS

ORGANIZATION	Plans and Controls	System Analysis	System Engineering	Detail Engineering	Prototype Fabrication	Prototype Test	Subcontracts Control	Customer Liaison (Contract)	Customer Liaison (Extra-Contract)	Production	System Test	Etc.—
● Company (Division)												
Chief Executive	A					I	I	I		I		
Controller	C					I	I			I		
Manager of R&D		I	C	P,A	P	I				I		
Materiel Director			I			I	C		I	I		
Production Manager		I	I	I		I				P	I	
Marketing Director			I			I		I	P	I		
Director, Product Assurance			I	C		P				C	P	
Etc.—												
● Project												
Manager	A	A	C	I	C	C	A	I	I	C	C	
Controls Manager	P	I	I	I		I	C	C		I	I	
Chief Engineer	I	P	P,A	C	C	I	I	C		I	I	
Subcontracts Manager			I			I	P			I	I	
Manufacturing Representative				I	I					C	I	
Marketing Representative						I		I	C	I		
Contracts Administrator						I	I	P	I	I		
Test & Reliability Manager						A				A		
Etc.—												

P—Prime responsibility   I—Information to   C—Coordinated with   A—Approval authority ple. Thus, in the flow of work, system analysis and system engineering functions are performed by the project office; detail engineering and prototype fabrication and inspection are a function of engineering research or subcontractor organizations; and system test is a responsibility of the project office. The project office therefore determines the work to be done and determines whether its specifications have been met, although the greatest effort in terms of manpower and dollars is performed by functional and subcontractor organizations.

The In-House Organization. A key question in project management is how to control project operations while cutting across departmental and divisional lines within the project manager's company. The basis for this relationship is a work authorization (WA), which clearly states what is to be accomplished and the level of dollars and manpower allotted by months or other periods of time. The WA must be agreed to, after discussion and negotiation, by both project and functional parties; if agreement cannot be reached (a not unusual situation where stiff competition, tight funding, and a fixed-price contract are involved), the project manager should refer the matter to higher common authority with his recommendations and basis for them. It is fundamental to planning, control, and the success of the project that disputes involving WA's be resolved *early,* before substantial costs are incurred.

The project manager has a number of tools in addition to the work authorization for gaining the active support of in-house project elements, however.

1. The project manager is, in effect, the customer of in-house project elements; his control of project funds is a powerful "persuasive" lever.

2. In companies which recognize the importance of the project manager's role and appreciate that he needs functional management support, the project manager has a clearly stated charter and position guide which cut through much of the underbrush of confusion and misunderstanding that otherwise tends to arise.

3. A well-planned and continuing employee information program, including an initial orientation of each individual, periodic status reports and presentations, and a "promotion" campaign, is an effective, supplementary tool.

4. Weekly meetings (technical, schedule, and cost) of project and task managers are essential to in-house control.

5. Periodic presentation of project status to company management is necessary, both to keep company management informed and to request assistance if necessary. A major aircraft producer

holds project status reviews every Saturday morning; few problems arise which are not soon corrected.

6. An arrangement whereby project engineers are responsible to both functional management (for all purposes other than work contributing directly to project accomplishment) and project management (for work contributing directly to the project) gives the project manager an important administrative control. A developer of propulsion systems effectively uses this dual responsibility concept.

Subcontractor Control. Subcontracts and outside purchases generally account for 50 percent or more of expenditures on development projects. Standard items and subcontract items of lesser dollar amount are procured through the company's purchasing or materiel organization. As to major subcontracts, however, the matter of whether materiel or the project office or engineering has cognizance is often poorly defined but is of prime importance in successful performance on these contracts.

To give proper direction to the subcontractor, the matter of responsibilities must be clearly defined for (1) technical aspects, (2) schedules, (3) cost aspects, and (4) contract administration. It is apparent that a contract administrator (normally assigned to the materiel function) will usually handle matters pertaining to contract administration, and that a project engineer will direct the technical aspects. It is in the areas of responsibility for schedule and cost, and the role of the project office, that confusion often arises. Whether the project engineer or subcontract administrator will monitor and control schedule and cost and whether the project office has a director of subcontracts to whom these people are fully or partially responsible must be clearly defined and must be made crystal clear to the subcontractor. A failure to define these responsibilities invites subcontract problems.

The mechanics of subcontractor control are generally similar to those of overall project control: a sound *plan* for achieving technical, delivery, and cost objectives; regular *measurements* of achievement and expenditures against the plan; and corrective *action* where deviations appear. The format and periods of plans and reports must be compatible with those required by the project manager's customer, because they are "feeder" information for his project control and progress reports.

Timeliness in taking corrective action is particularly important in subcontracts control, because later the project manager has fewer and fewer opportunities to influence a sub's responsiveness. Greatest control is exercised at the time of source selection; then in order come contract negotiation, post-award conference, and the first two or three months of working with the subcontractor. If by this time the prime has not established a firm leader-follower relationship, he is in for trouble. Later, because of the elapsed time invested in the sub, as well as resources committed, it may be almost impossible to terminate the sub's contract even though he is performing unsatisfactorily.

The Project Team. Collectively, the project office, in-house functional elements working on the project, and the subcontractors comprise the project team. Motivating these diverse organizations to work as a team requires clear objectives, full communications, and full use of available incentives. Fortunately for the project manager, the purposes and objectives of most R&D projects are almost self-evident, and are much clearer than those of functional operations. The reasons for high reliability and quality, tight scheduling, and cost and funding limitations are almost immediately apparent to an experienced project team. The nature of this collective undertaking is the basis for developing a strong project organization.

The project manager normally uses this common-interest basis to foster a team spirit through such means as:

- Constant visual awareness—mockups, pictures, plant newspaper articles, and the like—of the end product.
- Keeping team members fully and regularly informed about developments, project status, and customer reactions.
- Advising responsible individuals of particularly good or weak performances, with copies to higher management as appropriate.
- Regularly scheduled progress, technical, and cost reviews whose purpose is to ferret out problem areas and take early corrective action.
- Personal visits to work areas.
- Developing friendly competition between project elements, on bases such as "progress for the money spent."
- Making sure that channels of communication are established between project elements.

There will be occasions, however, when a balky subcontractor or unresponsive in-house department needs a different approach. The project manager in these instances may have to withhold funds until the problem is resolved, might request higher-management assistance, or, as a last resort, may request action by his customer.

In summary, the project manager has available a number of techniques for controlling in-house and subcontract work toward achievement of project objectives. It is apparent, however, that *simplicity* of project organization, *clear relations* between project elements, and *full communications* are absolute necessities, rather than merely desirable techniques, in project management. As for authority, the project manager would do well to *assume authority* in those areas where his authority is not defined. Where the choice must be made, project objectives rather than friendship must be the project manager's guide.

18

Organization Alternatives for Project Managers*

Robert Youker

In the past ten years interest has grown in techniques and approaches for management of temporary projects (in contrast to ongoing operations). There has been an explosion of literature dealing with these techniques and strategies, and more recently, we have seen the beginnings of organized academic research on various aspects of project management.

However, in discussions and in the literature we still seem to be confused about the exact meaning of some terms. This is particularly true in the area of alternative approaches for the management of projects.

Functional Organizations

The most prevalent organizational structure in the world today is the basic hierarchical structure. This is the standard pyramid with top management at the top of the chart and middle and lower management spreading out down the pyramid. The organization is usually broken down into different functional units, such as engineering, research, accounting, and administration.

The hierarchical structure was originally based on such management theories as specialization, line and staff relations, authority

*Adapted from *Project Management Quarterly,* Vol. VIII, No. 1, by permission of Project Management Institute, P. O. Box 43, Drexel Hill, Pennsylvania 19026.

and responsibility, and span of control. According to the doctrine of specialization, the major functional subunits are staffed by such disciplines as engineering and accounting. It is considered easier to manage specialists if they are grouped together and if the department head has training and experience in that particular discipline.

The strength of the functional organization is in its centralization of similar resources. For example, the engineering department provides a secure and comfortable organizational arrangement with well-defined career paths for a young engineer. Mutual support is provided by physical proximity.

The functional organization also has a number of weaknesses. When it is involved in multiple projects, conflicts invariably arise over the relative priorities of these projects in the competition for resources. Also, the functional department based on a technical specialty often places more emphasis on its own specialty than on the goals of the project. Lack of motivation and inertia are other problems.

However, many companies use the functional organization for their project work as well as their standard operations. The world is a complicated place. In addition to discipline and function, other nuclei for organizational structures include products, technologies, customers, and geographic location.

Project Organizations

The opposite of the hierarchical, functional organization is the single-purpose project or vertical organization. In a projectized organization, all the resources necessary to attain a specific objective are separated from the regular functional structure and set up as a self-contained unit headed by a project manager. The project manager is given considerable authority over the project and may acquire resources from either inside or outside the overall organization. All personnel on the project are under the direct authority of the project manager for the duration of the project.

In effect, a large organization sets up a smaller, temporary, special-purpose structure with a specific objective. It is interesting to note that the internal structure of the project organization is functional, that is, that the project team is divided into various functional areas.

Note that the term here is "project organization," not "project management." You can manage projects with all three types of organizational structure. The advantages of the project organization come from the singleness of purpose and the unity of command. An esprit de corps is developed through the clear understanding of, and focus on, the single objective. Informal communication is effective in a close-knit team, and the project manager has all the necessary resources under his direct control.

The functional, hierarchical organization is organized around technical inputs, such as engineering and marketing. The project organization is a single-purpose structure organized around project outputs, such as a new dam or a new product. Both of these are unidimensional structures in a multidimensional world. The problem in each is to get a proper balance between the long-term objective of functional departments in building technical expertise and the short-term objectives of the project.

Criteria for Selecting an Organizational Structure

In the field of management, zealots like to say that their particular model is best. Neophytes want a simple and unambiguous answer. Experienced and thoughtful observers, however, know that no one particular approach is perfect for all situations. The current vogue in management literature is the contingency model. This theory states that the best solution is contingent upon the key factors in the environment in which the solution will have to operate.

The same is true for the choice of an organizational structure. What we need, then, is a list of key factors that will help us to choose the right organizational structure for the given conditions on a specific project with a given organization and a particular environment. A set of such factors is listed in Figure 1.

For example, an organization developing many new but small projects with standard technology would most likely find a functional structure best. On the other hand, a company with a long, large, complex, and important project should favor the project organizational structure. A firm in the pharmaceutical business with many complicated technologies would probably go to a matrix structure.

It is possible to use all three structures in the same company on different projects. All three structures might also be used on the same project at different levels—for example, an overall matrix structure for the project with a functional substructure in engineering and a project organization in another functional sub-area.

Before we can make a final choice, however, we must consider the following additional factors:

1. What is the relationship between organizational design, the

Criteria for Organization Design Decisions

	Functional	Favors Matrix	Project
Uncertainty	Low	High	High
Technology	Standard	Complicated	New
Complexity	Low	Medium	High
Duration	Short	Medium	Long
Size	Small	Medium	Large
Importance	Low	Medium	High
Customer	Diverse	Medium	One
Interdependency (Within)	Low	Medium	High
Interdependence (Between)	High	Medium	Low
Time Criticality	Low	Medium	High
Resource Criticality	Depends	Depends	Depends
Differentiation	Low	High	Medium

Figure 1

skills of the project manager, and the project planning and reporting system?

2. Are there ways we can improve coordination and commitment in the functional structure without moving to a project or matrix structure?

3. What variations exist in the matrix structure and what are the advantages of each variation?

Project Managers and Organizational Design

It is not possible to decide on the organizational design without also deciding whom to select as the project manager and what kind of design you want for the planning and reporting systems. These decisions are closely interrelated. For example, a successful project organization requires a project manager with the broad skills of a general manager. He must combine technical knowledge of the subject matter with management abilities before he can lead the entire project team. It makes no sense to select a project organization form if such a project manager is not available.

The planning and reporting system in a project organization can be fairly simple because the team is in close proximity. The opposite is true in the management of projects through a functional organization. Information in the form of plans, schedules, budgets, and reports is the key medium for integrating a functional organization. Therefore, a more sophisticated planning and reporting system is required in a functional organization than in a project organization.

Improving Lateral Communications in the Functional Structure

Organizations typically turn to a project organization or a matrix organization because the normal functional structure has failed on a series of projects. It is not necessary, however, to "throw the baby out with the bath water." Before giving up on the functional organization, analyze the real problems and see if steps can be taken short of reorganization. Some results of a reorganization may be favorable, but other unintended but logical consequences are certain to be unfavorable.

Methods of lateral or horizontal communication need to be developed across functional department boundaries. Alternative approaches for lateral communication include:

1. Such procedures as plans, budgets, schedules, and review meetings.
2. Direct contact between managers.
3. Informal liaison roles.
4. Teams.

These are integrating mechanisms short of the establishment of a matrix organization. They help to break down the barriers that seem to separate different disciplines, departments, and geographic locations.

Weak to Strong Matrix—A Continuum

The three major organizational forms—functional, matrix, and project—may be presented as a continuum ranging from functional at one end to project at the other end. (Figure 2). The matrix form falls in between and includes a wide variety of structures, from a weak matrix near functional to a strong matrix near project. The continuum in Figure 2 is based on the percentage of personnel who work in their own functional department versus the percentage of personnel who are full-time members of the project team. Note that in a functional organization the project team has no personnel of its own. The dividing line between functional and matrix is the point at which an individual is appointed with part-time responsibility for coordination across functional department lines.

ORGANIZATIONAL CONTINUUM

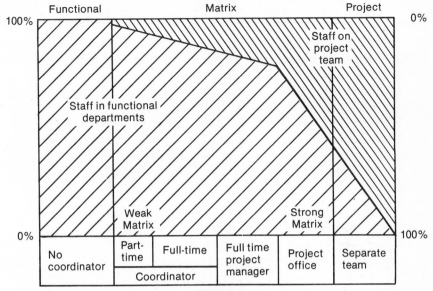

Figure 2

The bottom line of Figure 2 shows that a weak matrix has a part-time coordinator. The matrix gets stronger as you move from full-time coordinator to full-time project manager and finally to a project office that includes such personnel as systems engineers, cost analysts, and schedule analysts. The difference between a coordinator and a manager is the difference between mere integration and actual decision-making.

On the far right we have the project organization. Ordinarily, there is a clear distinction between a strong matrix in which most of the work is still being performed in the functional departments and a project organization in which the majority of the personnel are on the project team.

It is rare for a project organization to have all the personnel on its team. Usually some functions, such as accounting or maintenance, would still be performed by the functional structure.

Some persons have taken issue with the use of the term "strong matrix." They say that a strong matrix comes from an even balance of power between the functional departments and the project office. That may be true in some instances, but not always. Strong and weak are not used in the sense of good and bad. Rather, they refer to the relative size and power of the integrative function in the matrix.

Measuring Authority: Functional vs. Project Staff

Another way to differentiate between a strong matrix and a weak matrix is to analyze the relative degree of power between the functional departments and the project staff. We could construct another continuum with function on the left and project on the right. For a given project we would decide where the power rests on the continuum for decisions over project objectives, budgets, cost control, quality, time schedule, resources, personnel selection, and liaison with top management. On any given project the power will be strongly functional for some factors and strongly project for others. However, a profile line can be drawn from top to bottom that would indicate whether the trend is to the left (weak) or to the right (strong).

Making Matrix Management Work

Matrix management is a controversial concept. Some people have had bad experiences operating in a matrix. Others have had a great deal of success. It does require careful definition of authority and responsibility as well as strenuous efforts toward coordination and diplomacy. The matrix is basically a balance of power between the goals of the functional structure and of a specific project.

Overloaded Functional Departments

One key problem with matrix organizations is that they tend to overload the functional departments with work. If a functional department makes a commitment to work more man-hours on projects than it has available, conflicts over priorities between projects are inevitable. This problem can be alleviated, if not solved, by better planning.

A matrix organization will not work effectively unless a matrix strategic plan setting priorities on objectives and a matrix budget allocating resources also exist. For example, the project manager for Project A will add horizontally across functional departments to get his total budget. In a similar manner, the vice-president of manufacturing must add vertically across all the projects for which he has committed funds and resources as well as his strictly departmental efforts. The matrix budget must add up to 100 percent in both directions. The usual picture is that the functional departments are overcommitted and show required man-hours of perhaps 120 percent of actual man-hours available. When this happens, politics and disappointment become inevitable.

The golden rule in matrix management states, "He who has the gold makes the rules." If a project manager does not control the budget, he can only beg for handouts from the functional departments. A matrix budget assigns resources to the project manager for purchases from the functional departments. Making up such a budget takes careful work during long-range and annual planning. Regular updating of the matrix plan and budget are also necessary.

Survival Techniques in the Matrix

A common picture of the project coordinator in a matrix organization is of a frustrated diplomat struggling to cajole the functional departments into performing the work on schedule and within budget. His position is difficult, but the following approaches can help:

1. It is important to have a charter from top management defining responsibilities and authority for the project manager as well as the role of the functional departments.

2. The project coordinator or manager must anticipate conflicts in the matrix. Conflict is inevitable with dual authority, but it can be constructively channeled.

3. Since conflict is inevitable, it is important to take positive steps to develop teamwork. Regular luncheons or social gatherings help to foster a team spirit. In recent years, the behavioral sciences have developed a number of specific techniques for alleviating or using conflict effectively. Training programs for matrix managers should include experiences with such techniques.

4. The project coordinator's main power comes from the approved objectives, plans, and budgets for the project. Use these documents to hold departments to their commitments.

5. It is vital that the functional department head be committed to the plans and schedules for the project as well as the lower-level task leaders. Functional managers should review and sign off on these documents.

6. It is usually best to avoid direct conflict with the functional department heads. The matrix manager should use his boss when a situation threatens to get out of hand.

7. It is important to remember that the project coordinator is concerned with "what" is to be done, not "how." Use a management-by-objectives approach and do not supervise the functional departments too closely.

8. Many of the problems of matrix management flow from the uncertainty inherent in the project environment. By definition, a

project is, to some extent, a "new" effort. Careful and continuous planning can help reduce uncertainty.

No one perfect organizational structure for managing projects exists. The functional, the project, and the different matrix structures all have strengths and weaknesses. The final choice should come after weighing various factors in the nature of the task, the needs of the organization, and the environment of the project.

The functional structure will work for many projects in many organizations, especially if lateral communications can be improved through integrating mechanisms and procedures short of hiring a matrix coordinator.

When a matrix approach is chosen, the entire organization must put a great deal of effort into it to make it work. In particular, the project coordinator or project manager in the matrix must be carefully chosen and trained. His interpersonal skills are more important than his technical knowledge.

In many situations, a project organization may appear to be the simplest solution from the viewpoint of the project manager. However, the functional managers or top management may not find it to be the best long-range or most strategic decision.

The program manager must have a technical deputy he trusts—someone responsible for assuring that subsystem elements are more than merely compatible. They must be designed as part of a harmonious system and not an assemblage. The need for a technical deputy does not suggest that the program manager can or should avoid all technical problems. System engineering is only one of a lot of things he cannot avoid, but he cannot be the system engineer and also give all other matters the attention they require.

—*LMI Introduction to*
Military Program Management

As a true entrepreneur, a venture manager has an opportunity that rarely exists for anyone in an established company, for he can command a new enterprise from its early phases through commercialism. Obviously, such an experience is excellent training for many top management positions in a corporation. Unfortunately, the way people too frequently are trained for high-level jobs is just as impractical as it would be to train a symphony orchestra conductor by having him play a violin for five years, a flute for three years, and then asking him to conduct the whole orchestra. How much better training it would be to have him first conduct a university orchestra, and then a community symphony, before taking on the New York Philharmonic!

—*Russell W. Peterson, "New Venture*
Management in a Large Company," Harvard
Business Review, *May–June 1967, p. 72.*

19

The Effective Management of Conflict in Project-Oriented Work Environments*

Dr. Hans J. Thamhain†
Dr. David L. Wilemon‡

To successfully manage complex tasks, project managers must successfully deal with a number of managerial issues. First, they must develop support for their projects from key interfaces within their organizations. Second, they must effectively deal with the inevitable conflict situations which arise in administering their projects.

Project managers often operate in an environment conducive to the generation of intense conflict situations. The nature of project management, the need to elicit support from various organizational units and personnel, the frequently ambiguous authority definition of the project manager, and the temporary nature of projects all contribute to the conflicts which project managers experience in the performance of their roles.

A number of conclusions can be derived from this study which potentially can increase the project manager's effectiveness in the management of conflict and in eliciting support for his project.

Project managers need to use their expertise judiciously. If

*Extract from *Defense Management Journal,* July 1975, pp. 29–40.
†General Electric Co.
‡Syracuse University.

overused, it can be detrimental and demotivating to project participants since it may discount their contribution; expertise which is wisely used can be important in developing respect and support for project managers.

Conflict with support functional departments is a major concern for many project managers. For the various categories—conflicts over schedules, project priorities, manpower resources, technical opinions, administrative procedures, personalities and cost—the study revealed the highest conflict intensity occurred with the functional support departments. The project manager usually has less control over supporting functional departments than over his assigned personnel or immediate team members, which may contribute to conflict. Moreover, conflict often develops due to the functional department's own priorities, which can impact on any of the conflict categories.

To minimize conflict in these seven areas requires careful planning by the project manager. Effective planning early in the life cycle of a project can assist in forecasting and thus, perhaps, minimizing a number of potential problem areas likely to produce conflict in subsequent phases. Consequently, contingency plans should be developed as early as possible in the life cycle of a project. Top management involvement and commitment in the project also may help reduce some of the conflicts. Good planning is often given insufficient attention by project managers.

Since there are a number of involved parties in a project, it is important that key decisions which affect the project be communicated to all project-related personnel.[1] By openly communicating the objectives and necessary subtasks involved in a project, there is a higher potential for minimizing detrimental, unproductive conflict. Regularly scheduled status review meetings can be an important vehicle for communicating important project-related issues.

Project managers need to be aware of their conflict resolution style and its potential effect on key interfaces. As the study suggests, forcing and withdrawal modes appear to increase conflict with functional support departments and assigned personnel, while confrontation, compromise, and smoothing tend to reduce conflict. Again, it is important for project managers to know whether conflict should be minimized or induced. In some instances managers may deliberately induce conflict in their decision-making process to gain new information and provoke constructive dialogue.

A definite relationship appears to exist between the specific influence mode project managers employ and the intensity of con-

[1]D. L. Wilemon, "Managing Conflict on Project Teams," *Management Journal*, Summer 1974, pp. 28–34.

flict experienced with interfaces. Our findings suggest, for example, that the greater the work challenge provided by a manager, the less conflict he experiences with assigned project personnel. One approach is to stimulate interest in the project by matching the needs of supporting personnel with the specific work requirements of the project.

Conflict with functional departments also may be induced by the project manager who overly relies on penalties and authority. Often the overuse of authority and penalties has a negative effect in establishing a climate of mutual support, cooperation and respect.

In summary, project managers must be aware not only of the management styles they use in eliciting support, but also of the effect of the conflict resolution approaches they employ. For the project manager each set of skills is critical for effective project performance. If a project manager is initially skillful in eliciting support but cannot manage the inevitable conflict situations which develop in the course of his projects, his effectiveness as a manager will erode.

$$\star \quad \star \quad \star \quad \star \quad \star$$

Common Characteristics of Project Managers. . . . • Ingenuity • Dedication • Well-rounded background • Ability to instill confidence • Good physical health and condition • Good communicator • Ability to get the most out of people • Authority: *not* a problem . . . . *And Operating Practices* • Concentration on objectives • Willingness to take risks • Into details to the greatest possible extent • Sound plans and timely controls • Maintain a time reserve and a money reserve • Timeliness in making decisions • "Big Picture" awareness.

—Anonymous

20

Synthesis*

Erasmus H. Kloman

What is the essence of the management learning experience gained in the Surveyor and Lunar Orbiter undertakings? Can this experience be synthesized into meaningful and significant concepts relevant to the management of future undertakings? How important is the "management" of the project relative to other factors such as environment and the state of the technology? Are there apparent means suggested by Surveyor and Lunar Orbiter for transfer of learning experience? Is the experience applicable exclusively to similar advanced-technology research and development projects, or can there be lateral transference to the broader field of management in general?

What emerges perhaps most forcefully from a broad retrospective view is the importance of the human aspects of organization and management. Both projects demonstrated the critical nature of human skills, interpersonal relations, compatibility between individual managers, and teamwork. The Surveyor experience brought out these lessons, for the most part, by demonstrating the effects of gaps or barriers in the total web of managerial relationships. Many of the difficulties of the Surveyor project can be traced to individual and institutional discords that stood in the way of communication and agreement based on mutual interest in resolving project problems. Despite all the formal reporting systems, communications in the early stages of Surveyor were generally inadequate, both within and between the participating organizations. Individual managers in the various customer and contractor organizations were often sur-

*Extract from *Unmanned Space Project Management* (Washington, D.C.: National Aeronautics and Space Administration, 1972), pp. 39–41.

prised by a failure of their counterparts to follow what seemed to be the obvious course to get the job done.

Lunar Orbiter demonstrated the importance of leadership commitment to a project. When all levels of management fully support an endeavor, the odds for its successful completion obviously improve. In an environment marked by mutual respect and confidence of all participating organizations, Lunar Orbiter maintained its schedules and avoided many of the kinds of trouble that beset advanced research and development projects.

Surveyor demonstrated the depth of trouble a project can encounter when the full column of management support is incomplete. The general management structure of the Surveyor project at both the Jet Propulsion Laboratory and Hughes Aircraft Co. tended to be too removed from the project and too little committed to its necessary priorities. As one of the consequences, a multiple tier of suspicion and mistrust developed among the participants. Midway in the project, massive corrective measures, sometimes to the point of overcompensation, had to be instituted to assure the success of the Surveyor missions. Surveyor managers applied elaborate, detailed, and costly formal reporting systems in their attempts to keep the project on track. Lunar Orbiter managers, by contrast, had learned to reduce the amount of formal reporting and maximize the value of the informal links between project counterparts.

People make organizations; different kinds of people make different kinds of organizations. The field center personnel assigned to Surveyor were, by dint of circumstances of the time, very different from the kinds assigned to Lunar Orbiter. There was considerable reluctance at JPL to jeopardize professional careers in a project assignment. The professional staff charged with responsibility for Surveyor tended to be highly specialized in various research fields of science or engineering. The professional staff from which the Lunar Orbiter team was selected was eager to accept the challenge of the first spaceflight project assigned to them. Whereas the best talents were not applied to Surveyor until relatively late in the project's development, some of the best talents were assigned to Lunar Orbiter at the outset.

As between the prime contractors, the differences in makeup of Surveyor and Lunar Orbiter personnel were mainly in the degree of prior project experience. Personnel assigned to Surveyor were, for the most part, not trained in that type of project activity and few had the systems management capability needed. For Lunar Orbiter, large numbers of qualified technicians and managerial personnel who had worked with each other on prior projects were available. They began, moreover, with three years' more learning experience.

The different attitudes of Surveyor and Lunar Orbiter personnel upon the completion of their respective projects is significant. Some personnel at JPL still tended to regard their Surveyor experience as a sidetrack in their career advancement. Some felt that not enough effort had been made to apply their experience effectively in new assignments. Among Lunar Orbiter personnel, on the contrary, there was almost universal feeling that this project involvement had been a net plus in their careers.

Association with a successful undertaking breeds pride and confidence. Lunar Orbiter teams acquired a positive outlook almost from the beginning. For years Surveyor teams were harassed by serious technical problems, doubts about the technical feasibility of the entire undertaking, and second-class citizenship within their immediate environment.

The lesson here is obviously not that technical organizations should limit new undertakings to the least risky or demanding enterprises. Tough technical challenges must continue to be accepted by organizations aspiring to lead in technical endeavor. Perhaps the lesson centers on how the requirer and the producer reach agreement on their contract. General management of customer and contractor organizations must agree beforehand on the method of dealing with questions posed by sometimes conflicting priorities in allocating manpower and resources. Although it is far easier to make such a general observation in hindsight than to deal with such issues in practice, the assignment of priorities and allocation of resources by general management undoubtedly may be a determining factor in a project's outcome.

Many of the organizations and individuals engaged in space-flight projects such as Surveyor and Lunar Orbiter have moved on to work in nonspace-related fields. Despite the differences in technologies or differing environments surrounding their new enterprises, what they have learned about managing projects is still broadly applicable to their new ventures. The management skills represented in organizing and directing a space exploration project are not *sui generis.* Rather, they are a combination of common sense, managerial sensitivity, and technical competence adaptable to rapidly changing situations.

Although each manager setting out on a new task may view his assignment as a completely new departure, he is actually part of a continuum. Just as he brings to his task his own past knowledge and experience, so his colleagues bring theirs. The successful project manager is one who is able to provide the kind of leadership that effectively taps this experience, focusing a common effort upon common goals through a progression of commonly accepted intermediary steps.

Section 4—

CONTRACTING

Introduction

> Contract action shall be a major responsibility of the
> program manager.
>> —DOD Directive 5000.1,
>> Major System Acquisition

From time to time arguments appear as to why the PM should also be a contracting officer; just change hats and he can assume either role.

The realities of both responsibilities argue otherwise.

The PM has too many broad responsibilities to be deeply involved in contracting. And contracting as a field of expertise is too specialized and dynamic for him to gain equal footing with the careerists.

But the PM and his program office should be familiar with the basics of contracting. And particularly they must *read the contract!* Otherwise it is only a matter of time before they gain more experience than they want:

> Education is what you get by reading the contract.
> Experience is what you get from not reading it.

Not everyone on a project team needs to read the whole contract. But the key people do. And project engineers in industry should read the abstracts pertinent to their technical efforts. Often in industry and in government people rely on what someone says the contract says, rather than referring to the only true guidance, the contract.

William Thybony's article on the basics of contracting is an outstanding overview of contracting. This kind of background knowledge is essential for anyone in or doing business with the Federal Government.

Throughout this section, incidentally, reference is made to "procurement," the term used in the past and one that implies an active role. The current official term is "acquisition," which implies a passive role, as if a person or an agency might acquire something of value by just stumbling across it or by a "midnight requisition."

Incentive contracts, either fixed-price incentive or cost plus incentive fee, are the types generally used in systems contracting. The essence of cost targets and cost-sharing arrangements is discussed in "Incentive Contracting."

On most systems acquisitions more than half the value of a prime contract is subcontracted. The problem confronting the PM is how to keep some control over this part of his responsibilities when he has no privity of contract with his subcontractors. Curiously, little has been written in this area. The third article in this section gives guidance that should be of value in this dilemma.

In the final two selections Gen. Donald Nunn discusses contract administration from an overall management perspective, and W. J. Willoughby comments on how contracting can help improve reliability and maintainability, topics of increasing concern as systems become more complex.

The intent of these selections, collectively, is to provide a basic understanding of the link between the two parties to a contract.

21

What's Happened to the Basics*

William W. Thybony

Important principles may and must be inflexible.[1]
—Abraham Lincoln

During an era when procurement officials, professionals, and technicians, both in government and industry, are deeply and almost totally absorbed with complex problems and exotic (and often confusing) policy and procedural requirements, it is rare to focus the spotlight on the basics of Federal procurement. Often they are only backstage scenery. Today's paper implosion on the individual makes it next to impossible to sit back and relate the solutions of daily problems to the bedrock of procurement doctrine. And yet it is a discipline that needs cultivation.

The magnitude, complexity, and diversity of government procurement involves a huge cooperative effort and requires a high degree of understanding and education. Its impact on the level and trend of overall economic activity in the United States is considerable, and Federal procurement programs affect almost all business firms directly or indirectly. The government as a customer is engaged in millions of procurement actions each year, utilizing public funds which comprise a great share of the tax dollar. The great size of such an undertaking in itself solidifies the need to examine the basics.

The procurement process is beset with a good number of problems that could have been avoided. The seriousness of many would have been less, if at the outset good judgment and foresight based

*Extract from *National Contract Management Journal,* Vol. 5, No. 4, pp. 71–83.
[1]Last public address, April 16, 1865.

on the fundamentals of government contracting had been used. Often, those in the government procurement business, whether on the buyer or seller side, become so specialized that after time goes by they lose sight of the fundamentals. Knowledge of the basics and application on a day-by-day basis is essential. It is elementary not only to the novice, but to professionals of long standing experience as well, to be on solid ground.

Current dialogue and debate is drawn to the prevailing sophisticated modes of: cost accounting standards, major systems acquisition, research and development contracting, management systems, parametric cost estimating, pie cost, independent research and development, return on investment, design-to-cost, "should cost," cost sharing, technical transfusion, appeals, claims, defective pricing, industrial funding, patent policy, rights in technical data, consequential damages, economic price adjustments, etc., etc. Granted, all important—and yet many of today's issues could be simpler and procurements made sounder if they rested on a firm foundation of the basics.

What Are the Basics?

The basics of Federal procurement have grown and matured over the years through a maze of not only varied legislative, but administrative efforts as well, to develop a system providing safeguards against graft, favoritism, questionable ethics, war profiteering, collusion, and inefficiency, and to protect the integrity of the competitive and public bidding system once established.

What then are the real basics? Here again there will not be full agreement. Why? Because they are not compiled in any one law or regulation, and opinions of individuals will vary depending on their specialization, knowledge, and the divergent missions of their organizations.

However, in spite of this and from a broad and objective perspective, the condensation set forth below is offered as representative of the basics of Federal procurement. There can't be any quarrel with the statements included—there may be dispute as to whether the list is all-inclusive. Miss any one of the following and you're in trouble.

1. The power of the United States to contract is based on the general and implied powers contained in the Constitution of the United States.

2. The President of the United States, as the nation's Chief

Executive Officer, is responsible for government purchasing functions.

3. The Administrator for Federal Procurement Policy (head of the Office of Federal Procurement Policy in the Office of Management and Budget) by law provides overall direction of government procurement policy.

4. Upon entering a contract the government becomes subject to the rule of Federal law as a private individual.[2]

5. The U. S. government as a contractor is not liable for its sovereign acts.[3]

6. No contract or purchase on behalf of the United States can be made unless it is authorized by law or is under an appropriation adequate to its fulfillment. A contract liability expires when the appropriation is exhausted.[4]

7. Expenditures or contract obligations in excess of funds appropriated are prohibited.[5]

8. Federal agencies may make use of funds only for the purpose appropriated, in the absence of specific authority for another purpose.[6]

9. No contractor can be required to perform a government contract in a manner prohibited by law or in response to coercion or promised reward by a government official or employee.

10. No official or employee of the government may give away any vested right of the government.

11. The government contracting officer is the agent of the government under any government contract. His authority is limited. A government contracting officer may bind the government only to the extent of his actual authority, whether it be expressed or implied. Authority may be implied from a duty imposed upon the government agent or from some express authority given to him.

12. The risk of dealing with a government agent not authorized to act is on the contractor. Unlike a private contractor, when a government agent does not have actual authority to act, the government is not bound by his acts. The Supreme Court has said:

> Although a private agent, acting in violation of specific instructions, yet within the scope of his general authority, may bind his principal, the rule as to the effect of the like act of a public agent is otherwise, for the reason that it is better that an individual should occasionally

[2]*U.S.* v. *Allegheny County,* 322 U.S. 174 (1944), and *in re American Boiler Works,* 220 F. 2d 319 (1955).
[3]*Jones* v. *United States,* 1 Ct. Cl. 383, 385 (1965).
[4]42 U.S.C. 11, *Shipman* v. *United States,* 18 Ct. Cl. 138 (1883), 37 Comp. Gen. 199 (1957).
[5]31 U.S.C. 665 (a), ("Antideficiency Act").
[6]28 Comp. Gen. 38 (1948).

suffer from the mistakes of public officers or agents, than to adopt a rule which, through improper combinations or collusion might be turned to the detriment and injury of the public.[7]

13. The government is required to acquire goods, services, and facilities of the requisite quality and within the time needed at the lowest reasonable cost, utilizing competitive procurement methods to the maximum extent practicable.

14. The government relies upon the private enterprise system to supply its needs, except where it is in the national interest for the government to provide directly the products or services it uses.[8]

15. The two principal methods of procurement and forming of contracts are formal advertising and negotiation. Formal advertising is the preferred method, unless it is not feasible or practicable and one of the statutory exceptions to formal advertising is applicable —then the procurement may be negotiated.[9] (The Commission on Government Procurement concluded that statutory changes should be made which would require formal advertising when conditions justify its use, but that negotiated procurement should be authorized and recognized as an acceptable and normal alternative to formal advertising. H. R. 9061 would have implemented the Commission's recommendations in this respect by authorizing the following methods of procurement: small purchase procedures, formal advertising, competitive negotiation, and noncompetitive negotiation. Similar recommendations have been made in the past. Notable among them are recommendations contained in the National Security Industrial (NSIA) Defense Acquisition study,[10] and in an article by Robert B. Hall, U.S. General Accounting Office.[11])

16. Known qualified suppliers are given an equal chance to compete.

17. In negotiated procurements, written or oral discussions are conducted with responsible offerors within a competitive range, price and other factors considered.

18. Contract awards are made only to firms submitting bids or offers which are the most advantageous to the government, price and other factors considered.

19. Contracts are not awarded unless the price is deemed to be reasonable.

20. Normally, reasonableness of price is based on adequate

[7] *Whiteside* v. *United States,* 93 U.S. 247, 258 (1876), U.S. Supreme Court.
[8] Office of Management and Budget (OMB) Circular No. A-76, August 30, 1967.
[9] 10 U.S.C. 2304, 41 U.S.C. 253.
[10] Recommendation 32, National Security Industrial Association Defense Acquisition Study, July 1970.
[11] "The Armed Services Procurement Act of 1947 Should Be Reformed," Robert B. Hall, U.S. General Accounting Office, *National Contract Management Journal,* Vol. 3, No. 1, Spring 1969.

price competition (forces of competition in the market place) and is determined by price analysis.

21. Generally, in negotiated procurements where price has not been based on the competitive forces of the market place, offerors are required to submit cost or pricing data to assure reasonableness of price or cost estimates and to form a basis for cost analysis. (The "Truth in Negotiations Act" briefly stated requires that prior to the awards of noncompetitive contracts and all contract modifications exceeding $100,000, prime contractors and subcontractors will have to submit to the buyer cost or pricing data certified as to its accuracy, completeness and currency. It allows the government to reduce the contract price of the prime contract if it is later determined that the data submitted as of the date of the price agreement were not accurate, complete and current (defective data). Only downward adjustments of price are considered.)

22. Contracts are priced separately and independently, and no consideration is given to losses or profits realized or anticipated in the performance of other contracts.

23. Contracts are awarded only to those who are responsive to the government's requirements and are technically and financially able to perform.

24. Government contracts promote equal employment opportunities for all persons, regardless of race, color, religion, sex, or national origin.

25. Government contracting promotes small business, including minority business enterprises.[12]

26. U.S. domestic source products are preferred over foreign products.[13]

27. Fair dealing and equitable relationships are fostered between the parties.

28. Items supplied by a contractor are inspected and accepted by the government before payment of invoices.

29. Legal and administrative remedies are designed to provide for fair and equitable treatment of the contracting parties.

Donald N. Pitts, TRW, writing in a Newsletter of the National Contract Management Association states: "I urge all in the government contracting community to promote the concept and to apply their professional experience to the development of a set of Federal Procurement Principles, which ultimately must be established. Only by establishing and building up from a solid foundation can we ever hope to achieve greater efficiency in the expenditure of public funds in government procurement."[14]

[12]15 U.S.C. 631–647 (Small Business Act of 1953, as amended).
[13]41 U.S.C. 10 (a)–(d) (Buy American Act).
[14]"More Comments: Federal Procurement Principles," Donald N. Pitts, TRW, *National Contract Management Association News Letter*, March 1972.

What Is a Contract?

A contract is the prime instrument used by the government to obtain supplies and services from private business firms and other organizations. Generally, the law that determines the essential validity of government contracts is similar to that which governs private contracts.

In this sense, a contract is an agreement which creates an obligation. Its essentials are competent parties, subject matter, a legal consideration, mutuality of agreement, and mutuality of obligation.[15] In its simplest form it is nothing more than a system of legally enforceable rights and obligations.

Contracts require the essential elements of offer and acceptance. These elements constitute the means by which a contract is consummated and the absence of either element prevents the formation of a contract. In government procurements, the invitation for bids, request for quotations or proposals constitutes a request by the government for offers of a certain nature. The bid or proposal submitted by the party solicited is in fact the offer and the subsequent contract award constitutes acceptance. An offer cannot be revoked after its acceptance without the acceptor's consent; but it may be revoked at any time before acceptance, even though it allows a specific time for acceptance, unless it is under seal or supported by a consideration. While under ordinary principles an offeror may withdraw or modify his offer at any time prior to acceptance, a distinction has been drawn when an offer in the form of a bid is made to the government. In that situation, where there is no mistake, or unreasonable delay, the offer may be withdrawn or modified as a matter of right only until the date and hour set for opening of bids. Subsequent to bid opening, the government has the power to award a contract, on the basis of the offer submitted, for a specific period of time.[16]

Most commercial relationships expressed in contracts are relatively simple compared to the usual government contracts, which are normally complex, lengthy documents whose award and performance are controlled by equally complex statutes and regulations. Also, there are essential differences in government contracts, as compared to commercial agreements, which make them unique.

For instance, the government may change its mind and unilaterally terminate a contract for its own convenience; it may issue changes in delivery points, method of shipment, and specifications during performance without the contractor's consent; and if the

[15]17 Corpus Juris Secundum, Contracts §50.
[16]Government Contract Principles, Office of General Counsel, U.S. General Accounting Office, November 1970.

company has a dispute with the government contracting officer, the decision may be appealed, but it is resolved by one party to the contract—the government, through its Board of Contract Appeals. And an apparent contract is not a contract if the contracting officer acted beyond his authority, even though the contractor relied to his detriment upon unauthorized representations. The courts have reasoned that the risk of doing business with an authorized contracting officer should, as a matter of policy, fall on the individual contractor rather than the general public.

In brief, the prerequisites for the formation of a government contract are: (1) any formal execution as required by statute or regulation; (2) a specific appropriation adequate to the contract or general contractual authorization; (3) the agent of government has actual authority or his act is ratified by a person with authority; and (4) the resultant contract is not prohibited by some statute or regulation pursuant to a statute.[17]

The primary procurement regulations differ somewhat in their definitions of a contract.

The Federal Procurement Regulations state that "contract" means establishment of a binding legal relation basically obligating the seller to furnish personal property or nonpersonal services (including construction) and the buyer to pay therefor. It includes all types of commitments which obligate the government to an expenditure of funds and which, except as otherwise authorized, are in writing. In addition to a two-signature document, it includes all transactions resulting from acceptance of offers by awards or notices of awards; agreements and job orders or task letters issued thereunder; letter contracts; letters of intent; and orders, such as purchase orders, under which the contract becomes effective by written acceptance or performance. It also includes contract modifications.[18]

The Armed Services Procurement Regulation defines "contracts" as meaning all types of agreements and orders for the procurement of supplies or services. It includes awards and notices of award; contracts of a fixed-price, cost, cost-plus-a-fixed-fee, or incentive type; contracts providing for the issuance of job orders, task orders, or task letters thereunder; letter contracts; and purchase orders. It also includes supplemental agreements with respect to any of the foregoing.[19]

A wide variety of types of contracts are authorized for government contracting.[20] They are normally classified according to compensation for cost of performance and the amount and type

[17]Corpus Juris Secundum, Contracts §50.
[18]FPR 1.1.208.
[19]ASPR 1–201.4.
[20]FPR Subpart 1–3.4; ASPR §III, Part 4.

of profit incentive offered the contractor to meet or exceed specified targets.

The firm fixed-price type of contract is the most preferred since the contractor accepts full cost responsibility, and the relationship between cost control and profit dollars is established at the outset of the contract.

At the other end of the range from firm fixed-price, in relation to financial risk placed on contractors, is the cost-plus-a-fixed-fee type of contract where profit rather than price is fixed and the contractor's cost responsibility is minimal. In between are the various incentive contracts which provide for varying degrees of contractor cost responsibility, depending upon the degree of uncertainty involved in contract performance.

Other than in formally advertised procurements, in which firm fixed-price is required (or fixed-price with escalation in certain circumstances), the selection of contract type is generally considered a matter for negotiation and requires the use of judgment and depends on a variety of factors. Type of contract and pricing are interrelated and considered together in negotiation. However, in practice the government normally prescribes the type of contract to be used.

Cost-plus-a-percentage of cost contracts are prohibited by law.

The spectrum of authorized types of contracts for Federal procurement and a mini-sketch of each are as follows:

1. *Firm Fixed-Price.* (One price for contract period.)

2. *Fixed-Price with Escalation.* (Price adjusted as specified contingencies occur such as when wage rates and specific material costs fluctuate.)

3. *Fixed-Price Incentive.* (Fixed-price with incentive provided by allowing profit to be adjusted based on relationship of final negotiated total cost to total target costs.)

4. *Fixed-Price with Price Redetermination.* (Fixed-price with initial price adjusted as actual costs are known.)

5. *Cost-Sharing.* (Contractor receives no fee and is reimbursed only for an agreed portion of his allocable and allowable costs.)

6. *Cost.* (Allocable and allowable costs are reimbursed and contractor receives no fee.)

7. *Cost-Plus-Incentive-Fee.* (Allocable and allowable costs are reimbursed with provision for a fee which is adjusted by formula in accordance with the relationship which total allowable costs bear to target cost.)

8. *Cost-Plus-Award-Fee.* (Allocable and allowable costs reimbursed with special fee provision—fee includes a fixed amount and an amount awarded for excellent performance.)

9. *Cost-Plus-A-Fixed-Fee.* (Allocable and allowable costs are reimbursed and provision for the payment of a fixed fee to the contractor.)

10. *Time and Materials.* (Payment based on fixed hourly labor rate and materials at cost.)

11. *Labor-Hour.* (Payment based on fixed hourly labor rate.)

12. *Indefinite Delivery.* (Fixed-price, but "open" with respect to quantities or time of delivery. Three types: definite quantity, requirements, and indefinite quantity.)

13. *Letter Contract.* (Preliminary contractual instrument permitting production to start prior to the finalization of a definitive contract.)

Selection of contract type is determined by such factors as the financial liability of the government, the adequacy of cost information furnished by the contractor, the nature of the work, associated risks, and current market conditions.

Many serious problems would be prevented if the contractor was completely familiar with all of the provisions in his government contract. It is imperative that he know precisely what is required of him; he should know his rights and responsibilities.

Too frequently a government contractor has learned too late that prescribed contract "boilerplate," although a formality, means what it says, and that its stringent provisions may be invoked against him. It is basic to know that the government is not allowed to have a heart in administering contracts. A contractor must produce strictly in accordance with the specifications of his agreement with the government and within the delivery time specified, or he may have his contract terminated for default with consequences that could be disastrous for him.

What Are the Ethics?

Corollary to the basics of procurement policy are the basic standards of conduct relating to the public/private interface.

Businessmen selling to the government and government employees assume responsibilities of ethical conduct which are greater than found in the private commercial world. In government procurement, the principles of honesty, integrity, fair dealings and public confidence are requisite. The involvement of public interests and the expenditure of public funds demand an impeccable standard of conduct.

The underlying policy for government officials and employees is that: where government is based on the consent of the governed, every citizen is entitled to have complete confidence in the integrity of his government, and each individual officer, employee, or advisor of government must help to earn and must honor that trust by his own integrity and conduct in all official actions.

In consideration of the paramount importance for maintaining the highest possible standard of excellence of human conduct in government/contractor relationships, a large body of laws, executive orders, regulations, and directives dealing with ethical practices and the conduct of individuals has evolved over the years. However, not all of the ground rules are in writing; some are based on custom and require the use of common sense and the exercise of sound judgment.

From the mass of requirements and prohibitions, a pattern for guidance unfolds, although it is cautioned that pertinent statutes and directives must be known and complied with. The following is a compendium which embraces the cardinal principles of required and acceptable ethical practices:

1. A government employee should not:

a. Solicit or accept directly or indirectly, any gift, gratuity, favor, entertainment, loan, or any other thing of monetary value, either directly or indirectly from any individual or organization which has, or is seeking to obtain, contractual or other business or financial relationships with his agency.

b. Give preferential treatment or special favors to anyone, whether for remuneration or not.

c. Lose complete independence or impartiality of action.

d. Affect adversely the confidence of the public in the integrity of the government.

e. Use any information coming to him confidentially in the performance of government duties as a means for making private profit.

f. Have a direct or indirect financial interest that conflicts substantially, or appears to conflict substantially, with his official duties and responsibilities.

g. Engage in, directly or indirectly, a financial transaction as a result of, or primarily relying on, non-public information obtained through his official employment.

h. Receive any salary or anything of monetary value from a private source as compensation for his services to the government.

i. Recommend or suggest the use of any nongovernment person or organization offering services as intermediary, consultant, agent, representative, attorney, expediter, or specialist, for the purpose of assisting in any negotiations, transactions, or other business with his agency.

j. Knowingly, and wilfully, conceal or cover up a material fact, or make any false or fictitious statement in connection with any official matter, document, or record.

k. Wilfully and unlawfully conceal, remove, mutilate, falsify, or destroy any government document or record.

l. Make private promises of any kind binding upon the duties of office, since a government employee has no private word which can be binding on public duty.

2. A government employee should:

a. Put loyalty to the highest moral principles and to country above loyalty to persons, party, or government department.

b. Expose corruption whenever discovered.

c. Conduct himself in such manner that his work is effectively accomplished while observing the requirements for courtesy, consideration, and promptness in dealing with the public and other government personnel.

d. Perform business dealings with contractors and potential suppliers in a manner above reproach in every respect, and assure that his conduct is such that he would have no reticence in making a full public disclosure of his actions.

e. Refrain from any private business or professional activity which would place him in a position where there is a conflict between his private interests and the public interests of the United States, including the avoidance of an appearance of such a conflict.

f. Conduct all business with government suppliers on an arms length relationship basis.

3. Contractors are prohibited from:

a. Offering or giving gratuities, such as entertainment or gifts, to any officer or employee of the government with a view toward securing contracts or securing favorable treatment with respect to the awarding or amending, or the making of determination with respect to the performing of such contracts.

b. Knowingly promising or offering compensation to a government employee or officer for any services rendered by him.

c. Bribing public officials, such as giving or promising anything of value to an officer or employee of the government with the intent to influence any official act or to influence such employee to commit or allow any fraud upon the government or to influence any such employee to violate his lawful duty.

d. Employing or retaining any person to solicit or secure a contract under an agreement or understanding for a commission, percentage, or contingent fee (except bona fide employees or bona fide established commercial or selling agencies maintained by the contractor for the purpose of securing the pertinent business).

 e. Submitting false or fraudulent claims or statements to the government.

 f. Submitting bids or proposals which have not been arrived at independently from consultations or agreements with competitors for the purpose of restricting competition.

 The Federal Procurement Regulations and the Armed Services Procurement Regulation state that the term "improper influence" means influence, direct or indirect, which induces or tends to induce consideration or action by any employee or officer of the United States with respect to any government contract on any basis other than the merits of the matter.

 There are many areas not precisely covered by law or regulation or contract clause. These are the areas where good judgment has to be exercised. For instance, common courtesies and amenities are not gratuities if they are not offered with a view of obtaining favorable treatment in procurements. However, since it is not always possible to know the intent of the giver or the recipient, gifts or other favors even though small in value should not be given or offered to avoid embarrassment or need for explanation. It is far more prudent to lean in the direction of conservatism and discretion. It is emphasized that even the appearance of trying to influence or being influenced or the appearance of a possible conflict of interest should be fervently shunned.

Conclusion

 What's happened to the basics? Not a thing. They haven't vanished—they've been with us right along. It's whether we consciously apply them to our problems, whether every training course is introduced by them, whether we recognize in them the roots of our professional knowledge.

 The basics aren't balloons of tokenism. They are the respectable pillars of procurement.

✷ ✷ ✷ ✷ ✷

Remember that the only really firm basis you have for dealing with the contractor is the contract.

          —Ship Acquisition Reef Points

22

Incentive Contracting*

Ralph Burdick

The purpose of this article is to offer a few ideas for consideration when structuring an incentive contract matrix. In the opinion of this writer, the basic purpose of an incentive contract is to motivate a contractor towards meeting planned and specific objectives. If we don't carefully examine and determine what these objectives are and convey them to the contractor by means of a carefully structured incentive matrix, then obviously the benefits of this contract type are reduced or lost altogether. These are statements of the obvious but nevertheless there are too many instances where ceiling amounts and cost sharing percentages, for example, result from an arbitrary selection of values and not the result of careful analysis and planning related to the instant procurement. Also it seems that incorporation of technical performance incentives into incentive matrices is seldom done and in many instances this may be a valuable tool to counterbalance the cost incentive and improve reliability and quality.

Realistic Cost Targets

An incentive contract, irrespective of whether a cost or fixed price type (CPIF or FPI, respectively) should be fair to both parties and therefore should be based on the best possible assessment and establishment of a target cost for which there is a 50–50 percent possibility that final cost will be less than or greater than target cost.

*Extract from *Procurement Newsletter*, Spring 1977, p. A-3.

This amount may be based on adequate price competition or, if adequate price competition is absent, should be based on the results of a thorough cost and price analysis. Additionally, an appropriate assessment should be made regarding what the range of reasonable probable final cost outcome may be (upper and lower amounts which are not necessarily equal in difference from the target cost).

Computation of Cost Sharing Percent

In the case of FPI contracts, there are several methods for structuring an incentive matrix. The judgment may be made as to what profit amount the contractor should be allowed if his costs equal the aforementioned upper dollar amount (the sum of the upper dollar amount and profit being the ceiling price). In addition, a fair target profit amount should be established. Computation of the cost sharing line for a cost overrun is not difficult and is an exercise in arithmetic once the target cost, upper amount of probable cost overrun and profit thereon as well as profit at target cost have been established. (Divide computed difference in profit by computed difference in cost.) The derived cost sharing percent (e.g., 70/30 percent—70 percent government and 30 percent contractor) may also be applied to any cost underrun or compute the cost sharing percentage using a method similar to that discussed for a cost overrun.

In any event the selection of cost sharing ratios and ceiling amount should be the result of a careful and rational process related to the instant procurement and not the result of an arbitrary or preconceived notion of what percentage seems appropriate.

FPI contracting, unlike CPIF, provides no minimum and maximum profit/fee amounts and includes a ceiling price. It should be noted that the ceiling price, in addition to limiting the government obligation, has the effect of changing the cost sharing percent (share line) at a point between target cost and ceiling price known as the "point of total assumption (PTA)" to 0/100 percent sharing (0 percent government and 100 percent contractor). This means in effect that each dollar expended between PTA and ceiling and thereafter by the contractor decreases his profit by a dollar ($ for $) with it becoming a loss contract when costs exceed the ceiling price.

CPIF contracting differs from FPI for the reason that usually a minimum fee and always a maximum fee are stipulated without imposition of a ceiling price. Care must be exercised in developing the cost sharing percent—cost sharing line—to assure that the cost sharing applies throughout the estimated dollar range of final probable cost outcome (known as "range of incentive effectiveness"—RIE). Failure to do this (which is not uncommon) may result in a CPIF contract after a minimal cost overrun or underrun and therefore removing all incentive for a contractor to further control costs. In circumstances where a CPIF contract is indicated (e.g., in preference to FPI because the effort is engineering development or operational systems development) every consideration should be given to technical performance incentives to balance the cost incentive.

In a real sense, it all goes back to fundamentals. If the program manager, the technical people, the lawyer, and the contracting officer communicate with each other, the right contracting methods can be found. If they do not communicate the facts and the real intent, problems are inevitable.

—LMI Introduction to
Military Program Management

The contract type shall be consistent with the system program characteristics and shall give particular emphasis to the issues of risk and uncertainty to the contractor and the government. The cost type contract is preferred when the required development is a major part of the task and areas of risk remain. Fixed-type contracts should be used when the areas of risk have been resolved and the development objectives have been demonstrated successfully.

—DOD Directive 5000.2,
Major System Acquisition Process

The SPD must take a vital and active interest in the key procurement factors which affect his program.

—Gen. James Ferguson,
USAF, AFSC Commander

23

The Program Manager and the Subcontractor: Hands On or Hands Off?*

J. S. Baumgartner

On almost every defense system acquisition program, subcontracts account for more than half of the prime contractor's costs. One prime contractor, for example, subcontracts 66 percent of a missile program while two others have subcontracted 60 to 70 percent of aircraft and destroyer programs, respectively.

A general idea of the value of subcontracts can be gained from a recent report of the General Accounting Office (GAO).[1] The Comptroller General estimates that 116 Army, Navy and Air Force programs will cost more than $153 billion. Even after deducting prime contractors' fees or profits and general and administrative expenses, it is apparent that a major part of this outlay will go to subcontractors. And therein lies a key question for the DOD program manager: How can he control these costs when he has no direct access to subcontractors?

The DOD program manager's contract, being with the prime contractor, precludes a direct legal relationship with subcontractors. He has no privity of contract with them and must avoid putting himself in a position where he, in effect, relieves the prime contractor of responsibility and liability for subcontractors' performance.

*Defense Management Journal, July 1973, pp. 48–51.
[1]"Cost Growth in Major Weapon Systems," Report by the Comptroller General to the Committee on Armed Services, House of Representatives, March 26, 1973, p. 1.

This is well understood by DOD program managers who have a good appreciation for chain of command.

"Hands off" seems to have become the guiding doctrine in the program manager's relationship with subcontractors. But with the great emphasis on costs in acquisition, how can the program manager afford *not* to get more involved in subcontractor control? In short, where in practice is the dividing line between hands on and hands off?

Guidance and Doctrine

Official and unofficial guidance is remarkably sparse on subcontracts, particularly regarding the management aspects as distinguished from the legal relationship.

Section XXV of the Armed Services Procurement Regulation (ASPR) treats subcontracts briefly. One section of the regulation deals with evaluating and reviewing prime contractors' procurement systems. Another section concerns the government's right to approve subcontracts proposed by the prime contractor.

Tucked away in the next to last paragraph of Military Standard 881 on Work Breakdown Structure (WBS) is another statement regarding subcontracts: "The prime contractor shall be responsible for traceable summarizations of subcontractor data supporting his prime contract WBS elements. The prime contractor may negotiate any WBS with a subcontractor that permits the prime contractor to fulfill his contract WBS requirements and which provides adequate control of the subcontractor."

Beyond these two directives are incidental references to subcontracts in documents such as DOD Instruction 7000.2, "Performance Measurement for Selected Acquisitions," and the Handbook on Cost Information Reports. The role of the DOD program manager in subcontractor management, however, has received scant attention.

Reasons for Subcontracting

It is apparent that whatever action the DOD program manager takes with regard to subcontractors must be exercised through his prime contractor. This article will consider some of the measures he can take to ensure adequate control.

At the outset, a natural question arises: Why do prime contractors subcontract so much of their work?

First, there are fewer defense systems being procured although systems' dollar magnitude has increased. This means there are fewer prime contractors. As a result many former prime contractors are increasingly assuming a subcontractor role, as well as occasionally being a prime contractor.

Another reason for subcontracting is that as systems have grown in complexity, prime contractors have necessarily subcontracted for subsystems outside their in-house expertise. Propulsion, guidance and control and electronic subsystems, for example, are typically subcontracted by airframe contractors.

Subcontracting gives a prime contractor flexibility in coping with the accordion-like requirements of defense procurement while maintaining a relatively stable in-house base of skills and facilities. It dampens the effect of a company's expanding and contracting to accommodate changing DOD requirements.

Whatever the reason for subcontracting, subcontracts are often so large that they are, in fact, subprograms projectized and managed in a manner similar to that of the prime contractors and the military services. Subcontractors two and three tiers below the prime may also have a program manager, program organization, and plans, controls and objectives corresponding to those of the DOD program manager and his counterpart in industry, the prime contractor program manager. The techniques and principles of program management apply at these lower levels, just as they do at the level of the DOD program manager.

Who Manages the Subcontractors?

Let's look now at some actions the DOD program manager can take to ensure that his program's subcontracted dollar is well spent, without his becoming directly involved with the subcontractor.

Sometimes the fault for loss of subcontractors' control of costs is traceable to the prime contractor and, more specifically, to the matter of who in the prime's organization has responsibility for what. On a large aerospace program a few years ago a company's program engineer for propulsion assumed that he had full responsibility for both in-house and subcontract propulsion work because a documented company policy assigned this responsibility to the program engineer. At the same time a subcontract administrator in the prime contractor organization assumed *he* had full responsibility for propulsion subcontracts on the program because another numbered company policy assigned responsibility for subcontracts to the procurement organization. Company management was (and may still be) unaware of these conflicting directives. The net result was that, although it was clear to the individuals involved who was responsible for strictly technical and subcontract administration aspects, neither was directly responsible for cost or schedule management and neither took effective steps to control the two propulsion subcontractors. The company's program manager, more interested in technical aspects than in cost and controls, assumed no direct responsibility for subcontract management. Costs galloped out of control while progress inched along on subcontractors' work.

Eventually the program manager and his government counterpart were both replaced, largely because subcontract overruns contributed to a general loss of control.

If responsibility for subcontract or subprogram control is poorly defined in the prime contractor's organization, it is easy to imagine how confusing—and costly—this lack of definition is to the subcontractor who may be subject to conflicting directions from the prime's program manager, program engineer, subcontract administrator, general manager, director of procurement and perhaps his controller.

The DOD program manager can preclude this situation by obtaining from the prime contractor a documented statement saying who has specific responsibilities for cost, schedule and technical performance on each subcontract, and the prime program manager's responsibilities for subcontractor performance. Equally important, the DOD program manager should verify that subcontractors also receive such a statement; otherwise the effects of fragmented responsibility are sure to hit him in the pocketbook sooner or later.

Plans and Controls

The Cost/Schedule Control Systems Criteria (C/SCSC) can aid greatly in subcontract control if a subcontractor has a validated C/SCSC system. Many prime contractors, in fact, prefer to team with a subcontractor who has a validated cost/schedule control system because it provides greater visibility into program status and subcontract administration is less costly. C/SCSC also helps to ensure that the subcontractor's plan is practical, comprehensive and meshes with the prime's program plan.

There is another area which might be termed "rigor" that is important in the prime contractor's management of subprograms.

A subprogram manager learns very quickly whether his customer, the prime contractor's program manager, has tight or loose reins, just as the prime contractor discovers this about his Defense Department counterpart. Where responsiveness is demanded, the subcontractor will be more apt to stay on top of his work. Laxness on the other hand invites unresponsiveness, and usually higher costs. "Rigor" here does not mean detail. It means the insistence on the prime and the subcontractor each doing what they said they were going to do.

Bearing in mind that the DOD program manager must take action through the prime contractor, some of the measures he can take to ensure rigorous management are these:

• Verifying the prime receives subcontractors' planning documents and reports *on the day they are due,* rather than the following day or later—and ensuring corrective action is taken if they are not promptly received.

• Detecting informal reports or reports other than those required by the prime's contract with the subcontractor. The existence of preliminary or working reports usually indicates those required by contract have deteriorated to eyewash (". . . the reliability problem reported in June is being resolved through aggressive management action. . . .").

• Determining the effectiveness of corrective actions taken by the prime when the subcontractor reports deviations from his approved plan.

• Reviewing the subcontractor's reports, on a spot-check basis at the prime's facility, for meaning and timeliness; and comparing these reports with the prime's report to the government for the same period.

By rotating his staff through attendance at the prime contractor's facility, the DOD program manager can greatly increase his visibility into how his program's dollar is being managed.

As a corollary, the prime contractor's program manager will almost always become more attentive to managing his subcontractors when he knows his customer has this visibility.

Progress Reviews

Occasionally, early in his program, the DOD program manager should pick up his phone and ask his prime contractor counterpart, "Charlie? I'd like to sit in on your next progress review with Delta (subcontractor) on the guidance subsystem. Is that okay with you?" His industry counterpart may be thinking, "Progress review? I don't know about any progress review." But, quick on his feet, he responds, "Sure thing, Fred. I'm not sure just when my guys have it scheduled, but I'll get back in touch with you." Then he scrambles to schedule a review, sets up an agenda, and calls back. "Hello, Fred?

Our next regular quarterly review is scheduled at Delta for the 11th of next month. Why don't you come out and join us there?"

In accompanying the prime on his visit to the subcontractor, the DOD program manager must scrupulously avoid giving direction to the subcontractor but he can ask any number of questions. Based on his staff's review of the prime's subcontract management and on the DCAS or plant representative's surveillance, he will know what questions to ask and how to evaluate the answers.

If the subcontractor has a project control center, he can also ask to review the subcontractor's plans and controls, including the plans and controls of lower tier subcontractors. And the DOD program manager can, of course, at any time give pertinent directions to the prime contractor's program manager.

Summary

The most effective action in subcontracts management by DOD is the point at which the subcontractor is selected. After this, time effectively locks in a subcontractor, just as it does a prime contractor.

There are subsequent actions the DOD program manager can take in subcontractor management, even though he has no privity of contract and must exercise control through his prime contractor. He can (must) ascertain that responsibility for subcontractor management is clearly defined, for both the prime and subcontractor organizations. He can determine the effectiveness of the subcontractor's plans and controls, and the prime's rigor in demanding the subcontractor meet program requirements. He can also take part as an observer in reviews of subcontractors' performance, in company with the prime.

These measures are not, of course, all-inclusive. But they are indicative of steps the DOD program manager can take in controlling the bulk of his contract costs, while keeping a "hands off" attitude toward subcontractors. The magnitude of defense procurement and the ever present money crunch demand that the DOD program manager find ways to get the most for his program's subcontract dollar.

Source selection is the most critical decision point in life with a sub-contractor. An effective post-award conference is probably the next most important point in getting subcontract results. Once this relationship is underway, effective plans and controls, and a constant scrutiny of subcontractor status, are essential if the PM is to detect unreported problems before they erupt into a catastrophe.

—John Stanley Baumgartner

24

New Ways to Spell "Contract Mismanagement"*

Government Executive

As he did in an interview recently, Air Force Contract Management Division Commander, Major General Donald G. Nunn, might be expected to say, "Good contract management is becoming more and more important." Benign as that may sound, what he follows it up with isn't: "Industry mismanagement of prime contract dollars subcontracted out or spent on overhead costs is exceeded only by the government's."

Though it might seem so, he's not trying to pick a fight with everybody. In fact, what he's trying to do is get industry suppliers as concerned about the Air Force's problems as the Air Force is. "Our problem basically is that the members of the military-industrial complex—and, let's face it, that's what we are—don't sit down and talk to each other honestly and directly."

When there's communication at all, he adds, "we've got the wrong people talking to each other. The marketing guy from industry is talking to his old buddy in the service. The quality control guy is talking to his counterpart; engineers to engineers, and so on. But the decision-makers aren't talking to each other."

Aerospace industry management, he believes, "spends too much time trying to get new programs rather than on managing well the ones they have." His case in point: the high-level company official who said his job was to "bring $1 million a day of new business into the firm."

*Government Executive, December 1973, pp. 52–56.

"Then why," Nunn asked, "do you show up on the wiring diagram looking like you're in charge here? And, if you're not, who's worrying about the programs you have today?" His own experience just reinforces his frustration. "I write all my own letters to company presidents. I get an answer back 99 times out of 100 from the company lawyers." His aggravation is hardly surprising.

The Contract Management Division's (CMD) job, in simplest terms: "Help the system program director bring his program in on target; and see to it that contractors under CMD cognizance live up to their contractual promises." That responsibility covers more than 9,000 contracts worth in excess of $35 billion; systems and projects under development not only for the Air Force but for Army, Navy and the National Aeronautics and Space Administration.

Monitoring an annual expenditure of nearly $5 billion, CMD is headquartered at Kirtland Air Force Base, New Mexico (near Albuquerque); runs three test site contract management offices; and has Air Force Plant Representative Offices (AFPRO's) located in some twenty key prime contractor plants around the nation.

The AFPRO's are the heart of CMD. In officialese, their job is to "serve as the inplant extension of the System Program Office (SPO), providing on-site services in engineering, manufacturing operations, quality assurance, flight acceptance, safety, contract management, overhead control, subcontract surveillance and industrial materiel management." In other words, says Nunn, "Our job is to see that the contractors manage well."

But, he says, there "isn't one thing the best SPO combined with the best plant rep can do that will correct an award to a poor contractor." And a lot of contractors, he believes, aren't managing very well.

"I don't want to twist this out of perspective. We don't do our job very well either." But, he notes, in Project ACE, Air Force Chief of Staff George Brown "is more critical than anybody else has ever been of the Air Force total acquisition system." (ACE, for Acquisition Cost Evaluation, was started by Brown last March. Its goal: come up with policies and programs that will inspire cost cutting over the entire spectrum of Air Force weapon systems ownership from creation to replacement.)

In light of that, Nunn can't understand "why contractors are not running hard to improve cost and management performance so they can take credit for a change for doing something without being forced to do it." Instead of that, he says, "we're wasting time going to conventions, talking about the same problems we were talking about fifteen years ago—and nobody's *doing anything.*" Result: progress "is taking too long."

It seems very clear to him, for instance, that "Cost today is spelled with a capital 'C.' It's not just a buzz word we give lip service to." But he thinks few members of the aerospace industry really recognize that; "mostly just those hanging by their toenails, scrapping for survivability—and that's the wrong time to fight cost."

He freely admits, "Until I got this job (three years ago), the closest I had been to procurement was on the buying side and then only on the periphery (three tours at, first, the old Ballistic Missile Division of Air Force Systems Command, second, the Electrical System Division of AFSC, and third, the present-day Space and Missile Systems Organization of AFSC). With a military background largely in the Comptroller field—except for a civilian stint between World War II and Korea as a mink rancher—Nunn found, when he took over CMD, "It was easy to ask dumb questions." But he also found, "Some of the answers I got back weren't very smart, either."

What he worries about, he says, are not only the problems in his own area but "the problems of the boss. Those bigger problems are the ones I can't solve. And I would be terribly arrogant if I said I know the answers. But what I do know is there has to be a better way than what we're doing now."

One of the boss' problems: "Rising cost is pricing us out of business. And Congress is showing a complete impatience with our lack of improvement." Moreover, "We don't have much time to straighten out. We have a much more difficult time today convincing the committees and the Body of Congress that we've done our homework thoroughly. It has made them more conscious, more concerned that what we tell them about system cost, delivery and performance is right and not a hope."

Stirring a Ruckus

Yet, he has found, trying to get a handle on the answers is tough. For one thing: "It's hard to find the company man in charge when we have a fundamental management problem."

For another, he thinks there is something basically wrong in the relationship between the aerospace industry and the government. "They're either in love with each other or they're perpetual adversaries, pointing a finger of blame. Both these extremes are wrong. Our differences are mutual problems."

His message doesn't seem to have been heard too well. "I tell contractors, 'If you've got a problem, pick up the phone and call me.' In three years, I think I've had a total of about three calls from decision-makers." Another facet of the irritation: contractor failure "to tell me some new document isn't worth the paper it's written on; or to tell me what will happen if I press them into something."

Greeted with silence, Nunn says, "we'll assume we've done right and charge straight ahead. But it shouldn't be important if I'm right. The important thing is that we both be right. If I do something wrong, and they don't tell me, we both lose." He admits to making some mistakes in his job, "things I had to go back and change when it became obvious they weren't going to work. Somebody smarter than me should have told me at the outset and saved us all a lot of time and money."

In sum, "This 'low profile' idea of industry's is a lot of nonsense —with me anyway. If a contractor can get to the right level, and the Secretary of Defense is not it, he can get an audience and justice." His case in point: recently at CMD he got what was labelled "a draft" of a Military Standard 1520 (a quality control standard). He made some changes and CMD sent it all around for comments.

"I really stirred up a ruckus. I didn't know the 'Quality Assurance' boys had been working on that with AIA and USIA for over two years. Their representatives came down and we spent nearly three hours on it." Result: Nunn agreed to about 90 percent of the changes industry wanted, even though some of his own people were against them mostly because it would mean a change in CMD's way of doing business. "Because of that meeting, we got a better document with more common sense in it."

Unfortunately, he says, "That's the only time that's happened in three years—and I'm sure we've done a lot in that time that they didn't like." His point: the industry doesn't bring the problem to CMD. "Instead they take it to an association, and they, in turn, go to the highest level they can go in government—and not a heck of a lot happens."

Industry is likely to hear more from General Nunn in the future. His Brown-ordered drive to get a fix on subcontractor and overhead cost is the reason. Already, through the Aerospace Industries Association, industry has essentially said that's "none of the Air Force's business; that we're trying to run their business for them."

And Nunn grants the Air Force hasn't covered those areas too well in the past. "We've had no guidebook for our people on good and bad contractor judgment. Maybe that's the reason nobody looked at total contract management, the whole 100 percent, before. I have yet to hear even the NCMA (National Contract Management Association) talk about sub-contract management. They never have to my knowledge."

"There is very little talent around," he says, "for managing subs in spite of the fact that most problems start at the subcontractor level, sometimes two or three tiers down." Partly, he says, the problem is there because the industry has been allowed to develop some bad habits.

For one: the contract prime usually puts only a quality assurance guy in the sub's plant, "on the theory, I suppose, that if they let a firm fixed-price contract to reputable subs, that's all they have to do. But the really important questions of cost and good management aren't being watched."

"They say it will cost money to do that. I agree; but it costs more money when parts don't show up, when plants have to work around the clock to catch up, when poor workmanship is accepted. Good management is cheap, regardless of what it costs; because mismanagement costs a heck of a lot more." For that same reason, he admires Admiral Rickover. "He's about the only outspoken man we've had telling industry we're not just buying a piece of hardware; we're also buying management."

Aerospace Companies

In his drive to get visibility on what amounts to upwards of 75 percent of Air Force weapon system procurement dollars (overhead and subcontracting), Nunn already is going to put his emphasis on people rather than paperwork. "We backed away from management visibility on the C-5, and it didn't seem to solve the management problems." Besides, he says, "Some people think they'll get in trouble if they exercise judgment. So they write regulations and manuals out of the gazoo. All that does is stop people from thinking."

One thing he is changing: "When I got to CMD, we had only one person looking at subcontractor cost; and we didn't have any looking solely at overhead. So we had maybe 130 people in CMD (including part time people) looking at 75 cents of our dollar. The rest of our 3,600 looking at the 25 cents." It is clearly the Air Force's intent to find out how well contractors are managing this 75 cents.

Another change: Nunn has told the people in one AFPRO from now on they would have no prescribed duties except one. Each is to stake out an area of the plant "and know everything that's going on in that square." It's too early to tell what that will produce in the way of revelations about overhead and other questionable costs. But, reportedly, AFPRO morale has already improved.

Nunn is not particularly optimistic about industry management picking up his lead. "They have the same problem we do: a guy at corporate level will write a great instruction and two years later the worker on the floor hasn't seen it, yet."

Besides, "Aerospace company management has come mostly from one of two places: marketing or engineering. But if you're going to improve productivity, you're going to have to get somebody up top who knows manufacturing." Even on the government side, he says, "We don't have many people who can really do a good 'should cost' exercise or evaluation of contractor efficiency—especially in manufacturing processes. If the Air Force ever had it, we lost it somewhere."

Nunn is trying to get it back, which is why going "after the other 75 cents" places a tremendous burden on CMD. But the main uphill struggle he sees is "changing attitudes. When for 15 years you haven't demanded performance, haven't challenged their professional pride, that's very hard to awaken."

$$\star \quad \star \quad \star \quad \star \quad \star$$

Timely negotiation of a formal agreement between the system program office (SPO) and contract administration office (CAO) helps to satisfy several important aspects of good planning. A dialogue is established between SPO functional elements and their counterparts in the CAO. Each party knows what to expect from the other. Duplication is prevented while complete contractual administration is enhanced. The SPO learns what the CAO can do to assist in administering the contract. The CAO may use proposed agreements to identify needed additional expertise.

—TIG Brief, no. 12, vol. XXIX,
June 17, 1977, p. 18

Constructive changes can easily take place in the informal process of program management—in meetings and by correspondence—especially when the program manager or his deputy is involved. Such changes are prone to arise in situations where a contract is viewed (as some technical people view it) as a fussy necessity and something to be largely ignored.

There are three things a program manager can do to control these changes. First, he can make his position on the importance of the contract terms clear to his own staff and the contractor. If the program manager intends that there be no informal changes, he had better make it clear to everyone. Second, he can practice what he preaches. Third, he can encourage (even demand) active participation by his legal and contract advisers in the day-to-day operations and activities of the program office.

—LMI Introduction to
Military Program Management

25

The Procurement Role in Reliability and Maintainability*

W. J. Willoughby†

What is the procurement function's role in impacting and influencing reliability and maintainability improvement? *Everyone* involved with the contractual side of procurement should insure that *the requirements in the Requests for Proposals* and ultimately appearing in negotiated contracts are (1) enforceable, (2) realistic, and (3) enforced. In addition, each should assure that the means to measure contractor progress against these requirements clearly support timely enforcement. The following are representative of the necessary actions:

• If a specification includes numerical reliability and maintainability requirements, it is necessary that the factory demonstration test be timely and be conducted under environmental conditions duplicating the expected Fleet environments, including operation and maintenance by trained but inexperienced personnel. Existing military standards for reliability demonstration are unsuited to this task as currently applied, therefore required test conditions should be included in detail in the contract specifications.

• If a specification includes a disciplines and controls approach to reliability for the related engineering and manufacturing activities in lieu of (or in addition to) numerical requirements, *the means to audit compliance should be clearly defined.* Typical audit tools include (1) design reviews, at which specified technical documentation neces-

*Extract from *Procurement Newsletter,* Fall/Winter 1975, p. B-9.
†DCNM (Reliability & Maintainability) Headquarters Naval Material Command.

sarily generated by the contractor in conducting his work is examined for adequacy by knowledgeable Navy engineers; and (2) technical data, submitted by the contractor in accordance with the Contract Data Requirements List and the Data Item Descriptions.

• Contracts should reserve approval authority for the Navy for the test results and/or the audited documents, and the possible rejection actions should be clearly identified, ranging the full spectrum from correction and resubmission within a specified time limit, to contract termination.

• A requirement for identifying how the contractor will conduct his reliability effort should appear in every Request for Proposal, with the stipulation that it be submitted *with proposals,* to be evaluated as a significantly weighted source selection factor. It is too late to avoid major deficiencies in approach when the selected contractor is not required to reveal this approach until 30 to 180 days after contract award.

Procurement officers are not expected to be technically well-versed enough to correct deficiencies in the specification reliability and maintainability requirements, although this should not be beyond their realm of understanding. For this, they can rely on the cognizant project and technical support offices. They can, however, spot glaring omissions of realistic and enforceable requirements. *They can also verify that each enforceable requirement is backed up by a test, a key milestone review, or a CDRL data item, appropriate and adequate to measure contractor performance vis-a-vis each requirement.*

The Naval Material Command is in the process of implementing a number of new initiatives to upgrade the procurement of reliable and maintainable products, with the guidance and approval of the Deputy Chief of Naval Material for Reliability and Maintainability (NAVMAT 06). Among these initiatives are new policy instruments and awareness programs aimed at project officials and their technical support personnel. Procurement officials are the third group in this triumvirate. As all come to understand the problem and pull together as a team to solve it, the improved products the Naval Material Command delivers will restore to the Fleet unsurpassed levels of combat effectiveness at a price the American taxpayers can afford.

The whole point of a development process is to get something that we haven't got, something that we have never seen, and something which we don't really know can be produced.

—*Hon. Robert A. Frosch*

Section 5—

PROGRAM PLANNING

Introduction

The past two decades' record shows that most program failures are due not to weak execution but to poor planning: unrealistic, inflexible, uncoordinated, or just plain lack of planning. The usual excuse for shooting off without an adequate plan is, "We don't want to do anything that will slow down the work!" Or the run on the sponsor's checkbook.

Program planning has improved in recent years, however, as the relationship between plans and "actuals" en route to a PM's cost, schedule, and technical performance objectives becomes more fully appreciated.

A basic but often overlooked point is the necessity for the PM to define the need stated in the user's requirement. Sometimes the need as stated is different from what the user would like to have, as the first reading brings out. Jack Penick's penetrating view of shortcomings in planning is worth reviewing—several times.

The extent of systems engineering often is the fundamental difference between "system management" and "project management" as the terms are used in practice. Drumheller, Godden, and Schwegler cite the contents of a system engineering management plan, which forms the basis for the development of the major end items to be produced. Related to this plan and dependent upon it is the work breakdown structure or WBS. This is the "what" that forms the framework upon which budgets, schedules, and responsibilities are hung.

The WBS often is a sure indicator as to whether a program is in trouble, even though problems have not surfaced. WBSs that are unrealistic or a combination of functional structure and deliverable items (mixing the "who" and "what") or that exist in tandem with two or more WBSs on a program are a basic source of cost and technical problems. The article by Nucci and Jackson provides excellent guidance in developing or evaluating a WBS.

The final article in this section is on software, which has an increasing impact on systems cost and operational effectiveness.

This topic is discussed further in Section 8. The emphasis in this section is on planning for software.

Where most programs go wrong is at the beginning, not having adequate plans for getting "from here to there." These five selections offer guidelines for getting "there" intact.

I must be able to reach down to any level of Special Projects Office activity and find a plan and a performance report that logically and clearly can be related to the total job we have to do.

—*Adm. William F. Raborn*

26

Project Planning and Control*

John Stanley Baumgartner

Most difficulties in project operation, such as schedule slippages, personnel and organization problems, excessive expenditures, and the effects of unexpected changes, are directly traceable to weaknesses in planning. Personnel and organization problems, for instance, usually stem from not clearly defining relationships between the project and functional organizations and from inadequate orientation on project objectives, the project team, and where the individual fits into the project organization. Time and money problems frequently arise because schedules and budgets are not sufficiently realistic or because they are not maintained vigorously enough.

Planning is particularly important in research and development project management because usually there is no other experience factor to rely on for comparing "actuals" versus previous experience, as there is in manufacturing. The plan itself, in R&D project management, is the standard against which deviations are measured; these deviations in turn indicate where management should take action. Management action in guiding project operations toward time, cost, and technical objectives is therefore highly dependent on a sound, comprehensive, flexible plan.

A "plan for planning" is extremely important in defining what the project plan or plans will consist of, who is responsible for each part of the plan, and due dates for development and revisions of each part.

*Extract from *Handbook of Business Administration* (New York: McGraw-Hill Book Co., 1967), pp. 5–70 to 5–75.

Problem Areas

Several far-reaching problem areas merit particular attention in planning.

1. Confusion and loss of project control are often due to faulty work breakdown structure and to confused project/functional administrative practices. The work breakdown structure (project, task, subtask, black box, and so on) must include, for each "piece" of work, a statement of what is to be done; who the responsible manager is; how much time and money are to be allotted for the work; and what technical performance is to be achieved. Allotting a lump sum of funds to a functional department responsible for two or more project tasks virtually ensures loss of project control over these tasks. In large R&D organizations, the project manager may unintentionally contribute to this loss of control by working primarily through functional management rather than through the project organizational structure.

2. Related to the preceding point, and probably the most difficult problem in project management, is the matter of project/functional responsibilities and authority. Who has authority, for instance, over the design engineer in an electronics development department who is working on a communication link for a project? There is no commonly accepted "solution" in defining this relationship, nor is this fact particularly pertinent. What is important is that the working arrangement, whatever it may be, must be clearly understood and practiced by the project manager, the department manager, and the engineer himself. In determining this arrangement, physical location, maintaining technical proficiency, and responsibility for periodic reviews become important considerations.

3. Both cumulative and rate (of progress, expenditures, manpower application, and the like) plans may be necessary to detect trends requiring management action.

4. Personnel indoctrination and a systematic means of keeping personnel informed warrant thorough and effective planning. The project manager who finds that project operations seem to have bogged down after an early, enthusiastic period has probably overlooked the importance of making his people as effective as possible.

5. Plans must be flexible without being detailed to the extent that they become straitjackets. A straitjacket plan in a rapid-moving project situation invites its being rejected.

As in any kind of planning, the plan is more realistic and more enthusiastically carried out when the "doers" take an effective part in planning.

Project Control

What are project controls, and what is their purpose? Briefly, the purpose of controls is to show the project manager whether he is "on the beam" as he proceeds toward the technical, time, and cost objectives of the project, and to show him where to take corrective action if there are significant deviations. Controls, to be effective, must lead directly to action by the project or other manager; gathering of data which is merely "nice to know" or which a contractor believes will please his customer, regardless of its utility value, is an extravagance that few competitive organizations can afford.

Management action is highlighted by comparing "actuals" versus plans—actual versus scheduled progress, actual versus budgeted costs, and actual versus planned manpower, for example. On projects which extend over a year or more, it frequently is helpful to have both a cumulative and a rate of expenditure control. For instance, the actual cumulative application (man-months) of electronic design engineers may be within the total manpower budgeted to the current time; but detecting and working out "bugs" may require an increase in manpower at a time when the funding allotment requires a decrease. This divergence is readily apparent when comparing planned *rates* of manpower application, but is more difficult to detect when comparing only *cumulative* application. On a project involving many tasks in-house and out-of-house, controls of this type are useful in pointing out deviations early, when the project manager can take corrective action fairly easily.

Comparison of actuals versus plan for time and cost factors individually is relatively straightforward. PERT (program evaluation and review technique), CPM (critical path method), Gantt (bar) charting, and other techniques provide means of measuring actual versus scheduled *progress*. The company's controller reports on actual *manpower* and *dollar* expenditures which, when compared with worksheet or customer-approved budgets, provide action indicators for these two factors. The project manager needs to know also, however, whether he is getting satisfactory *achievement* for his money.

A continual comparison of progress versus cost versus technical performance is essential to sound control of project operations. For instance, a project task is not necessarily in financial trouble when actual expenditures exceed the budget, because progress may be correspondingly ahead of schedule. Nor is a missile necessarily over its cost and schedule problems when it arrives at a launch pad on schedule and within budget. If it blows up on the pad, the technical performance factor negates the apparent effectiveness of the administrative controls. Thus it is necessary to integrate these factors

—time, cost, and technical performance—to evaluate true status and to detect trends. The question the project manager must answer is whether he is getting his money's worth at each point in time; and what the trend is, at each level of effort, if he is getting his money's worth. For a meaningful evaluation, it is apparent that each work package must have its own technical objectives and plan, schedule, and budget, and that the format of reports must enable him to make a comparison among these factors.

Two general techniques are intended to evaluate time-cost status versus the plan. The more prominent of these is PERT/cost, an outgrowth of PERT. Backed by the Department of Defense and NASA, this technique provides the project manager with a mass of data on cost and progress for work packages at several levels (e.g., project, task, subtask, black box). In spite of its official backing, however, the technique has generally been unsatisfactory in practice because of its cost and complexity. Its major weakness as a useful tool is that, even if and when programming and other technical difficulties in the technique are overcome, the massive data confronting the project manager still must somehow be analyzed in terms of what they mean to him. The project manager is in effect told, "Here are all the data you need. You figure out what they mean." Analysis of these data frequently amounts merely to substantiating obvious situations which the project manager had known for some time.

The other general approach in integrating time-cost factors is a comparison of input versus output, a technique successfully used by several major defense companies. Input is generally measured in dollars (actual versus planned), and output is measured in progress versus schedule. The two ratios are compared, and relative progress for the money on each work package is derived. This information indicates to the project manager where he is or is not getting his money's worth, where he should reallocate funds, and what kinds of action to take. Using the status index—a concise numerical indicator of output/input, or efficiency—the project manager can forecast "money's worth" and also evaluate the effectiveness of project planning.

The project manager must also evaluate technical achievement along with progress and cost. Usually technical achievement is compared with scheduled milestones to give a technical performance/schedule comparison.

In summary, effective project controls show the project manager where and what kinds of action he should take to meet his project objectives. A comparison of actual progress, costs, manpower, and so on, versus the plan provides basic data for action; but true project control requires consideration of the interactions of time, money, and technical achievement. Only when the project manager knows whether he is getting his money's worth will he be in full control of project operations.

$$* \quad * \quad * \quad * \quad *$$

Nothing chastens a planner more than the knowledge that he will have to carry out the plan.

—*Gen. James M. Gavin*

Programs shall be structured and resources allocated to ensure that the successful demonstration of program objectives is the pacing activity. Schedules and funding plans shall be prepared to accommodate areas of program uncertainty and risk. Schedules shall be subject to trade-off as much as any program constraint to permit task accomplishment without unnecessary concurrency.

—*DOD Directive 5000.1,*
Major System Acquisitions

27

The Critical Step: The Initial Program Management Plan*

Lieutenant Colonel Ronald J. Penick

Peter C. Sandretto proposes in his book, *The Economic Management of Research and Engineering,* that

> "After all has been said and done about systems to control engineering costs and performance after the decision is made to embark on a project, it is the project plan, prepared before starting the work, that determines to a major extent the outcome of a project in terms of time, costs and technical performance.
>
> Almost universally, there has been a lack of realization that once a project plan is accepted, the die is cast. Further action can help to steer the course of the project and possibly conduct a rescue from disaster, but the road sign to the disaster point was erected when the project plan was written."[1]

A brief survey of Program Management Plans supports Sandretto's hypothesis. The opinions of today's program managers regarding the necessity and utility of this critical document, the Program Management Plan (PMP), vary throughout the continuum of "never use it" to "it's my program Bible—absolutely indispensible."

While it is obvious that the development of a perfect PMP will not guarantee that the program will be successful, it is reasonable to conclude that a poor, incomplete PMP will guarantee unnecessary difficulties in successful program completion.

*Extract from Study Project Report, Defense Systems Management College, November 1976. Italics added.
[1]Sandretto, p. 256.

PMP Formulation

Before we can analyze the PMP and identify the factors which address the question of why some PMP's are bad, it is critical to understand the functions which make up the PMP and the elements of each function. Furthermore, it is essential to have a full understanding of the dependency hierarchy of these functional elements and their various interrelationships.

The PMP development process can be divided into two functions, program planning and program controlling. The program planning function consists of three elements—assumptions, planning and programming; likewise, the controlling function can be divided into three elements—scheduling, costing and resource allocation. For purposes of this discussion, the following definitions will be used for these six elements:

- Assumptions—uncertain or nonvalidated information which forms the basis for subsequent action.
- Planning—identifying all actions required to proceed from where you are to where you wish to be.
- Programming—ordering all required actions into a logical sequence.
- Scheduling—the assignment of quantitative time values to an action or series of actions.
- Costing—cost of completing any given action or series of actions.
- Resource allocation—allocating money and manpower to an action or series of actions in order to implement that action or series of actions.

The first function in program planning is making assumptions. Obviously many assumptions are routinely made in any planning process. The two major assumptions required in order to proceed with the development of the PMP are the assumption regarding the threat definition and the assumption regarding the technical base.

Assumptions. The nature of the threat is the most basic assumption because the definitization of any plan requires that an end objective be well defined. In context of a PMP for a weapon system acquisition, the end objective is the development and deployment of a specific weapon system to negate an assumed threat to the security of the United States. The difficulty of precisely defining the kinds of, and capabilities of, weapon systems a potential enemy will have five, ten or twenty years from now is enormous, but even if you can predict the equipment part of his threat, it is even more difficult to forecast the strategic and technical approach that an assumed enemy would take in using such weaponry. It is not surprising then, when asked to define the threat, the potential user responds with a very hazy, sketchy description of what he thinks he wants. Such documents usually contain appropriate caveats which absolve the user of the final responsibility for the development of an end product, which could be useless when built to meet the user's stated requirements.

If the PM is knowledgeable and persistent, the potential user will finally agree that his assumptions and perception represent the best estimate of the requirement. What this means is that the user representative agrees that the *PM's assumptions and threat definition* are as good as the user could define. With the signing of this memorandum of agreement between the PM and a representative of the potential using agency, the PM accepts full responsibility for making sure that the end product he intends to develop will meet this assumed threat at some future date, even though the threat which materializes may only vaguely resemble the intial assumed threat.

The next area which usually requires a set of assumptions is the technical base available to the PM. Here the PM is likely to assume a far more mature technology base than actually exists. This is caused partly by the total absence of any organization which can give the PM a clear, factual statement of the technology base available. In order to obtain this information, the PM must communicate directly with the development scientists and engineers. But they, by the very nature of their professions, are optimists. Thus the PM always starts with an optimistic evaluation. Once again he is faced with the task of establishing his assumptions regarding the technical base.

Planning. The objective of planning is, given the assumed technical base, to identify all actions required to develop and deploy the weapon system. Not only must technical problems and solutions be identified, but also management actions and alternatives. Inadequate attention to either portion of this process almost guarantees serious difficulties in execution of the plan. In this process it is common to find that for some actions there are no reasonable alternatives. These items become critical go, no go decision points in the program and require special attention.

This list should include anticipated documentation efforts, discrete technical efforts, testing, safety programs, deployment transition efforts, supporting research and development efforts, etc., without regard to how they will be sequenced, funded or executed. This step is the most critical part of the PMP development process, for once the PMP is developed and published there will be no time to repeat this process. It is now or never!

The second part of the planning process is fairly straightforward—identifying who could perform each of the action items. One way to accomplish this is to develop a matrix structure with "what" on one axis and "who" on the other axis. By "who," it is intended that all proposed agencies be identified for initial consideration. This should include contractors, government agencies, and the program management office itself. "What" is the technical and managerial actions required. Once the "whats" and "whos" are identified, the filling in of the matrix is straightforward and proceeds rapidly.

The critical nature of the planning element cannot be overemphasized. It is here that most plans have failed. For example, a preconceived notion of how and what almost always eliminates consideration of alternatives. The lack of alternatives results in failure to recognize critical items which require early and constant attention and usually results in failure to identify better ways of accomplishing the objective.

Programming. The programming function is relatively easy. Setting the action items into a sequential format is normally obvious and can be done in a short time. Nonetheless, this process requires close attention since the sequence of events is the primary factor in the next effort, development of control tactics. Here the first business strategy is developed. Questions such as (a) in-house or contractual? (b) one or more agencies in competition or parallel efforts? (c) development of alternatives? need to be answered at this point. By the time this phase is developed, the PMP framework is beginning to take recognizable form and it is ready for the PM to develop the control function.

The Control Function

The only elements the PM can directly control are money, manpower and time, and he has only minimal direct control of the time element. However, scheduling is considered a control function since time is a visible, measurable quantity.

Schedule. For each action item a time-to-complete estimate must be developed and assigned. Although by now it has usually been decided what the most likely approach will be, it is still too early to eliminate the options and contingency items. All of these must be evaluated in terms of money, manpower and time. Having time quantified the programmed plan (the sequenced plan) the format may be changed from the matrix into a detailed time phased network, simply as a matter of convenience and clarity of presentation. Now it begins to look like a decision tree skeleton, and is becoming a document from which the PM begins to do some serious evaluation of alternatives.

Costing. Cost estimating undoubtedly causes the PM more headaches than any other element of the PMP because of the nature of the art of cost estimating. But he has no choice but to develop cost estimates because it is the cost and schedule estimates which provide the basis for proposing the business strategy and tactics.

The cost estimates should be reasonably accurate for those actions scheduled for completion within the first year or two. Beyond two years, the cost estimates will be more and more difficult to obtain. In today's environment of pressure to use life cycle costs and unit costs as decision points for go, no go decisions, these tend to be enormously underestimated. The prudent manager will document his assumptions and data sources for these estimates, be reasonably pessimistic and assign a probable margin of error to these estimates. Whether the PM likes it or not, the fact is that once the schedules and cost estimates developed in this initial PMP are published, these values become firm input to higher headquarters, DOD and Congress.

Resource Allocation. The next step is to allocate manpower to each action item. Normally, this starts with the structuring and sizing of the program office itself. Each action item is now considered and manpower resource allocations identified. When there is reasonable doubt that government manpower will be available for a given action, contractual manpower should be assigned to it.

Following this allocation of manpower, it may be necessary to iterate some cost estimates. Once the PM is satisfied with the final cost estimates, the budgeting process is quite easy. By this time, a preferred series of actions is visible and the primary budget is the simple sum of the cost estimates for each action scheduled for each fiscal year. Furthermore, the expected costs of alternative actions are available for the PM to negotiate from as the budgeting process continues. The final budget, of course, should include reasonable contingency funds to cover unexpected events which are certain to occur throughout the lifetime of the program.

The real value of the PMP developed in this way becomes quickly evident as the PM begins to defend his program management philosophy, the manning of his program management office, and the submission and defense of his budget requests. This PMP provides most of the input for his Advanced Procurement Plan (APP), Decision Coordinating Paper (DCP) and other key documents. But most importantly, the PM has established a firm basis for credibility for future dealings with the program team members and higher authorities by documenting his perception of the problem and how he plans to solve it.

PMP Format

One of the authorities delegated to the PM is the authority to decide the format of his program PMP. Most PMP documents combine the planning function data and the control function data into a single volume. This however restricts distribution to within the government, thereby keeping a large portion of the total team uninformed. If the planning function data and schedule data were published as a single volume, this could be given to interested potential contractors and it would be possible to ask for contractual support in developing this portion of the PMP.

Assuming that the PMP will be published in more than one volume and using AFSCP 800-3 (1:A4-1) as a model, the following topics could be assigned to each of three proposed volumes.

Volume I—Program Plan, Schedules and Milestones. This volume should address all topics except those identified in Volumes II and III.

Volume II—Budgets and Fiscal Plans. This volume should address Financial and Procurement Strategy including the detailed rationale for the fiscal data. This volume would also include cost estimate data.

Volume III—Manpower and Organization. Manpower, organization and training should be detailed in this volume.

"Why must the initial PMP be so extensive and detailed?" The answer is that the PM must understand the nature and number of subsequent documents which are dependent upon the PMP. We have alluded to some, including the budget, the APP and the DCP. But there are many more, some of which are part of a document chain having broad impact, especially if the PMP is for a large major weapon system.

Changes to the information within the published PMP often have significant impact throughout DOD and Congressional fiscal committees. When these changes occur, the program manager spends a great amount of time answering questions and criticism from the agencies that depend on the PMP for information. *Once a program is initiated, all of the information which should be in the initial PMP will be addressed, sooner or later.* If the time is later, the PM will pay a severe price in time by simply trying to research and answer the inevitable questions one at a time.

De-Optimizing Factors

PMs offer a wide variety of reasons for deficient PMP's, including:

- Inside-Out Approach
- Preconceived Solution
- "My Plan" Syndrome
- Inadequate Threat Definition
- Inadequate Technical Base
- Inadequate Staff Support
- Time Pressure
- Wrong Priority

Inside-Out Approach. This is undoubtedly the most frequent cause of bad PMP's. This procedure is to start with a given set of control elements and an assumed threat and try to build a plan to fit. The starting point is a directive from higher authority which appoints a PM or task force leader, gives him a directive to set up an office and develop a PMP which will deliver a new military widget for field deployment in five years. The PMP is due in ninety days and the PM is authorized five people and $250,000 for the first fiscal year. And "Oh, by the way, the total cost should be about 'n' millions of dollars." At this point, the PM goes to Headquarters and pleads his case for not being able to do this. Headquarters acknowledges that may be true but "try anyway." The military "can-do" attitude takes over and the PM mashes together a PMP which meets all of the initial requirements. Since only the PM has to approve the PMP, he does not have to tell anybody that the schedule is impossible, the plan is poorly conceived and the estimated cost is a factor of four too low. He has complied with the directive and he can always correct the plan later when he has more time to think about it.

Preconceived Solution. One of the most dangerous approaches to developing the PMP is where the solution is preconceived. In this case, alternatives are rarely developed and since the path is already "known," schedules and resources will be highly optimistic. When difficulties develop in the program, there is either a scramble to develop an alternative or, more likely, the PM will insist that with more resources and time he will overcome his problems. Preconceived solution PMP's must be avoided if cost and performance tradeoffs are to be a viable part of the weapons acquisition process.

My Plan Syndrome. Deeply rooted in the "Program Manager" philosophy is the charter of PM independence regarding how he runs his program. Some PM's interpret this to mean total autonomy within their program, including the development and publication of the PMP. AFSCP 800-3 clearly states that its contents are not directive upon the PM but are to be used as guidance in the development of the PMP. Subsequently, the PM is forced to demonstrate that he has a master plan, so he submits a plan with only enough information in it to get the inquirer off his back. While his intent is to prevent higher authority from managing his program, by withholding information he is also depriving his team members of the information they need to support his program. This approach creates unnecessary management difficulties.

Inadequate Threat Definition. A threat is a logically-defined military deficiency which is forecast for some future date.

Since the new PM is usually hesitant to challenge the threat, he assumes it is valid and sets about developing his PMP in order to get his new program underway "as soon as possible." *The minute this PM signs off on this threat definition he has just made a basic assumption which now becomes associated with him and not the analysis organization who suddenly retreats to the supportive role.*

Inadequate Technical Base. Rarely are errors about the actual status of the technical base fatal to a program. In most cases the PM suddenly inherits a more extensive development program than he anticipated, with the usual schedule slips and program cost growth.

Technical risk is a problem area the PM expects to handle throughout the development process. But the manager who develops a plan with serious errors in his technical base assumptions is inviting trouble from the beginning.

Inadequate Staff Support. Quite often, the proposed program management office has not been officially established when the initial PMP is being developed. A small task force and a PM designee or task force leader are tasked with writing the PMP. *The team charged with this effort has an obligation to identify and use all of the expertise available, and particularly those organizations which will subsequently be involved in the program.* For example, all functional support organizations such as engineering, safety, procurement, intelligence agencies, user command, personnel manpower evaluation teams, and even potential contractors should be requested or directed to help develop the PMP. If these organizations are involved in development of the initial plan they become committed to the program and will support it with considerably more enthusiasm than they will if asked to join the team later.

Time Pressure. From the first, the PM is under severe time pressures. These pressures are almost invariably caused by an assumption which establishes a very arbitrary, but firm, date of deployment of the new weapon system. The typical PM responds to this urgency by reducing the time allocated to developing the PMP to as little as possible. The damage is done when it is published and accepted as the PM's best plan.

Wrong Priority. Normally, when a PM is appointed to start a new program, he is immediately flooded with a deluge of requests for budget, manpower requests, plans, and even the first Decision Coordinating Paper (DCP). The PM is likely to assign work priorities which will satisfy the most people in the very near term. In doing so, he often gives the PMP far less than the priority it so desperately needs. As a result, budgets, both current year and out year, organization decisions, manpower requests, etc., are "temporarily" submitted while the PMP is developed. Much to the surprise of the PM, he soon finds that the "temporary" submissions have shown up in many key documents. Thus a new, unexpected problem arises, getting those numbers changed, which requires the talents of the very people who are trying to develop the PMP. *Finding himself in this vicious circle, the PM may never recover enough to fully develop an adequate PMP.*

Despite all of the de-optimizing factors which exist, however, with some understanding of the process and a few changes in the way the PM develops the PMP, it can be a good plan and the most valuable document in the program management office.

$$\star \quad \star \quad \star \quad \star \quad \star$$

The implications for system program plans are obvious: schedule slippages and added, unexpected costs are all but inevitable in these later phases—time and money need to be squirreled away in each of the major program phases for the rainy day that is certainly coming. This essential slack is easiest to hide when it is built into the early program plans.

A further implication is obvious: sub-system hardware tests must be pushed upstream to resolve as much uncertainty as possible in subsystem elements before the program is besieged with system problems. A good risk analysis and risk reduction program plan already embrace this need.

—LMI Introduction to
Military Program Management

28

System Engineering Process*

E. Oakley Drumheller, Jr.
Forrest L. Godden, Jr.
John F. Schwegler

System engineering management is one of the major functions of project management. It is closely interrelated with configuration management, product assurance, integrated logistic support, and cost/schedule planning and control. There are various levels of system engineering management. These range from top level management exercised by the materiel developer to the most detailed level to which the performance and design requirements of system elements are controlled by the contractor or equivalent government agency.

The following requirements should be documented in a System Engineering Management Plan to assure effective system engineering management:

• Mission Requirements/Constraints. Interpretation, clarification, and validation of basic inputs to the system engineering process.

• Responsibility/Authority. Identification of organizations and key personnel for managing system engineering efforts, and definition of responsibilities, lines of formal communications, and functions of personnel associated with system engineering policy.

• Resource Allocation. Allocation of funds, schedule, and expertise necessary to achieve effective system engineering.

*Extract from *Defense Industry Bulletin*, Winter 1971, pp. 8, 9.

• Procedures. Process for accomplishing system engineering through all phases of the program.

• Documentation Format. Procedures for initiation and management of all system engineering documentation.

• Design Reviews. Schedules and procedures for comprehensive examination and review of all aspects of the design.

• Interdisciplinary Integration. Procedures to assure design compatibility from the standpoint of all pertinent engineering and scientific disciplines.

• Engineering Decision Process. Formal internal procedures using system effectiveness models, tradeoff studies, risk analysis and other models.

• Program Assurance. Selection of technical measures to be excuted to reduce risks and unknowns associated with critical areas of the program.

• Change Control. Formal internal procedures necessary to control all technical data that has an impact upon configuration, performance requirements, design constraints, or functional/physical interfaces.

• Work Breakdown Structure. Structure of products and services comprising the entire work effort.

• Training methods and procedures that will be used to train selected personnel in the system engineering process, methodology and rationale.

• Technical Performance Measurement. Identification of items having significant impact upon system effectiveness; identification and quantification of parameters having significant impact on system effectiveness; establishment of analytical or test criteria for the estimation or measurement of technical performance; estimates or measures, evaluations and forecasts of all significant technical performance characteristics of the system through the design activity.

• Tailoring. Deletions, alterations, or additions of requirements to adapt to the peculiarities of specific systems or subsystems.

• Milestones/Schedules. Identification and establishment of cost, time and performance accomplishments essential at a specified point in time to meet the objectives of the system engineering effort.

This article has discussed what system engineering entails, but why do we really need it?

Since the Korean conflict, the importance and complexity of engineering specialties have required increased specialization in weapon system acquisition procedures. Separately procured components may not function as planned when incorporated into the total weapon system. Personnel training may not be appropriate for the operation to be performed. Schedules and budgets may be excluded from consideration.

To remedy these deficiencies, procurement practices have had to be reviewed and revised.

The design, development, and management of today's complex weapon systems require the use of new approaches, new tools and new techniques. System engineering responds to this challenge.

$$\star \quad \star \quad \star \quad \star \quad \star$$

The user is the program manager's customer. The user may not be the direct source of the system requirements and may be represented by a requirements activity. In that event, the program manager has two customers—and a more complex problem of coordination. The whole purpose of weapon system development is to satisfy the user's need. The program manager has to face the fact that he may have an unhappy customer from the beginning. Moreover, the customer will become even more unhappy when problems which will inevitably arise during development force him to retreat still farther from the system capability he wants. Trade-offs will have to be made throughout the development process. Since the user is the customer, he must participate in the trade-off decisions. If the program manager attempts to make these decisions unilaterally for the user he is courting disaster.

—LMI Introduction to
Military Program Management

It's the results that count; if it works right and the costs are right, you'll have a happy client.

—Robert K. Duke, Fluor Corp.

Successful management of system acquisition depends upon competent people, defined responsibilities and authority, realistic objectives, rational priorities and recognition that programs are different and require management flexibility.

—DOD Directive 5000.1,
Major System Acquisitions

29

Work Breakdown Structures for Defense Materiel Items*

E. J. Nucci

A. L. Jackson, Jr.

The concept of using a work breakdown structure (WBS) in project planning and control is not new. In fact, WBS has been used extensively as a management tool by the Defense Department and its industrial contractors in developing and acquiring military systems and equipment for some time.

In essence, a WBS effort focuses on systematically dividing the total job at hand into manageable pieces, which together constitute some total product desired. This is a normal, logical approach to any problem or project, especially one that is large or complex.

Experience with this tool revealed, however, that the principal managers in a project—development, production, financial, procurement, logistics, etc. (often called "functional managers")—were tailoring breakdown structures to their own individual functional needs. From this there emerged a recognition of the desirability, even necessity, for a WBS system that would provide for a specific contract/project; a single WBS that could serve as a common framework for all the functional managers without disturbing their individual needs. Accordingly, a new, unifying dimension of the concept was added by DOD Directive 5010.20, "Work Breakdown Structures for Defense Materiel Items," dated July 31, 1968.

This article is a review of the background events leading up to

*Extract from *Defense Industry Bulletin,* February 1969, pp. 22–28.

the need for such a policy directive, and the purposes and relationships of the WBS's in the area of system/project management, systems engineering, configuration management, integrated logistic support, procurement, and cost and information reporting.

What Is WBS?

As the term implies, WBS is a technique for breaking down a total job into its component elements, which then can be displayed in a manner to show the relationship of these elements to each other and to the whole. The WBS display is much like the familiar organization charts used to show the complete structure of a large firm, its organizational sub-elements and their interrelationships. In the context of a system/project, WBS provides a schematic portrayal of the products (hardware, software, services, and other work tasks) that completely defines the system/project. This structure results from the project engineering effort during development and production of the given system/project.

Background

In the past decade the development and production of military systems and support equipment have been characterized by an increasing trend toward greater functional complexity and a demand for higher readiness capability. The attendant problems led functional managers to develop new techniques and methods aimed at improving technical and management control of programs and projects. Many of these techniques, e.g., cost reporting, configuration management, specification tree, contract line item structure, PERT/Cost, employed a form or structure similar to those used in WBS.

There was a valid need for these and other techniques, and benefits to be gained from their use. Basically, however, they were developed independently and were applied as separate requirements in contracts. Thus, a single contract often contained several different, unrelated breakdown structures in addition to the basic WBS.

Under these circumstances, an opportunity was seen to improve overall project management by providing functional managers with a common reference base for communicating and making decisions of mutual interest. Accordingly, the principals concerned with research and development, financial management, and procurement/production in the Office of the Secretary of Defense agreed on the desirability of a uniform WBS that would satisfy all management functions, and on the need to determine whether or not existing practices were causing special problems. In August 1965 the Director of Defense Research and Engineering initiated a study to analyze existing WBS practices and requirements, which had the following basic objectives:

- To develop guidelines for the preparation and application of a WBS for a single project that would satisfy multiple user needs in DOD and industry, as regards both management planning and control within a project and external information reporting.
- To develop a practical minimum of uniform WBS's that could be applied to the widest possible variety of both large and small system/projects.

As part of the study, WBS's of some 70 different system/projects were analyzed. From the study and other experiences, a set of problems were identified as relating to existing practices:

Misunderstandings and Confusion Caused by WBS Practices. The variations and inconsistencies in how the various DOD agencies were applying WBS's in contracts (with differing element definitions, varying structural arrangements, etc.) caused confusion and delay both for DOD and contractors. They were particularly burdensome for the large number of contractors that did business with more than one DOD customer.

Inability to Evaluate Comparable Efforts. It was difficult to compare and evaluate planned work efforts and products in competitive proposals owing to the lack of uniform terminology and definition of scope of WBS elements. Similarly, the comparability of efforts between similar systems/projects was difficult to determine. Also, as a corollary, it was hard to transfer experience gained on one program to a similar follow-on program.

Inability to Evaluate Completeness of Project. Project managers were having difficulty in determining the completeness of the project work when they did not have a checklist of all the work to be considered in the system design and management.

Burden on Contractors of Overlapping Management Reporting Requirements. Where contracts included several (up to seven) unrelated breakdown structures (to satisfy different management control and reporting requirements), contractors were having to reorient and regroup their management data and control systems. Often they had to establish redundant data collection and reporting procedures which were not related to the way the work was being accomplished.

Constraints on Design and Development. WBS's were causing constraints on the design and development process, as well as on project management, in those cases where they were being included in contracts at too low a level of detail.

To begin to find a solution to these problems, the study recommended a set of policies and guidelines for the structuring and application of WBS's in projects for systems and major equipments. A draft DOD directive on WBS policies was proposed, along with a draft military standard for applying these policies in contracts.

The suitability of WBS's prepared and used in accordance with the criteria set forth in these preliminary documents was then demonstrated by a pilot test in which they were applied and analyzed in relation to three different major system developments. Further, these documents were reviewed, and an unusual degree of concurrence was achieved as to their need throughout DOD and industry. When reviewed as part of the DOD/CODSIA[1] study of management systems control, three task groups validated their need and specifically endorsed the proposed product-oriented type WBS.

Finally, the two documents served as the basis for DOD efforts to develop DOD Directive 5010.20, "Work Breakdown Structures for Defense Materiel Items," and the MIL-STD-881 (same title) which was coordinated with industry through CODSIA before publication.

Gains Expected From New Policy Guidance

Both DOD and industrial contractors should benefit from the new policy guidance on WBS, because it was developed to solve and prevent the recurrence of mutual problems that have arisen in current programs. The following benefits are envisaged:

• Contractors will not be burdened with several unrelated breakdown structures in a single contract, let alone the unwarranted differing WBS requirements from their many DOD customers.

• Ability to compare similar work efforts will be improved, and experience will be transferable to similar new programs.

• The total project's visibility to management will be increased, and all management information will stem from a single framework related to how the work is accomplished.

• The cost of satisfying management's information needs for new programs will be reduced.

• Managers will operate at levels necessary to assure program success and yet preserve the flexibility needed in design, development and production for achieving the desired product.

• Improved defense systems will be acquired at a lower total cost.

[1]DOD/CODSIA (Council of Defense and Space Industries Association) Advisory Committee for Management Systems Control, Final Report "Management Systems Control," Dated March 1968.

Application of WBS's

Since management control and project element visibility are the principal objectives of WBS, its greatest value is realized when it is applied to large, complex projects. For this reason, the DOD directive requires that the WBS concept be applied to all new major defense systems and equipments (or major modifications) in engineering development or in operational systems development,[2] and to the production following these development projects. However, the application of a WBS, wholly or in part, may be directed by the responsible DOD agency or by the Director of Defense Research and Engineering to other systems or equipments in engineering development, operational systems development, or follow-on production.

How Are WBS's Prepared?

Before pursuing this discussion further, it is important to understand the basic construction of the four principal WBS's that are applicable:

- Summary WBS.
- Project Summary WBS.
- Contract WBS.
- Project WBS.

Each of these structures is composed of a set of *elements* that make up an identifiable product, a set of data, or a collection of services.

Summary WBS. The set of *generalized* structures (shown in Figure 1) are the Summary WBS's for the seven principal categories of defense materiel system/projects—aircraft, missiles, space, ships, surface vehicles, electronics and ordnance. While a complete WBS is the entire "family tree" down to the required level of detail, a Summary WBS relates only to the upper three levels of that "tree." These top levels are prescribed in MIL-STD-881 as to element terminology, definition and placement in the "tree" structure.

Project Summary WBS. This type of WBS is a *tailored* one, prepared by the customer, the DOD component (Army, Navy, Air Force or Defense Agency), by selecting elements applicable to a particular project from one or more of the Summary WBS's shown in Figure 1 to match the project's objectives. Where elements of the Summary

---

[2]Engineering development and operational systems development are development efforts wherein the hardware is engineered for service use (DOD Directive 3200.6).

WBS are insufficient because of a unique configuration or other special features of the project, additional or substitute WBS elements may be used to make up a Project Summary WBS. Also, items known to be critical to the project may be included as elements in the summary levels or in any lower level as needed.

The first structure in a project is ordinarily a *preliminary* Project Summary WBS developed from the results of the preliminary systems engineering conducted during concept formulation[3] or equivalent effort. The *preliminary* Project Summary WBS is an input and a basis for contract definition[4] or equivalent effort; changes, if any, in the WBS's resulting from this effort are adopted to establish the *approved* Project Summary WBS.

Contract WBS. Appropriate elements selected from the approved Project Summary WBS are then compiled and used in the Requests for Proposal (RFP's) for the various follow-on development efforts. Necessary adjustments may be made on the basis of contractors' proposals and contract negotiations. During the contract work, the development contractor(s)—or an equivalent in-house activity—by breaking the job into smaller pieces extend the WBS elements negotiated into the contracts, and so develop the Contract WBS's which contain the additional levels necessary to the individual contract effort. The Contract WBS thus portrays all products and work to be accomplished under a specific contract. Note that the elements in the lower WBS levels are defined by the contractor.

Project WBS. The Project WBS, which the DOD component prepares before production, is developed by merging the various Contract WBS's with the Project Summary WBS. Changes to the WBS made during production will be reflected in the Contract WBS and the Project WBS.

MIL-STD-881 contains the guidance needed to prepare and apply WBS's during the various phases of systems acquisition.

How Is WBS Used?

WBS provides project managers and other interested parties, on a continuing basis, with a visible framework and display of all products and services comprising the entire work effort related to a specific project. It is used as a common base for controlling and

---

[3]Concept Formulation. The comprehensive system studies and experimental hardware efforts necessary to provide the technical, economic and military bases for a conditional decision to initiate engineering development (DOD Directive 3200.9).

[4]Contract Definition. The initial phase of engineering development to verify or accomplish preliminary design and engineering, develop the necessary performance specifications and management plan to form the basis of a firm contract for the full-scale engineering development (DOD Directive 3200.9).

Figure 1 — SUMMARY WORK BREAKDOWN STRUCTURES (SUMMARY WBS)

CATEGORIES OF DEFENSE MATERIEL ITEMS

AIRCRAFT

Level 1   AIRCRAFT SYSTEM
  Level 2   AIR VEHICLE
    Level 3   Airframe
          Power Plant
          Other Propulsion
          Communications
          Navigation/Guidance
          Fire Control
          Penetration Aids
          Reconnaissance Equipment
          Automatic Flight Control
          Anti-Submarine Warfare
            Equipment
          Central Integrated Checkout
          Armament
          Weapons Delivery Equipment
          Auxiliary Electronics
            Equipment

Level 2 PECULIAR SUPPORT EQUIPMENT	COMMON SUPPORT EQUIPMENT	SYSTEMS TEST & EVALUATION
Level 3 Organizational/ Intermediate Depot	Organizational/ Intermediate Depot	Development Tests Technical Evaluation Operational Evaluation Test & Evaluation Support Mock-Ups Test Facilities

MISSILES

Level 1   MISSILE SYSTEM
  Level 2   AIR VEHICLE
    Level 3   Integration & Assembly
          Propulsion (For Single Stage Only)
          Stage I
          Stage II
          Stage III
          Stage IV
          Guidance and Control
          Launched Payload
          Payload Shroud
          Airborne Test or Training Equipment
          Auxiliary Equipment

COMMAND & LAUNCH EQUIPMENT
  Integration & Assembly
  Surveillance, Identification and
    Tracking Sensors
  Data Processing
  Launch and Guidance Control
  Launcher Equipment
  Communications
    Auxiliary Equipment

See Ⓐ above for additional required elements.

SPACE

Level 1   SPACE SYSTEM
  Level 2   SPACE VEHICLE
    Level 3   Integration & Assembly
          Spacecraft
          Propulsion Module
          Payload
          Payload Shroud
          Re-entry Vehicle
          Orbit Injection/Dispenser

LAUNCH/STAGE VEHICLE
  Integration & Assembly
  Stage I
  Stage II
  Stage III
  Stage IV
  Guidance and Control

GROUND COMMUNICATIONS, COMMAND AND CONTROL EQUIPMENT (PECULIAR)
  Surveillance, Identification and Tracking
    Sensors
  Communications
  Command and Control
  Data Processing Equipment
  Launch Equipment
  Auxiliary Equipment

FLIGHT SUPPORT OPERATIONS AND SERVICES
  Launch Operations
    and Services
  Flight Operations
    and Services
  Recovery Operations
    and Services

SHIPS

Level 1   SHIP SYSTEM
  Level 2   SHIP
    Level 3   Hull Structure
          Propulsion
          Electric Plant
          Communication and Control
          Auxiliary Systems
          Outfit and Furnishings
          Armament
          Integration Engineering
          Ship Assembly

See Ⓐ above for additional required elements.

SURFACE VEHICLE

Level 1   SURFACE VEHICLE SYSTEM
  Level 2   PRIMARY VEHICLE
    Level 3   Integration and Assembly
          Hull/Frame
          Suspension/Steering
          Power Package/Drive Train
          Auxiliary Automotive Systems
          Turret Assembly
          Armament
          Body/Cab
          Special Equipment
          Communications and Navigation
            Equipment

SECONDARY VEHICLE
  (Same as Primary Vehicle)

See Ⓐ above for additional required elements.

ELECTRONICS

Level 1   ELECTRONICS SYSTEM*
  Level 2   PRIME MISSION PRODUCT(S)
    Level 3   Integration and Assembly
          Sensors
          Communications
          Automatic Data Processing
            Equipment
          Computer Programs
          Data Displays
          Auxiliary Equipment

*VEHICLE/SITE/PLATFORM
  Select Level 2 and
  Level 3 from other
  Categories

*For electronic systems
  vehicle or platform
  can be any one of the
  Level 2 vehicles for
  the other categories.

See Ⓐ above for additional required elements.

ORDNANCE

Level 1   ORDNANCE SYSTEM
  Level 2   LAUNCH SYSTEM
    Level 3   Integration and Assembly
          Launcher
          Carriage
          Fire Control
          Ready Magazine(s)
          Adaptor Kits

COMPLETE ROUND
  Integration and Assembly
  Structure
  Warhead
  Fuze
  Safety/Arm
  Guidance and Control
  Propellant/Propulsion

See Ⓐ above for additional required elements.

FOR CATEGORIES OF DEFENSE MATERIEL ITEMS

Ⓐ **APPLICABLE TO ALL CATEGORIES (Select as appropriate)**

SYSTEM/PROJECT MANAGEMENT	TRAINING	DATA	OPERATIONAL/SITE ACTIVATION	INDUSTRIAL FACILITIES	SPARES & REPAIR PARTS
System Engineering Management/System Engineering Supporting Project Management Activities	Equipment Services Facilities	Technical Orders & Manuals Engineering Data Management Data Data Depository	Site Construction System Assembly, Installation & Checkout on Site Site/Ship/Vehicle Conversion Contractor Technical Support	Construction/Conversion/Expansion Equipment Acquisition or Modernization Maintenance	Specify by Hardware Element

> See Ⓐ above for additional required elements.

1. Other Level 2&3 elements may be added if necessary (See DOD Directive 5010.20)
2. See MIL-STD-881 for detailed definition of WBS elements

reporting the progress and status of engineering efforts, resource allocations, cost estimates, expenditures, and procurement actions throughout development and production. In summary, WBS is used as a common framework to satisfy the needs of the various functional managers—technical, financial, procurement/production, and logistics—involved in a project. These uses are detailed more specifically in the following paragraphs which relate WBS to several important activities pursued in the course of a project.

System/Project Management. This is the area in which WBS has the greatest use or variety of purpose, because the system/project manager is concerned with all principal areas of management. Since WBS portrays the products and services comprising all work related to the project, the system/project manager uses WBS first to review and assure the completeness of systems engineering in terms of hardware, software, facilities and systems support. Once this breakdown is established, the evolving WBS is used in planning and assigning responsibilities and schedules for accomplishment of the work, including the activities and efforts of interface support groups. The same framework also provides a basis for planning "in-house" and contract efforts, and for allocating resources.

Since the breakdown results from systems engineering (which reflects the performance allocated to the components of the system/project), WBS provides an excellent framework for monitoring performance, cost and schedule throughout the program. As an allied benefit, the WBS display is a convenient method of highlighting critical items or areas of the project to ensure that they receive the necessary attention by management.

The preliminary Project Summary WBS is submitted as part of the system/project Technical Development Plan and will be evaluated as part of the project approval process. Further, the System/Project Master Plan will include the Project Summary WBS.

It is significant that, while the detailed levels of WBS are always to be available to the system/project manager, DOD management control (aside from critical items) is established through the summary levels of WBS. This provides for adequate management control while retaining contractor flexibility in accomplishing the work (a factor discussed later in connection with cost and management information reporting).

Systems Engineering. WBS provides a visible documentation of the results and status of systems engineering at any point in time. It has the following uses:

• As a vehicle to summarize all products and services comprising the project's total engineering effort (including the necessary support and other tasks), and to display the relationship of these component efforts to each other and to the whole engineering activity.

• As a tool in reviewing the completeness of the total project engineering effort.

• As a means of highlighting critical items of the project.

• As a framework for developing the system/project "specification tree" needed to describe the configuration base lines.

• As the common framework and basis for monitoring technical performance, cost and schedule; and for making it possible to trace requirements and functions to the hardware.

• As a means of communicating the results of systems engineering to subsequent phases of the acquisition process.

When used as in the last item, the various WBS's are intended to evolve with project engineering and not steer it. WBS is not to be allowed to interfere with the flexibility needed by the development or production agency to achieve the desired product. Accordingly, the preliminary Project Summary WBS should be viewed simply as a means of communicating to the contract definition contractor the results of preliminary systems engineering during concept formulation. In no way should this WBS constrain the system definition process. In fact, contractors are encouraged to propose alternative solutions aimed at obtaining an improved product.

Similarly, summary levels of a WBS selected for use in the Request for Proposal in engineering development and operational systems development should be reviewed and adjusted so as to be compatible with the bidder's proposed efforts, provided that they remain consistent with project needs. Aside from government-furnished equipment and specified critical WBS elements negotiated into the contract work statement, the contractor must have complete flexibility in extending WBS to show how his work is to be done, and thus complete the Contract WBS.

Configuration Management. As a framework portraying the products and services comprising the system/project at any point in time, WBS also reflects the configuration breakdown. Through the function of configuration management, these same problems are described, their physical and functional characteristics being controlled in a set of specifications and other descriptive technical documents. This composite array of specifications forms the specification tree of the system/project, which is directly related to WBS.

Another notable correlation is that all items identified in contracts as "configuration items," those subject to configuration management, are elements in the Project Summary and Contract WBS's. On the other hand, all WBS elements are not necessarily subject to configuration management. A Contract WBS, therefore, includes at least as many levels of WBS as are necessary to identify all configuration items.

Integrated Logistic Support (ILS). In view of recently increased management attention to ILS, the WBS concept provides another mechanism by which the consideration of support requirements for system/project engineering can be assured. Accordingly, the elements needed to satisfy logistic management requirements—support equipment, facilities, repair parts, etc.—are included in the Summary WBS (Figure 1) for use in the Project Summary WBS. Below the Summary WBS levels, there may be situations in which logistics management and reporting can best be accomplished by utilizing some identifiable combination of elements related to those of the Project Summary WBS.

Procurement/Production. The deliverable output of a contract consists of products and services, and WBS elements are established in those terms. Because of this congruity, WBS can be used as a convenient means of relating the products and services of a procurement to the natural breakdown dictated by the project's systems engineering. The Project Summary WBS can be used to formulate work statements and establish the contract line items or end items. Government-furnished equipment is also directly related to the Contract WBS. The product orientation of WBS also makes it possible to relate all contractually required technical and management reports to the Project Summary and Contract WBS's. Further, this same framework can be used for monitoring contract compliance in terms of technical performance, cost and delivery schedules. In addition, the technical data packages deliverable under the contract can be related to the summary levels of the Contract WBS.

While the foregoing contractual aspects are related to WBS, a one-to-one correlation is not necessarily required. The contract negotiator may find that the best contractual arrangement and the best contract price may be obtained by combining certain WBS elements. The contract negotiator must be free to work on the basis of a contract structure that will help him achieve a contract that has favorable terms for both the government and its contractor. However, this latitude must not be allowed to compromise the effectiveness of the contracted work, or system performance, which are the prime factors determining the system's ultimate real value to the government. The contract line items, end items, or work-statement tasks, therefore, should be either WBS elements or some identifiable combination of WBS elements related to the Project Summary WBS.

Consequently, WBS serves to integrate the work effort and procurement details. Only one WBS is established and used from the issuance of each Request for Proposal throughout the ensuing contract.

Cost and Management Information Reporting. Since the reporting of management information is related to hardware and services, WBS again provides a natural vehicle for this reporting. Establishing these reporting requirements on the framework of WBS means that managers can use the same data that were generated in the engineering and work process. The organization of reporting requirements before the WBS approved for the project has been developed, however, is not to be construed by either government or contractor as determining how the system or equipment is to be designed and built.

The fact that WBS's relating to various weapon and support systems represent a uniform basis for collecting cost data makes it possible to compare the cost of like weapons and equipments, and to better estimate the cost of similar future programs. The success of these cost comparisons, however, will depend largely on ability to uniformly apply accurate definitions of the scope of WBS elements. This is one objective of the WBS-element definitions established and required by MIL-STD-881.

With respect to schedule monitoring and reporting, WBS again provides a common framework which permits the use of engineering management information for business management.

WBS also provides a discrete mechanism for implementing the basic principle that all management and cost reporting must be restricted to as high a level as is practical for assuring the program's success, while retaining flexibility of operation. Only summarized data is required to monitor the contractor's progress, but relevant detail is to be available if the need arises. In WBS, this relates to the summary levels and to critical items at lower levels. Thus the contractor has complete freedom and flexibility in his own internal management, and the amount of reporting is reduced.

WBS: A Tool for Top Management

The top managers of both DOD and defense contractors need adequate continual visibility of entire projects, with timely knowledge of project performance. They also need timely data on the occurrence of problems and the cause of these problems. In fact, what is needed is a means for detecting or predicting these problems much earlier than it has been done in the past.

In WBS, management visibility and data reporting are established in a fashion which is directly related to the systems engineering and the manner in which the work is to be accomplished. Accordingly, WBS is viewed as a necessary tool for helping to satisfy these top management needs. The payoff to this improved management approach will be the improvement of DOD's ability to achieve the operational performance and readiness it needs at the lowest possible cost.

Milestone 0—Program Initiation
Milestone I—Demonstration and Validation
Milestone II—Full-Scale Engineering Development
Milestone III—Production and Deployment

—DOD Directive 5000.1,
Major System Acquisitions

The success of a program is often established or destroyed in its initial stage—by its concept, its RFP, the program plan and its funding. We must give this part of the process more explicit attention.

—Statement of Principles for
DOD Research and Development

30

Software Visibility and the Program Manager*

Lieutenant Colonel Alan J. Driscoll

As software has become a large segment of weapon system development, the problems of software cost, schedule, and performance have become critical to the successful fielding of most weapon systems. The cost, schedule, and performance problems have pervaded all phases of software development and have resulted from some seemingly unsolvable problems and various sins of omission as well as commission. Among the more important difficulties have been: (1) poor requirements definition; (2) inadequate system engineering; (3) inability to track software development progress, particularly during the implementation and verification phases; (4) inadequate change and configuration control (hence changes drive costs and schedules beyond acceptable limits); (5) improper matching of test and verification with requirements; and (6) nonavailability of support software when needed, resulting in maintenance problems and higher maintenance costs.

Software does not have exclusive rights to these problems; hardware is often subject to the same problems. However, software has been prone to the greater suffering because of the failure on the part of personnel having cognizance to recognize the importance of software. There are ways to alleviate most of the problems. If the Program Manager is going to control software cost, schedule, and performance, he must recognize the potential for problems to occur

*Extract from *Defense Systems Management Review,* Vol. I, No. 2, Spring 1977, p. 25.

and take preventative action. Significant steps the Program Manager can take include:

(1) Get the user involved early. Require an early statement of user requirements and meaningful user participation in design reviews.

(2) Insist on full incorporation of software into the system requirement analysis process. Software must be engineered as an integral part of the weapon system.

(3) Place software at a high level in the WBS and remove it from the category of "data."

(4) Make full use of planning aids such as the program management plan and the CRISP (Computer Resources Integrated Support Plan) to ensure all members of the program management team know what is expected and required.

(5) Make support software a deliverable item and when applicable make it a configuration item. This is particularly appropriate when software is to be transferred to a support or using command.

(6) Organize the Program Office to provide adequate technical support for software. Assign responsibility and accountability for this support to someone other than the Program Manager, who cannot be the integrator.

(7) Plan the total program budget to provide adequate funds to implement the total software development program.

One thing that is present in all aspects of what the Program Manager must do to obtain software is planning. There is an old saying in the Real Estate business that tells the three most important things to consider when buying a house: location, location, and location. An analagous comment on software would be that the Program Manager who wants adequate software would do well to pay prime attention to planning, planning, and planning. Experience has shown that if the plan does not include software in the System Requirement Analysis, it will not be included; if you do not plan for the use of a High Order Language, there may not be enough computer memory to handle the software; if the plan does not provide for allocation of funds to support proper software development, funds will not be available for use.

A primary point is this: The Program Manager can do little to alleviate problems of inadequate software and lack of control late in the development effort. The proper steps must be implemented in the early stages to assure the availability of software at a later date. The extent to which a Program Manager has control of software is a direct function of how well he plans for software development.

Section 6—

TIME MANAGEMENT

Introduction

This section encompasses six different views of time, a basic factor in undertaking a project. There are two common themes: how best to use the time available, and the importance of time relative to cost and operational life.

Interestingly, the Acquisition Cycle Task Force concludes in the first reading that it takes longer in general to get things done than it used to. And it finds that the reason for delays, particularly in defense systems, is in the decision-making process, rather than in actually doing the work. These stretch-outs affect not only costs and technical performance but also project survival, as illustrated by the B-1 program.

Time as it affects return on investment is the theme of the second selection: The less time it takes to field a system, particularly one of high technological content, the longer its span of operational life. This is a principle keenly appreciated by managers of commercial and industrial projects but often overlooked in defense.

In the third selection, Major John Douglass discusses the program integrated master schedule from the practical viewpoint of an experienced program planner. The next two articles pertain to scheduling techniques in development (network scheduling) and in production.

Network scheduling has an interesting history itself, aside from how Columbus might have used it in the fourth selection. PERT and CPM (critical path method) were developed in the late 1950s and were credited with saving a great deal of time on major defense systems, including two years' saving on the Polaris missile. Almost everyone jumped aboard the PERT/CPM bandwagon. PERT-niks sprouted like weeds, to the extent that to this day many people not involved in systems management equate project/systems management to PERT or CPM.

Network scheduling has been applied in situations where it was never intended, however. And cost planning and control were hung on the PERT framework (PERT-cost) with dismal results. As a result of overburdening these useful techniques, they came to be gradually rejected in practice by the services. DOD seems to have thrown away their good aspects along with the bad. Industry, on the other hand, continues to derive a great deal of benefit from them.

The fifth selection concerns line of balance, the scheduling technique commonly used in production. In the final selection Major Ted Brostrom looks at where one's time goes in the program office, and how to use it effectively. Simply stated, the project manager needs to find 20 percent of the items that will yield 80 percent of the results, and then spend 80 percent of his time on those items; sound, practical advice to us all.

Here then are six views of time and how to use it.

$$\star \quad \star \quad \star \quad \star \quad \star$$

All businessmen are concerned, and properly so, about the long time it takes to move a new development from its inception to a profit status. But frequently forgotten is the fact that a month's delay in the early stages of development is exactly as long as a month's delay in the later stages. While it may *seem* innocuous to put off a decision for a month or two in the early years of a project with an uncertain future, that delay may turn out to be just as costly as is procrastination when the final decisions are made. In short, a sense of urgency is essential to decision making in *all* stages of a new venture, not just the later stages.
—*Russell W. Peterson, "New Venture Management in a Large Company,"* Harvard Business Review, *May–June 1967, p. 72.*

The natural tendency of scientists and engineers, whether in industry or in government, is to seek technical perfection. The natural consequence of this tendency is that they regard schedules as of secondary importance. Someone has to emphasize the fact that schedules are important—perhaps even more important than the last measure of small improvement in technical performance. In the words of one program manager:

> Design engineers will fiddle and tinker forever. If you let them alone, you are guaranteed to have schedule slippages and cost problems. Nothing will come out of the end of the pipe unless you push it out. One technique that works for me when I see them at the fiddling stage—making things a little better and not worrying about the schedule—is to shove an absolute deadline on them and tell them that we will just have to go with what is available to them. As a matter of fact, it is often surprising how much they squeeze out of the last few weeks. They just don't like the idea of your going with less than the best.
> —*LMI Introduction to Military Program Management*

31

Report of the Acquisition Cycle Task Force*

The following items are among the key findings and conclusions in the Acquisition Cycle Task Force's report to the Chairman of the Defense Science Board, Spring 1978.

During the Summer Study, the Task Force came to the conclusion that:

- It takes longer to get things done in the DOD (and elsewhere in the U.S.) than it used to.
- The increased delays seem to occur in the decision process rather than in the time to do the actual work.

It was determined on the basis of a number of weapon system acquisition program case studies that it doesn't actually take any longer to *do* something; it just takes longer to obtain the necessary approvals and acquire funding to do it and get to the deployment stage once the development is finished. These decision delays do not take the form simply of more time for the decision maker to decide; they are manifested by additional complication in the decision process—more levels of review and approval, additional steps in the system definition and development process and therefore more decision points, demands for more analyses, more studies, more justification, more tests, and more evaluation of results.

In general, the length of time it takes to do something is dependent both on how hard it is to do it and on how badly society wants to have it done. It is not apparently inherently more difficult to do

*Extract from *Report of the Acquisition Cycle Task Force,* March 15, 1978. The Task Force consisted of senior individuals in DOD and industry, chaired by Dr. Richard D. DeLauer of TRW.

things than it used to be. Although the things we do today are often larger and more complex, we bring better tools and better knowledge to the task. The trouble lies rather in the growing lack of desire of the society to do certain kinds of things, such as to build modern weapon systems or to construct nuclear power plants.

It is fairly clear that the underlying desire of the U.S. society for new weapon systems has been diminishing for many years if we take out the short-term variations due to wars, overt Russian actions, and internal politics. In recent years, there has been a certain level of funding available each year for defense procurement. The present level of funding allows us to acquire a certain number of things each year, and then the money is all spent and no more is available until the next year.

The time it takes, therefore, to get military equipment into the hands of the forces in the field is dependent almost entirely on when the money becomes available to buy it. It is only loosely dependent, if at all, on when the development program started, on how much gold-plating there is in the decision process, or on who happens to be sitting in the Pentagon.

There are enormous numbers of perceived mission needs and a great number of good ideas for meeting them at any time within the DOD. In general, the DOD does not commit substantial funds to development unless there is some reason to expect that procurement funds will be available when the development is complete— in fact, such funds are often set aside in the out-year budgets. Unfortunately, everything always seems to cost more than predicted, so when the development has been completed, the money is frequently—if not usually—no longer available for production of the system or equipment. Other demands have eaten up the money and the price tag on the new system has gone up.

It is of course rare that the circumstances are this clean, and rarer still to face up to them in precisely these terms. The more usual course of action is to determine that the development is not complete (it never is) and that there are still unanswered questions (there always are) and to send the developer back to do some more work. In fact, with only a little thought, it is usually possible to change the requirements for the system and thereby postpone the production decision for quite a while.

If these delays in the acquisition cycle cost us no more than time, they might not be very serious, at least in some instances. Unfortunately, delays do in fact cost more than time; they also cost money because of the expense of keeping the development effort going. Even worse, costs would not seem to be the most serious result of delay. The most serious problems result from what might be termed the second order effects of the process. Among these effects are:

1. *Results are often unsatisfactory.* When the system finally appears in the field, it is often obsolescent technically and no longer matches the perceived operational requirement.

2. *Desirable system flexibility is sometimes lost.* To ask for flexibility during system definition and development is to admit uncertainty, and survival through the approval process appears to demand system optimization to meet a specific need many years in the future. It is then difficult to change the design during the long life of the program to meet the changing perceptions of that future.

3. *Systems become over-complicated.* Since it takes so long and costs so much, there are great pressures to make the system do "everything." The need to obtain so many approvals tends to make the situation worse since the system becomes the sum of all the minimum demands of each approver. Multi-service programs are particularly bad from this point of view.

4. *Too many technical risks are taken.* This leads to cost and schedule overruns and to high retrofit and maintenance costs. Once again, since it takes so long to get the system, the designers reach for the latest technology so as to avoid obsolescence insofar as possible. The latest technology is often not ready for inclusion and the resulting problems must be solved at a late stage in the program at great expense.

5. *Short-term improvements are dying out.* There is a growing belief that it takes at least eight years to do anything; therefore, there is no value in taking small, evolutionary steps to improve the performance of existing operational systems. It also is believed to take longer to develop a big fix than a little one. Therefore, the user must make do with what he has until 1985 or so. In some ways, this is the most troubling of the second-order effects, as it leads to frustration and cynicism in both the user and the developer communities.

6. *The problem is getting worse.* Senior people who look at these difficulties tend to mistake the symptoms for the problems. The natural human reaction is to assume the troubles arise from inadequate preliminary study and program definition (e.g., the "plan your work—work your plan" syndrome), and they insist on more and earlier review and approval at more frequent intervals. This hurts rather than helps since the difficulty arises not from unwillingness to plan sensibly, but from inability to do so over too long a period of time. Additional early review and approval further lengthens this time and makes the problem progressively worse.

The proper action should be to improve the efficiency of the development process, probably by reducing the time to develop rather than increasing it as we seem to be doing now. Perhaps we should transfer money from the R&D account to the procurement accounts thus buying more things while supporting fewer in development. Perhaps we should simply stop more things we can't afford rather than letting them drag on. Perhaps we should really mean it when we say we want less expensive systems.

Concurrency

One of the arguments which has been advanced against concurrency is that the quality of the delivered product is questionable as the degree of concurrency becomes significant. No clear correlation between concurrency and poor quality of the end product could be discerned from the data examined by the Task Force. On the contrary, the argument can be made that some of the most highly concurrent programs were also the most successful in terms of meeting schedule and cost goals as well as established system performance objectives (e.g., F-5E, Polaris, Minuteman, Boeing 727).

In addition to the "poor quality" argument, the other major contention is that the money expended in making preparations for production is wasted if the program is cancelled. An often-cited example is the Condor program, where approximately one-quarter of the $300 million expended before the program was cancelled was procurement funds. In the case of Condor, however, the information presented to the Task Force (by the contractor's program manager) made it clear that the final decision to cancel the program was made on grounds other than lack of success because of concurrency, and in addition the convoluted nature of the program's history makes it very difficult to determine for just what category the funding was actually spent in many cases.

However, when considering all programs, the total amount which has been "wasted" is obviously a very small percentage of the total procurement budget, and it appears to have been more than offset by the following:

- Concurrency provides a smooth transition from development to production.
- Concurrency minimizes the acquisition time span.
- Finally, properly done, concurrency drives the total system to be ready—training, logistics, support services, etc.

On the basis of the data and information available to the Task Force, including discussions with knowledgeable and experienced people, the following conclusions are offered with respect to concurrency:

- Concurrency is the normal way of doing business in the commercial business world.

- There is no convincing evidence that concurrency necessarily adversely affects program outcome in terms of cost, performance, or field utility.
- The transition from development to production is smoothed significantly by the right degree of concurrency.
- The acquisition time span from FSD to IOC can be minimized if concurrency is properly employed.
- Program tradeoff flexibility must be available to support successful development progress in a concurrent program.
- Assuming the intent to deploy clearly exists at the start of FSD, concurrency is highly desirable.
- The degree of concurrency should reflect the extent of risk.
- Low-rate initial production is desirable with operational suitability testing preceding the high-rate production go-ahead.

Early Deployment

The Task Force concluded that there is considerable evidence to support the claim that early deployment is frequently a useful and valuable practice, particularly in those cases where less than the ultimate system performance is acceptable in the initially-deployed units. Several examples support this finding: Minuteman I, where the first wing did not meet the range specification; Polaris A1, which also did not possess the full specified range; and the 425L system, which represented a significant reduction in operational capability over that originally envisioned in the initial performance requirements. Each of these systems served a very useful operational function, and provided a valuable operational capability and experience until subsequently replaced by an upgraded version with greater performance than the initially-deployed system.

Early deployment also permits a shortened acquisition time for the initial operational capability, which also has considerable value in terms of dollars spent:

- A shorter acquisition cycle avoids costly and usually unnecessary gold-plating.
- It means a shorter period of time during which the overhead costs associated with the acquisition of the system must be carried.
- It means a shorter time for costs to increase due to the effects of inflation.
- It permits the realization of more efficient production rates in most instances.

Early deployment and a shorter acquisition time also enhance the ability of the Services to match or achieve superiority over a changing threat. The shorter acquisition time which permits earlier deployment also puts the end product in the hands of the user for a longer period of time before it is no longer adequate to meet the threat—a longer useful life before obsolescence which results in a greater "return on investment" when the cost of acquisition is amortized over a longer operational lifetime.

The External Environment

Probability of Program Cancellation. The Task Force concluded that there is a definite indication that, due to the influence of external forces and influences, the longer a program stays in full scale development, the greater are its chances of being cancelled prior to completion. Primarily as a result of changes in personnel and viewpoints within DOD, in the Congress, in the Executive Branch external to DOD, and in the public sector, there is frequently a shift in the perception of priorities, attitudes, and appreciation of the external threat which caused the program to be approved for development in the first place. Such changes often result in major redirection of the program, with attendant increases in overall cost and significant delays in the schedule for completion of the acquisition cycle.

Programs are often cancelled only after they have been subjected to a series of costly and time-consuming redirections, and many are subsequently re-initiated at some later time under a new name. The B-1 program, as a typical current example, was continued for a period of approximately fifteen years, with a total expenditure on the order of $4 billion before it was finally brought to a virtual halt by Executive Order in mid-1977. If a requirement for an advanced manned penetrating strategic bomber is adopted at some time more than perhaps two or three years in the future, it is likely that very little of the time and money expended on the B-1 will be salvageable for applicability to the new program.

One conclusion that was drawn from this examination of the effect of external influences on the probability of program cancellation is that the likelihood of a program ever being completed decreases as it passes through more than one "administration" which, for lesser systems, may be the tenure of the military SPO, and for major, national systems such as the B-1, may be the tenure of a political administration, i.e., of the top federal elected officials in the Executive Branch. Thus, there is clearly significant potential advantage, in terms of shortening the acquisition cycle within which a particular mission need is to be satisfied, as well as in terms of conserving considerable national resources which must be expended to satisfy that need, in completing approved programs as quickly as is consistent with the practicalities of the scientific and engineering risks associated with meeting the need.

$$\star \quad \star \quad \star \quad \star \quad \star$$

Time defeats technology . . . .

—John Richardson, Hughes Aircraft Company

Among Soviet systems based on well-known technology that U.S. officials see as threatening is the family of new Russian ICBMs. As unsettling as the missiles themselves, officials say, is the progress made by the Soviets in improving their accuracy. Soviet work has proceeded much faster than observers expected a year or two ago.

—Aerospace Daily
August 10, 1976, p. 241.

Allied with the problem of administrative lead time is the danger of bureaucratic apathy affecting the program office. Its symptoms are long review and approval chains, slow responses to correspondence, a reluctance to seek or approve waivers from standard procedures, and a faith that the way something has always been done in the past must be the right way to do it. It is a sure sign that the steam is going out of the organization.

An occasional look at some routing sheets and at referenced dates in correspondence is about all that is needed to uncover the problem. An intolerance for the symptoms—especially for expressions of faith in the excellence of current practices —will go far to preserve the free spirit that is one of the important assets of program management.

—LMI Introduction to
Military Program Management

32

Comment on the Value of Time in Defense Systems Acquisition*

J. S. Baumgartner

As the pendulum in defense systems acquisition swings steadily nearer to full emphasis on costs, and away from the value of time, there is a strong possibility that we may be approaching the point where we will get less, rather than more, value for our defense dollar. And we may be unlearning some of the wisdom gained from hard lessons of the past.

A basic reason for adopting project management in tackling the difficult, unique tasks in producing a system is to eliminate unnecessary delays in accomplishing the job at hand. Time is a resource in systems management, to be treated with indifference or used well like any other resource. Before the pendulum swings too far, it may be well to consider the economic value of time as it relates to both the immediate costs incurred by relaxing procurement schedules, and to the greater but less obvious costs of reducing the operational life of the resulting system.

First, though, it should be recognized that technical performance, although not discussed here, is "first among equals" in the cost-time-performance trilogy that are the project manager's objectives. And it should also be understood that the economic reasons for adopting a tight schedule do not usually apply to a project that is well under way: change to an on-going schedule, whether a speed-up or a slow-down, is expensive. But for projects not yet in

*Defense Management Journal, July 1972, pp. 53–56.

full swing, it is important to recognize that time has an economic value, and that we may be taking time too much for granted.

Rationale for Relaxing the Project Schedule

The reasons for stretching out project schedules are worth noting.

• Foremost is the cost of concurrency—overlaps in development and production. There is no question that a heavy premium is paid for excessive concurrency. Redesign after a product is in production involves retooling, replanning, and reprocurement of materials, and extensive retrofit or modification. However, what is considered a vice in the 1970s has in the past been a virtue whenever the pendulum has suddenly swung toward the importance of time: "Get it out the door, never mind what it costs!"

• Secondly, a better product can be expected if it is more thoroughly debugged and tested. In the past, time allotted for testing has often been squeezed too much. Independent of the time factor, tests often did not sufficiently simulate the realistic environment in which the system would have to operate. However a system does not really get "wrung out" until it is in the user's hands, regardless of the extent of debugging beforehand. A more relaxed development schedule may invite additional engineering changes and system complexity which, in turn, requires more debugging.

• Thirdly, it is hoped that other countries will reciprocate.

Value of Time

These arguments for proceeding with reduced urgency on any given project are plausible and have been generally adopted. But granted that excessive concurrency causes additional costs, a stretched out schedule is not necessarily a low-cost one, because it incurs two kinds of cost penalties: the near-term penalties associated with a longer acquisition period, and the longer-term penalty of reduced value of the system because of a shorter operational life.

Of the near-term penalties, probably the most obvious cost increase due to a stretch-out is inflation. A one-year stretch in the schedule increases costs by 3 to 6 percent.

Lengthening the schedule also invites additional engineering changes, those inevitable product modifications that add to both the cost and complexity of a system. Like inflation, changes are a factor of time—the longer the schedule, the more changes will be adopted; and the more changes, the higher final costs will be.

Another adverse effect of lengthening a project schedule is the fact that key personnel are more likely to change. The effect on project cost is difficult to assess, but former Deputy Secretary of Defense David Packard repeatedly cited the importance of keeping program managers on the job longer.[1] Aside from the fact that project managers and their key people have built up a high degree of rapport with various members of the project team and with higher Defense Department levels, they also have a perspective based on system requirements and early start-up pangs that is difficult to pass on to their replacements. A related effect is the "father of the system" syndrome, the possibility that replacements may seek to put their personal stamp on the project by accepting changes more readily than their predecessors. Changing a winning lineup also may have an adverse effect on morale.

A more subtle effect on costs is delayed decisions—waiting to assemble 90 percent of the factors bearing on a decision, rather than going ahead on the basis of 80 percent of the facts. The desire to be "right" is natural, particularly when the spotlight of public and Congressional opinion glares harshly on the inner workings of project management. But it is often more costly to wait and be right—and a prolonged schedule lends itself to this tendency—than it is to go ahead and make a decision that is nearly the same; or on occasion, even wrong.

Another cost that should be recognized is the increased chance that a project will be cancelled due to obsolescence or competing technology. History shows that sooner or later stretch-outs invite cancellation; and, although much is learned and subsystems developed may have an application on other systems, the value of a cancelled project is minimal compared to carrying it to fruition.

Product Life of Non-Defense Products

A point having more impact on the *value* of a system is the matter of how long its useful life will be. Leading producers of commercial and industrial products have become well aware of the importance of bringing new products to market—"deploying" them —without delay, in order to gain the greatest return on the heavy investment costs involved in new product development and production. The increasingly shortened life of products is indicated by a study which says, "In the next three years alone, about 75 percent

[1]David Packard, "Toward Better Management of the Development and Acquisition of New Weapon Systems," *Defense Management Journal*, Fall 1971, p. 3, adapted from testimony before the House Appropriation Committee, March 18, 1971.

of the nation's growth in sales volume can be expected to come from new products."[2] Other studies show the life of new products is only three to five years.

Adding six months to two years to the useful life of a sophisticated product, whether it is contractually acquired like an F-15 or a proprietary product such as a computer, yields obvious benefits in terms of return on investment. The competitive advantages resulting from availability of the item can sometimes be enormous.

A major west coast producer of computers and scientific test equipment is keenly aware of the impact of time on product life. A typical product has only an 18-month life span, due to competition and the effects of technological advance. The problem is that it takes almost 18 months to develop the product. In this 36-month cycle, from start to finish of the product, every month consumed in development and initial production shortens its product life by a corresponding amount of time. The most costly schedule, however, is not where the company (whose batting average happens to be very good) starts 18 months late; in this case it would merely have lost a profit opportunity. The most costly schedule is one that causes the product to get on the market six to nine months after the competition, when the company has incurred the heavy expenses of development and production start-up, but is too late to reach the break-even point.

Product Life of Military Systems

Making use of time to increase the life of a system applies to military products as well as to commercial/industrial ones. Concentration on product cost, without considering the life of the resulting product, overlooks a key point: whether the military buyer obtains value for his dollar. The most costly system, in terms of value, is one that appears when it no longer fulfills a useful purpose, even though it has been produced at a minimum cost. At the other end of the value scale is the product that has maximum useful life.

To illustrate the value of time in military systems development and operational use, let's assume that an aircraft project began in 1970. By 1985 it is expected that the aircraft will be technologically obsolete. Development and production can proceed on either a tightly compressed schedule, allowing a longer operational life, or on a relaxed, cost-emphasis schedule, with reduced operational life but a lower acquisition cost.

The relaxed, cost-emphasis schedule might look like Figure 1. In this case, development is nearly complete before the plane goes

[2]"Management of New Products," Booz-Allen & Hamilton, Inc., Chicago, 1968, p. 2.

into production; there is a minimum of concurrency. Production, in turn, phases into operational use on a well planned basis. As a result, costs are held to a minimum, say $1 billion.

| DEVELOPMENT | PRODUCTION | OPERATIONAL USE |

1970   1980   1985

Figure 1

On the other hand, tight scheduling, with production overlapping development and operational use overlapping production, will cause costs to rise sharply, perhaps 50 percent higher because of redesign and production changes required. The schedule in this case might look like Figure 2. In the first case, acquisition costs have been held down to $1 billion compared to costs of $1.5 billion in the second case. Critics of defense procurement would say, "Obviously the cost-emphasis route is the way to go." But in terms of value, considering what the taxpayer receives for his money, this is a doubtful conclusion. In the first case, the relaxed scheduling produces an aircraft with only a 5-year operational life, an acquisition cost of $200 million per year of operational use of the aircraft.

| DEVEL. | PROD. | OPERATIONAL USE |

1970   1975   1985

Figure 2

In the second case (time-emphasis scheduling), the stringent schedule causes costs to rise to $1.5 billion, but the aircraft has a 10-year life. The acquisition cost is $150 million per year of operational use.

It can be objected that in this example the cost figures and years' operational use are warped to make a point for tight scheduling. For example, it could be pointed out that, if the plane is operational until 1990, the acquisition cost per year of useful life is $100 million under *either* cost-emphasis or time-emphasis scheduling; and, if the plane is operational longer than that, lower cost as well as greater value will accrue from cost-emphasis scheduling. It is important to the concept of value, therefore, to determine with some accuracy what the added costs of tight scheduling may be, and what operational life may be expected from a system.

Operational system life will vary, of course, depending on the pertinent life factors and growth potential of each particular system.

But increased costs resulting from compressed scheduling can be estimated in a generally applicable way; and they appear to be considerably less than the 50 percent assumed in the foregoing example.

Cost Growth

A Comptroller General report of March 1971 provides a clue as to the premium paid for time-emphasis scheduling.[3] This report covers 70 major systems, 61 having been in development or production for some time (and, therefore, better reflecting the cost of earlier, time-emphasis scheduling than the report released in May 1972). The increase in cost reported for these 61 systems (less increases for quantity changes) is 21 percent for the then-current estimates through program completion as compared to the original development estimates. This growth includes increases due to inflation, engineering changes, and revisions to correct previous estimates.

If project schedules had been tightly compressed, as they were after December 1941 (World War II), June 1950 (Korea), October 1957 (Sputnik), and 1965 (Vietnam), the premium paid would probably have been greater than this 21 percent. But offsetting this premium in the case of cost-emphasis scheduling are the combined effects of greater inflation, additional engineering changes, increased complexity of the system, personnel changes, and delayed decisions previously mentioned.

The net effect of time-emphasis scheduling is probably a cost premium on the order of 10 to 20 percent. And in most cases this is more than offset by the value obtained through longer operational life of the acquired system.

As the pendulum swings increasingly toward emphasis on costs and de-emphasis on time, it is well to recognize that in the process we may be getting less value for our tax dollar. Logical, orderly project scheduling may reduce the costs of concurrency; but a tight schedule, with its inherently greater acquisition costs, may well give a longer product life and, thus, greater economic value.

And this is looking at time from only the standpoint of economics.

Having a necessary system in being, rather than playing the expensive game of catch-up, might in the future, as in the past, be insurance for survival.

[3]Comptroller General's Report to the Congress, "Acquisition of Major Weapon Systems," March 18, 1971, p. 58; and covering the period through June 30, 1970.

33

Development of an Integrated Master Schedule for Weapon System Acquisition*

Major John Wade Douglass

The master schedule for a program should serve as a time reference baseline for the program. In order to do this it must be kept up to date with the approved program for cost, schedule and performance. By approved program I mean the officially-approved schedule which will achieve approved performance levels within approved cost allocations. Maintenance of the master baseline is a task akin to that inherent in configuration control. There will be many changes in any development program and these changes grow through an individual life cycle of their own.

Program changes, whatever their source, start as proposals, grow into a firm plan, and eventually are incorporated into the program as approved changes. When to plot these is a question of judgment and should reflect the policy of the program manager. Each change should be plotted as a proposed or tentative change until the change is approved.

A permanent record of each change should be maintained and illustrated where required. If the program has slipped, the slip should be shown until it no longer serves a purpose to do so.

*Extract from Study Project Report, *Development of an Integrated Master Schedule for Weapon System Acquisition,* Defense Systems Management College, May 1977, pp. 7, 28–30, 35.

Schedule Discipline

The degree of schedule discipline imposed within the program office can be a major factor in the use of the master schedule. Whenever copies of the master schedule are made they should be dated and should be authenticated by the signature of the program director or his appointed schedule manager. Undated and unauthenticated schedules should not be released outside the program office.

These are simple rules but many programs do not follow them and consequently suffer from the unauthorized release of schedule information that is not integrated into the master schedule and not approved by the program manager.

Program Reviews

The master schedule can serve as the framework for periodic program reviews within the program office. If constructed properly, the schedule will illustrate the top few levels of the Program Work Breakdown Structure (WBS) and therefore will likely be compatible with the program's Cost/Schedule Control System reporting.

Program reviews can serve as an excellent forum for the resolution of schedule conflicts and the genesis for controlled change to the schedule from within the program office. Most of the important leaders on the program office team are present at these reviews and therefore proposed schedule changes or slips can receive wide dissemination within the organization in this forum.

"What If" Exercises

The master schedule can serve as the framework for the "what if" exercises that are imposed on programs from outside the program office. Schedule changes can be plotted manually using overlays to the master. The use of the same grid coordinates in an overlay fashion allows the program office to see clearly and graphically the effect of compressions or extensions of the various submilestones on the program.

Without the master to utilize as a baseline, these exercises tend to require much longer to accomplish and often overlook important variances from the established program baseline schedule or plan.

Program Briefings

The master schedule can also serve as the baseline for program reviews at higher headquarters and other places external to the program office. Most programs have certain key milestones which are taken from the master schedule and presented in summary form on view graphs or slides. If these do not show the detail required to make a point the time span of the slide can be reduced down to the point where the details are visible.

The master schedule can be transported with the team accomplishing the briefing, but this is not recommended. The handling is usually very hard on the paper and almost always results in a redrawing requirement. Remember this schedule is usually 7' × 10' to as large as 10' × 15' in size.

Conclusion

I would like to leave the program manager with the following messages:

1. If you don't have an integrated schedule that you control and developed *within the program office,* you're headed for trouble.

2. Don't over-estimate the job. A couple of smart people can do amazing things given a week to ten days.

3. Don't try to get too fancy too fast. Keep it simple until you know your people have mastered the program and the basics of the process.

4. Use the schedule as a core management tool and make it compatible with your WBS and contract structure.

5. Instill *discipline* in your people. Do not allow program schedule changes to get out of the program office until you've approved them. Make sure everyone has the same schedule.

6. Plan for the unknown. Do not approach complex events like source selections or DSARC gates with a viewgraph-level plan. How would you feel if your contractor did it that way?

7. Do not accept no for an answer when you ask to have such a schedule completed. The week I wrote this I had the opportunity to chat with the Chief of Program Control on a major Joint Service Program. He told me that he had a person working for six months to get a schedule for his program and never could get it done. It *can* be done. And if it's not, sooner or later the price will be paid.

34

The Enterprise of the Indies*

The network scheduling technique presented here, critical path method (CPM) to a time scale, is applied to what might now seem a small project, though one of vast historic significance. Actually it applies also to the largest projects and is in common use in industry. Although it has a practical limit of 200 to 300 activities, CPM to a time scale is a superb top-level scheduling technique because of three major advantages:

1. It communicates. The critical path and time-relationships of all activities are clearly apparent.

2. It motivates. Activities are related to a time scale or scales (calendar dates, time from start, and time to completion). This attribute is often lost in other network techniques, such as PERT. A benefit often realized in industry is tapping the resourcefulness of the project team because they can see where the constraints are, and can devise ways to overcome them.

3. The amount and location of slack time are clearly apparent. This enables a PM to see where he can make trade-offs in order to reduce costs; how to avoid or minimize overtime and under-utilization of resources, for example.

With these capabilities the PM can assess and minimize risks. This is what one Cristobal Colon tried to do, given the likelihood of his disappearing from the face of the earth.

*Based on a case by James H. Carbone and Daniel J. Strauss.

In 1491, their Royal Majesties Ferdinand and Isabella, by the Grace of God King and Queen of Castile, Leon, Aragon, Sicily, etc., etc., were up to their royal ears in strife. The King had assembled the flower of Spanish knighthood in his efforts to supplant the Moorish crescent with the cross in Granada, and was directing the siege from a fortified camp erected outside the city. Preoccupied though he was, Ferdinand nevertheless took time to receive one Cristobal Colon, again.

Six years earlier the King and Queen had received this same Colon and listened to his request for royal patronage for an Enterprise of the Indies. They referred his ideas and propositions to a special commission of "learned men and mariners." After four years of deliberation and efforts to learn more specifically what Colon had in mind, the commission returned its findings. As might have been predicted, Columbus' request was denied on the grounds that (1) a voyage to Asia would require three years; (2) the Western Ocean is infinite and perhaps unnavigable; (3) if he reached the Antipodes (the land on the other side of the globe from Europe), he could not get back; (4) there are no Antipodes because the greater part of the globe is covered with water and because Saint Augustine said so; (5) of the five zones, only three are habitable; (6) so many centuries after the Creation, it was unlikely that anyone could find hitherto unknown lands of any value.

Ferdinand nevertheless had meanwhile ordered municipal and local officials to furnish free board and lodging to "Cristobal Colon who has come to our court." With this support, and being lodged and fed at public expense, Columbus persisted in his enterprise, in spite of the learned commission's findings. Now he was at Santa Fe, the camp where the king was directing the siege, to press for royal backing.

Early in 1492 the siege of Granada was won "by the cross," and with the collapse of the Moorish kingdom, Ferdinand had an opportunity to weigh Columbus' request. The result: request denied again.

Columbus resolved to go to France for the support he needed and to "bestow the glory and riches of his expedition upon a receptive monarch." But enroute to France he was intercepted by a royal messenger. Queen Isabella had been persuaded by supporters of Columbus to back his enterprise—at least in part by the rationale that a small investment could bring great returns. After three additional months of discussions and administrative delay, Columbus obtained the necessary royal support.

On Wednesday, 23 May 1492, "in the church of St. George of this town of Palos, in the presence of Fr. Juan Perez and of the mayor

and councilors," Cristobal Colon gave and presented to the afore-
said the following letter of their Highnesses:

> "Ferdinand and Isabella, by the Grace of God King and Queen of
> Castile, Leon, Aragon, Sicily, Etc., to you Diego Rodriguez Prioto and
> all the other inhabitants of the town of Palos, greeting and grace.
>
> "Know ye that whereas for certain things done and committed
> by you to our disservice you were condemned and obligated by our
> Council to provide for us a twelvemonth with two equipped caravels
> at your own proper charge and expense. . . . And whereas we have
> now commanded Cristobal Colon to go with three *carabelas de armada*
> as our Captain of same, toward certain regions of the Ocean Sea, to
> perform certain things for our service, and we desire that he take with
> him the said two caravels with which you are thus required to serve
> us; therefore we command that within six weeks of receiving this our
> letter . . . you have all ready and prepared two equipped caravels, as
> you are required by virtue of the said sentence, to depart with the said
> Cristobal Colon whither we have commanded him to go . . . and we
> have commanded him to give you advance pay for four months for
> the people who are to sail aboard the said caravels at the rate to be
> paid to the other people who are to be in the said three [sic] caravels,
> and in the other caravel that we have commanded him to take, what-
> ever is commonly and customarily paid on this coast to the people
> who go to sea in a fleet. . . .
>
> "Given in our City of Granada, on the 30th day of April, year of
> our Lord Jesus Christ 1492."

The town fathers, who were held responsible for complying
with the sentence served upon Palos, promptly resolved any ambi-
guity in the royal letter by establishing the following statement of
work:

> Supply two caravel ships (not three). Supply reconditioning
> services and provisions for a voyage to "certain regions of the
> Ocean Sea," i.e., the Orient. Provide crews for the two caravel
> ships. Complete such preparations *in forty-two days.*

The mayor of Palos, who would be personally guilty of compounded "disservices" if the caravel project went awry, petitioned
their Majesties for an extension of the preparation period to allow
an additional thirty days. Over the objections of Admiral Columbus, who wanted to avoid any royal change of mind that might
terminate his adventure before it started, the petition was granted,
subject to presenting to their Majesties' representative an acceptable
rationale (master milestone chart) clearly identifying the work to be
performed, scheduling of the work, and an explanation of why the
additional time would be required.

Due to delays in coordination, delays in sending messages back and forth, and delays in preliminary planning, actual work on the project did not start until June 24. By then, only forty days remained in which to complete the work before the scheduled sailing.

Meanwhile, in order to meet the difficult schedule, chandlers, shipwrights, sailmakers, timber merchants, cartographers, bakers, physicians, metalsmiths, chronologers, caulkers, coopers, compass makers and others were designated to contribute their special skills in the preparations. Each realized that his support was required as penalty for Palos' "disservice" to Ferdinand and Isabella.

Project Tasks

Preparation for The Enterprise of the Indies involved three major tasks. A work breakdown structure was prepared as shown in Figure 1 below.

Crew Task

Notwithstanding the perils of the voyage on the uncharted Ocean Sea, a capable crew had to be recruited and signed on. All civil and criminal prosecutions were to be suspended against anyone

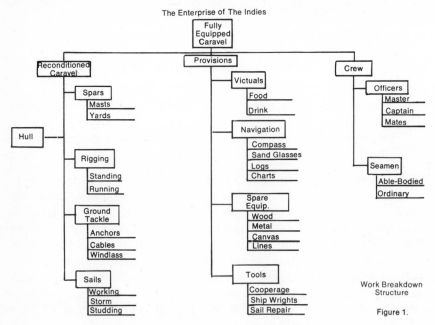

Work Breakdown Structure

Figure 1.

who agreed to ship with Admiral Columbus. The fleet required a total of thirty officers and sixty seamen.

Provisioning Task

Provisioning posed a problem. Provisions were available from the citizens of Palos by royal command, but how much provisioning would be needed? How long would the voyage to the Indies require? Since the carrying capacity of the caravel was limited, the right mix of provisions, materials, equipment and supplies would have to be selected to sustain twenty-five crewmen and officers for an indeterminate period, under unknown sailing conditions, for each of the two caravels.

Scheduling

The Mayor of Palos sought a means to assure himself that his tenure as Mayor and his liberty would not be terminated. He recognized that he could perform the tasks for the two ships simultaneously, so that the schedule for one ship would serve the other also.

A network of activities, like that in Figure 2, was prepared to show the various activities and to determine interdependencies.

The critical path showed that fifty-three days would be required, unless changes were made to reduce the time required for preparation. It was clear that risks in recruiting officers and seamen were necessary, even though the quality of the crew would suffer. Reconditioning the hull would also have to be done in less time; it was decided that working at night as well as daytime would be necessary to shorten the reconditioning period. And Admiral Columbus agreed, reluctantly, to shorten the time for sea trials from seven days to three days.

Finally, a revised network was developed that looked like the one in Figure 3.

If all went as planned, the caravels would be ready for the voyage within forty days. Based on this, the sailing was set for early on the morning of August 3.

It was expected that additional provisioning could be obtained at San Sebastian in the Canary Islands. Thereafter there was only the unknown, and the dread of falling off the edge of the world.

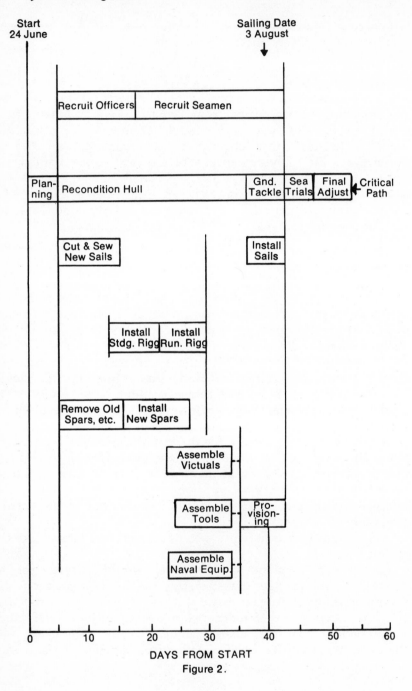

Figure 2.

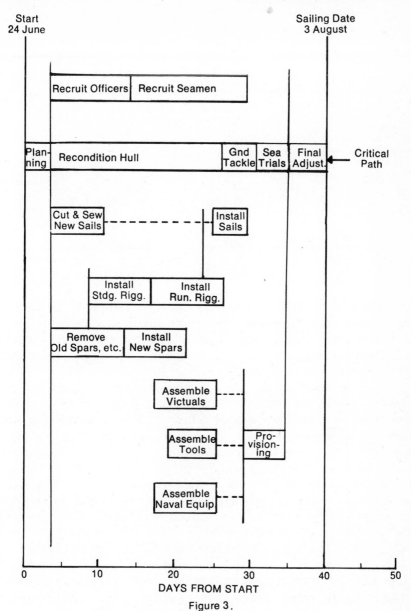

Figure 3.

35

Line of Balance*

Commander Gerald J. Chasko

Line of Balance (LOB) is a management technique for collect-ing, measuring, interpreting and presenting in graphic form infor-mation relating to time and accomplishment during production. It shows the progress, status, timing and phasing of interrelated project activities.

LOB is based on the idea of management by exception and deals only with the main checkpoints of a project or those which potentially govern the over-all schedule. It is a monitoring and reporting technique that provides feedback information to a man-agement control system. The information provides management with a means of measuring where a project is with respect to where it ought to be. In addition, management receives timely information concerning critical areas where the project is, or will be, behind schedule. This information can be used to determine those areas of the process which need corrective action. Successively updated studies provide checks on the effectiveness of remedial action.

Although it can be used on one-time projects like building a plant, LOB has proven most useful in production programs from the point when incoming or raw materials arrive to the shipment of the end product. Without a computer controlled production process, Line of Balance doesn't lend itself readily to day-by-day updating, but a monthly or weekly check is usually enough to keep the pro-cess on schedule. If the project seriously falls behind schedule, management will know it—and know why—far enough in advance to make smooth adjustments.

*Defense Systems Management College paper, September 1, 1978.

Reporting to customers or top management is quick, inexpensive and graphic. The charts used for analysis and trouble shooting are suitable for at-a-glance status reporting. A set of clear, simple charts is easier to understand than a list of facts and figures, and charts are faster and more reliable than oral reports.

A Line of Balance study has four elements: (1) the objectives of the project; (2) the program or plan and a schedule for achieving it; (3) the current program progress or status; and (4) a comparison between where the program is and where it's supposed to be. The first step in using LOB is to gather and organize the needed material into three charts. Once this is done you can "strike the line of balance" whenever necessary to keep track of the program. The three charts are interdependent and they can be plotted on one sheet of paper.

The first phase of the study is to set down the objective. The objective of a production process is the required delivery schedule. The delivery information used in a Line of Balance analysis is of two kinds: (1) the planned schedule showing the contractual delivery requirement; and (2) the actual deliveries made by the producer up to the time of the study. Planned and actual deliveries are always collected and plotted in cumulative end items per unit of time (Figure 1). Include any end items that may have already been shipped before the study. Actual and planned deliveries are both put on the same chart. In Figure 1 for example, the schedule calls for five end items in December, three more in January, seven in February, etc. Actual deliveries however show five shipped in January, two a month later and so on. Note that all entries are cumulative.

The horizontal difference between the two curves shows how far actual deliveries lag scheduled deliveries in terms of time. The vertical distance shows how many items are overdue. The difference in slope of the curves shows the lag in the production rate.

Next, the production plan must be defined. The production plan is a graphic flow chart of selected production activities plotted against the lead time required before shipment. The monitoring of progress is done using key plant operations or assembly points in the manufacturing cycle, known as control points. Start at the point of shipment and work backwards on a scale of time, using working days, weeks, months or any appropriate units. Remember that in a five-day-week operation, a month is 22 working days. Time for in-plant transfer and storage in addition to processing time must also be allowed for. Only major or limiting steps in the process need be considered for the program, for example, places where money is tied up or where machine speeds are a controlling factor. Figure 2

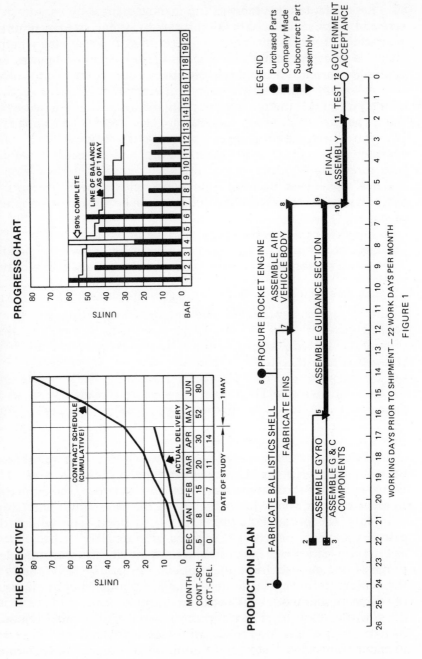

SAMPLE LINE OF BALANCE CHART

FIGURE 1

lists the control points for the sample study. Set each one down in terms of working days of lead time needed prior to shipment of the final item. These main events are given symbols that show whether they involve purchased items, subcontracted parts or pieces and assemblies produced in house. Assemblies break down into subassemblies, these into parts or operations and so on; and the production plan can be constructed to any or all of these levels of equipment (see Figure 1).

DESCRIPTION	CONTROL POINT NUMBER
Begin Ballistic Shell Fabrication	1
Receive Gyro Components	2
Receive G & C Components	3
Begin Fin Fabrication	4
Begin Guidance Section Assembly	5
Receive Rocket Engines	6
Begin Air Vehicle Body Assembly	7
Complete Air Vehicle Body Assembly	8
Complete Guidance Section	9
Start Final Assembly	10
Complete Final Air Vehicle Assembly	11
Government Acceptance	12

Figure 2

The more steps that are monitored, the more sensitive the charts are, but they are also more complicated. The number of control points on a single chart generally should not exceed 50. If there are over 50, subsidiary plans can be used to feed the main one. Then each chart can be kept simple and easy to follow. The "shipping date" of the subsidiary charts will be the date on which the sub-project must be ready to join the overall plan.

On the planning chart, each monitored step is numbered (left to right), the step with the longest lead time being No. 1, and the shipping date having the highest number. If two steps are done at the same time, number them top to bottom.

The planning chart shows the inter-relationships and sequence of all the major steps, and their individual lead times. It takes a good understanding of the manufacturing processes involved, and sound judgment to know which and how many steps to monitor.

The third element of the study is to fix the date of the study and plot the progress or status of activities as of that date. The number of parts or subassemblies at each monitored point is counted in terms of end-product units. These quantities are shown with bar graphs (Figure 1), keyed by number to the check-points on the program chart. If there are temporary shortages or fall-downs, an outline bar may be used to show the number of parts virtually complete, and a solid bar to show the ones actually finished.

The fourth phase is to "strike the line of balance." The line of balance indicates at what level each bar on the status chart should be if the job is to stay on schedule. In different words, it specifies the quantities of end item sets for each control point which must be available in order for progress on the program to remain in phase with the objective. Normally, the line steps downward to the right. If the line just hits the top of each of the bars, the program is exactly on schedule. The line shows at once just where quantities are off and where they are likely to be off in the future. Bars that don't reach the line of balance represent shortages; those that pass through it show excesses (probably caused by over-production or over-zealous purchasing).

To strike the line of balance, plot how many units should be at each check-point as of the date of the study. First, from the program chart (Figure 1), pick off the lead time for the first check-point. In the example shown, this is 24 working days (number 1— a company made part). This lead time is plotted on the objective chart to the right of the study date. In this case, the study date is May 1, so the lead-time date for check-point 1 falls early in June, 24 working days later. Next, extend this point vertically until it hits the schedule (objective) line. Here, the contact point falls at about 54 units. From the contact point, move horizontally across to the progress chart. Draw a line where the status bar of check-point 1 is cut. This is the balance line for that check-point.

The same thing is done with each of the other check-points. Points 2 and 3, for instance, have lead times of 22 days; point 5 has 16 days, etc. When all the points have been extended from the objective chart to the progress chart, and the horizontal balance lines have been connected, there will be a set of steps, sloping down to the right. This is the line balance as of the study date.

Interpreting the Line-of-Balance charts is fairly simple. The progress chart indicates which bars failed to reach the Line of Balance; that is, what check-points have shortages. By checking back with the program chart, you can see how these problem points affect the over-all job. Normally, you start at the end of the process and work backwards toward the beginning—toward the longest-lead-time items.

In the example, the shipping point is No. 12. Its bar doesn't reach the line of balance, so you're behind schedule there. Points 11 and 10 are also short. However, Point 9 is on schedule. Since 10 depends on 9 and 8, you know 8 is the offender. Both 8 and 7 are short, but there are more than enough purchased items at control point 6. What's the problem with 7? Trace it back to 4, which is seriously short. It is obvious that not having enough completed fins is holding up the whole process. Control points 2, 3 and 5 are short, but are not directly responsible for the failure to meet the delivery schedule. The problem with the fins should be addressed before management attention is devoted to other "short" operations. The overages at 1 and 6 may be examined from the point of view of inventory control.

Whatever corrective actions are taken, the next line of balance will help to evaluate their effectiveness.

After 1935 costs weren't particularly important. What mattered was *time.* We worked three shifts a day. Everything was *time.* Quantity and time. It turned out that we probably produced at the lowest cost too; but the emphasis was on time.
—*Jeffrey Quill, Spitfire development testing*

In those days, concurrency was a *good* word.
—*John T. Cosby, F-111 aircraft program*

Crash programs are common in the (Soviet) strategic sector. Ustinov frequently double-teams a project at least through the research and development stage.
—Fortune, *Aug. 1, 1969, p. 122*

36

Effective Time Management in the Project Office*

Major Theodore M. Brostrom

The purpose of this study is to find out if project managers have enough time to adequately manage their projects. If it is confirmed that a problem exists, then an attempt will be made to define the problem, identify the major impediments to the effective use of time available to the project manager and to determine what can be done to alleviate or manage those impediments. This study will conclude with a set of principles or guidelines to help the project manager make the most effective use of his time. Finally, if we can twist Peter Drucker's words around ("Time is our scarcest resource, and unless it is managed nothing else can be managed"), this study should allow a project manager to say: "Since I can manage my scarcest resource (time), then I should be able to manage the project."

Time Wasters

To give some idea of the time wasters faced by managers, consider the partial list that follows: unclear objectives, poor information, procrastination, lack of feedback, too much reading, interruptions, telephone, no time planning, meetings, beautiful secretaries, lack of delegation, lack of self-discipline, visitors, lack of priorities, junk mail, poor filing, fatigue, red tape, coffee breaks,

*Extract from study report, *Effective Time Management in the Project Office,* Defense Systems Management College, November 1976, pp. 2, 3, 14–16, 35–37.

244

socializing, mistakes, pet projects, can't say no, poor communication, span of control, crisis management, peer demands, and so on.[1]

Some of the time wasters listed above are certainly familiar to the vast majority of managers. This then assists in redefining the objective of this study. Peter Drucker said that "poor management wastes everybody's time—but above all, it wastes the manager's time."[2] If wasting time is doing nothing, then doing something that accomplished some goals would be effective use of time. It has been suggested that a very stimulating exercise is for one to write his obituary—for now and for some time in the future. After finishing with the statistics and family items a basic question will remain: "What did you do?" Was time used effectively?[3]

The Internal Monkey Wrench

When one is asked to identify the major time wasters, he (or she) will usually generate external causes first, such as the telephone, meetings, visitors, paperwork, and delays. After considerable discussion of the problems encountered in time management a new source is invariably surfaced—the man within, who generates such time wasters as lack of delegation, lack of plans and priorities, the open door policy, and procrastination.[4] It takes a willingness to be self-critical, to see how much of our ineffectiveness is caused by ourselves. When one can admit error with impunity, the real reason comes to light. The cartoon character Pogo said: "We has met the enemy and they is us."[5]

This ability to overcome procrastination or breaking bad time management habits requires that one be able to look in the mirror for that Pogo in us. The basic ingredient for success in getting things done is determination. There is no secret—just the one word—determination. If the need for success, money, position, power, fame or anything else is great enough, then the conditions are present for doing something about it.[6] To get started, one must ask himself the right question: "Since I'm going to do it eventually, do I really want to pay the price of delay?"[7]

[1]Mackenzie, R. Alec, *The Time Trap—Managing Your Way Out.* New York: American Management Association, Inc., 1972, p. 5.

[2]Drucker, Peter F., *The Effective Executive.* New York: Harper & Row, Publishers, Incorporated, 1967, pp. 46–47.

[3]Feldman, Edwin B., *How To Use Your Time To Get Things Done.* New York: Frederick Fell Publishers, Inc., 1968, p. 60.

[4]Mackenzie, *op. cit.,* p. 4.

[5]*Ibid.,* p. 7.

[6]Feldman, *op. cit.,* p. 28.

[7]Lakein, Alan, How To Get Control of Your Time and Your Life. Scarborough, Canada: New American Library of Canada Limited, 1974, p. 136.

Synthesis: Time Management Principles for the PM

The principles that follow are a synthesis of the literature that was reviewed and the result of the two surveys that were conducted as a part of this study. The principles do not represent a "cookbook" approach to time management, because there is no one best way to manage time.

The first principle consists of understanding the nature of the Pareto Principle (80% of the value is derived from 20% of the items) and its application to time management. Simply stated, the project manager needs to find those 20% of the items that will yield 80% of the results, and then spend 80% of his time on those items. The identification of those items leads to the second principle.

The second principle involves the determination and prioritization of goals for the project. The project manager should write down exactly what ends he wishes to achieve. All goals should be prioritized as to their relative level of importance with A goals most important, B goals next, and C goals having the least importance. While doing this one must keep in mind the first principle involving Pareto. Then with approximately 20% of the goals identified as A goals, the project manager needs to prioritize the A goals with A-1 being most important, A-2 second most important, A-3 third most important, and so forth.

The third principle consists of listing all activities to accomplish the A-1 goal, all activities to accomplish the A-2 goal, A-3 goal, and so forth. Then the project manager needs to prioritize each of the *activities* for the A-1 goal, the A-2 goal, A-3 goal, and so forth. Keep in mind that one can "do" activities but not goals. At this point a list of activities should be developed for each of the A goals with A-1.1 being the number one activity for the A-1 goal, A-1.2 the second most important activity for the A-1 goal, A-1.3 the third most important activity, and so on.

The fourth principle is to schedule the A-1 activities into the most productive part of the business time schedule and in "chunks" of time required to accomplish the activity (i.e., A-1.1: 1000–1015 hours, A-1.2: 1015–1045, A-1.3: 1100–1130, and so forth). These first four principles will be labeled the planning phase of time management.

The fifth principle is to make time for the planning and scheduling of activities (principles 1–4) by following these work procedures.[8]

---

[8]Lakein, Alan, "How To Use Your Time Wisely." *U.S. News & World Report.* (January 19, 1976), p. 46.

1. Delegate everything that is possible to delegate, including meetings and readings. Insure understanding of delegated task.
2. Generate as little paper work as possible; continually question the need for reports. Practice waste basketing; avoid the "squirrel complex." Get rid of everything possible as soon as possible.
3. Use "body English" to save precious minutes. Do not sit down in other peoples' offices unless prepared for a long visit. By standing, one communicates a sense of urgency. If sitting, move to the edge of the chair.
4. Get the maximum mileage from your secretary. Insist that people schedule appointments through her and that she is kept apprised of appointments you have made. Let your secretary serve as a "buffer" and "screen" for the numerous phone calls, visitors, and correspondence impinging on you, the project manager. Dictate your letters to her—keep letters short and to the point. Use an electronic dictation system if available.
6. Handle paper work once only. Answer as many letters as possible on the spot. Avoid memos and a holding file like the plague. Move actions along.
7. Concentrate on one activity at a time.
8. Do not permit telephone intrusion. If the phone rings on the way to an appointment, keep going. If you answer, the pressure will show in your voice, the call will be handled poorly, and you'll be late for the appointment.
9. Cancel or do not attend meetings if there is not a need, if the right people are not going to attend, or the necessary information is not available.
10. Put "waiting time" to good use by reading or relaxing.
11. Plan the activities schedule the first thing during the day while fresh.
12. Develop an appreciation of time management considerations in subordinates by respecting their time (not dropping in unexpectedly). Mention to your superiors and higher echelon staffers the time management procedures you have instituted (e.g., morning meetings: 0800–1000, afternoons 1400–1445, correspondence, etc.)
13. Distinguish between important and urgent. Urgent is seldom important and the important is seldom urgent.
14. Have a light lunch so as not to get sleepy in the afternoon.

Section 7 —

COST AND FISCAL MANAGEMENT

Introduction

The processes by which industrial programs are financed and the budget processes by which defense programs are financed vary greatly from one organization to another. The Navy process for example differs considerably from those of the Army and Air Force. For this reason, little of a generally applicable nature has been written regarding fiscal processes.

Navy Captain Robert J. O'Shaughnessy makes this comment, however, which has general significance in defense programs management:

> The Navy budget process is complicated, fast moving and no place for the novice. It is dynamic and changing. Three principal budget activities are taking place concurrently:
> Execution of current and prior year budgets.
> Justification of the budget for the next year.
> Formulation of the budget for the year following.
> For the Navy program manager, an understanding of the budget dynamics, timeliness of response and continuous rejustification for his program are prerequisites for the survival of his program. If he doesn't understand the Navy budget process, it is almost a sure bet that his program will be underfunded or cut. Even with the knowledge of how the system works, his program may be cut because a Navy program of higher priority requires funding. He must realize that if this happens, he will have to restructure his program accordingly. However, if he loses funds because of inadequate justification or poor timing, then he must take the blame. [From a paper written at the Defense Systems Management College.]

Another program manager describes the competition for funds this way:

> If you want to protect your program, you have to fight for it. You especially have to fight for funds. One or another program is always in trouble and someone is sure to be looking for money. They want to swap their problems for your money. It may be a provincial attitude, but I think a program manager is expected to push for his

program. That means two things: first, grab for your money; second, get it into contracts and work orders as soon as possible. You have to plan and schedule your contract actions early in the fiscal year. You have to make sure you are moving your money out as planned. [From *Introduction to Military Program Management* by the Logistics Management Institute.]

Industrial program managers have a less difficult time in the fiscal arena, and consequently can spend proportionately more time on other aspects of their programs. In Defense, however, the budget crunch is reflected in "One Plane, One Tank, One Ship: Trend for the Future?" by Norman Augustine, former Assistant Secretary of the Army for Research and Development.

An approach to cost control, on the other hand, has become widely adopted, and a commonly-used language has evolved during the 1970s. This is the "criteria" approach, developed initially in the Air Force Systems Command and subsequently adopted throughout DOD and among defense industry contractors, and emerging in civil agencies as a preferred way to control program costs. What this approach is and how it is implemented are the subject of "C/SCSC: Alive and Well." Related to C/SCSC is the matter of how to analyze cost and schedule information produced by a system that meets the required management criteria or tests. Gen. John R. Guthrie's remarks at a 1978 conference on this topic are given in the next selection. Gen. George Sammet then portrays how a senior logistics commander rides herd on his programs on a continuing basis. The techniques used are of value to top management in either industry or government.

Life cycle costs, including costs of development, production, and operation and support (O&S), are receiving greater attention than ever because it is recognized that additional costs incurred in development often result in lower production costs and lower costs of ownership. Don Earles presents ways of estimating life cycle costs and their use in source selection in the final selection.

✷ ✷ ✷ ✷ ✷

It is customary in democratic countries to deplore expenditure on armament as conflicting with the requirements of the social services. There is a tendency to forget that the most important social service that a government can do for its people is to keep them alive and free.

—*Sir John Slessor*

37

One Plane, One Tank, One Ship: Trend for the Future?*

Honorable Norman R. Augustine†

During the 1920's, President Calvin Coolidge, apparently distressed over the burdens of procuring three additional military aircraft, mused: "Why can't the Army buy just one aeroplane and let the aviators take turns flying it?" In the 1970's, we are rapidly approaching the point where we will quite literally be able to *afford* only one aircraft—or, for that matter, one tank and one ship. Unfortunately, President Coolidge is proving to be less a skeptic than a prophet.

Figures 1, 2 and 3 indicate the consistency with which the cost of each of these three basic kinds of military hardware has risen in recent decades. Such a trend cannot be sustained much longer. This is not merely due to a redirection of management—much more fundamental is that this trend cannot continue without violating certain basic laws of mathematics.

The unit cost of major items of military hardware has been increasing at a significantly faster pace than the DOD budget itself, or for that matter, the Gross National Product. It is a relatively straightforward calculation to show that if the trends which have prevailed so consistently over the last half-century were to continue for a few more decades, we will reach a point in the year 2036 where the Defense Department will literally be able to afford only one aircraft. Fortunately, by sharing this aircraft among the military

*Defense Management Journal, April 1975, pp. 34–40.
†Assistant Secretary of the Army (Research and Development).

services on alternate days of the week, it will be possible to accrue enough money to replace it roughly every fifteen years thereafter. By devoting the entire GNP to aircraft procurement, we can delay this singular event by only 83 years.

The year 2036, it should be noted, is well within the lifetime of our population today. It is about as far into the future as World War I is in the past.

Much the same prognosis applies to other types of military hardware, with our being limited to a single tank just nine years before we are reduced to one airplane.

The problem is quite analogous to that which arose in connection with the exploding growth in scientific and engineering manpower in this country during the past century. This rate had been so extraordinary as compared with the growth in total population that any moderately exuberant observer would have had to predict there would soon be more scientists and engineers than people!

Self-Correction. That such trends are self-correcting is evident. The only question is whether we as managers will lead in

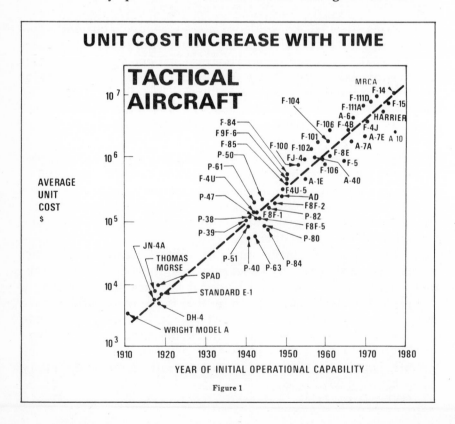

Figure 1

taking the corrective steps or whether we will merely become witnesses of the inevitable rectification.

That self-correcting forces are already at work is suggested by a comparison of defense procurement in 1974 with that of exactly three decades earlier, i.e., at the peak of World War II. These periods happen to be characterized by roughly the same total defense budgets as measured in current dollars, but there the similarity ends. At the peak of World War II, we were producing 50,000 tactical aircraft, 20,000 tanks and 80,000 artillery pieces a year. In 1974, we have struggled to produce 450 tanks, 600 aircraft and no artillery pieces.

The problem is compounded by the increasing loss rates which must be expected in modern warfare because of high precision weapons. What the future holds in this regard may have been glimpsed in the October 1973 War; a conventional war wherein neither major power was directly involved. Yet, in this war, Egypt and Syria *lost* about as many tanks as the U.S. *owns* throughout Europe, including our prepositioned stocks. They *lost* more artillery pieces than we *have* today in Europe. And all this took place in just

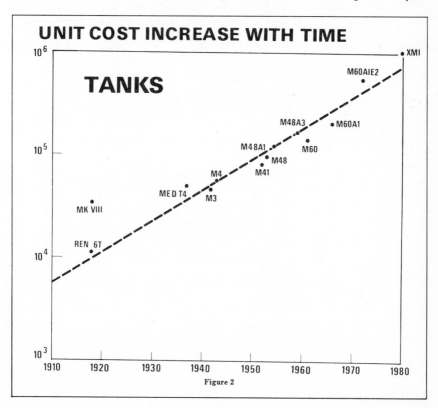

Figure 2

19 days without tactical airpower having had the occasion to make *its* full impact felt. On today's battlefield a fundamental change has taken place: What can be seen can be hit. What can be hit can be destroyed.

Safety in Numbers. Just how important is numerical superiority on this battlefield? Certainly, qualitative superiority can go a long way toward offsetting numerical disadvantages. The atomic bomb is, perhaps, the extreme example of this. But setting aside the case of weapons of mass destruction, it would appear that qualitative superiority has some very real limitations.

In 1916 the British engineer, F. W. Lanchester, showed that to match a foe with twice as many weapons as one's own, one must possess weapons not of twice the quality of the enemy's but rather *four* times the quality. That is, quantitative superiority is favored by the presence of a "square" law, whereas the advantages of qualitative superiority assert themselves only linearly. Because of the limited applicability of the case analyzed by Lanchester, it has often been argued that the proper exponent is something less than two but certainly greater than one.

Nonetheless, it is very difficult indeed to offset major numerical disadvantages with quality alone—and nearly impossible to do so

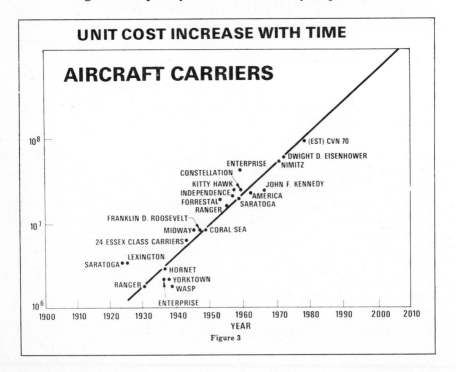

Figure 3

when the enemy combines quantitative superiority with reasonably high *individual* weapon effectiveness. This point has certainly not been missed by the Soviet Union which has not only amassed very large forces but has embraced Lanchester's principle by including it in such publications as *Anti-tank Warfare,* by Biryukov and Melnikov.

The applicability of Lanchester's analysis is, of course, affected by the tactical situations. For example, it is generally assumed that forces on the defense are favored by a factor of three to five in terms of required strength to produce a stalemate. Lanchester's analysis applies principally to a case wherein shifting tactical situations tend to counter-balance such effects. As the Secretary of Defense has noted, when Daniel Boone, who shot 50 bears a year, was replaced by 50 hunters, each of whom shot only two bears a year, there is no record of the bears celebrating the decline of human marksmanship.

Seeking Balance. Although the trend of increasing unit cost of military hardware will inevitably play a decisive role in force structuring in the future, there is today another even more dominant factor—personnel costs. People-related costs consume approximately 56 percent of the current DOD budget. In the case of the Army budget, personnel costs exceed 69 percent. In contrast, the corresponding figure for the USSR is about 30 to 35 percent. Perhaps that explains, in part, how the Soviet Union manages to maintain such large forces with ever increasing quality.

The dilemma, then, is how to maintain our already marginally adequate military manpower and equipment levels while simultaneously providing funds to assure those who wear our country's uniform of the standard of living their talents would demand in civilian endeavors. This, as in any free society, we must be prepared to do.

Just how important "non-hardware" costs have become can be seen from Figure 4, which views the "lifetime" cost of ownership (20-year basis) of one type of *equipment-heavy* division; namely, an armored division. A division completely outfitted with today's material (M-16 rifles, CHAPARRAL missiles, TOW/COBRA gunships, M60A1 tanks, M551 Reconnaissance Vehicles, TOW missiles, etc.) costs only about six percent more than the same division would if outfitted with the equipment of about a decade ago (M-14 rifles, Twin-40 anti-aircraft guns, Huey gunships, M60A1 tanks, M41 light tanks, 120mm recoilless rifles, etc.). When general support costs are amortized against the cost of ownership of the division, this difference is even further diminished. Thus, within reasonable limits, "the cost of a division is the cost of a division," and one might as well have well-equipped divisions, *distinct, however, from gold-plated divisions.*

A Word of Caution. Although it still appears beneficial to procure high quality equipment, there is an important side-effect of sophistication which should not be overlooked. This side-effect evidences itself as unreliability, which is perhaps the greatest penalty of overcomplexity to have thus far made itself evident as the dynamics of weapon system unit cost growth evolve. The inside of a tank today resembles the sophisticated aircraft systems of only a few years ago.

During the past decade the Soviet Union appears also to have moved toward increasingly complex systems, with the SA-6 air defense missile system, the BMP fighting vehicle and the ZSU-23-4 air defense gun noted in the October 1973 War being prime examples. Although undeniably highly capable, it is doubtful that any of these systems could, in their present form, have survived a DSARC!

How, then, does one tell when the point of design ingenuity has been surpassed and the point of undue sophistication approached? In this regard, it is instructive to consider two fairly basic pieces of foreign hardware: the Russian standard bayonet and the Israeli Galil rifle.

The Russians, apparently taking a page from Napoleon who once noted that one "can do almost anything with a bayonet except sit on it!", have combined a wire cutter into their standard bayonet

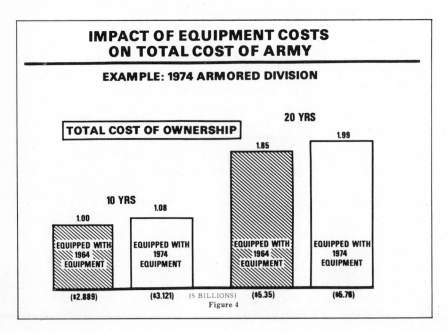

Figure 4

and electrically insulated the hilt and scabbard. It has been estimated it would cost our Army over $4 million simply to provide this wire cutting capability to its forces.

In the case of Israeli rifles, most systems analysts, as well as those experienced as Congressional witnesses, would be disheartened indeed to note that it contains a built-in bottle opener! On the other hand, if Israeli soldiers will not refrain from damaging moderately expensive ammunition clips when doubling their use as a bottle opener, who is to say that it is not cost effective to go ahead and provide a built-in bottle opener?

Perhaps the most portentous example of all is the fact that the bulkhead hand grips on the Soviet ZSU-23-4 vehicle are electrically warmed.

Highly Leveraged R&D. The yearly cost of inflation in the "people" part of the DOD budget is now of the same order of magnitude as the total amount being spent on research and development. It would thus appear that there are enormous gains to be made from devoting R&D dollars directly to reducing the manpower demands associated with performing a given mission, rather than simply to increasing hardware effectiveness as has generally been the case in the past. An example of what potentially can be accomplished is suggested by the SAM-D program. When completed, this program will replace ten different kinds of radar with a single type of radar, will permit a reduction in troops from 18,434 to 10,440 in the field Army alone and will reduce the number of individual stockage items from 86,415 to 16,193, all while dramatically increasing the effectiveness of our air defenses.

Other examples could include TACFIRE, an automated artillery direction system, and the Cannon Launched Guided Projectile, CLGP. This latter development promises to give to artillery, essentially for the first time in history, the capability to efficiently attack fixed and moving *hard point* targets with indirect fire. The savings in people this economy of firepower could entail will cascade itself all the way back through the support system. For example, if ten percent of the targets to be engaged were point targets capable of being attacked with CLGP, with all other targets being engaged with conventional ammunition, the savings achievable in the logistic pipeline alone amount to about five transportation companies and two ammunition companies, or about 1,200 spaces, when fighting a NATO war.

It is instructive to consider the benefits of reducing the personnel support associated with various specific types of units, say a LANCE battalion. If one could, through the prudent expenditure of R&D, reduce the unit cost of the LANCE missile by twenty percent, it would be possible to add one-fourth of a battalion to the eight battalions now programmed for our forces with the realized savings. On the other hand, if this same R&D could be focused on reducing the non-missile costs within a LANCE battalion by the same percent, it would be possible to increase the number of units deployed by about 1–½ battalions.

In the past, efforts to trade more effective equipment for manpower have not been notably successful. Perhaps one reason for this is that the net result of such proposed trades was usually to reduce overall manpower strength in the services. Justifiable concern was thereby raised as to the potential consequences of equipment failure if we were to become so heavily dependent upon hardware, especially when that hardware is available in such limited quantities.

Secretary Schlesinger, on the other hand, has found a very effective means of overcoming this problem in an analogous area, that of reducing the size of headquarters. In this latter instance he has directed the military services to reduce the size of their overhead structure but, this time, the guidance is that, in general, for each man saved in a headquarters the services may add a man in a combat unit. As a direct consequence of this policy the Army, for example, is moving toward a leaner, tougher fighting force of sixteen divisions rather than the prior thirteen divisions, *all within the same manpower end strength.* This same policy, were it to be applied within the material process, could produce correspondingly great benefits.

As but one example of this potential payoff, the introduction of the TACFIRE automated artillery control system, with its inherent multiple backup modes that assure "graceful" degradation when malfunctions occur, could permit sizeable savings in manpower *that could then be translated into procuring additional artillery batteries.* This latter action is the essential element if we are to provide the needed motivation to streamline and, at the same time, avoid a highly brittle, overly automation-dependent force.

A Glimpse at the Future

It is inevitable that the past trend in rising equipment costs must decelerate and that numerical sufficiency cannot indefinitely continue to play a secondary role to qualitative superiority. Nonetheless, selective qualitative gains remain an essential goal, with especially high leverage being achieved through research and development dedicated to the reduction of manpower and other support demands with the efficiencies thereby realized being transformed into additional fighting elements. Thus, in the years ahead, we could profitably shift the focus of our R&D from near-total concentration on increasing performance to a more balanced attack which includes, as one element, a major assault on support costs.

$$\star \quad \star \quad \star \quad \star \quad \star$$

I see no basis for the notion that we tend to overdo the military aspects. To the contrary, the nation has repeatedly neglected to provide a military basis to match its policy or to cope with aggressive forces.

—*Dean Acheson*

Our Army declined to the point where it was ranked seventeenth in combat capability in the world by 1933. Lack of funds for weapons system development was one of the primary reasons for the low rating. Armor is a case in point. Tanks had played an important part in a number of battles in France during the war, and some European powers were proceeding to develop and improve their armored forces at a rapid pace. The US Army budget for armor concept development in 1920 was $500. In 1934 the Army possessed a grand total of twelve modern tanks; the rest could not be depended upon to make it into battle, much less fight effectively. . . . The Army carefully guarded and maintained the little equipment allotted it. General George C. Marshall recalled signing a report of a $28 property loss twelve times, and seeing 28 other signatures on it. Promotions were hard to come by. An enlistee counted himself lucky if he made PFC in three years. An officer could expect to make captain at age 39, and remain in company grade until almost age 50. Dwight D. Eisenhower was a major for 16 years during this period.

—Commanders Call,
DA Pamphlet 360-816, Winter 1973

And some experts suggest that the Soviet military burden has actually continued on a steadily rising course—to a 1975 GNP share of 14 percent to 15 percent from a 1960 level of eight percent to nine percent. This would mean that the Soviets have been placing an increasingly high priority on military strength at the very time when the superpowers were supposedly ushering in a new period of detente.

—*"The CIA's Goof in Assessing the Soviets,"*
Business Week, *Feb. 28, 1977, p. 96*

Soviet soldiers are profoundly grateful to the people, the Party and government for providing the Armed Forces with first-rate weapons, combat equipment and every-thing necessary for combat training, service and every day routine.

—*Marshal A. A. Grechko,* The Armed
Forces of the Soviet State

38

C/SCSC: Alive and Well*

J. Stanley Baumgartner

"Major, are you trying to tell us, one of the world's largest corporations, how to manage? If you want us to try this C/SCSC system on your program—and we think we've done pretty well without it for a long time—it'll cost you two and a half million dollars."

This response was typical of industry's reaction to the cost/schedule control systems criteria (C/SCSC), circa 1967, and to its Air Force predecessor, the cost/schedule planning and control specification. A number of individuals within the Defense Department also had reservations about the concept.

Five years later, the corporation was visited again by the same officer and he found it had implemented C/SCSC across the board in the division concerned, on commercial as well as on defense projects. "What did it cost?" he inquired. "Well, a little less than a quarter of a million," a company spokesman acknowledged, "including our commercial programs."

This change in attitude toward C/SCSC is not unusual. The problem was that many people thought it was another system, a management veneer, that would be imposed with varying degrees of success and then scrapped.

What was not understood in those days is that C/SCSC is not a system. It is *criteria* or a set of standards that a contractor's management system, whatever it may be, must meet in undertaking development of a major defense program. "Criteria" is the key word in C/SCSC.

*From *Defense Management Journal,* April 1974, pp. 32–35; and paper presented at the Fifth Internet World Congress, Birmingham, England, September 14, 1976.

Essentially what C/SCSC does is ensure that data provided by a contractor, such as his monthly cost performance report, is accurate and timely. Cost and schedule deviations can then be traced to their source and action taken. But C/SCSC, alone, provides no project operations data nor does it require that any be collected.

There are some 35 of these criteria in the C/SCSC Joint Implementation Guide.[1] They define the standards a contractor's management system must meet regarding organization, planning and budgeting, accounting, analysis, revision and access to data.

Within the past four years, performance measurement or the "criteria" approach to project management has been widely adopted on major U.S. defense projects. More than a hundred key facilities, representing practically every major defense contractor, have been accepted by the Defense Department as meeting the standards or tests required for effective project management. Companies are adopting the same standards of project management on proprietary products. And even government-controlled facilities, usually the last to adopt innovations, are using this approach.

The path toward acceptance of cost/schedule control systems criteria (C/SCSC) has not been easy however. In fact large segments of the Defense Department and practically all of industry initially looked upon C/SCSC as another plague. They were intent on scuttling the concept when it appeared in the late '60s.

Adopting the Criteria

Recognizing a need for better visibility of program status and for more reliable data, the Air Force in the latter 1960's was determined to "go" with the criteria approach. Industry, thinking it was another here-today, gone-tomorrow management cult, was equally determined to resist. This impasse lasted for two or three years.

Finally, in 1969, one contractor realized, "These guys aren't going to go away." The management of one of his divisions pushed for compliance with the criteria, made the relatively few changes required and, in April of that year, the division's management control system was validated as complying with C/SCSC.

This caused a major change as others recognized that C/SCSC was here to stay. The problem then was to ensure that a contractor was, in fact, using his own management system, rather than trying to duplicate the first contractor's validated system. Surprising to most contractors since that time has been the fact that a good

[1]The pamphlet "Cost/Schedule Control Systems Criteria Joint Implementation Guide," AMCP 37–5, NAVMAT P-5240, AFSCP/AFLCP 173–5, March 31, 1972, is available from the Superintendent of Documents, U.S. Government Printing Office, Washington, D.C. 20402; order no. 0870–0318; price $1.25. (Revised October 1, 1976.)

existing system is generally 90 percent satisfactory insofar as the criteria are concerned.

Many companies also apply their Defense Department-approved systems to commercial and industrial projects because of the improved visibility provided. Others have requested validation reviews even though they did not have contractual requirements for C/SCSC-compliant systems.

From the number of validations and planned demonstrations, it is obvious that a major part of the defense contracting community, prime and subcontractors, have been covered by the criteria. Along the way, though, industry raised a good point, "If this is so good for us, DOD, why don't you try it yourself?" The cognizant focal points of the military services gulped, recognizing that in-house applications might well prove more difficult than those in industry, and bit the bullet.

In particular, the Army set about applying the criteria approach to its arsenals, research and development centers and ammunition plants. Somewhat surprisingly the validation teams were met with open-mindedness, then cooperation and then enthusiasm as managers of facilities began to understand the criteria and to realize the benefits of increased visibility. The same rigor and standards applied to industry are used in these in-house validations.

Understanding of Criteria

There is something a bit mysterious about C/SCSC. Why do organizations in industry and in the government embrace the criteria concept? What is different about this approach compared to previous management practices? What are the benefits and costs?

To answer these questions, it is necessary first to have some understanding of "criteria." For example, one of the planning and budgeting criteria in the C/SCSC Joint Implementation Guide says, "Schedule the authorized work in a manner which describes the sequence of work and identifies the significant task interdependencies required to meet the development, production and delivery requirements of the contract." It says nothing about *what* scheduling technique must be used. This is left to the contractor who may apply whatever technique he chooses so long as it meets this standard.

Another criteria in the Guide, part of the organization group, requires a contractor to integrate his planning, scheduling, budgeting, work authorization and cost accumulation systems with each other, with his work breakdown structure and with his organizational structure. Without this integration, a contractor might plan his work according to technical work to be done, accumulate costs by his functional organization structure, and budget his work according to what funds are available. This situation often existed in the past and is a reason costs sometimes galloped out of control.

Only two things are essentially new or different about C/SCSC from management approaches of the past, aside from its not being a system. One of these is the requirement that management controls must "play" together, as indicated previously. This integration and the use of only one work breakdown structure were new to many organizations, including some of the largest and most experienced defense producers.

The other difference is the concept of earned value, or budgeted cost for work performed (BCWP) as it is known in C/SCSC terminology. Previously a program manager could measure progress against a predetermined schedule and measure actual costs for work performed (ACWP) against a budget. The problem was that the program manager could not determine, for the money spent, whether or not he was getting the progress he should have obtained. How much should he have spent for the progress achieved and how did this compare with what he actually spent? Often he tried to evaluate value by making a "seat of the pants guesstimate," based on percent of funds expended. This is like trying to determine the value of a purchase based on the balance available in a person's checkbook.

Concept of Earned Value

C/SCSC introduced the concept of earned value which enables program managers in industry and the government to determine, with considerable accuracy, the status of their programs and sub-elements costwise. They do this by comparing BCWP and ACWP. By comparing BCWP with the budgeted cost of work scheduled (BCWS), they can measure actual and planned progress in terms of the cost to come from a behind schedule position to on schedule.

The diagram below is a concise graphic portrayal of these comparisons.

	BC	WS	Schedule deviation (work
Cost deviation (budgeted	BC	WP	scheduled vs. work performed)
cost vs. actual cost)	AC	WP	

Where BCWS is the Budgeted Cost of Work Scheduled, BCWP is the Budgeted Cost of Work Performed. ACWP is the Actual Cost of Work Performed.

Although C/SCSC does not require any reports per se (its purpose being to insure timeliness and validity of reports), the Cost Performance Report (CPR) is normally a contractual requirement on major projects. An extract of a CPR illustrates the use of BCWP (Col. 3) or earned value in problem analysis:

ITEM	Budgeted Cost		Actual Cost	Variance	
	Wk.Sch-eduled	Wk.Per-formed	Per-form'd	Sche-dule	Cost
(1)	(2)	(3)	(4)	(5)	(6)
Work Breakdown Structure					
Propulsion	134	119	195	(15)	(76)
Guidance & Control	112	119	163	7	(44)
Communications	38	12	9	(26)	3
Integr. & Assy.	415	382	421	(33)	(39)
Development Tests	1160	1148	1194	(12)	(46)

Dividing BCWP by ACWP gives a cost performance index (CPI), where 1.00 is "par." An index below this indicates less progress for the money than planned; an index above 1.00 indicates greater progress for the money than planned. The problem areas, those having more than, say, 15 percent negative variance, almost jump out at the analyst:

Propulsion, with a CPI of .61
Guidance and Control, CPI of .73

Indices can (and should) be made for cost and schedule performance for both the latest reported period and for the cumulative period to date.

Given the system discipline required in application of the criteria, the project manager can isolate cost problems, spot trends, confirm schedule problems and assess their magnitude, and determine where action is most needed. The solution of problems, of course, requires sound management, as always. But C/SCSC and related reports are a powerful tool when used by knowledgeable project managers.

If terms like BCWP, BCWS and ACWP sound like jargon that will soon go out of style, two points are worth noting. One is that they have been in widespread use for some years and are destined to be in use for a long time because of general acceptance of the criteria approach. The other is that the terms are used and their meaning is well understood by decision makers at high levels of DOD.

Benefits

What benefits result from C/SCSC, and what does it do for the project manager? Its main purpose is to assist the PM in keeping within his target cost. This of course is a difficult task, given the challenge inherent in any development-type project and inflation. However, a leading corporation reports cost underruns on three major defense projects of .3%, 1.5%, and .7% using C/SCSC. This same corporation, originally one of the holdouts against adoption of the criteria, now applies the C/SCSC approach to many of its proprietary programs. Other users of approved systems report similar results.

• During a C/SCSC demonstration, it was discovered that a contractor's manloading curves exceeded the available budget. As a result, five percent of his personnel were released from the program at a savings of $5 million.

• On a large aircraft development program the cost per aircraft was reduced by $2.1 million when cost visibility enabled the program manager to reduce the use of titanium with only slight effect on performance.

• A contractor on an electronic system traced a problem to a particular individual who had made a mistake that cost $300,000. The contractor estimated that, without a validated system, he would not have detected the problem until during the test phase when it would have cost $2.5 to $3 million.

• On another contract, cost and schedule variances were traced to a rotor blade problem. The contractor was able to redirect his effort and used a different material for the blades.

• In one instance, DOD saved $5 million when a cost performance report showed an overhead cost that should have been billed to a commercial activity.

• On a missile program, completed two weeks early with a $2 million underrun, the general manager was able to discover and assess the cost magnitude of a serious schedule slippage in time to take corrective action.

Some other benefits of C/SCSC are identification of problems not previously recognized; the ability to trace problems to their source; determining the cost impact of problems; and objective rather than subjective assessment of program status.

Interestingly, the two main benefits in contractors' eyes, even on retrofit applications, are greatly improved overall system discipline and detailed forward planning and budgeting.[2]

Problems

Compared to initial resistance to the criteria, present problems are relatively minor. The fundamental problem has been a lack of understanding in industry and the government of C/SCSC and how it works. The joint logistics commanders recognized this and established management courses to overcome the problem. In the past eighteen months, there has been a significant change in attitude toward C/SCSC.

One of the early problems, for instance, was rigidity on the part of government validation teams as to length of work packages and levels of the work breakdown structures. These teams have subsequently adopted a more flexible position without sacrificing the intent of the criteria. Another problem was that initial applications were retrofits to programs that had been under way for some time. These retrofits were difficult and painful compared to applications at the beginning of a program. Another problem is the effort required to understand the terminology (BCWS, BCWP, ACWP, cost accounts) and to apply these terms in practice.

Cost

The contractor's absolute cost of revising his system to meet the criteria is difficult to measure, but it is generally estimated to be less than a quarter million dollars. Information from several companies indicated there was no cost involved other than the initial computerizing effort. The same number of personnel would be involved on some other technique and C/SCSC is considered by far the best.

The cost is usually less than one-half of one percent of a program, including the nonrecurring costs. This is to be expected, since most of the elements of a compliant system are usually already in use. The best indicator of cost versus benefits, however, is the fact that an increasing number of companies use their validated systems to control commercial and industrial programs.

---

[2]"The Effect of the C/SCSC on Contractor Planning and Control," doctoral dissertation by Lt. Col. Leonard S. Marrella, The George Washington University, Washington, D.C. February 1973, p. 174.

Lessons on Implementation

The criteria approach to project plans and controls almost failed in its early implementation because of an assumption in industry that this was merely another management veneer that, like others, would come and go. Because of Internet 76's interest in new management techniques several observations based on experience with C/SCSC are offered.

• The implementer or developer of a management concept must know the problem he is addressing. This seems to be simplicity itself. Often however a technique fails because its developer starts with a solution and then looks for areas or problems where it might be applied.

• The technique must be sound in concept, and worthwhile to the extent that implementation offers benefits worth several multiples of the cost and turbulence caused by the changes involved.

• Implementers must be convinced of the applicability and importance of the technique. Without the perseverence of the Air Force Systems Command, standing firm for several years against strong opposition, C/SCSC would have fallen by the wayside.

• An effective program of education for the parties concerned is a "must," and this reflects the need for top management support. Initially there was a great lack of understanding of C/SCSC in both industry and the Defense Department. This was subsequently overcome only by a strong educational effort.

• Well-trained and well-organized practitioners are needed, preferably before they begin implementing the proposed technique. On-the-job training is too expensive in terms of mistakes and shattered confidence.

• There is a need to be flexible and adjust to practicalities in implementation (the early C/SCSC validation teams seem, in retrospect, to have been overly rigid), but to hold firm to principles involved.

Outlook

C/SCSC is required on all major defense programs, and is applied on a selective basis to others that fall below the "major" thresholds. The 35 criteria originally developed have remained intact and have met the test of time.

A major part of C/SCSC implementation has been accomplished and attention has been given to surveillance of approved systems by a Joint Surveillance Guide and instruction in this phase.

The area now receiving much-needed attention is use of data: how to analyze the cost performance report and other information (including technical performance information) for management action. All this is for the purpose of enabling the project manager to achieve his cost, schedule and performance objectives.

C/SCSC is no panacea. Good management and technical excellence are required as much as ever. But invariably, as managers realize its potential as a management tool, they find they have better visibility and control.

C/SCSC is going to be around for a long time, partly because it is so logical. But mainly, because it produces results.

$$\star \quad \star \quad \star \quad \star \quad \star$$

What is it that the Defense Department really expects from C/SCSC? Primarily I think we expect to gain confidence in a contractor's management system; to feel assured that we will not be blissfully under the impression that costs and schedule are going as planned only to be surprised and jolted late in the game by the revelation of huge overruns. More specifically, we look to C/SCSC to assure us and our contractors that the work to be accomplished is being properly planned and controlled in sufficient detail; that accomplishment is based on an objectively-determined earned value; that the system has disciplines which achieve proper baseline control; and that there is consistently accurate and objective reporting of progress data and estimates-to-complete.

We look for the system to provide the contractor and the government not only with valid data but also with adequate analysis of the data. This includes the cost impact of known problems; the identification of other problems not previously disclosed in the normal day-to-day contacts the tracing of significant problems to their source; analysis of their impact on the contract and the program; and the plan for solving the problems.

—Gen. John R. Guthrie, USA

39

Cost Performance Analysis*

General John R. Guthrie†

I welcome this opportunity to share with you some of my views (and those of DARCOM). I need not tell you that the whole area of cost measurement and control, specifically including cost performance analysis, presents great challenges and great opportunities to us who are working in support of our nation. *I'm convinced that one of the most important and useful of our approaches to better cost control has been the application of the DOD Cost/Schedule Control Systems Criteria (C/SCSC) which, as you know, is intended to assure the adequacy of contractor management control systems and the generation of valid data.* The analysis of that data is important because it is that analysis which permits our contractors and managers, whether from industry, from our arsenals, from our government-owned contractor-operated ammunition plants, or our project management offices, to make better management decisions and to exercise more effective cost control.

Background

In order for the Department of Defense to meet the Soviet challenge, we in the materiel business must design and manufacture capable equipment and get it to our forces in the field in the minimum time and at an affordable cost. Effective cooperation between government and industry has therefore never been more important than it is today.

*Extract from Keynote Address, Cost Performance Analysis Conference, March 6, 1978.
†Commanding General, U.S. Army Material Development and Readiness Command (DARCOM).

The Soviet Union today is engaged in a massive, all encompassing force modernization program. They are increasing the sophistication and performance of their equipment, while the quantity available and their production rates remain high. We no longer can be said to have qualitative superiority in any meaningful sense. Across the board, their equipment is as good as ours and they have a formidable edge in numbers.

The nature of the threat, therefore, demands that we capitalize on using our greatest asset, the superiority of our science and technology to modernize our forces in the most practical way. It is here that industry know-how can make its greatest contribution. But only if we keep costs under control.

As a nation, we are dedicated to an adequate defense posture. I'm gratified to read in the paper this morning that one of the recent polls indicates that we are becoming increasingly dedicated to that posture. But we are also dedicated to using our tax dollars effectively and efficiently. The President, the Secretary of Defense, the Secretaries of the Military Services, the Chiefs of Staff, and the Joint Logistics Commanders are all demanding that we spend money wisely and well. And I know that you and I, as taxpayers, support our efforts to assure that we receive the maximum benefit from each tax dollar. One of these efforts is in the area of cost performance measurement and analysis.

Early Experience

When I first reported to the Army Materiel Command (AMC) in 1958, we were, like everyone else at that time, experiencing numerous problems associated with schedule slippages and cost overruns. And there were, unfortunately, many too many "surprises." Reliable and timely cost performance information was hard to obtain and even when it was available, we really hadn't developed our skills sufficiently to make proper analyses of what we had.

After I became the Deputy Commander for Materiel Acquisition in 1971, General Miley, who was then commanding AMC, told me that the Air Force had an officer named Col. Driessnack (now Lt. Gen. H. H. Driessnack, Air Force Comptroller) aggressively pursuing a program called C/SCSC. I was instructed to find an Army officer who could do the same thing for the Army. So I found Len Marrella (Col. L. S. Marrella, now Project Manager, Army Gun Air Defense Systems) who is, I believe, the only individual who has obtained his Doctor's degree by writing his doctoral dissertation on this subject, and I tasked him with getting the Army moving on

C/SCSC. By that time we had begun applying the Criteria to our new large development and production contracts (except, of course, those that were firm-fixed price). We also began and have continued to apply the Criteria to some of our in-house operations, to some of our government-owned contractor-operated ammunition plants, and even to some of our laboratories. As a result of C/SCSC application on our contracts, we had good reason to believe that our contractors on these new programs would be using sound, effective cost and schedule control systems. We knew they would be able to generate and use valid cost and schedule performance data and would be able to provide this data, in summarized form, to our Project Managers by use of the Cost Performance Report.

Now, obtaining valid data is vitally important, but it serves us poorly if we cannot or do not use it effectively. *The great potential for better cost and schedule control is lost if the data is not analyzed and made to produce essential management information needed by the Project Manager and senior managers.* We recognized and acknowledged this as an area of weakness which had to be corrected.

O.K., so much for the background. Let me now move to the present. Where are we today?

I would like to say to you what I said to Project Managers in DARCOM at the first Project Managers' Conference we had after my return. I said my perception (and I underline perception, because it is purely that, not quantified and purely a subjective "gut" feeling) was that, after the first three or four months back in this DARCOM environment, there was much less emphasis on cost control within our organization than there had been four years ago when I had left. *So I have been trying to place increased emphasis at all levels on this subject,* and I'm hoping that my presence here today will help to cement that.

Controlling Our Acquisition Costs

How do we approach this business of controlling our acquisition costs? Well first we must recognize that some dollars are much easier to control than others. When we are buying commercial or low technology items we can predict our costs, use firm-fixed-price contracts, and have relatively little worry about surprises and overruns. But when we are pushing the state-of-the-art, or when the costs are not predictable, we assume part or all of the cost risk, and when we do, there is great potential for costs to run out of control.

So we need to know that our contractors are controlling costs; and we look to C/SCSC to assure us that the contractor has a management system which is capable of generating the data he needs for effective cost control. We then look to the effective analysis of the Cost Performance Report to give our managers the information they need in order to exercise cost control.

We are currently applying C/SCSC and obtaining Cost Performance Reports on more than twenty of the Army's largest acquisition contracts, including the XM-1 Tank, the Advanced Attack Helicopter, the Black Hawk Utility Tactical Transport Helicopter, the Patriot Surface-to-Air Missile System, and the Fighting Vehicle Systems (Infantry Vehicle and Cavalry Vehicle). Most of the programs which do not use C/SCSC and CPR are those which have firm-fixed price contracts, or which are composed of a number of relatively low-dollar-value contracts.

C/SCSC Benefits

While the benefits of C/SCSC are mainly intangible, they are real. The contractor with a C/SCSC-compliant system must methodically plan, budget, and schedule his work, and a disciplined system of tracking provides early visibility of cost and schedule variances. This in turn can permit prompt corrective actions, thus avoiding major problems later on. But there's really no way of knowing what those major problems would have been, nor what the resultant effect would have been, had we not had C/SCSC applied. So the dollars saved or costs avoided can't really be calculated.

Despite this, let me mention just a few specific instances where tangible benefits have been reported. One of the most dramatic is in the case of a large aerospace contractor who said a saving of more than $1 million in the first year cost of his development contract was achieved before the work had progressed very far. To meet C/SCSC, of course, the work had to be planned in advance. When the engineering manager reviewed his planning, he found that over $1 million worth of the planned design effort for the first year was unnecessary and could be deleted.

In a reversal of this situation, there's the experience of a helicopter contractor whose forward planning required by C/SCSC made him immediately aware that a subcontract for flight controls would cost well over a million dollars more than had been estimated in his proposal. With this early warning, corrective action could be taken early in the contract. There are in fact a considerable number of instances where the early planning to develop a cost baseline for a contract has provided prompt evidence that the contractor would be unable to meet his contract target cost, and the project manager was able to revise his fiscal planning accordingly.

Let me give you two other examples. In the Material area, there are also specific instances of savings. An automotive engine contractor, in laying out his C/SCSC-required material plans, discovered a duplication of items required. This was due in part to multiple material plans and lack of coordination between his departments. The procurement of duplicate items was eliminated at a saving of several hundred thousand dollars. Similarly, a large missile contractor informed us that as a result of the planning disciplines associated with C/SCSC, they discovered and cancelled an order for almost $2 million of unneeded heat shield material, which, due to short shelf life, would have had to be scrapped.

The same contractor told us that the material system's capability to measure usage, as required by C/SCSC, highlighted a relatively serious shortage in transistors for the autopilot. The alarm came early enough that a new set of priorities could be worked out with the vendor without incurring penalties. This prevented a schedule slippage on the autopilots and avoided about $500,000 of cost which would otherwise have been incurred for overtime, revision of internal planning, additional test equipment, and so on.

A clear indication of the net benefits of the C/SCSC approach is found in the steadily increasing number of contractors who use the C/SCSC disciplines where there is no C/SCSC requirement in the contract, e.g., on their work for commercial customers. We consider that this confirms the conclusion of an in-depth study done several years ago by Len Marrella, whom I previously mentioned. As far as I know, that is the only extensive definitive study which has been made. Its major finding was that C/SCSC was, on balance, cost-effective even in those early days when we and industry still had a lot to learn about how best to implement C/SCSC, and how best to use the Cost Performance Report and Cost Performance data as a powerful management tool.

C/SCSC Accomplishments

Over the years we've applied C/SCSC to over 100 Army contracts, and the Air Force and Navy implementations are equally impressive. By now it would seem that most of the major defense contractors have C/SCSC compliant management systems. Yet, new contracts go to new contractors often enough that the C/SCSC implementers in all three services are as busy or busier today than ever. So far the Army has accepted sixty management control systems after thorough review, and 43 more applications of C/SCSC on subsequent contracts at facilities with accepted systems.

Twenty-nine more are currently being worked on. The figures for the other services are also substantial.

Incidentally, I think it's appropriate to note that the 10th anniversary of C/SCSC came last December. It passed without the acknowledgement it probably deserved. That C/SCSC has survived and flourished is good evidence that it is an effective and practical way to assure good contract cost visibility while giving the contractor flexibility in managing his internal operations.

Cost Performance Analysis and Cost Growth

We cannot, however, rest on our laurels and be complacent. There's always the need and the opportunity to improve; and we have continued dialog with industry toward this end. New ideas need to be proposed, understood and questioned. Analysis methods and techniques which help one project office may be just what another project office has been seeking. As time goes on, various analytic approaches get refined and new ones are tried. We must keep abreast of the times.

In that connection, the Cost Performance Report (CPR) is of prime importance to project managers, but its usefulness doesn't end there. There is a high-level interest in the summarized data from the CPR. When our project managers give their formal briefing to me or my deputies, one segment addresses the CPR data (for those contractors who have C/SCSC compliant systems). Likewise the Department of the Army Program Report and the Selected Acquisition Reports contain a portion addressing the contractor cost and schedule performance as reported in the CPR.

From time to time, as you know, information appears in the press based on these Selected Acquisition Reports. Invariably, the press reports dramatic increases in the estimated cost at completion. I recognize that the greatest part of these increases in projected costs is usually due to inflation or to increases in the planned quantities, and not inefficiency. But I would caution that we be sure we not use those excuses as "cop-outs" for careful analysis of projected cost increases. It's too much to expect C/SCSC to eliminate these increases.

Actual cost control is through management decisions. C/SCSC and CPR are only useful management tools to provide information which may be used either poorly or wisely by the managers. When someone exclaims about the size of an overrun on a contract requiring C/SCSC, it is necessary to ask, "Isn't it probable that without this requirement, the cost and schedule variances would not yet have surfaced and that, therefore, the overruns and the end result might have been even larger?" In any event, the trend of overruns, as a percent of contract value, has been down in recent years as compared for example with 1972.

My deputy for Materiel Development, General Baer, gets CPR-based information every month, along with an independent analysis of the CPR focusing on the factors and reasons for cost and schedule variances, the actions taken and planned by the managers and, most important, the validity of the contractor and project manager estimates of cost at completion. The C/SCSC focal point in my Headquarters also uses this information for review of the SAR and the Department of the Army Program Report submissions. *So you can see that analysis is an important function at all levels from the contractor through the project manager, DARCOM Headquarters, Department of the Army, the Office of Secretary of Defense, and on across the river to Capitol Hill.*

Estimated Final Cost

All the contract status information on the CPR provides a basis for verifying the contractor's estimate of cost at completion, or for developing an independent estimate thereof. It is most important that you understand the various techniques and methods for developing estimates at completion (and also that you understand their limitations). *Early visibility of cost and schedule problems must result in the reassessment of the ultimate cost and timely changes to program budgets and fiscal plans.*

A few years ago, we had a couple of large helicopter programs, each showing a sizeable cumulative cost variance. In each case, the project manager briefing our Headquarters predicted his contract would be completed by his contractor at the contract target cost. When these predictions were challenged and examined, it was found they were based on undue optimism. The cost performance index required for the remaining work on both of these contracts was entirely unrealistic. Fortunately, it was not too late to take action. Each program was restructured and rebudgeted. It was as a result of these experiences that we initiated our monthly Headquarters review of CPR's focusing on the validity of the contractor and project manager estimates of final contract cost. Here, as everywhere, the dangers of looking through pink, rosy spectacles are always present.

Excessive Data

Another challenge is to seek and obtain from the contractors only that amount of information needed for effective management control. All too often we had placed burdensome and costly requirements for detailed data we have neither the ability nor the capability to use. Sometimes we prescribe work breakdown structures to lower levels than are justified. We must scrutinize these requirements carefully.

In years past, I'm told, it was all too common for project managers to have such large quantities of the most detailed data that it was simply not possible to use it at all. Our basic premise now is that when C/SCSC gives us assurance the contractor is using a good management control system, the Government Project Manager needs only summarized data. We must never forget how data multiplies as one goes to lower breakdown structure (WBS) levels. One contractor has shown us thirteen WBS elements at the third level exploding into ninety-nine at the fourth level. We must be careful not to prescribe the work breakdown structure to too low a level. We must obtain detailed data at those lower levels only in exceptional circumstances, as, for example, when a specific problem area has surfaced and is being tracked.

Cost/Schedule of Non-Major Contracts

While the C/SCSC and CPR's help us in the management of our major contracts, we now have a new tool to help us with our non-major contracts. This, of course, is the Cost/Schedule Status Report (C/SSR), which is essentially a tailored-down CPR. Many of our projects in the Army are made up of a multitude of comparatively small contracts instead of a few large ones. Nonetheless, the potential for overruns is always present and the need for valid cost data is, therefore, just as important. So analysis of the C/SSR takes its place alongside that of the CPR to enhance further our capability for effective control.

It's important to be concerned about the quality of the data on the C/SSR. Since a CPR results from a management system which meets C/SCSC, we can be reasonably sure about the validity of the data it contains. But C/SSR involves no C/SCSC validation. The contractor has greater flexibility in generating and reporting the data. If either he or the project manager simply assumes that the numbers on the C/SSR are valid, they could be badly misled into wrong conclusions and decisions and poor program management.

Before a contract including C/SSR is awarded, it is necessary to understand how the contractor proposes to develop the data for the report and to negotiate with him if his proposal is deemed inadequate. Then, following contract award, it's a good idea to visit the plant to gain familiarity with the development of the data, and to obtain assurance it is being developed as agreed to.

DARCOM has been working with the other military departments, and with OSD, DCAS, DCAA, and industry on the development of uniform, comprehensive C/SSR guidance. The Guide is called "Cost/Schedule Management of Non-Major Contracts." This document, together with the C/SCSC Joint Implementation Guide, will give our acquisition managers guidance across the entire spectrum of cost reimbursement and cost incentivized contracts.

Summary and Closing Remarks

As far as the Army is concerned, I assure you that I intend to assure that our project managers and other managers use cost and schedule performance data fully and effectively, and all of us here today must have the same objective clearly in mind.

This gathering of representatives from the military departments, defense agencies, and industry underlines the importance of cross-fertilization. We have all had our successes and we have all had our share of failures. We need to share our experiences and extract as much as we can from the "Lessons Learned," both the good and the bad. That is why this conference is important.

$$\star \quad \star \quad \star \quad \star \quad \star$$

We finish each bloody war with a feeling of acute revulsion against this savage form of human behavior. And yet on each occasion we confuse military preparedness with the causes of war and then drift almost deliberately into another catastrophe.

—*General of the Army George C. Marshall*

U.S. policymakers now know that the Soviet Union has devoted a greater effort to armaments than was previously thought and that it is a lot harder to estimate this effort accurately than was previously thought. This carries the further implication that the Soviet Union may have more and better weapons than the CIA has yet acknowledged.

—*"The CIA's Goof in Assessing the Soviets,"* Business Week, *Feb. 28, 1977, p. 103*

40

Cost/Schedule Control Systems Criteria: Practical Army-Industry Approach to Acquisition Management*

Major General George Sammet, Jr.

What is it that the Army really expects from C/SCSC? Primarily, we expect to gain confidence in a contractor's management system; to feel assured that we will not be under the impression that costs and schedule are going as planned—only to be surprised and jolted by the revelation of huge overruns.

More specifically we look to C/SCSC to assure us and our contractors that the work to be accomplished is being properly planned and controlled in sufficient detail; that accomplishment is based on an objectively determined earned value; that the system has disciplines which achieve proper baseline control; and that there is consistently accurate and objective reporting of progress data and estimates-to-complete.

The Army looks for the C/SCSC complaint management system to provide the contractor and the government not only with valid data but also with adequate analysis of the data. This includes the cost impact of known problems; the identifications of other problems not previously disclosed in the normal day-to-day contracts; the tracing of significant problems to their source; analysis of

*Army Research and Development News Magazine, November-December 1974, pp. 13–15.

their impact on the contract and the program; and the plan for solving the problems.

A basic and most important expectation is that the management system which meets C/SCSC is the one which is in fact used to manage the contract rather than an "eye wash" system imposed simply to meet a contractual requirement. In fact, an "eye wash" system cannot meet the requirement which says that "the contractor shall establish, maintain and *use . . .* systems meeting the criteria."

In the past, we in the Military Departments, along with our counterparts in industry, have been guilty of a number of sins, many of which can be grouped into the category of poor cost and schedule control. We were so caught up in pushing the frontiers of technology and the state-of-the-art, and in obtaining the last drop of added technical performance, that we neglected to focus adequately on the cost and schedule objectives and constraints.

You have all heard the horror stories about suddenly discovered overruns that surfaced too late to allow any alternatives beyond pouring in more funds. When we had to face reality, there was only one other alternative—cancel the program. That is what happened to the Cheyenne Helicopter and Main Battle Tank programs.

What led us down the wrong path? In addition to our technological myopia, many of our contractors were using rubber baselines, i.e., adjusting their plans to correspond more nearly with the actuals; working out today's problems with funds budgeted for future work; making subjective estimates of accomplishment; equating rate of expenditure with accomplishment; and using systems with lax reporting and no methodical variance analysis.

It became apparent that program managers who have a handle on where their programs are in terms of cost and schedule, who know the value of the work accomplished for the dollars spent, are able to manage their programs better—because they are aware sooner of cost problems and their impact.

The problem at the DARCOM level was to get all project managers into a position where they all have and use good, timely information, with emphasis on *use.*

When it was shown that C/SCSC and the associated Cost Performance Report (CPR) would have given us an objective status of projects at all times—that we would have had warning of pending cost and schedule difficulties and their magnitude, and that costs for C/SCSC and the related CPR are relatively low—it was decided to accelerate implementation of C/SCSC and to emphasize it with the project managers. Action was taken to:

• Develop a reporting system which would quickly provide HQ DARCOM with objective cost and schedule data based on C/SCSC, and with the Cost Performance Reports (CPR's) as the primary ingredients of the reporting system.

• Conduct a complete study of the numerous reports being submitted to HQ DARCOM to determine their utility—who uses them and what decisions are made based on them.

• Establish a control room in which all major programs are charted on viewgraphs each month. There are six basic charts displayed for each program.

A typical cost and schedule variance chart is shown in Figure 1. On this chart we have cost variance in dollars and schedule variance in both dollars and time. This is a simple chart—and it is no easy matter to keep it that way. C/SCSC proponents seem to want to show you everything on one chart; then it gets so busy it becomes part of the problem instead of a part of the solution. The point is, it is necessary to guard against a tendency to get too detailed in the display of data to management.

The chart (Figure 1) shows cost and schedule variance from a controlled baseline. That's important. Rubber baselines are not per-

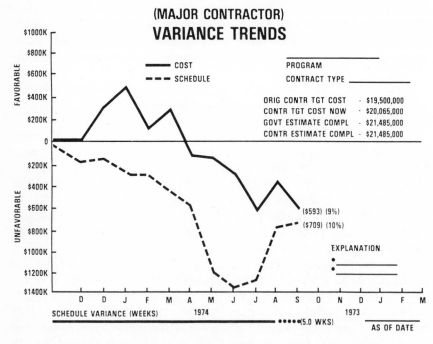

Figure 1

mitted. On the bottom it shows the C/SCSC schedule variance as a function of time—and it shows the variance in terms of percent of the total contract.

The next chart (Figure 2) shows the availability and application of contractor management reserve. It follows that if we are going to track cost and schedule variance, we need to know the status of the management reserve. We recognize that a straight line application of reserve over the length of the contract is not realistic. It does give us a point of reference and that is all it does.

The comparison of these two charts (cost and schedule variance, plus a track of management reserve) gives a good, quick picture of the dollar status of the contract.

That, however, is inadequate because it does not give us the whole story. Simply put, it does us no good to monitor cost and schedule in a vacuum. We must also track technical performance. What good is a piece of equipment brought in on schedule and within cost if it does not function properly?

Two charts are used to track technical performance. These differ with each program but a typical chart for a combat vehicle is shown in Figure 3. We merely list the bands of performance in the contract. In this case they are weight, speed, acceleration, and range.

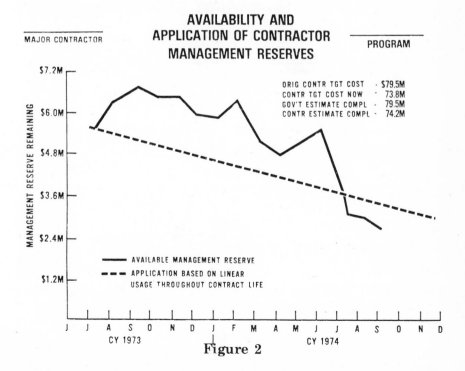

Figure 2

Performance below the horizontal line in each instance is unfavorable and is shown in red.

The other technical chart we watch is one on Reliability (Figure 4). This chart has some weaknesses but as of this moment we have not figured out a way to do it better.

We also track manpower loading because it can be an important indicator. Engineering Manpower is shown in Figure 5. We have a baseline (the original plan for manpower utilization), the manpower actually used, and a projected utilization. When we see a negative variance in engineer manpower, it is a clue to an existing or pending technical problem. If the projected line is still negative, it tells us we are not yet near a solution.

Another chart (Figure 6) on manpower is very similar. It reflects total manpower. We use it the same way and any variances in these are checked out closely—because variances not in Engineering could mean a problem in one of the other areas of direct labor, or else an overhead problem. Further, this type chart assures us that the manpower loading reflects peaks or valleys in activity—like testing or phasing down near the end of the contract.

This high-level reporting system based on C/SCSC has solved one major problem—how to keep on top of many programs on a

PERFORMANCE STATUS

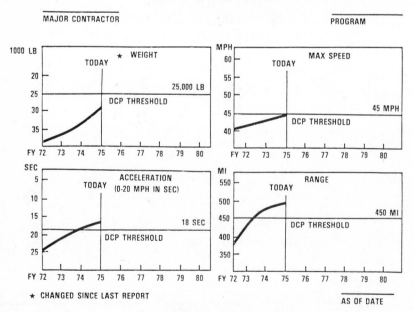

Figure 3

continuing basis. When negative variance red lines appear on the charts, emphasis is placed very quickly on those problem programs.

This approach has enabled us to bring to bear the old management principle—"that which the boss checks is also checked by everybody else." We now have a situation where the project managers check cost and schedule variances each month. In fact, it is really surprising how many similar systems based on the CPR have sprouted up in the project management offices.

In addition, this system provides us with enough data to enable us to eliminate many reports and reduce the number of formal program reviews. Some lessons learned in establishing this system were:

• The charts must be simple. You must remember that as you progress up the ladder of management, the manager's time becomes more important, almost critical, because of the greater scope of responsibility. No matter how good your management system is, no matter how good your analysis is, if you cannot get your message across quickly and clearly, your efforts are not productive. A graphic display is a simple, quick way of doing it.

• The CPR's must be analyzed and the data reduced quickly to graphic form to keep the information current. If this is not done, the

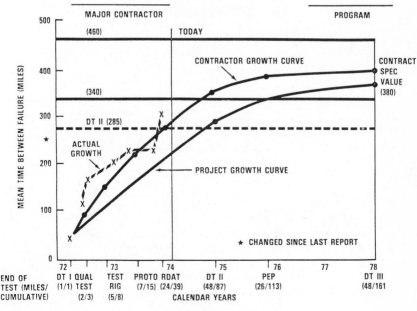

SYSTEM RELIABILITY GROWTH

Figure 4

information loses its impact because it is old, and it does not permit the manager to get a feel for the cost and schedule impact of technical problems which almost always surface before the CPR data is produced.

• The right people in the organization have to do the job. Analyzing CPR data, displaying it graphically, and having it briefed by people who understand it, is a job for experts. The people who do your analyzing must be trained in the theory and discipline of C/SCSC.

We expect to see a broadened application of the CPR type of reporting to cover the need for effective cost and schedule control of smaller contracts. The Cost/Schedule Status Report (C/SSR) (Figure 7) has been specifically designed to meet this need. It should provide a practical tool for tracking cost and schedule performance on those contracts above $2 million and over one year in duration, on which application of the CPR is not appropriate.

In other words, on most of our large contracts we will require C/SCSC and the CPR. There may be some where the CPR will be required, even though for some reason C/SCSC is not a requirement. The smaller ones will be candidates for the C/SSR.

Up to now we have expected our DARCOM managers to con-

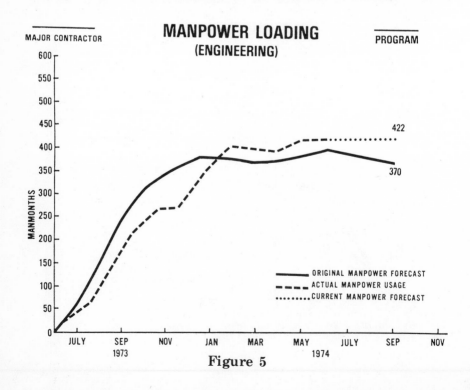

Figure 5

sider any contract if it is a cost-reimbursable type of contract, and on this type over $25 million is a sure thing.

What's new about C/SSR? It fills a gap, provides a "tailoring-down" of the CPR so that enough data can be obtained to manage a small contract without the "overkill" that would result from a CPR. In essence, it is simply the abbreviated first page of the CPR showing cost and schedule performance-to-date for summarized Work Breakdown Structure elements and the latest estimated-cost-at-completion compared to the budgeted cost-at-completion.

The data will be sufficient to allow the same tracking of cost and schedule variances that we now have using the CPR. However, the use of the C/SSR does not require that the contractor meet the C/SCSC requirements or use C/SCSC disciplines.

This obviates the need for the comprehensive C/SCSC reviews. But if C/SSR is to serve its purpose, there is a responsibility on the part of contractors to report conscientiously and candidly.

We are already in process of applying C/SSR to a project where it is badly needed. This project has a large number of rather small contracts—too small to make C/SCSC and CPR reasonable. We are expecting the C/SSR to give them a handle on cost and schedule status that up to now has been sadly lacking.

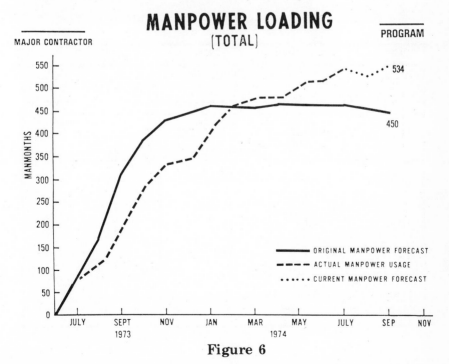

Figure 6

Although we are making progress, it seems appropriate to identify some of the areas requiring additional thought.

First, there is the question of overhead. We know that an awful
lot of the dollars go into overhead. Is it controlled? Is it controlled
well? Can it be measured? How? Getting a better handle on overhead can be a most profitable endeavor.

Second, design-to-cost is now to be reckoned with. Previously,
the objective was to control development cost. The purpose of
C/SCSC is to help keep development cost down but, with design-
to-cost ceilings, it may be desirable to increase the development
cost. Is C/SCSC then incompatible with design-to-cost? Can they
coexist? Of what use is C/SCSC in the design-to-cost environment?

Third, OK, you have implemented C/SCSC. You are getting a
lot of good valid data. You know the value of the work that is being
accomplished, and how it compares with the actual cost. Now what?
Are you getting full benefit from the data? How is it analyzed?
What techniques do you use to forecast what is ahead? Do you
derive useful information for better decision-making?

Fourth, can your management control system be improved?
It may meet all the C/SCSC requirements, but this does not
mean it cannot be improved. Have you overreacted to require-

COST/SCHEDULE STATUS REPORT

Contractor		Contract		Program		Report Period		
CONTRACT DATA								
Orig. Target Cost		Contract Changes ($)	Current Target Cost		Auth. Unpriced Work		Contr. Budg. Baseline	
PERFORMANCE DATA								
WORK BREAKDOWN STRUCTURE	CUMULATIVE TO DATE					AT COMPLETION		
	BUDGETED COST			VARIANCE				
	WORK SCHED	WORK PERF	ACTUAL COST	COST	SCHED	BUDGETED	LATEST ESTIMATE	VARIANCE
GEN & ADMIN								
UNDISTRIB. BUDG.	/////	/////	/////	/////	/////			/////
MGMT. RESERVE	/////	/////	/////	/////	/////		/////	
TOTAL								

Figure 7

ments? Are you doing more paperwork than necessary? Is there a better way?

Fifth, as a spin-off of this, are you able to show the "man who bends the iron," the bench engineer, how this discipline can help him? If you can convince this working engineer, our job will be considerably easier.

Sixth, we still struggle with the validity of the EAC (Estimated Cost at Completion). Is what we are getting valid? Are our contractors doing the type and caliber of planning that facilitates development of good EAC's? Are our tools for analyzing costs and projecting the EAC adequate?

The question, "Why is C/SCSC of benefit to the Army?" may be answered in summary as follows:

- It forces detailed forward planning—the breakdown of the work, the scheduling, and the establishment of time-phased budgets.
- It gives an accurate and objective status of where we stand on the contract performance. This is important. It does not produce a subjective estimate. Rather, it compares the actual cost of the work performed to what it should have cost to accomplish the amount of work; it compares the value of the work accomplished to the value of the work that should have been accomplished.
- It permits us to get a cost impact of known problems and their cumulative effect in cost and time.
- It provides a means of tracing problems to their source—the lower level hardware elements and organizational elements.

These are not all the benefits of C/SCSC, but they are the most important to me.

C/SCSC: This is the key to good financial management.

          —*Maj. Gen. Ben Bellis, F-15 SPD*

41

Techniques for a Multifaceted Discipline*

Don Earles

Life cycle costing is a costing discipline, a procurement technique, an acquisition consideration and a tradeoff tool.

As a costing discipline it is primarily concerned with operating and support (O&S) cost-estimating methods. As a procurement technique it is concerned with minimizing total life costs for component procurements. As an acquisition consideration its primary concerns are source selection and the balancing of acquisition and ownership costs. As a tradeoff tool its primary concerns are repair levels and the impact of specific design features on operating and support costs.

Customer/Contractor Interface

The customer defines the mission to be performed and its associated operational scenario. This definition is based on direct consideration of force plans, current programming and budgets, and existing indirect support burden. The customer also establishes acquisition logic—prototype, dual prototype and fly off—and the affordable "design to" unit production price.

Given mission requirements, the contractor determines required performance and synthesizes a system design. He formulates concepts for hardware mechanization and conducts producibility,

*Extract from *Defense Management Journal,* January 1976, pp. 38–47.

reliability, maintainability, and maintenance analyses. From these analyses, production units are priced, spares and repair parts are costed, and manning, training and associated tools, test equipment and data costs are estimated.

Estimating by Analogy

All cost estimating is done by analogy to known similar historical experience. The following estimating methods are used:

- Per unit catalog price or planning factor.
- Cost-to-cost estimating relationships.
- Non-cost-to-cost estimating relationships.
- Specific analogy.
- Expert opinion.

Per unit catalog price, planning factor and expert opinion costing are self-explanatory.

In "cost-to-cost" estimating, the desired item cost is estimated as a function of some other cost.

In "non-cost-to-cost" estimating, costs are estimated as a function of one or more non-cost parameters of the system, such as performance, weight, size or operating characteristics.

In specific analogy, costing estimates are made by analogy to some prior similar equipment or system. The new and the analogous systems are likened in terms of performance, design, manufacturing or operating characteristics.

Customers estimate primarily with cost-to-cost or non-cost-to-cost estimating relationships. Contractors estimate primarily by specific analogies. Both use catalog pricing, planning factors and expert opinion.

No Standard Models

Life cycle costing models have progressed along four lines— total cost models, logistic support models, design trade models and level of repair models. Each of these models uses as input some form of cost estimates arrived at by the above methods. Except for level of repair models (MIL-STD-1390), there are no standard life cycle costing models. Some models, like the Air Force logistic support cost model, have become relatively standard, but even that model exists in several versions and must be tailored for each new application.

Cost estimates should be structured to reflect cost accounting. This is a requirement for the cost estimates that support bid prices.

It should also apply to life cycle cost estimates. Since operating and support costs are funded by appropriation and budgeted by program activity, they should be estimated that way.

Logistic support cost models pertain only to the operational phase of life cycle costs. They generally operate at the line replaceable unit (LRU) level of equipment—the level of equipment that is removed and replaced to make an "on-line" or "on-equipment" repair. Each of the services has developed detailed logistic support cost models which are primarily used for comparisons of support costs for competing contractor designs. Many people refer to these models as life cycle cost models, which they are not, even though they are correctly used in life cycle costing.

Detailed equations have been developed for most of the cost elements. Those equations are dependent on knowledge of the system hardware mechanization concept. Design to cost, with its need for a preliminary producibility analysis, has made that knowledge now feasible early in the acquisition cycle.

Program Applications

Life cycle costing is done throughout the acquisition cycle. It starts with a conceptual phase baseline estimate which is validated by an independent cost estimate (ICE) either developed or approved by the Cost Analysis Improvement Group (CAIG) and submitted to the Defense Systems Acquisition Review Council (DSARC). The baseline estimate is updated for each DSARC review as is the independent cost estimate. By the second review, a design to cost goal is established. All cost estimating and accounting is done against a single Work Breakdown Structure (WBS). Incurred costs are monitored by Cost/Schedule Control Systems (C/SCS) that have been certified as meeting established government criteria. Data for the development of cost-estimating relationships are collected with Contractor Cost Data Reporting Systems (CCDRS). Both C/SCS criteria and the CCDRS apply only to development and investment costs. Specific requirements and criteria for operating and support cost monitoring and reporting have yet to be developed.

Costing Varies With Decision

Guidance for system level life cycle costing is contained in DOD Guide LCC-3 and CAIG cost-estimating criteria memorandums and cost development guides. LCC-3 recommends that models used for estimating life cycle costs be tailored to the decisions to be made.

It is possible that LCC estimates made by contractors for source selection competitions consider one set of factors while LCC estimates made by the Contracting Service for DSARC review consider another.

Source Selection

To compare contractor LCC estimates, the customer must provide the specific life cycle cost estimating models used. Only those costs that differ as a consequence of selecting a given bidder must be included. For instance, costs of direct operating and support cost personnel should probably be considered, whereas administrative and base support personnel costs might be the same regardless of contractor selected.

Life cycle cost estimates presented at the DSARC review must encompass all costs to be incurred by the government as a consequence of authorizing the development. Based on CAIG guidance, those costs include all organizations, intermediate and depot maintenance and supply operations, and personnel support including training, medical services and transfers. Base support such as billeting, messing, security, motor pools or communications may or may not be included, depending on the specific case. Command overhead, retired pay, family housing or DOD contingency funds are not included.

End Goal

Using definitions and models provided by the customer, it is entirely feasible to conduct a design competition which includes as a source selection factor the lowest life cycle cost. However, contractors can only be accountable for costs directly resulting from their designs. Total cost responsibility remains with the customer. The customer must design system requirements to meet affordable total life cycle costs. Contractors can then design hardware to meet the requirements of minimum acceptable performance, reliability and availability; the maximum acceptable unit production price, including installation if applicable; and the maximum acceptable direct operating and support costs, including warranties if applicable.

Section 8—

TECHNICAL PERFORMANCE MANAGEMENT

Introduction

Unlike time and cost, which can be measured in one dimension, technical performance is a multidimensional challenge. Trade-offs may be made not only between elements of performance, such as speed and range, but also between such characteristics as performance and reliability and maintainability.

Of increasing concern and attention is readiness or availability. The readiness of radar in a certain aircraft is about 60 percent, meaning, as the chief of the logistics command concerned points out, that almost two are required for every one that is operational. Here indeed is an expensive piece of hardware, expensive particularly in terms of skilled manpower required at the operational site.

The close interrelationship between cost and performance thus continues into operational use. And while it has often been said that cost equals or exceeds technical performance in importance as a program manager's goal, most of us have reservations about this statement. After all, if a PM gets his missile, for instance, to the launch platform on time and within his budget, but the missile then fails, how can he claim that he has in fact met his time and cost objectives?

The range of topics encompassed by technical performance management is indicated by the coverage of selections in this section: readiness versus performance, engineering management versus cost and schedule management, specifications and standards, designing to cost, software development, configuration management, reliability, logistics considerations, testing and producibility. And this is not all-inclusive. Risk assessment and technical performance *measurement* are not included, because literature on risk assessment is almost nil, and because no one dimension lends itself to technical performance measurement. The closest measure of technical achievement at this time is relating this factor to milestones, which is only an indirect evaluation.

Cost is an increasingly important design parameter, and sometimes technical problems surface through cost and schedule analysis. More often the reverse is true, however; technical performance problems are detected in normal daily contacts, and their relative importance and magnitude are reflected through cost and schedule reports. The article by Erickson and Wosina, "Designing to Cost On the XM 1," shows a great deal of insight into management of design-to-cost (DTC) as a program objective. For example, "The only real answer to the dilemma posed by the inevitable conflict between combat effectiveness and DTC (design to cost) depends on the depth of management commitment and on the technological creativity of the design team."

Systems software is also becoming recognized as a very expensive and elusive item of program management. Dr. Alvin Nashman discusses this topic in Chapter 46. But software management remains a black art. Dr. Ruth M. Davis, Deputy Under Secretary of Defense for Research and Advanced Technology, says this about software management:

> . . . software is the most unsafe, the least understood, and the most expensive component of total computer system costs. Software development costs are now almost 90 percent of total computer system costs. This percentage will probably increase along with the absolute costs of software, since software design, development, and testing [are] the most highly labor-intensive component[s] of computer system products. The really useful and exciting advances in computing probably will proceed only at the same pace as advances in software engineering. This is distressingly slow. . . . technological developments, especially in the past fifteen years, have dramatically reduced the cost of computer circuitry and increased hardware capability. A microprocessor costing about $20 today has the computing power of a large computer that cost $1 million twenty years ago. The cost of software has shown the opposite trend; it has risen continuously. The estimated cost of software development, testing and maintenance for the Federal government is $4 billion per year (1977). The government in 1977 owned about $25 billion worth of currently used software. . . . Overruns of 100 percent in both cost and the time to develop software have not been unusual occurrences. In fact, there have been cases of total failure to develop systems. . . . The cost of maintaining software is estimated to account for about 75 percent of software costs. Much of this expense is attributable to time spent in fixing up software that was not correctly developed in the first place. [From "Reducing Software Management Risks" by Dr. Ruth M. Davis, Deputy Under Secretary of Defense for Research and Advanced Technology, *Defense Systems Management Review,* Vol. 1, No. 6, Summer 1978, pp. 18–20.]

Related to software is the value of adequate testing, as discussed by Admiral Kollmorgen. But as brought out in the report of the Acquisition Cycle Task Force (Chapter 31), the analysis of test results could well be done in parallel in order to save time.

And, finally, Dr. John S. Foster, former Deputy Secretary of Defense for Research and Engineering, outlines major considerations in systems engineering, including a truth discovered during World War II when General Electric first systematized value engineering: "We must learn that the simpler and less expensive products are often the best products."

$$\star \quad \star \quad \star \quad \star \quad \star$$

Contemporary scientific-technological progress is marked by the fact that it is the chief cause for weapons and combat equipment becoming rapidly obsolete. Consequently, these weapons have to be replaced more rapidly.

—Marshal A. A. Grechko,
The Armed Forces of the Soviet State

Whatever the shortcomings of the Senior Soviet military planners, they are not backward in their approach to technological advance. Almost everything is to be sacrificed for better arms and equipment. The wretched state of their housing and the lack of comforts that are available in much poorer countries are testimony of their monomaniacal pursuit of the very best in military hardware.

—Hon. Edward A. Miller, Assistant Secretary
of the Army (Research and Development),
and Lt. Gen. Howard H. Cooksey,
DCS Research, Development and Acquisition

42

Balancing Readiness and Performance*

Admiral Frederick H. Michaelis†

In the continuing task of procuring weapon systems for the fleet, the Navy has recently developed a greater appreciation for a broadened spectrum of basic design parameters. Where once raw performance capability of a weapon system was of paramount importance, today a system's readiness on a 24-hour-a-day, 7-day-a-week basis throughout its life cycle must be carefully weighed and kept in balance with that performance. Consequently, trade-offs among performance, reliability, and maintainability are becoming a way of life. Because the Navy must cope with resource constraints, it is therefore imperative that reliability and maintainability be incorporated into the basic design effort.

To trade off performance for improved reliability and maintainability within a given dollar constraint requires careful use of modern analytical tools. Visibility must be given to the efficacy of dollars put into initial procurement costs as opposed to dollars put into operating costs. In considering a logistic support subsystem peculiar to a particular weapon system, the interfaces with the overall Navy logistic system must be explored. Moreover, costs generated in such areas as personnel, training, material, and transportation must be identified. While the necessary analytical and econometric tools exist today in such techniques as Design to Cost (DTC) and Life Cycle Cost (LCC), they need further refinement and a sufficient data base must be developed.

*Defense Management Journal, January 1977, p. 46.
†Chief of Naval Material.

The Navy uses cost analysis and control techniques to enable acquisition managers to incorporate DTC and LCC requirements into their programs. The latest revision to the *Joint Navy/Army/Air Force Design to Cost Guide, Life Cycle as a Design Parameter* is one example. Formal instruction in basic LCC techniques is also provided in the Navy Logistics Management School for program management personnel.

One current application of these techniques is implementation of early "phase cost control" on the F-18 aircraft program using incentives based upon LCC program constraints and reliability improvement warranties. The F-18 project office has instituted a formal LCC management program to track the airplane's performance and capitalize on every opportunity to reduce operations and support costs.

Even when the first-generation system hardware design can no longer be changed, it is necessary to continually improve reliability and readiness through refinement of maintenance and other support elements. Downstream cost visibility can be provided by collecting operating and support cost data with existing Navy data collection and processing systems. This important effort, called Visibility and Management of Support Costs, will provide data to aid in planning decisions, design improvements, selection of alternative logistic strategies, and projection of meaningful budgets.

By developing LCC estimates for various alternatives and effectively using cost visibility and control, the Navy now has the means as well as the will to increase the purchasing power of defense dollars and to maximize the Navy's principal goal: *combat readiness* to conduct prompt and sustained combat at sea in support of our national interests.

$$\star \quad \star \quad \star \quad \star \quad \star$$

In considering the path covered by the Soviet Armed Forces, one cannot help but be struck by the enormous changes which have taken place in their technical equipping. The selfless labor of the Soviet people and their creative thinking allowed the Armed Forces to take a giant step forward from the field three-incher to the intercontinental missile, from the towed machine gun to the powerful tank, from slow moving aircraft to supersonic aircraft, and from unsophisticated submarines to the atomic missile carriers—the genuine masters of the ocean depths and expanses.

—*Marshal A. A. Grechko,*
The Armed Forces of the Soviet State

43

Engineering Management*

6.1 *Relationship of Technical Program Planning to Cost and Schedule Planning. The technical program* planning function defines the detailed planning requirements. *It forms the basis for allocation of resources, scheduling of task elements, assignments of authority and responsibility, and the timely integration of all aspects of the technical program.* This planning function is carried out to the prescribed contractual levels and integrated with the cost and schedule control system criteria. The allocated resources become the budgeted cost. This relationship pertains both to initial program definition and to the redefinition which is a part of the decision and control process.

6.2 *Relationship of Technical Performance Measurement (TPM) to Cost and Schedule Performance Measurement.* The purpose of performance measurement is to: (1) provide visibility of actual vs. planned performance, (2) provide early detection or prediction of problems which require management attention, and (3) support assessment of the program impact of proposed change alternatives. TPM assesses the technical characteristics of the system and identifies problems through engineering analyses or tests which indicate performance being achieved for comparison with performance values allocated or specified in contractual documents. Cost/schedule performance measurement assesses the program effort from the point of view of the schedule of increments of work and the cost of accomplishing those increments. By comparing the planned value of work accomplished with both the planned value of work scheduled and the actual cost of work accomplished, problems may surface in the schedule and cost areas. *In addition to problems due to unrealistic cost and schedule planning, cost/schedule performance measurement may show up technical inadequacies, just as technical problems identified through TPM can surface*

*Extract from Military Standard 499A (USAF), May 1, 1974.

302

inadequacies in budget of time and dollars. Basically, however, *cost and schedule performance measurement assumes adequacy of design* to meet technical requirements of the system element under consideration; TPM is the complementary function to verify such adequacy. Further, by assessing design adequacy, TPM can deal with the work planned to complete major design and development milestones which need to be changed and thereby provide the basis for forecasting cost and schedule impacts. TPM assessment points should be planned to coincide with the planned completion of significant design and development tasks, or aggregation of tasks. This will facilitate the verification of the results achieved in the completed task in terms of its technical requirements. Thus, *TPM and cost/schedule performance measurement are complementary in serving the purpose of program performance measurement.*

$$\star \quad \star \quad \star \quad \star \quad \star$$

To be effective, cost-performance trade-offs must be made as early in the program as possible—preferably in the conceptual and demonstration and validation phases —before specifications are finalized, contractor statements of work are written, and full-scale engineering development initiated.

—TIG Brief 21, Nov. 4, 1977, p. 13

I have discussed project management with many project managers and prospective project managers during my tenure as Deputy Secretary of Defense. The project manager is responsible in a unique sense for all that goes on in the program which he manages. Many factors affect a project—some of which the manager has control over while others are beyond his control and require close coordination with others.

It is incumbent upon you as a project manager to run your project as you deem best and if decisions are made or resources not provided (either in manpower, contracts or finances) which preclude your carrying out your program as approved, then your responsibility is to bring this to light at the highest levels of the Defense Department. Similarly if problems occur in your project which in your opinion require my attention it is important that this be done at a time early enough for constructive help to be provided.

—W. P. Clements, Deputy Secretary of Defense

44

Tailoring Specifications and Standards to Today's Needs*

Lester Fox
Jeffrey S. Allan

What's wrong with military specifications and standards? Why have these documents been criticized over the years by the defense industry, program managers, and military users? Both Congress and the General Accounting Office have condemned specifications and standards as sources of poor performance, goldplating, excessive delays, and unnecessary costs. But is the real problem the documents and the way they are written, or is it the way they are used?

DSB Task Force

In July 1974, at the request of the Deputy Secretary of Defense, the Defense Science Board created a task force on specifications and standards to answer these specific questions. With representation from the Office of the Secretary of Defense, the three military departments, the Defense Logistics Agency, and industry, the task force had as its primary objective the development of recommendations for improving the origination, generation, maintenance, and application of specifications and standards.

The resulting study found that although some improvement in the substantive content of military and federal specifications and

*Extract from *Defense Management Journal,* October 1977, pp. 10–16.

standards was possible in all areas, the benefits derived from such improvement would not be as significant or achievable in the near term as those which could be achieved from an improved climate of application. Specifically, the task force determined that excessive costs arose when the specifications and standards imposed on a contract required change by contractors from their accustomed and proven methods of doing business; were given their most stringent interpretations; were too rigidly or prematurely applied in the acquisition cycle; were input-oriented rather than objective-oriented; were applied without limiting incorporation by reference to lower-tier documents called out in the top-level documents; or were used in a climate requiring excessive demonstration of compliance through prescribed procedural approaches. Misuses included misapplications, overapplication, underapplication, untimely application, and misinterpretation.

Unnecessary Requirements

Although the structure and layout of specifications and standards sometimes contributed to their misapplication, investigation revealed that the flexibility and levels of applicability written into specifications and standards were consistently ignored, resulting in inappropriate, excessive, and costly contract requirements. Specifications and standards were treated as if they were sacred. Contractors and government managers were found to be equally at fault, but for different reasons.

Government managers responsible for generating requirements took great pains to avoid the risk of failure, often going to extremes to preclude that risk; while contractors were constrained by the pressures of a highly competitive marketplace to comply indiscriminately with requirements even when those requirements were obsolete, redundant, or not cost-effective. In most cases, little analysis had been done to evaluate the costs of certain specifications as opposed to their benefits. The result was a tendency toward an overly conservative and unnecessarily expensive application of military specifications and standards.

Of the more than 40,000 documents catalogued in the DOD Index of Specifications and Standards covering both hardware and management subjects, the task force determined that nonhardware specifications and standards had the greatest potential for misuse. Typically, in addition to improving the potential for quality performance, specifications serve as a primer of good management practices for the inexperienced. Many of the military's management standardization documents, however, required contractors to develop a set of procedures (for quality control, reliability, or configuration management, for example) different from acceptable procedures already established within their organization.

Based on these findings, the task force recommended a twofold approach to improve the climate for applying specifications and standards. First, it advocated increased emphasis on tailoring requirements to specific system needs prior to contractual application. Specifications and standards reviews, for example, should be conducted by the government prior to issuing the request for proposals. During these reviews, attention should be focused on ensuring not only that all facets of the program are adequately addressed, but also that only the most appropriate documents are selected and only their essential requirements invoked. Contractors should be encouraged to propose cost-effective alternatives to government requirements. In concert with the design-to-cost philosophy, contractor flexibility should be promoted and encouraged.

The second recommendation was to strengthen top-level DOD management of specifications and standards. The task force concluded that closer management attention should be aimed at controlling the format, content, and proliferation of those specifications and standards that had the greatest potential for misuse. Improved feedback mechanisms should be developed to couple specification preparers with government and industry specification users. New specifications and standards should be structured to facilitate their tailoring.

Tailoring Philosophy

The concept of tailoring contractual requirements to satisfy system requirements is not new. It is basic, good management. At the outset of any new defense system development program, it is not practicable to define and describe all technical requirements down to the last detail which ultimately will be required for production of the system. The development of the definitive detail into the system specification is a progressive, evolutionary process which continues throughout the development and into the production phases of the program. At every major milestone in program development, reviews are conducted to ensure that all aspects of system requirements have been or will be adequately addressed. All military specifications and standards which enhance the success of the program are incorporated into the system specification and associated statement of work.

In the past, this evolutionary process focused on military specifications and standards as a whole unless major deficiencies were found within required standardization documents. The detailed challenge of individual requirements to detect redundant, unnecessary, or untimely demands contained within essential specifications is typically not addressed.

The current DOD emphasis on specifications and standards not only expands upon previous practices but focuses on specific, formalized tailoring and application. This involves four basic steps:

- Selecting those documents that may have application to a particular acquisition program.
- Identifying from these the ones that have specific application.
- Tailoring each document to include only the minimum necessary requirements in the solicitation or contract.
- Specifically tailoring these requirements to support the particular system during acquisition and life cycle ownership.

A degree of caution must be exercised in achieving the desired balance between performance and life cycle cost. While it is essential that specifications and standards be applied in a prudent and cost-effective manner, essential operational capability requirements must not be sacrificed.

The process described is particularly applicable in the selection and use of nonproduct specifications and standards in a given materiel acquisition program. On the other hand, product specifications such as those for parts, material, components, and equipments are not as susceptible to tailoring when selected for use in a materiel acquisition, since they have been developed around a specific set of design or performance characteristics. The process of tailoring the requirements contained in the product specification would normally be accomplished during the development and promulgation of the document, independent of a specific acquisition program. For that reason, the decision regarding the use of product specifications in materiel acquisitions is normally a matter of adopting it in full or rejecting it completely. This does not mean that product specifications cannot be tailored for use in a particular acquisition program; they can and should be when conditions warrant such action.

Improving Control

The investigation conducted by the Defense Science Board task force highlighted the need for closer management attention on controlling the format, content, proliferation, and application of nonproduct specifications and standards. The defense standardization program is commodity-oriented and defined by federal supply classes. The noncommodity-oriented standardization documents (those not fitting within specific FCSs) had been somewhat neglected, resulting in overlapping, repetitive documentation and voids. To correct this problem, the task force recommended that a comprehensive, top-level management program be initiated which would identify specific management standardization areas; integrate all ongoing projects in these areas together with their objectives, schedules, and required resources; and define future necessary projects and requirements for improving documentation control.

The task force developed an initial listing of nine DOD standardization areas needing immediate attention:

- General design requirement specification
- Environmental requirements and test methods
- Reliability and maintainability
- Quality control
- Human factors and safety
- Documentation
- Configuration control
- Integrated logistic support
- Packing, packaging, preservation, and transportation.

"The current DOD emphasis on specifications and standards not only expands upon previous practices but focuses on specific, formalized tailoring and application."

In December 1976, the Defense Materiel Specifications and Standards Office assigned to various lead-service activities the centralized management responsibility for developing DOD program plans to accomplish interservice standardization of appropriate documents. For each of the assigned areas, the lead-service activities are required to prepare, coordinate and provide DMSSO with a five-year standardization documentation program plan to:

- Identify existing military documents and related data item descriptions.
- Assess the status of these documents with respect to current military requirements and the state-of-the-art.
- Highlight voids in document requirements.
- Plan for deleting unnecessary requirements, eliminating duplication, and consolidating specifications, standards, and related documents.

- Restructure and develop specifications and standards for cost-effective application.

DMSSO also expanded the list of areas needing improved management attention. These included such nonproduct-oriented disciplines as nondestructive testing and inspection, thermal joining of metals, soldering, electromagnetic compatibility, and long-haul communications. A reliability standardization document program plan was approved by the Defense Materiel Specifications and Standards Board, and draft program plans were developed for nearly all of the remaining areas.

In conjunction with the emphasis placed on restructuring specifications and standards to make them more conducive to selective application and tailoring, the concept of sectionalization was introduced. In simplest terms, this promotes the construction of standardization documents to simplify the tailoring process by specifically grouping all mandatory requirements, specifically identifying optional requirements, ranges, variables, and the like, and structuring each requirement to be independent of any other requirement in the document. The purpose and objective of each separately structured requirement are defined together with a statement of how it should be utilized in acquisition programs. This sectionalization approach has been utilized successfully on such documents as MIL-STD-202, "Test Methods for Electronic and Electrical Component Parts," and MIL-STD-810, "Environmental Test Methods," and the expansion of the concept and its application to other standardization areas is being fostered.

Program Assessment

Results from major defense system reviews conducted by the DMSSO have been encouraging. Because of the DOD emphasis on specification tailoring and selective application, flexibility provisions were incorporated into the solicitation and contractual packages for major acquisition programs such as the Navy's Electronic Warfare Suite and the Army's Single Channel Ground and Airborne Radio Subsystem (SINCGARS) and Advanced Attack Helicopter programs.

Competing contractors for the EW suite and the AAH were provided with considerable design latitude during the development of their system specifications. In issuing the RFP for the prototype EW suite development contract, the Naval Electronics Systems Command clearly specified mandatory operational performance requirements. Many of the military specifications and standards cited in the statement of work, however, were provided to the contractors to be used as technical guidelines. In a similar vein, the AAH competing contractors were encouraged to submit waivers, deletions, and alternatives to specifications and standards cited in the government-prepared system specification which the contractor felt were cost-effective and appropriate.

The SINCGARS program extended the specifications and standards flexibility provisions to include contractual latitude in the submission of technical data. Offerors were requested to propose alternative data items, cross-referenced to stated requirements, with justification and cost estimates for the Army Electronics Command's evaluation.

Progress is clearly being made in improving the climate of specifications and standards application, tailoring and control. A comprehensive program has been initiated to control and coordinate requirements cited in management-oriented documents. The gulf between specification preparers and specification users is being narrowed. Flexibility, judgment, and contractual latitude have been introduced in the application of specifications, but there is still room for significant improvement. The leadership of managers at all levels is needed to educate and motivate both government and contractor personnel in the continued, cost-effective development and application of specifications and standards.

✳ ✳ ✳ ✳ ✳

The practice of blindly applying specifications and standards to their fullest extent is viewed as a conservative approach toward achieving program success or as an attempt to extract the remaining few percent of capability. This process accomplishes little if the result is a dollar inflated product beyond the reach of an already strained defense budget, even for a product possessing capability in excess of that required to accomplish mission objectives.

—*W. P. Clements, Deputy Secretary of Defense*

45

Designing to Cost on the XM1*

Robert P. Erickson
John W. Wosina

Most weapon system management innovations seem to go through three stages of evolution before they reach maturity, and Design to Cost has been no exception.

The first stage is a public relations effort, during which proponents of the innovation describe it in glowing but sometimes over-simplified terms, while the people who will have to implement it groan as they realize that one more unadjustable requirement is about to be added to their already ponderous burdens.

The second stage is a test for seriousness of intent, a period of "creative chaos" during which the over-simplifications of the first stage come into conflict with the real life dynamics of ongoing programs, and compromises are made on both sides.

The third and final stage (assuming the innovation has survived the second) is one of consolidation and regrouping. As the smoke of battle thins and the realization begins to grow that the programs are still alive and well despite the new innovation, program managers begin to compare notes and even to brag a little about how well the innovation works on their program.

Inconsistencies between programs are reviewed, and the rapidly maturing innovation is honed into a useful tool—sometimes exceeding the capability envisioned by its original innovators.

At Chrysler Defense Division, the *XM1 Main Battle Tank* Design to Cost effort has progressed to the third stage, and is not only alive

*Government Executive, May 1976, pp. 40–43.

and well, but is contributing significantly to program decision making. The intent of this article is to summarize its evolution on the XM1 Program in the hope that Chrysler's experience may assist in the achievement of a consistent industry-wide understanding of this important tool.

Management Approach

As a condition of the XM1 Prototype Validation Phase contract, a Design to Cost (average unit production cost) ceiling of $450,000 in fiscal year 1972 dollars was established for the defined quantities, rates and schedule for the production tanks. (The $450,000 DTC ceiling is the total DTC of $507,790 less government-furnished equipment and therefore is the contractor's manufacturing cost.) Other fixed values for XM1 included reliability, availability, maintainability and durability (RAM-D), weight, width, height and development schedules. Within these non-degradable values, combat performance had to be optimized to offer significant gains in effectiveness over existing tank systems.

In addition to these contractual constraints, Chrysler management imposed two others on its XM1 Task Force:

• Develop a Life Cycle Cost (LCC) model, reflecting Chrysler tank experience and including Army data, to avoid potential imbalance between DTC and the other costs of ownership.

• Identify and track any differences between the production configuration and the prototypes. This constraint, which required imposition of relatively tight configuration management controls, was considered essential to assure integrity of the DTC baseline.

Because of the tradeoff conflicts inherent in such contractual and self-imposed constraints, Chrysler imposed a formal system engineering management effort on its Validation Phase Program. This effort, particularly the disciplined correlation that was achieved between the budgets, schedules and technical targets for the tank's assemblies and components, proved invaluable in the Design to Cost approach.

Push Decisions Down

As part of its system engineering activity, Chrysler divided its Validation Phase into four sub-phases, each terminating in a full-scale program review to which the Army XM1 Program Management Office was invited to participate in an observer role. During the first sub-phase, Preliminary Design, much flexibility was permitted by the Chrysler Program Manager in order to allow the greatest exercise of technical ingenuity on the part of the design staff. During the second (Detailed Design) and third (Test and Evaluation) sub-phases, the relative flexibility rapidly diminished as the detailed design interfaces firmed up. During the fourth sub-phase (Delivery) the Validation Phase learning was applied to the deliverable vehicles, and to the next phase proposal.

The degree of flexibility permitted in each phase was controlled by the authorized reissuance of the system engineering design sheets, which were revised as required at each major program review and agreed to by the responsible subsystem design manager and the program manager.

The overriding purpose of Chrysler's system engineering program was to force technical decision making down to the level of the engineer responsible for meeting technical and cost requirements. This was accomplished, once the general conceptual approach was determined at the Program Management level, by allocating performance, RAM-D, and Design to Cost targets and interface boundaries to each design manager. These allocations formed the decision framework within which the engineering staff exercised its creativeness in adapting its individual technologies.

The most important benefits of DTC are realized only when the creative designer thinks in cost terms as he shapes his technology to the needs of the program. To help him think in these terms, a methodical dialogue was established between the designers and the production cost estimators. The subsystem design manager responsible for deciding upon the final configuration arbitrated between design and production personnel as alternatives were generated to reduce cost without degrading performance or RAM-D.

From these sessions evolved many truly creative solutions that quite often not only reduced cost but increased effectiveness.

The Program Planning and Control function within the XM1 Program organization was responsible for monitoring DTC estimates. As the design was released, its cost was estimated, fed back into the computerized tracking system, summarized and correlated with the target apportionments. Trends and projections of the accumulating data were also fed into the Technical Performance Measurement function of System Engineering and integrated into the continuing overall design evaluation.

The organizational responsibility for major tradeoffs, including the special considerations of DTC, was assigned to a Tradeoff Board headed by the program manager and staffed by the key personnel representing the various views in conflict. The Tradeoff Board was brought into play whenever the subsystem design manager could no longer meet his objectives within the agreed upon allocations. It also ensured the optimum use of DTC dollars that became available whenever design goals were satisfied below the agreed upon DTC allocations.

Solving Early Problems

Last, but by no means least, the integrity of the entire system of DTC responsibility and methodology could only be assured by an unmistakable commitment by the management not only of Chrysler but of its major subcontractors. This commitment was expressed not just in words but in the technical decisions that were ultimately forced by DTC.

Because of the immaturity of DTC at the beginning of the XM1 Validation Phase, the formula for converting—or deflating—current dollars back into fiscal year 1972 dollars was oversimplified and rudimentary, being based primarily on standard Bureau of Labor statistics. As this formula can exercise significant leverage on the ultimate acceptance of the XM1 production cost estimates, it was obvious that a more accurate representation of inflationary growth needed to be developed.

A new deflator model was evolved for XM1 and authorized by the Army Development and Readiness Command. This model is sensitive to indices that more closely reflect the economic fluctuations within the materials and labor categories involved in XM1. It is being reviewed jointly and periodically to assure the continuing accuracy of its relationship with the economy.

Other early problems arose that are no doubt typical of most programs, and adjustments were made in Chrysler's DTC approach to solve them. The main thrust of the government's DTC "education," for example, was directed mainly at the large prime contractors, and many of the subcontractors had only a hazy notion of its meaning and implications.

Chrysler found it necessary to meet with and obtain commitments to DTC from the top management of its major subcontractors, to provide seminars, and to send its specialists into the field to work with the subcontractors until a consistent understanding of the commitments involved was achieved. As a result of this effort, Chrysler's XM1 supplier team has contributed significantly to the achievement of XM1 DTC goals.

One early problem that plagued many other programs but fortunately did not show up on XM1 (because of the tight program discipline imposed by the Army Program Manager) was the traditional practice of allowing military and government personnel to involve themselves in contractor design decisions. While the experience of such personnel is an extremely valuable asset to a program such as XM1, it must—to be effective—be integrated into the requirements baseline provided to the contractor and not into his solution process.

While from time to time Chrysler did ask the Army Program Manager to provide "juries" of user personnel to provide independent evaluation of the design, no attempt was made to interject subjective "requirements" into a decision process extremely sensitive to DTC considerations.

One of the principal characteristics of the early stages in DTC maturity is overconfidence. Initial interrogations of the design staff and periodic review of status and trends invariably reveal that there are and will be no problems in meeting the DTC commitment. It is only when the bathtub is almost full that its inability to hold the remaining cupfuls of water becomes readily apparent.

As every program manager knows, the credibility of commitments is inversely proportional to the number of variables remaining that can be changed. As the XM1 configuration crystallized and the more precisely defined commitments were re-accumulated, the iron grip of DTC began to make itself felt.

When faced with a DTC growth problem there are three basic avenues of approach, and they were all exercised in Chrysler's XM1 effort. The first avenue was to more precisely reapportion the targets and management reserve. Obviously, some of the earlier estimates were better than others.

Unforeseen problems arose in some areas while other areas fell on or below target. The targets were reapportioned—but only after the system level Critical Design Review confirmed the need—and reiterated until the system was in balance with the commitments and a reasonable contingency reserve was protected.

The next avenue of approach (and these avenues were explored in parallel, not in series) was an intense producibility engineering effort in those areas of the system where cost could be saved without affecting function. An example of this kind of impact on design came from a producibility review of the roadwheel design.

The original design required a single forging for the hub. As this involved expensive machining operations, producibility engineers recommended a two-piece forging that could subsequently be welded together. The cost savings in this technique was substantial, with no reduction in effectiveness or durability.

The third avenue required a re-evaluation of the creative process itself. When all the "fat" had been rendered out of the target apportionments and the basic design configuration, the only apparent source of further DTC savings was the reduction in combat performance.

Some early DTC arguments encouraged a reduction of performance on the basis that the weapon system designer typically provided too much capability, and should instead emulate the commercial equipment designer who provided just enough performance to satisfy the market need. This approach is dangerous in that a small but critical increment of combat performance sacrificed for a lower DTC could cost many lives and seriously damage our defense capability.

The only real answer to the dilemma posed by the inevitable conflict between combat effectiveness and DTC depends on the depth of management commitment and on the technological creativity of the design team. One of the hopes cherished by the early proponents of DTC was that it would force not a mere cheapening of hardware solutions but a search for new technology.

Producibility and intensive cost reduction efforts, while important, can only exert their influence within the frame of reference established by the designer's technological creativity. The real leverage is in the creative process itself, and this was exemplified, in one of many instances, by Chrysler's approach to XM1's fire control needs.

The basic firepower system of a tank—its main gun and turret—was classically aimed through an independent optics system. Because of the severe environment created by the lurching and vibration of a moving tank, it was only possible to aim and fire with great accuracy when the tank was stationary—leaving it vulnerable to reciprocal attack.

In recent years, the fire control systems that were developed and used on advanced U.S. M60 tanks integrated the aiming system with the gun and turret, and provided a stabilization system that enabled the gunner to aim and hold the gun on target while the tank was moving.

The most sophisticated fire control technology that had been integrated into a tank prior to XM1, i.e., the XM803, involved the gyro-stabilization of the gunner's sight in two axes: vertical and horizontal, and the slaving of the gun's vertical movement (elevation) and the turret's horizontal movement (azimuth) to this line of sight. The gun and turret were slaved by servo mechanisms to the optical system so that, as the gunner trained the sight on the target, the gun and turret duplicated the sight's movements while compensating in both axes—as instructed by a ballistics computer—for factors such as different types of ammunition and relative movements between the tank and its target.

As can be imagined, the inclusion of such systems significantly affects the cost of a tank; and the XM1 requirements for day and night accuracies, requiring as they do the inclusion of such features as laser range-finding and passive thermal imaging, could logically be expected to make fire control the single most expensive subsystem within the tank.

As the contractor's share of the unit cost of the tank had to be held at $450,000, this meant that a "normal" development approach (i.e., involving more complexity and cost) to the fire control requirements could only be satisfied at the expense of other subsystems—for example, the engine and drive train—within the tank.

A tank with too sophisticated a fire control system and too "cheap" an engine might find its superb ability to hit on the move hampered by its frequent and lengthy visits to the engine repair shop.

Chrysler's approach, based on its experience with stabilized M60 fire control systems, was to requestion the validity of many of the assumptions that tended to drive tank fire control systems toward extreme sophistication. Analysis showed, for example, that —because most of a tank's response to cross-country motion results in pitching movements directly impacting on gun elevation—the contribution of vertical (elevation) axis stabilization to accuracy was three times greater than the contribution made by horizontal axis stabilization.

Integration of both stabilization modes into a dual axis sight stabilization system, however, drove the costs far beyond what was considered reasonable for the benefits obtained. Chrysler therefore rejected the dual axis sight stabilization system and provided separate systems for gun/sight stabilization in elevation and turret stabilization in azimuth.

Design to Cost

The performance degradation suffered by this approach is negligible—and yet a substantial unit cost savings per tank is realized. Even with this savings, the Chrysler fire control system more than meets the Army's requirements for accuracy.

A further example of the innovative technology used to lower fire control DTC is Chrysler's choice of a digital ballistics computer. The digital computer outperforms the analog in the current specified application, provides far more flexibility and growth, includes a built-in automatic fault diagnostic capability, and yet is considerably below the cost of a competitive analog computer.

In addition to these fire control activities, the entire torsion bar suspension subsystem was redesigned, for DTC reasons, three times during the Validation Phase. It achieved its DTC target with a performance that more than satisfied the requirements, and throughout thousands of miles of severe testing experienced not a single torsion bar failure.

DTC, however, did not dominate every technical decision. Because of Chrysler's conviction that a proper balance must be maintained between DTC and Life Cycle Cost, it accepted an increase in engine DTC allocation because of the more than $150 million in Life Cycle Cost savings generated by the choice of a turbine engine.

Having gone through the vicissitudes normal to a new concept, DTC on the Chrysler XM1 has come through with flying colors. It has matured into a more effective discipline than was perhaps originally envisioned, and its impact has probably done more to shape the design economics of the XM1 than two years of "normal" development. It has evolved from a relatively simplistic and isolated production cost target to a much more credible number representing the best economic tradeoff between the costs of acquisition and the costs of operation and maintenance.

And within a total cost context more precisely defined and controlled than ever before, the Chrysler XM1 production design reflects a technological creativity that not only meets the Army's DTC target, but provides the performance desired by the Army to maintain a significant edge in the larger competitive arena of combat, where the worth of all weapon systems must ultimately be proven.

$$\ast \quad \ast \quad \ast \quad \ast \quad \ast$$

The Project Manager is . . . responsible for: achieving the technical performance objectives of the project . . . on schedule and at the lowest practicable cost, and maintaining a continuing and strong emphasis on the design-to-cost approach to hold down costs . . . [and for] assuring that planning is accomplished and that, except as otherwise directed, the execution of the project conforms to the plan. . . .

—*XM 1 Tank System*
Project Manager Charter

46

Software Development
Management*

Dr. Alvin E. Nashman†

The software industry is currently experiencing a very dynamic phase in its precipitous growth. Industry and government have begun to obtain a grasp of the software development problem and have made great strides in one of our most publicized contemporary problem areas—software reliability. It therefore seems appropriate, in light of current client interests, to examine in some detail in this paper the basic software development problem, current approaches to its solution and the manner in which these approaches relate to the ongoing central problem of staying within cost and schedule. It is not news that the software industry is under criticism for its frequently spectacular inability to provide effective and reliable software within a reasonable cost-envelope and time frame. Examples of major software systems, both military and civilian, which have not been able to perform to their advertised specifications, are all too numerous. In many of these cases, the dispute over the adequacy of systems performance had to be resolved through litigation, and in most instances, the supplier appears to be responsible.

*Extract from *Signal,* the official journal of the Armed Forces Communications and Electronics Association, February 1975, pp. 26–33.
†Vice President, Systems Group, Computer Sciences Corporation.

Essential Criteria

A client recently summed up the situation by saying that very few, if any, completed major software developments have met four recognized criteria for success. These criteria are:

- Preliminary cost estimates must be accurate within reasonable bounds.
- Production schedules must be met.
- The operational requirements and design performance criteria must be achieved.
- The product must be reasonably error-free and fundamentally dependable when installed in an operational environment.

The net effect of this indictment is a loss of confidence in software systems as highlighted in a recent statement made by Lieutenant General Lee M. Paschall, currently Director, Defense Communications Agency. With respect to automation, he stated, "Before a man can be put in a largely monitoring role, we need to build up far greater confidence in our software." Further, General Paschall indicated in strong terms that he believed that software is overly expensive, cumbersome, inflexible, and too full of errors in critical paths.

The importance of the problem is reflected in the size of the industry. The computer industry is currently about the eighth largest in the United States with sales running between 20 and 25 billion dollars annually. By 1990, the industry is expected to be the third largest with sales correspondingly higher. Of more than passing interest to the software industry is the ratio of software to hardware costs—currently averaging about three to one. For example, a recent Worldwide Military Command and Communication System (WWMCCS) buy had software and hardware costs of $800 and $300 million, respectively, near the 3:1 ratio. Rapid technological advances in computer hardware, with resultant decreases in cost and concomitant increases in computing power, have resulted in an overwhelming demand for automation. However, these rapid advances have not, until recently, been accompanied by a software implementation methodology which guides the total development in an orderly manner. We have used, and many are continuing to use, first-generation software development methodologies to program fourth-generation equipment.

The foregoing can be summarized: a problem exists; the stakes are high; the hour is late. Fortunately, we are not starting without precedent or dealing from ignorance. As alluded to in the opening paragraph, many advances have been made in the assurance and insurance of system quality.

Five Phases

Consider for a moment this approach to our critical problem: The life cycle of operational software can be divided into five major phases: concept, definition, development, evaluation, operation. Of these, development and evaluation are usually the major responsibility of the supplier with the client participating in the final verification and validation testing of the product. Various rules of thumb, backed by some historical data, indicate that the development phase, consisting of analysis, design and code, requires approximately 60 percent of the resource allocation (analysis and design 40 percent, code 20 percent) and that the evaluation (installation, integration and test) phase accounts for the remaining 40 percent. Typically, system development status is, at best, qualitative up to the point where the evaluation phase begins. As the integration and test proceeds from module through subsystem to system, the cost in manhours per program bug detected increases at an exponential rate. Given that approximately 60 percent of the resources are expended before any real qualitative measure of development status is attainable and that the costs of detecting errors increases exponentially, a methodology to reduce both the uncertainty and debug time is essential to a successful system development.

This reasoning has prompted industry to develop more effective coding techniques such as "top-down" and "structured" programming to reduce the number of errors in the code. Automatic debugging aids and structured test methods have been developed which both reduce the debug time and increase the level of confidence in the finished product. Government, on the other hand, has sponsored research in areas aimed at developing automatic verification and validation testing-methodologies to aid in the acceptance of the finished product. Out of these efforts has come the current concept of software reliability: how to develop, test for, and insure reliable software products. There is little doubt that the advent of this concept has served to increase our confidence in software products.

Let us assume, for the moment, that error-free code can be developed and that the added cost of this effort can be established. What have we gained with respect to our previously stated indictment encompassing industry's failure to meet the four basic criteria for success? Consider these criteria separately.

Preliminary Cost Estimates Must Be Accurate Within Reasonable Bounds. Even with the cost of reliability established, we have only solidified the 20 percent resource allocated to coding and somewhat reduced the uncertainty of the evaluation phase. There still remains the baseline cost and uncertainty associated with the analysis and design phase (40 percent) and the uncertainty of meeting operational requirements (Criterion 3).

Production Schedules Must Be Met. Again, we have addressed only 20 percent of the problem directly. The problem of establishing a quantitative measure of system status still evades us and much of the uncertainty surrounding the production schedules still remains.

Operational Requirements and Design Performance Criteria Must Be Achieved. Great strides have been made here with the advent of verification and validation testing. A much greater confidence in any system's ability to meet its basic specification is acquired. There does exist the problem, however, that the specifications may not properly reflect the system requirements and hence the system does not perform its intended function adequately. Whether because of ambiguous or inadequate specifications, such a problem seriously impacts system cost due to the pervasiveness of error propagation and the discovery of causative factors late in the development schedule.

The Product Must Be Reasonably Error-Free and Fundamentally Dependable. This criterion is addressed completely if we properly define error-free software. There are basically three types of software errors: (1) design error, (2) coding error, and (3) implementation error. While most software development techniques address the latter two, and even if the means are provided that minimize the occurrence of all three types, the responsiveness of error-conscious development and testing to our four criteria can be discerned to be incomplete. While the development of error-free software does address two of the four criteria, it has not been established that cost and schedule can be either estimated or controlled. Thus, we must conclude that while our efforts have served to increase the level of confidence in the software product, we have failed to adequately address the central problem of escalating costs.

To illustrate this further, consider a simple alternate form of system integration. Suppose that rather than postponing integration testing until code completion, a development scheme could be utilized which spreads the integration over a greater portion of the time schedule. The development/integration cycle would be formulated so that the most critical modules are developed, integrated, and tested first. Other modules would be integrated as they were developed, each being driven by a previously integrated module. Such an approach would permit thorough regression testing on the completed modules, give an early quantitative measure of system status and allow ample time for debugging. This is simply an example of system modulatization which is a fast growing approach to reliable programming and cost control for large systems. It provides customer visibility and increases confidence through the employment of the principle of "Build a Little, Test a Little." Could it be that this approach would be more cost effective than an imposed reliability program?

The point is that we have not exhausted the possibilities of developing quality software within the cost-schedule envelope. It is our contention that the combined efforts of government and industry will ultimately provide improved solutions to the problem outlined above. While our current efforts have been of tremendous value to the software community, the need to provide a means of attacking the problem in toto is an imperative requirement.

While we do not claim to have the final solution to this problem, we propose to postulate in this article several items which strengthen the software acquisition process. Regarding the five major phases of software life cycle, specifications are the only link between the concept and definition phases. We believe stronger specifications must be developed in order to insure successful results.

It is also apparent that a more structured software design concept is required to strengthen the transitional step from definition to development. We believe a unified methodology must be implemented which is effective both in terms of design-to-cost and reliability. Any acceptable methodology must also be compatible with existing efforts in this important area.

The four postulates that follow are not intended to be exhaustive by any means, but represent, in our opinion, areas of endeavor which could unite our efforts toward the solutions we seek relating to the cost and quality of software systems.

The Specifications Document Is Key to Effective Software Development. This postulate, almost trite, has nevertheless gone nearly unnoticed since very little attention has been devoted to it by the software community. Its importance in software reliability has been pointed out by Meeker and Ramamoorthy[1] who indicate that current vague definitions and measures of software reliability are due, in part, to the amorphous nature of the germane specifications. Meeker and Ramamoorthy also believe that future programs could be designed for completely-reliable operation if the specifications would for-

---

[1]Meeker, R. E., Jr., and Ramamoorthy, C. V., *A Study in Software Reliability and Evaluation*, TM No. 39, University of Texas-Austin, Texas, February 1973.

mally define the intent of the program. In their opinion, definitive specifications are fundamental to the evaluation process in that they become the "yardstick" of the test procedures.

Buckley,[2] in a recent report from the field, points out that many problems encountered in the TACFIRE system development could have been avoided had a complete, unambiguous set of specifications been available. The opinions of Meeker, Ramamoorthy and Buckley underscore the importance of the specifications document. This should be evident to all if it is realized that the specification document represents the only real interface between client and developer. Without a genuine basis from which to work, there is little that the client or developer can do to insure a common understanding of the system to be developed.

Finally, it is particularly noteworthy that all specifications represent an authoritative interpretation of system requirements, and, typically, offer a final opportunity to the developer to insure performance prior to acceptance of a completed system. For this reason, Meeker and Ramamoorthy recommend that the first step in any software development should be a verification of the supporting system specifications. We concur, and suggest that this is the appropriate point to find discrepancies, identify conflicts, and insure traceability through each level of the specification documents.

A verified specification document can become a baseline upon which the client, supplier, and ultimate user can confidently place their trust. The user, in that he knows what he is getting; the client, in that his final acceptance test has foundation; and the supplier, in that he knows his developed product will not contain a myriad of uncontrollable errors due to ambiguous or contradictory specifications.

Granted a premise that a specification verification methodology can be developed, the essential question then becomes one of implementation at critical points in the software product life cycle. The optimum situation would exist if completed specifications could be verified before contract award. Failing the attainment of this Utopia, it seems patently obvious that each level of specification should be verified (to both client and developer satisfaction) before any lower level documents are generated.

The Software Design Should Be a Traceable Representation of the Specifications. Just as the software specifications, properly verified, represent an interpretation of the system requirements, the software design should be an interpretation of the system specifications. The reasons for this are obvious from the standpoint of traceability, but, perhaps

[2]Buckley, Ltc. F. J., "Software Testing—A Report From the Field," Proceedings IEEE Symposium on Computer Software Reliability, 1973.

more importantly, the initial software design becomes the common language with which all the participants, clients and supplier alike, must converse. Why not then adopt, at the outset, a methodology of design whereby each understands the intent (traceability) and organization (configuration) of the software design? Such an approach simultaneously provides the basis for configuration, cost and schedule control, documentation, verification and validation testing, and perhaps, more importantly, management visibility. Buckley pointed out the need for visibility on the TACFIRE program and in his concluding remarks states, "The moral is, that continuous vigilance is the price of a good product. The customer (client) must, at the very beginning of a contract, obtain visibility into the contractor's efforts." Such a comment in itself should suffice to encourage the adoption of a unified development concept that bridges the gap between specification and finished code. Two of the other attributes of this methodology provide additional incentives. Configuration control and documentation have historically been an anathema to the software developer. Much of the busy work and drudgery involved in these areas could be circumvented by adopting a concept such as suggested here. Many software developers already implement portions of the suggestions contained in this paper. What remains to be done is the formalization, adoption and control of these diverse procedures.

An approach to this problem has been successfully developed and applied by CSC to a large weapons system development with conspicuous success. The process, called THREADS,[3] represents the system as a set of functional paths, is a reference unit for configuration management and performance measurement, is traceable to the specifications, is the common language between client and supplier, and provides any required level of visibility into the development process. THREADS solves the problem of communication and coordination of the elements of a development effort by tying them together through a common approach and discipline.

THREADS includes as its basic element a complete functional path through the system at the level under consideration. Therefore, the integration of a basic element means that an operational requirement has been integrated—a discrete quantitative measure of system status (a demonstrable satisfaction of a client requirement). For example, whenever 80 percent of these basic elements are integrated, the system is 80 percent complete without any qualitative measure, such as lines of code, being invoked. In addition, the early

---

[3]Computer Sciences Corporation, *A User's Guide to the THREADS Management System,* Moorestown, New Jersey, March 1974. THREADS descriptive documentation has been copyrighted by CSC.

integration of critical elements provides for a thorough regression testing of these elements, contributing significantly to system reliability. Indeed, we build a little, and test a little.

A Unified Software Development Methodology Is Compatible With Contemporary Reliability Enhancement Efforts. As pointed out earlier, the postulates presented herein do not represent a recommendation to change direction, but are merely an organization of our current efforts toward the common goal. Postulate I concerns the first two phases of the life cycle (concept and definition), Postulate II, parts of the second and third (definition and development), and Postulate III with parts of the third and fourth (development and evaluation). The adoption of Postulate II does not constrain coding or testing techniques in any way. For example, structured programming could begin with the functional interpretation described above and proceed as suggested by Dijkstra[4] and others. Proof of program correctness, structured test development, or other verification and validation aids fit well within the framework suggested and, since the framework is traceable to the specifications, actually enhances their capability. In fact, it is the basic simplicity of the methodology, complemented by any of the recent developments, that makes it so powerful. It would seem we can have our cake and eat it too: by employing the management controls so necessary to cost effective software development, we will simultaneously provide for the development of reliable software.

A Unified Software Development Methodology Is Compatible With Future Requirements. It may seem premature to look to the future while we are locked in contemporary problems, but if we had possessed more prescience ten years ago, our problems concerning the development of quality software might be less significant. Concerning the future, Dr. Malcolm R. Currie, Director of Defense Research and Engineering, recently said, "Design-to-cost must be evolved as a fundamental and flexible approach to our programs—it can be a central management tool and communication channel between the Defense Department and industry." Based on current emphasis toward automation and the increasing ratio of software to hardware cost, it seems inevitable that design-to-cost is the wave of the future.

Change impact assessment has become an integral part of most large system developments. Changes in budgets, requirements and schedules are an everyday occurrence. The need to respond quickly and accurately to changes is not unlike "designing-to-cost" where the supplier is asked to offer the best system that he can under constraints of schedule and cost. We recently encountered such a

[4]Dijkstra, E. W., Notes On Structured Programming, T. H. Report 70-WSK-03, Second Edition, April 1970.

situation on the weapons system development mentioned previously. Due to schedule changes, we were asked to reconfigure a significant part of the system. Furthermore, the particular functions comprising that delay were suggested to us. We made an analysis of the proposed delayed-functions using our THREADS data base. We discovered that delaying these particular functions resulted in considerably less real savings than had been assumed by the client. We then made a second analysis of the system, this time to identify exactly which functions should be delayed in order to accomplish the desired system cost savings. Effectively, we were designing-to-cost. Using our automated THREADS system we were able to completely reconfigure this major real-time system in three days with virtually no deviation from the schedule.

In each area of activity in which the software community is engaged, we should not lose sight of the overall problem of restraining the escalating cost of software products. It would be completely ineffective to have the capability to develop error-free software if the costs incurred are prohibitive. In addressing the past failures of the software community, it is apparent that inadequate specifications are the weak links in the chain and that verification of these basic elements of the system is essential. Finally, we believe the computer community should adopt a unified development methodology that is compatible with both basic management and current efforts to develop reliable software, and that provides visibility and traceability.

It is, therefore, critical to the various roles of the software community in the defense development arena, that we strive to develop cost effective, reliable management techniques. Whether our concern be with the development of complete and consistent high level system specifications or with the development of a reliable element of software, equivalent attention to solving problems inherent in project management is essential. It is imperative that we in the computer community work together to solve the historical problems of large-scale system development cost overruns while continuing to develop effective state-of-the-art systems.

47

Configuration Management: Creative Catalyst?*

Chester P. Buckland

Configuration management has the dubious distinction of being the number one damper of ambition in talented youth. In both industry and government, an assignment to that field may be greeted with all the enthusiasm of exile to Siberia.

Come to think of it, perhaps such assignments are a good way to identify young men who *are* talented and ambitious. If, after a few months of configuration management, they seem restless and dissatisfied, top management in both government and industry may have some budding executives on its payroll. They may be cut out for something more challenging to creative spirit.

Consider for a moment. Configuration management does not visibly create anything except paperwork: it merely provides a decision framework. By a set of baselines, established at prescribed times, it tells creative people that decisions have been made. A set of rigid controls prescribe that creative engineers may decide to create something different, only when the baseline decision has been formally changed. Finally, an encyclopedic set of records must be maintained showing that carefully deliberated decisions have been rigorously followed. The entire process, from conception to deployment, is meticulously documented. As a bold new project reaches fulfillment, the configuration specialist may feel that he has contributed nothing but the inevitable mountain of paper. Surely, promotions won't spring from that!

*Defense Industry Bulletin, Winter 1971, pp. 1–3.

But let's take another look. Suppose there were no configuration management. Suppose automobile manufacturers maintained no parts lists by yearly models and body styles. Suppose this were also true of refrigerators, washing machines and televisions. One of two things would happen. Either there would be no yearly models, or design changes would make routine repairs prohibitively expensive. The economics of mass production would maintain a collision course with advancing technology. Catastrophe is averted by implementing documented design decisions which permit mass production and technical progress to occur simultaneously. Manufacturers' parts lists are mute, but tangible, witnesses to an industrial matrimony at which configuration managers performed the rites.

Viewed in this light, configuration management emerges as a catalyst which amalgamates mass production and engineering advances. These partners are the very heart and soul of our "affluent society." But, like all catalysts, configuration management leaves no trace in the finished product. Its achievements reside in such prosaic documents as grease-smudged parts lists, dusty specifications, and faded blueprints. These unsung monuments proclaim many hours of soul searching deliberations whereby key decisions were announced.

Hence, these are the frustrations of talented and creative young minds who toiled through the catalytic process. Their sense of unfulfillment is in some sort of direct proportion to the sophistication of an end product. When a space vehicle is successfully launched, and performs some incredible mission, the headlines lavish praise on the scientists, the engineers, and the production wizards responsible. The configuration managers are only acknowledged, if at all, in some omnibus phrase as "the humble rank and file who labored incessantly to make this feat a success."

"Big Deal!" thinks the talented youth and lays plans for a changed assignment. The program manager's problems are thereby compounded by questions of human motivation.

As spectacular new systems become operational, the front page headlines disappear. Occasional press releases may refer to "tactical successes." They never mention the engineering change decisions that were required to make those successes possible. Specialized journals, which the public never sees, may contain glowing accounts of "operational readiness rates," "reliability," or better-than-expected "life-cycle costs." There is never a mention of the continued catalytic action which is indispensable, and inseparable, from these logistic phenomena. Dispatches from the front are never written by configuration managers.

Decision-Making Role

So, what does all this mean; and why is this article being written? It is being written to suggest possible ways to raise configuration management above the status of anonymous drudgery. One method is implicit in what has already been said. It should be relatively easy to dramatize the decision-making role that configuration managers play to allow mass production and technical progress to co-exist. But first we must set the stage.

Automobile manufacturers bring out yearly models for several reasons. First, the practice helps to maintain a high sales volume by appealing to a widespread desire to own the latest model. Second, in many cases a year's production roughly matches the useful life of a set of production tools, the foundation of mass production. Since tooling must be replaced, new styles are economically justified to satisfy the demand for distinction. Finally, the tooling life cycle is the logical time to incorporate new and improved designs, including technical advances.

Yearly models do not involve all parts of a car. Except for body styles, a major portion may remain unchanged for many years. Internal mechanical improvements may wait upon the exigencies of competition or public clamor. Heavy costs of new tool designs are thus avoided where they won't show. Hence, a given car may sport the latest garb but harbor components from many prior years. The inevitable result is a necessity for parts lists, that massive body of documentation which records the configuration of any given car. This is status accounting in its most prosaic form: the unsung product of configuration management.

Now for a simple test of its importance. Let the frustrated or skeptical young configuration manager assume that he has lost the gas tank cap on his car. Let him then go to the nearest well stocked service station and ask for a replacement. The attendant will ask for the car's year and model. With this information, the chances are excellent that with his parts list, showing the manufacturer's identifying number, a replacement cap will be readily found in the dealer's stock costing less than $2.50. Configuration status accounting has made the replacement a relatively quick and economical process. Mass production provided the economy, and advanced technology provided the latest design (perhaps even later than the original item).

Application to Military Items

Now let the tyro executive, the young configuration manager in this case, transfer his thinking to military items. In this field, "style" has no place, but advanced technology is all important. Military threats are not static. The stark facts of survival compel immediate response to improved enemy capability. Furthermore, technically improved weapons, which increase an existing margin of superiority, tend to keep an enemy off balance. Hence, the importance of simultaneous mass production and engineering advance. Hence, the paramount importance of configuration management's catalytic action which makes the simultaneous actions possible. As ambitious young men grasp this idea, frustration wanes. The reasons for configuration baselines, continuously identified by disciplined procedures, begin to emerge. MIL-S-83490 and MIL-STD-190 assume new vitality.

The gestation of improved weapons is a pageant of changes. The item ultimately delivered can be no sounder than the decisions made by the attending physician in his application of configuration control. Injudicious decisions, which violate the criteria of MIL-STD-480 and 481, will be memorialized by birth defects of operational shortcoming. Clearly, the decision-making contribution of configuration managers is not to be lightly ignored. Their genetic messages demand respect.

Through the infancy of system test, the adolescence of initial training, and the maturity of operational deployment, a system is logistically nourished. Initial sustenance may flow through the mammary glands of contracts for augmented contractor support. In other cases the catalytic action of configuration management produces initial support whereby all inherited and modified features of a system, produced by mass production, are reconciled. In short, initial spares are accurately representative of the delivered item. By continued application of configuration management, the anatomy of a weapon system is adapted to changing requirements. The logistic diet is judiciously prescribed by the "Data Elements and Related Features" of configuration status accounting. By MIL-STD-882, a wholesome interface is maintained between mass production industry and DOD's changing world. By adroit (but sometimes tedious) application, a truly remarkable union is effected.

If the union prospers, its praises flow. The headlines proclaim operational achievements. The journals disgorge statistical reports. Program managers get promoted. Configuration managers remain anonymous and continue to generate mountains of documents. Only rarely can they see over the top and behold the outcome of their labor. They remain unmotivated, because no one has thought to dramatize their contribution. The program manager who struggles to retain talent at the inception of a program may consider filling this void by enlightened indoctrination: *Extol the importance of catalysts!*

Consider the Parthenon

As this approach wears thin with the passage of time, another suggestion is offered. It draws upon history.

Other ages have had their notions of progress, and their ideas of "breakthroughs" in achieving it. In the Age of Pericles, 500 to 400 B.C., progress was measured by the development and perfection of new forms of artistic expression. Sculpture had started in Egypt as mere bas reliefs. It took centuries to learn how to carve statues "in the round," i.e., unsupported by a wall, cliff, or other adjacent element. Even then, statues were often held upright by serving as columns for temple roofs. The Cretans went a little farther. They managed some statues that stood alone, but arms, legs, and inanimate objects had to be close to the subject. A warrior with sword outstretched was beyond the "state of the art." The Greeks gave us the first truly great examples of "free-standing" statues. In their eyes, such masterpieces as "The Discus Thrower" were incredible achievements.

Their efforts were by no means limited to sculpture. Research and development were lavished on drama, poetry, and architecture. In the latter field, the Parthenon was probably their most spectacular achievement. Even in its present nearly ruined state, it commands our genuine admiration. Its construction incorporated, in one edifice, not only free-standing statues by the great Phidias, it contained dozens of them; and they were all masterpieces.

If you have visited the Parthenon or read about it, you know that there is not a straight, a vertical, nor a horizontal line in it. The steps across the front and rear are 110 feet long, but they are four inches higher in the center than at either end. The columns are neither straight nor vertical. They slope from each end of a colonnade toward the center. The sides are slightly curved, and taper toward the capitols. All of the other seemingly straight, vertical, or horizontal lines are similarly curved, ever so slightly.

Why? Because the architects, Callicrates and Ictinus, had learned by experience that straight lines, in a building of that size, produced an effect on the eye that was cold, harsh, and severe. They knew that the use of imperceptible curves produced an effect that was soft and aesthetically pleasing. The resulting temple was an artistic breakthrough of breakthroughs. It was as exciting to the Greeks of Pericles' day as a manned moon landing is to us.

But think of the tedious amount of detailed work—of configuration management—that must have been necessary to bring this about. Think of the "paper work" that was needed to tell each stonecutter and each mason *exactly* how to cut and assemble each massive piece of marble, so that the desired effect would, in fact, be achieved. The ambitious young men who handled the details must have had their moments of boredom and frustration, but the end result must have been inwardly rewarding. The verdict of history has been that their efforts were well worthwhile.

It really doesn't matter whether the end result of a long, difficult, and tedious task is a Greek temple, space vehicle, or something in between. If the resulting product represents progress, artistic or scientific, it must also represent exact and extensive planning. There can be no significant progress without it. This thought may come as a revelation and stimulating idea to unsung configuration managers. Perhaps they will see for the first time that they are not building mountains of documentation: they are assisting at the birth of a major achievement.

$$\star \quad \star \quad \star \quad \star \quad \star$$

Change control is based on two related precepts:

- Let a good thing alone
- What looks like a pussy cat may turn into a tiger.

—LMI Introduction to
Military Program Management

Change control implies these rules:

- An initial predisposition against changes. If in doubt, don't make the change.
- A detailed analysis of the direct and the likely impact of a change on all three program characteristics: performance, schedule, and cost—especially the last.
- A continuing predisposition against change after the analysis is completed. The probability is that things will turn out much worse than the analysis has predicted.

These rules have been followed by a number of military program managers who said that their change policy was to have no changes at all—and then back down from there only when there was overwhelming and convincing justification for, and evaluation of, proposed changes.

—LMI Introduction to
Military Program Management

48

R&D Emphasis on Reliability*

Robert N. Parker†

Experience has shown that reliability values reported from field service are generally lower—often much lower—than those predicted by design analysis or demonstrated by laboratory testing. This has led to optimistic projections of operational effectiveness and ownership cost. It can also lead managers down a "primrose path" during development, since predictions and demonstrations indicate that reliability requirements are being met. In point of fact, the opposite is the case. Field reliability problems encountered with recent generations of complex systems amply demonstrated this situation and helped catalyze the Office of Director, Defense Research and Engineering, to give major emphasis to reliability in new system development.

During the early stages of weapon system development, more emphasis is being placed on design as a means of achieving field reliability. An appreciation of the degree to which investment into initial system development efforts to achieve specified reliability values in the field is just beginning. In the recently awarded F-16 fire control radar development contract, provisions were added to accommodate 3,000 hours of reliability improvement testing. This provided the contractor with confidence to accept a production reliability improvement warranty program based on achieving field reliability. Other approaches used during the development program involve the use of contract incentives as well as specifications of test and evaluation conditions of system reliability in field reliability

*Defense Management Journal, April 1976, p. 19.
†Principal Deputy Director, Defense Research & Engineering

terms. An illustrative example of this approach is the newly initiated F-18 aircraft program which has a large percentage of the development contract fee linked to the successful demonstration of reliability.

Efforts are now under way in the Department of Defense (DOD) to establish a uniform set of reliability terms and definitions that can be tracked from the initial statement of an operational requirement, through all phases of research and development, and test and evaluation, to field service. A key initiative is the distinction between reliability as a factor in successful mission completion, and malfunctions that drive ownership cost. The recognition of this distinction will allow better cost/effectiveness trade-offs. For example, it will help to determine the real value of design redundancy which, while increasing the ability to complete a mission, may also increase the number of system malfunctions and thus adversely drive ownership costs by adding to system complexity and parts count.

DOD and industry also are jointly working towards increasing the realism of laboratory testing. The basic concept is to combine performance, reliability, and environmental testing, insofar as practical, in the same test chamber, and to program the chamber to simulate the real field environment rather than the artificial profiles defined by a general specification. Current avionics equipment recently tested under this concept demonstrated much closer correlation between laboratory and field failure rates and failure modes than that previously experienced. Most realistic test conditions also reduce the amount of test time required to demonstrate equipment reliability—by as much as 80 percent in the case of avionics.

Military Standard 781, "Reliability Tests—Exponential Distribution," is now being revised to incorporate this concept, and laboratory test realism as well as the relationship between laboratory and field results are now being addressed more intensively in Decision Coordinating Papers and at Defense Systems Acquisition Review Council reviews.

Emphasis is being removed from theoretical predictions of reliability growth based on design analysis, and placed on measured reliability improvement. The time saved by more realistic demonstration testing can be most profitably invested in "Test-Analyze-Find-And-Fix" (TAFF) testing under those same conditions.

The sampling of efforts that have been discussed is not expected to resolve all the problems associated with designing, developing, and delivering systems with higher field reliability. They do, however, offer some insight into the approaches now being developed to close the gap between specified reliability and field results. Emphasis on both reliability design and realistic testing during the early stages of system development is a key element. Based on recently reported experience, these approaches are proving fruitful.

The program manager and his top people should go into the field and work with the users. The product has to be sold. One program manager states:

> If you sit back and wait to hear how it goes, you will get flak you won't believe. Everyone up and down the line will get so upset with the shortcomings, real and imagined, that you won't even have a chance to be heard. Work with the user, explain why things are the way they are and the impact of changes on funds and schedule objectives, solicit his cooperation, and show an interest in getting the bad points fixed as soon as possible. The user is happier, and you can maintain the momentum of the program.
>
> *—LMI Introduction to*
> *Military Program Management*

49

Reliability by Design, Not by Chance*

Willis J. Willoughby

Reliability means many things to many people, depending on their points of view. Personal or corporate-level experience is perhaps the single most dominant reason for the general confusion concerning reliability. Experience with military systems requiring very high levels of safety, or with systems in private industry that are tightly linked to a profit and loss structure, usually results in an organized approach to a reliable product. Conversely, if some of these requirements have not been present or at least apparent, the organized approach rarely occurs. For example, the typical military acquisition manager may view reliability as a variation of cult magic, or at best a collection of imprecise mathematical processes designed and understood only by mathematicians. He may recognize little real-time, practical value in reliability, and may not see the reliability "discipline" as a means to advance or even assure the successful accomplishment of his assigned program.

In many instances his conclusion is generally justified. Too often the reliability requirement has not been truly coupled to the design effort, but instead has been designated for measurement or "demonstration" as a numerical objective at the conclusion of full-scale development. At best such a demonstration can only measure the worth of a design at a time when it is too costly and time-consuming to make any changes needed to correct a reliability

*Defense Management Journal, April 1976, pp. 12–18.

shortfall. More typically, reliability "demonstration" is highly questionable because of test conditions and sample sizes chosen. When only numerical reliability is specified as a requirement, it is used too often as an illusionary hurdle to be overcome by any means available other than fundamental design considerations. This is indeed a sad state of affairs since design reliability is the key to successful equipment operation throughout its specified lifetime.

The most common approach to specifying reliability requirements is shown below.

Current Typical Reliability Requirements

* Numerical requirements.
* Specification requirement simply to "conduct a reliability program in accordance with MIL-STD-785A."
* Contract data requirements (reliability program plan and reliability status reports).
* Factory reliability demonstration test (one or two units in MIL-STD-781B or similar environment).
* Factory "burn-in" and acceptance tests (every unit in MIL-STD-781B or similar environment).

This approach is guaranteed to perpetuate the present dilemma in which products are acquired whose reliabilities in the field are far below the specified reliability requirements—so far below that one may be led to believe that the requirements were never intended to be met in the field, but only in the factory. There are no specifications, and consequently no measurements, enforcement, and control, of the engineering and manufacturing disciplines which assure reliable products. This "numbers game" approach is *reliability by chance.*

Why Reliability?

The Navy, like the other military services, is faced with less-than-desired combat effectiveness levels and rising life cycle costs. This situation exists because reliability has not been properly specified and pursued; rather, the Navy has relied heavily on integrated logistic support. As a feature element in improving operational readiness, this approach has not proven effective in improving reliability for two principal reasons:

* Equipment reliability has been far worse than expected, thereby completely overburdening the logistic procurement system.
* The logistic distribution system has a pipeline that is growing both in length and diameter, requiring tremendous efforts to keep it filled in order to meet the needs of the Fleet.

As a result, the Navy now has aircraft, ships, and electronic systems which are very expensive to own when properly supported to meet substantial readiness requirements.

To repair some two million failures, the Navy is currently spending more than a half billion per year on spare parts alone— and this is a *peacetime* environment! *Combat* engagements would quickly sever this "umbilical to the beach."[1] The aircraft carrier JOHN F. KENNEDY, for example, has some 41,000 line items in its spares inventory, at an estimated value exceeding $60 million, solely to support its complement of aircraft. Adequate levels of operational readiness are being sustained only through the tireless efforts of overworked maintenance personnel and countless spare parts, much to the distress of those who operate the equipment. Furthermore, *readiness is not reliability!* A capability to launch a mission doesn't guarantee its successful completion if it involves unreliable hardware; repairs stop when the mission begins.

To reverse this situation, the Chief of Naval Material, Admiral Frederick H. Michaelis, is reordering the priorities of the Naval Material Command. In comparison to aerospace experience, particularly that of the National Aeronautics and Space Administration's Apollo Program, the shortcomings of current Navy programs are easily discernible, and the actions required to correct them are clear, albeit painful. The acquisition and deployment of reliable weapon systems offer the prospect of significant improvements in Fleet readiness and significant relief to the Navy's beleaguered Supply Corps. Nevertheless, the Navy's "new way of doing business" efforts that have been recently initiated first met with *fierce resistance,* both in the Navy and in industry. There is a considerable amount of inertia (a "business as usual" syndrome) and many traditions of past years yet to be overcome. The Navy has been procuring modern and sophisticated weapon systems utilizing outmoded reliability techniques that have not allowed the realization of the reliability benefits that the new technology has to offer.

A New Approach

The first step is a total dedication by the government and sincere response from industry. The broad changes in emphasis and actions which are essential to this effort and currently guide initiatives in the Naval Material Command are outlined below:

[1]Admiral Isaac C. Kidd used this phrase to describe the supply-and-depot-level maintenance pipeline during his tenure as Chief of Naval Material.

A New Approach to Reliable Systems

- Set essential reliability requirements.
- Place reliability criteria with performance requirements.
- Demand reliable design concepts.
- Minimize dependence on support.
- Ensure reliability by design, not by chance.

Note that no new policies are required or implied; these initiatives are entirely within the scope of existing Department of Defense and Navy policies, and simply reflect a new approach to implementing and utilizing existing instructions and directives at all defense management echelons.

Reliability Requirements

The reliability levels necessary to meet threat scenarios in the combat environment should be specified in the Operational Requirement (OR) and the Decision Coordinating Paper (DCP). While this is sometimes impractical until a concept is validated, the setting of essential numerical requirements frequently does not get the attention it demands at the higher defense management echelons. With the current emphasis on maximum combat effectiveness at minimum life cycle cost, it must be made clear that both of these parameters *become frozen* once firm reliability requirements are specified, and are never considered unless meaningfully enforced. It is essential that setting reliability levels in the OR and DCP become a concern of top management to the same extent as performance levels, instead of leaving this task to the project manager and the contractor. While it is often proposed that support cost data are unavailable for life cycle cost studies, more importantly what is missing is acquisition cost as a function of reliability. Since acquisition costs are in the real-time domain of the contractor, it may become necessary to request proposals for a range of reliability alternatives, in order to support life cycle cost analysis prior to source selection.

Reliability vs. Performance

Experience with some 500 major procurement actions in the Naval Material Command during the past two years reveals that performance has seldom been a limiting factor; indeed, performance has usually exceeded requirements. At the same time, however, reliability requirements, which in some instances were questionably low to begin with, are being missed by wide margins; yet many of these products will be in service for ten to twenty years or more. A high-performance product has little value, even as a deterrent, if it cannot consistently deliver this performance because it is either broken down or breaks down immediately upon being pressed into service.

General Samuel C. Phillips, USAF (former Apollo Program Director and former commander of the Air Force Systems Command before his recent retirement), has stated that "a designer may make reliability his initial consideration and then look for alternate approaches to achieving performance. . . ." Close scrutiny of many Navy weapon systems strongly supports the need for executing this position over the life cycle of these systems. Whatever necessary reliability levels may be initially established for a new OR, the Naval Material Command is now placing these alongside performance in planning the new program. Design simplicity and ruggedness, as well as adequate time to reach design maturity, are among the predictable results. Complex, high-risk, advanced concepts and parts, whose reliability "track records" have not yet been established, will seldom be justified as the Navy makes reliability its first consideration and then looks for alternatives to achieving performance; combat engagement is too late to discover whether or not systems are reliable.

Reliable Design Concepts

Attention to reliability begins in the earliest conceptualization of materials to meet Operational Requirements because the basic concept often "locks in" the inherent upper limits of reliability at levels which will clearly be unable to meet future operational needs in the field. For example, a multimission aircraft, dependent on a host of complex electronic systems, is predictably reliability-limited. An earth-spanning satellite communications system which employs aerospace design technology in the satellites but relies on standard reliability practices for the ground stations has immediate and long-range problems. Entire shipboard weapon suites which require a complex of digital computers for their operation are in the Fleet today. Ships propelled by a single variable-pitch screw are on the way. The Operational Requirements for most, if not all, of these products may leave no reasonable alternatives. Where this is the case, however, foremost emphasis on reliability is essential. To date, it has not received this priority, with few exceptions.

Support

The support function, specifically the maintenance and spare parts elements, may have been forced historically to grow in response to battle damage and deteriorating field reliability; however, it now encourages an imbalance in acquisition emphasis on performance *vis-a-vis* reliability. Support resources are strained severely by this *de facto* reliance on maintenance and spare parts. Reversing this situation requires that field reliability be measured in terms of "months between failures" rather than "hours between failures;"[2] but these more reliable products are going to cost more procurement dollars to acquire. However, the payoff in reduced support dollars will come when they reach the field, as commercial and aerospace products have amply demonstrated.

Reliability by Design

The alternative to *reliability by chance* is government specification of the engineering and manufacturing disciplines known to result in reliable products. In this context, numerical requirements revert to their proper role of aiding early product design planning and measuring progress as opposed to being the sole focus of government attention. The contractor's approach to reliability achievement is a concern and the business of the government customer. The implications of this role must be examined more closely.

The reliability of a product depends on its design. In every detail possible, the designer must know and use the environmental conditions in which the product will operate (such as levels of temperature, vibration, shock, humidity, salt fog or spray, and altitude) and the length of time in each; this information is included in the product definition and mission profile. Beginning in the conceptual phase of the procurement cycle, the designer must be required to emphasize simplicity in his design for these conditions, consider possible design alternatives, and institute checks to see that simplicity is achieved, because field retrofit to correct poor design is the most expensive and disruptive approach to reliability improvement.

Once the environmental specifications have been established, the selection and application of parts and materials then become critical and play a significant role in reliability achievement. Therefore, a vigorous parts program is essential to establish and maintain through organizational policy qualified parts lists, specification control drawings for parts procurements from approved sources, and

[2]General Phillips used the expression "months instead of hours" (between failures).

laboratory facilities for testing and screening of parts and materials which assure that electrical, mechanical, and thermal stresses on the product's parts are substantially below their design limits.

Adequate derating often can yield reliable products using inexpensive, widely available parts, while even the best parts will fail repeatedly if derating is inadequate. For example, in the rapidly escalating use of solid state electronic devices, including large-scale integrated circuits, a reduction of ten degrees Centigrade in the junction temperature (about five percent of the maximum rating) below seventy degrees Centigrade has been found to *double* the reliability of the device. The designer uses stress-analysis techniques to check the effectiveness of derating and the interactions of each part in his design; the design is then modified where necessary and the stress analysis is updated until every part meets or exceeds the contractor's derating requirements. But these requirements vary widely from one company to another, easily accounting for wide variations in reliability of similar products between contractors. Military procurements seldom invoke specific derating requirements, or often take notice of contractor policies at design reviews.

Another design technique for reliability involves redundancy, alternate and degraded backup modes of operation, and fail-safe concepts; the design engineer uses failure modes and effects analysis (FMEA) to evaluate these factors. The objective should be to minimize the number of single parts whose failure can cause mission failure or crew loss, and to single out those which are unavoidable as candidates for higher reliability requirements, tighter parts screening, and additional subassembly-level testing. Unfortunately, the FMEA is sometimes performed only because it is a contract data requirement, with the government evidencing little understanding of its importance; consequently, its results are infrequently put to use. It is therefore incumbent on the project office which specifies an FMEA to ensure that its results are fully factored into the engineering process.

Testing

When the design on paper has been certified to be satisfactory through a series of critical fact-searching design reviews, construction of one or more test articles begins.[3] The purpose of testing is to ensure that the design meets all stated performance specifications, including the reliability requirements. Any shortfall must

[3]In the case of ships, the test article is also the end item which will ultimately be delivered to the Government.

stimulate redesign until the requirements are met. A crucial factor in testing is the environment; only if the factory test conditions duplicate or exceed the field environment will the testing be truly effective in ensuring that specified performance and reliability requirements will be met after deployment. There are three major factors which play strong roles in ensuring the adequacy of testing:

• An accurate mission environmental profile.

• An integrated test plan which sets up a logical, progressive sequence of testing at increasing levels of assembly and environmental complexity in accordance with the mission profile.

• Operational test and evaluation by the government to give the product its first exposure to the real mission environment.

Testing is probably responsible, more than any other single factor, for the poor reliability of military procurements. In *reliability by chance,* it is the only means of measuring the contractor's accomplishment. The environmental qualification test usually measures the product's performance under conditions and levels which equal or even exceed the expected field environment. The length of this test, however, is negligible with respect to the product's reliability requirement; e.g., a 1,000-hour device may complete environmental qualification in one eight hour shift. In contrast, the long-duration test to measure the product's reliability is conducted under environmental conditions which bear *no* resemblance to the field environment. From a reliability viewpoint, this is the only hurdle the product must clear, and the contractor is therefore strongly motivated to design to the benign reliability test environment rather than to the field environment. Is it any wonder that there are sometimes ten to one differences between factory and field reliability? This situation is being corrected, and the first step is to modify the MIL-STD-781B test levels in favor of realistic environmental qualification test levels. The ultimate long-range objective should be one extended environmental test which qualifies both the performance and the reliability of the product.

Throughout the integrated test program, reliability is reflected by the product failures which may occur. Key elements of the reliability program at this point include:

• Logging every failure along with the technical data describing the test conditions at the time of failure.

• Determining and understanding the cause of every failure, by in-depth laboratory analysis if circumstances dictate.

• Taking appropriate corrective actions, by redesign or other means, to preclude the recurrence of the failure.

These actions should be continued until the average interval between new failures in the field environment equals or exceeds specification requirements. Even then, failure analysis and corrective action are essential for new failures, particularly in critical components as identified earlier in the failure modes and effects analysis.

Quality Assurance

When the design fully meets specification requirements in the test program and production is authorized by the government, quality assurance becomes the key factor in assuring that the reliability inherent in the final design is not compromised in the manufacturing process. Producibility problems as well as the effects of manufacturing processes dictate continuing testing of a burn-in and acceptance nature, with failure analysis and corrective action taken as necessary. This testing should also be conducted in field environmental conditions, with the exception of destructive conditions. Deployment of the first units may also reveal previously undetected reliability shortfalls upon full exposure of inexperienced operations and maintenance personnel. These failures should be few in number if the factory test program was properly conducted; nevertheless, they should receive the necessary analysis and corrective action by the contractor until in-service reliability stabilizes at satisfactory levels.

Conclusions

Military contractors, acknowledged experts in the techniques that result in reliable hardware, will find nothing technically new in this Navy approach to reliability improvement. They will find, however, that the Navy has established and is vigorously enforcing an engineering management process aimed at assuring the acquisition of reliable weapon systems. But before reliable weapon systems can be acquired routinely, and this must be the final objective, the following must occur:

• Defense management at all echelons must recognize that highly reliable weapon systems which require far less support are the only means to reach vital levels of combat effectiveness while holding the line on life cycle cost.

• This recognition must be manifested in requests for proposals, technical specifications, and contractual requirements which leave no doubt that reliability equals or exceeds performance in priority and importance to the government.

• These technical specifications and contractual requirements must state clearly the engineering design and manufacturing quality assurance disciplines which the government expects to be employed to achieve reliable products.

• The stated disciplines must produce visible and measurable results that the government and contractor alike may use to manage and control the timely execution of contracts.

• The government must include in the management and control of its procurements the strict enforcement of these disciplines.

The Naval Material Command is fully supporting these five principles guiding specific actions to reestablish credibility in acquiring reliable systems for the Fleet. The Navy recognizes that the approach followed in the past for specifying reliable military systems needs to be updated and that will not happen overnight. Nevertheless, there is a solid commitment to a comprehensive program which will substantially improve reliability and will result in a gradual lessening in the demand for spares. As this program is fully implemented, the improved products the Naval Material Command delivers will restore to the Fleet unsurpassed levels of combat effectiveness.

$$\ast \quad \ast \quad \ast \quad \ast \quad \ast$$

One program manager in industry sums up his approach to controlling optimism as pushing the worst case upon the engineers:

> First you ask what is the worst thing that could happen. Second, you ask why it cannot happen to us. Third, you ask how you will know it has happened —what event or test will tell you. Fourth, you ask what you are going to do if it happens. These questions wring out most of the optimism and you get a chance to look at some real engineering analysis and hard facts.
>
> —*LMI Introduction to*
> *Military Program Management*

50

Reliability, Availability & Maintainability*

Commander Gerald J. Chasko

"The high cost and complexity of modern military systems require the most efficient management possible to avoid wasting significant resources on inadequate equipment.

"Efficient systems management depends on the successful evaluation and integration of numerous different but interrelated system characteristics such as reliability, maintainability, performance and cost. If such evaluation and integration is to be accomplished in a scientific rather than intuitive manner, a method must be formulated to assess quantitatively the effects of each system characteristic on overall system effectiveness."[1]

The problem of relating availability, reliability and maintainability to other system parameters is just as real today as it was when the above statement was made twelve years ago. This paper discusses reliability, availability and maintainability in the context of System Effectiveness (SE) and describes their relationships to each other.

System Effectiveness

A weapon system is designed to perform a function or set of functions in order to meet a mission need. A common measure of

*Extract from Defense Systems Management College paper, September 1, 1978.
[1]Weapons System Effectiveness Industry Advisory Committee (WSEIAC) Final Reports, AFSC, January 1965.

how well the system performs its intended function is System Effectiveness (SE). Basically SE is concerned with the ability of the system to perform its mission successfully in its intended environment. System effectiveness is a function of Availability (A), Capability (C) and Dependability (D). The object of the SE function is to determine: (1) Is the system ready to perform its function? (2) Will it produce the desired effects? (3) How well will it perform during a mission?

Aside from special cases a system must be ready to begin performing its mission at some point in calendar time (which can be regarded as random for many defense systems). This ability is often called availability or operational readiness (the difference between these two terms will be discussed later). Then the system must perform its mission satisfactorily for a specified period of time (mission time). This ability is referred to as dependability or mission reliability. Finally the actual performance of the system in terms of its performance functions and the environment in which it is performed is called capability. (The terms design adequacy or utilization are used in other methods of measuring SE. They will not be included in this discussion.)

There are several currently used methodologies that are concerned with the above attributes in one way or another. As a result, many semantic barriers arise in talking of SE and its components since people may use the same words to mean different things and different words to mean the same thing. Terminology used in this discussion will be consistent with current DOD concepts of System Effectiveness as defined in MIL-STD-721B.

This document defines system effectiveness as "a measure of the degree to which an item can be expected to achieve a set of specific mission requirements and which may be expressed as a function of availability, dependability and capability." This definition may be expressed as:

$$E_s = F \text{ (CAD)}$$

A=AVAILABILITY: A measure of the degree to which an item is in the operable and committable state at the start of the mission, when the mission is called for at an unknown (random) point in time.

D=DEPENDABILITY: A measure of the item's operating condition at one or more points during the mission, including the effects of Reliability, Maintainability, and Survivability, given the item condition(s) at the start of the mission. It may be stated as the probability than an item will (a) enter or occupy any one of its required operational modes during a specified mission, (b) perform the functions associated with those operational modes.

C=CAPABILITY: A measure of the ability of an item to achieve mission objectives given the conditions during the mission.

These are usually expressed as probabilities, and although it may not be entirely clear from the definitions, the three terms are mutually exclusive and care must be exercised to ensure that the same data are not included in more than one term (in modeling SE for example). Further explanation may help clarify the terms.

Availability

Availability is simply the probability that the system is in "up" and ready status at the beginning of a mission when the mission occurs at a random point in time. Stated another way, is the equipment ready to operate within allowable response time with all mission-required functions capable of operating within design specifications? Availability of hardware is a function of the reliability and maintainability characteristics of the system (neglecting for the present, safety, survivability/vulnerability, logistics and human factors). For sufficiently long operating periods the availability of a system with zero warning time can be expressed as a relationship between uptime (reliability) and downtime (maintainability). Availability may also be defined as the ratio of the total time the system is capable of performing its function (uptime) to the total time when there is a demand for the system (uptime plus downtime).

Dependability

Availability as discussed above is a point concept; that is, it refers to the probability of a system being operable at a random point in time. The ability of the system to continue to perform reliably for the duration of the mission is measured by its dependability. Dependability is the probability that, given the system was available, it will continue to operate throughout the mission either without system-level failure or if it fails that it will be restored to operation within some critical time-interval which, if exceeded, would cause mission failure.

Operating over the desired period of time depends on clearly defining the system's operating profiles. If the system has a number of operational missions then the profile for each mission must be considered. The phrase "no system-level failures" means that the performance during the mission is within design specifications considering the effects of the environment. For instance, failure of a redundant item when only one of two is needed to produce the system output would not imply system failure. Failure of both, however, would produce system failure. Several dependability cases exist depending on the criteria for system failure. As in the case of availability, dependability is also a function of reliability, maintainability, human performance and other characteristics.

Capability

Capability is the probability that the system's designed performance will allow it to meet mission demands successfully *assuming that the system is Available and Dependable.* This term takes into account the adequacy of the system to perform its mission when operating within system design specifications and environment. The definition of capability implies that when the system is carrying out a mission where demands are within its design performance limits, and under environmental conditions that are within its specified limitations, that its capability is exactly what its designers computed or determined by test. This is rarely 1.0, as is sometimes assumed, except in vastly over-designed systems or very special cases.

Usually capability is less than theoretical computations or test results would indicate since demands or environment may not be precisely within specified limits, electromagnetic compatibility problems exist, or the human performance part of the capability term may have been overestimated. A major difficulty is in obtaining suitable data and frequently an estimation process must substitute for empirically-obtained data due to budget and schedule constraints imposed on typical programs.

The foregoing discussions on C, A and D assume that a defined specific mission profile is being analyzed. If a system is to be used for more than one type of mission, it is advisable to define system effectiveness with respect to each mission.

Reliability

Reliability (R) is "the probability that an item will perform its intended function for a specified interval under stated conditions." Reliability may be expressed in terms of mission reliability or hardware reliability (or both) and should be stated as a firm requirement rather than a goal. That is, contracts should contain quantitative reliability values which must be formally demonstrated. Mission reliability is normally expressed as a decimal fraction (.99, .95, .90, etc.) probability that a system will perform its function under specified conditions without failure for a specified time, i.e., the probability of success. As with the concept of SE, mission reliability must be associated with a specific mission or mission profile. When referring to the reliability of a system or piece of equipment, mean time between failures (MTBF) is a measure of how often repairs or spare parts are required. MTBF is a measure of hardware reliability and is computed by dividing total system operating time (or cycles) by the total number of failures which have occurred.

Once system level reliability requirements have been established, they must be allocated to subsystems parts and components. These component reliabilities are then combined to provide a prediction of total system reliability. A major tool for R allocation and prediction is the reliability block diagram. This is a block diagram of the system which defines the series and parallel structure of the system elements, and forms the basis for the mathematical reliability model. The R model states the probability of system failure during missions of stated duration. Detailed failure modes and effects analysis are further required to establish the relation between parts failures and consequences to mission success.

When predicted reliability is unsatisfactory, reliability improvement techniques such as redundancy, parts selection and screening and part/component derating are used to improve reliability. The most effective time to impact the ultimate reliability of a system is during detailed design since it becomes increasingly expensive to make design changes as hardware is fabricated, tested and produced. Design reviews and test programs provide a formalized periodic appraisal of the design to evaluate its progress. Reliability improvement is achieved through testing in an environment that duplicates or closely simulates the field environment, with thorough analysis of all failures and corrective action that provides a fundamental solution to the problem encountered in the test.

Ideally the R program should be a part of the overall effectiveness program in order to guarantee that the relevant trade-offs with other system attributes are accomplished. The design function of the reliability organization alternates with the modeling/evaluation function which is carried out in concert with maintainability, logistics, human factors, etc., within an overall system effectiveness analysis function.

Maintainability

In attempting to satisfy availability and dependability require-ments, a system could be made so reliable that failures are rare. (Space systems are an example.) However, this approach might not be feasible in all cases because the required technology may not be within the state of the art or because using highly reliable compo-nents would not be economical or cost effective. Another approach to satisfy these requirements would be to design a system so that failures might occur frequently but could be corrected in a short time. In this case, however, the maintenance resources required might not be cost-effective and a system that fails frequently, even though it's easily and quickly repaired, would probably be intoler-able to the user. The reliability engineer is concerned with increas-ing availability by increasing the system's uptime while the main-tainability engineer attempts to decrease system downtime.

Maintainability is defined as "a characteristic of design and installation which is expressed as the probability that an item will be retained in or restored to a specified condition within a given period of time, when maintenance is performed in accordance with prescribed procedures and resources." (MIL-STD-721.) Maintaina-bility engineering is concerned with the actions taken by a designer that will facilitate maintenance activities at the appropriate mainte-nance level.

Maintainability is well-established as an effectiveness disci-pline through the relation of one of its major parameters, mean time to repair (MTTR) to Availability and Dependability, as discussed earlier. In engineering programs, the maintainability function must work closely with the reliability functions to establish the optimal levels of system reliability and maintainability, e.g., reliability/availability/maintainability (RAM) analysis is carried out to estab-lish the most cost-effective combination of maintainability (MTTR) and reliability (MTBF) design features which meet the requirements for system Availability and Dependability. The opportunity for trade-off between the two functions is apparent in the $A = MTBF/(MTBF+MTTR)$ formulation of Availability and will be discussed in the section on trade-offs.

It is important here to distinguish between maintainability and maintenance. *Maintenance* is the set of actions necessary for retaining an item in, or restoring it to, a specified condition. It can be seen that maintainability is a system design parameter while maintenance actions are a result of the systems design. The purpose of maintaina-bility is to provide the required availability and dependability by maximizing ease of maintenance in a manner that is consistent with other system requirements and by minimizing support resources required. Typical maintainability activities include modeling, prediction, allocation, test/evaluation, maintenance concept and design specification, design review and other activities necessary to provide assurance that the system's maintainability characteristics are consistent with system effectiveness goals. Since the repair time of a system depends on (1) failure characteristics, (2) detail design features such as packaging, labeling, test points, etc., and (3) maintenance technician characteristics, the maintainability function overlaps those of several other functions including reliability, human factors and logistics, with which close liaison must be maintained. In fact, it is not uncommon to find similar requirements for analysis and design criteria related to the maintenance features of the system in the specifications and standards for human factors, maintainability and logistics support—all called out for the same acquisition program.

As with reliability, the maintainability organization alternates between a design function and an analysis/evaluation function which is carried out within the system effectiveness analysis program. When predictions indicate unacceptable levels of maintainability, it is the responsibility of the maintainability design function to recommend maintainability design approaches which will enable goals to be met. In addition to detail design recommendations involving test-point levels, marking/labeling, packaging, accessibility and various "human engineering" criteria which are well-documented in "M Criteria handbooks," trade-offs and other analyses are used to establish maintenance concepts—generally in cooperation with or as part of the Integrated Logistics Support function. The types of maintenance concept decisions made on the basis of modeling and analysis include: repair vs. discard of failed modules; location of module or equipment repair (shipboard, tender, depot, contractor, etc.); test point location; type and location of failure detection devices and test equipment (manual vs. automatic, special vs. general, built-in vs. portable, etc.); technician numbers and skill-levels; special support equipment, tools and jigs; location and types of maintenance data and instructions; level of modularization and degree of standardization; etc. Since these decisions have considerable impact on both effectiveness and cost, it is essential that the alternative maintenance concepts be evaluated within an overall cost-effectiveness context through exercise of the overall cost and system effectiveness models wherever possible. At minimum, suboptimization through lower-level trade-off analyses is required.

Time is an important design parameter of maintainability. In defining downtime for purposes of computing system availability, two types of maintenance activities were discussed: preventive maintenance and corrective maintenance. *Preventive maintenance* is maintenance performed on a scheduled basis for the purpose of *retaining* an item in a satisfactory operating condition. It includes servicing, inspection and periodic testing. *Corrective maintenance* is a maintenance performed to *restore* equipment to operating conditions after a failure or other malfunction has occurred. Corrective maintenance includes fault location, diagnosis, correction and checkout. Active maintenance time is that time that the maintenance technician is actively engaged in maintenance. During maintenance delay time the technician can do little or nothing towards actively restoring the equipment to operating condition. Delay time is a function of operating and environmental conditions and of the availability of support resources. Active maintenance time, however, is design controllable and an essential consideration in maintainability design.

Trade-Offs

It is possible to optimize maintainability requirements independently of other system parameters based solely on specified maintainability requirements. The same is true of reliability requirements. In both cases, however, we would be suboptimizing reliability and maintainability. If availability or dependability were specified as system effectiveness requirements, then the designer could make trade-offs between reliability and maintainability and achieve a higher level of system optimization than that of either reliability or maintainability.

A trade-off is nothing more than a selection among alternatives in order to optimize some system parameter which is a function of two or more variables which are being traded off. RAM trade-offs vary from reliability-maintainability-availability trades to level of repair analysis, repair/replace/discard decisions, skill level trade-offs, corrective vs. preventive maintenance, level of automation of test equipment and so on.

As discussed earlier, system availability is a function of MTBF (reliability) and MTTR (maintainability).

$$A_i = \frac{MTBF}{MTBF + MTTR}$$

In order to optimize availability it is desirable to increase MTBF and decrease MTTR. There are constraints which bound solutions considered in trade-off optimization. For example, there are limits to how much MTBF can be increased because of cost constraints or state of the art limitations. Similarly, very low MTTR values may be achieved by completely automatic test and checkout equipment but the resulting system might be too expensive.

$$\star \quad \star \quad \star \quad \star \quad \star$$

In fact, cost and time cannot be measured except against technical goals. The question of how much cost or how much time means nothing unless it is accompanied by "to achieve such and such a technical performance."

—*Peter C. Sandretto*

Program balance is the product of a conscious recognition that there is an inescapable interplay among the three basic program elements of technical performance, time, and cost. It is a product of an awareness that we cannot talk about what we want without also talking about when we want it and how much we can afford to spend on it. Program balance also involves an awareness that the balance which is struck at the beginning of the program seldom can be maintained throughout the development. New facts, new technology, new threats, unexpected costs—all upset the old balance and require a new balance to be struck.

—*LMI Introduction to*
Military Program Management

51

Logistics Management Challenges in Weapon System Design*

Honorable John S. Foster, Jr.†

I would like to separate my talk this morning into three major parts: first, a brief sketch of future trends in product development —or to say it another way—a description of new Defense Department approaches to the acquisition of major weapon systems; second, some of the more significant problems in achieving our objectives; and third, some of the things which logistic support people can do to help us, and to help themselves, as we design and produce the major defense weaponry of the future.

Let us then begin with the product of the future. It is most important to understand that nothing will improve, nothing will happen to better our future performance, unless we will it so— unless we dedicate ourselves to the job of seeing that it does occur. By the same token, that which is undesirable in the way we now conduct our business will remain with us unless we take positive action to get rid of it. Very simply stated, this means that the product of the 1970's will turn out to be exactly what we consciously make it to be—nothing more, nothing less.

Recently I had an opportunity to talk in Washington about six essential ways to maintain technological leadership in the service of our national goals. I would like to quote one of these six ways now, because it will explain the course of action which I feel we must take. I quote:

*Address to the Logistics Management Advisory Committee, National Security Industrial Association, June 29, 1970. Printed in *Defense Industry Bulletin,* September 1970, pp. 6–9.
†Director, Defense Research and Engineering.

". . . we must revamp—and thoroughly—the design philosophy in every corner of the Defense Department and defense industry. This task falls within my responsibilities—and there is no other matter about which I feel more strongly. We shall not in the future indulge in the present syndrome of incorporating into every system the most advanced technology, as soon as it seems to be available or merely because it is advanced. We shall ask only for what we really need— the minimum necessary performance—and we shall match, wherever possible, proven technology to that essential, realistic need. We shall insist relentlessly—as a point without peer in our management—that price has as much priority as performance. This does not rule out vigorous pursuit of new technology where that technology is required or can pay its way. And frequently new technology can be used to reduce costs. Yet we must design-to-a-price, a much lower price, or else we will not be able to afford what we need. Defense budgets are going down. The costs of what we need, just our essential needs, are going up. Our only solution is to make cost a principal design parameter. That is how we must define what is best. We have no other choice."

I have quoted from a talk I made some months ago in order to emphasize one of the most fundamental changes we must make in product character—that of treating cost as a major system objective. We have talked about this before, but we haven't really been successful in *doing* it. It is the *doing* that will cause some pain to everyone who gets involved, but especially to the engineering community. It will necessitate self-discipline and dedication of the highest order. It will cause a restructuring of our individual sets of priorities. It will necessitate the development of new capabilities and new points of view. We must learn that the simpler and less expensive products are often the best products—not shoddy goods at all.

Another major change in product character is that each must be adequate and acceptable in terms of mission worth but no more than that. This means that the translation of true operational need into stated operational requirements must also be scrutinized to ensure that we ask for no more than we need in the way of performance. Further, every stated operational requirement must be subject to re-evaluation as the engineering design emerges. It is at this point where, by virtue of actual tradeoff activity, we can evaluate the cost implications of the conversion of each individual stated operational requirement in terms of anticipated operational hardware. This is where tradeoffs can be meaningfully made—when price tags are attached to requirements, so that the most expensive ones become fully visible.

Another point that needs to be made is that all of us, including the Congress and the general public, must recognize that *total system cost* must go beyond mere acquisition cost and include the cost of ownership until the last operational unit is retired from service. This says that a price tag attached to a stated requirement should always include the total cost of ownership. When this occurs, we will be in a position to make meaningful tradeoffs between development, investment and operational saving, as well as between the desired performance parameters themselves.

This, I believe, brings us to a definition, broad as it may be, of product trends. We will no longer try to meet our increasing needs primarily by designing and fielding weapon systems which are increasingly complex and expensive; rather, we will prudently apply our creativity and technological skills in the direction of more system simplification. I am sure there are many who have the impression that it is easy to design a simple system, and most difficult to design a complex one. This might be true if the simple system reflects simple requirements, but a real challenge and real agony lie in translating a complex set of requirements into a simple system—a low-cost system—one which also embodies functional and operational excellence—one which is characterized by high reliability—one which is easy and inexpensive to maintain and to support—and one which can be efficiently and effectively used in its operating environment.

This is the only way we can afford what we need. It's just simply the way it's got to be.

The problem now is how to accomplish these seemingly impossible objectives. Possibly one of the best ways is to insist, particularly in the early stages, on a larger portion of our effort and time in recycling or refining the design to reduce cost and complexity. Expensive solutions are generally the result of first-time-around ideas. Simplified designs, with reduced costs, usually are the result of iterative design simplification efforts.

This brings me to my second broad subject. The composition and scope of today's engineering and scientific community has changed drastically in the last decade or two. The graduating engineer of today has many more fields of specialization in which to pursue his career. The active professional engineer or scientist is under constant pressure to continue his education in parallel with his work, and greater specialization is usually the result.

While this trend is appropriate and necessary to serve many needs of our country, I feel that the challenge and fascination of the field of general engineering or, more specifically, of system design, has too often been overlooked. Perhaps this intense specialization has become the norm just when we can least afford it in defense work—just when system complexity seems to be an unfortunate rule rather than a special exception, when system design seems to be driven by the available technology rather than the true need, and decisions are slowed by mountainous documentation.

I believe the difficulty of achieving a simple, cost-effective, functionally excellent product is increased by the seeming disappearance of the "total system designer." For example, it would be difficult to identify clear successors to the Kindelbergers, the Johnsons, the Heinemanns, or the Messerschmitts in today's engineering community. These people, total system designers in every sense of the word, may not have successors, even though we will need them desperately. These are the people who think from the beginning of the operational environment. These are the people who think from the beginning of logistic problems. These are the people who are concerned from the beginning with simplicity, cost, reliability, and all of the interlocking factors which decide whether a system will be good or bad.

So perhaps one of our problems is not only "to revamp our design philosophy," but to recreate a place in the sun for experienced, yet up-to-date people who will make reasoned judgments on total system design. We need creativity and imagination, vision and foresight, dedication and self-discipline. In the process of translating stated operational requirements into usable hardware, the decisions must benefit, not plague, the operating community.

Today, there appears to be too much tendency to pull together a team of specialists—the best technical experts in materials, in structures, in engines, avionics, data handling, etc. This is easy to do and it is often wrong. It can lead to the development of an overdesigned machine—one that is so complex that it can be made to work in the factory but not in the field. It will be a system that requires mountains of paper to describe, thousands of highly trained people to operate and maintain, and will not really suit our needs.

What we need are teams led by professionals in the broad art of basic design of military systems—men who know the strategy, the tactics, the nature of the weapons we have and those we will oppose, men who know the user's environment. Once these factors have been considered to scope the design, these broad-gauge leaders can then properly phase in the efforts of the specialists in each specific area, as they are needed.

To sum up my second point, it seems that we have the monumental task of changing both the *people* and the *environment* in order to achieve our product objectives.

As my third point, I submit that there are two broad areas in which logistic system people must be effective and that, if these areas are not distinctly clear in the minds of the logisticians, we will continue to address inadequately the fundamental design problem. We will continue to overkill with detail planning and overlook basic problem solving.

The formulation of a good logistic support system can be likened to the creation and development of a good engineering design. The system design process breaks down into two basic phases: first, the conceptual phase, including validation; and second, the full scale development phase—the "pick and shovel" phase. In system design, if we attempt prematurely to define detailed hardware, we begin to lose sight of the major parameters which we are struggling to achieve. For example, if we become engrossed in configuration end-item specifications before a solid configuration has emerged, the fundamental system objectives get lost in detail. I see the same thing happening in the logistic support system profession. The eagerness to define the system in detail has smothered and circumvented the conceptual creativity during the earlier stages, and has defeated the basic purpose of the entire logistic effort.

So I suggest that the first part of the logistics problem is to fix basic product characteristics that will make the system sensible from an operational point of view. The second part is to produce the detail planning, supporting procedures, and policies *after the original configuration has been set.*

This, to me, is the heart of Deputy Secretary of Defense Packard's two references to the logistic support problem in his important memorandum of May 28. I quote the first:

> "Consideration must be given *in development* to all matters necessary in a full operating system. This will include such things as maintenance, logistic support, training, etc."

I now quote the second:

> ". . . where these matters are dependent upon the final production design, *as much of this work as possible should be delayed until the production stage.*"

If these two different task areas can be understood and defined, I feel that the necessary interchange and joint sense of purpose between the engineering design community and the logistics system community can be developed and strengthened.

Engineers must be motivated to consider the operating environment in the same manner as they consider system weight, structural integrity, reliability and system cost. They must realize that the system they produce cannot be evaluated as a good system if, from the logistics point of view, it is too difficult or costly to support. I believe it is extremely important at the outset to set limits on what is considered too difficult, too costly, and to set minimum acceptable characteristics.

Logistics people must likewise be motivated to state their conceptual objectives in a manner and form meaningful to the engineer. When a designer is given a job to do, one of the first things he wants to know is how much time he has. Everything he does from then on may be constrained by time. He is further constrained by many other requirements, some which are adequately defined and often quantified, and others which are loosely described and hazy. The attention which he pays to his constraints is greatly influenced by the degree to which they are clear.

Weight, for example, is a relatively easy problem to address because it lends itself to clear understanding. Where system weight is a requirement, each designer begins his work with his own weight objective clearly in mind, regardless of level of detail. To a lesser degree he has some idea of the requirements for reliability. He knows what the system must do in terms of performance but, when it comes to the operating environment, he may have a hazy idea of what is needed. This then gives the designer a poor basis for performing the vital tradeoffs that must be made with other major system needs.

Logisticians will substantially advance their own cause and actually assist the beleaguered designer by making sure that logistic considerations, introduced in the early conceptual stage, are confined to those which directly contribute to the physical characteristics of the system hardware. By this I mean that the system design people should not be asked during the early development process to attempt a quantification or a detailed definition of spares requirements, of manning requirements that are not a system parameter, of maintenance levels, or of the personnel training problem. Very simply, we must allow the designer time to gather his thoughts and to put his best conceptual effort into the physical configuration of the system itself. This effort, therefore, must be constrained only by those parameters which are truly necessary as inputs to the basic system itself. It's the age-old, horse-sense story of doing first things first.

The best solution to this is to have designers who understand the implications of excessive spares, maintenance, or personnel training so that it is an inherent part of their initial thinking.

Earlier I mentioned the efforts of specialists in the system design. You know that as problems were recognized in such areas as reliability, maintainability, logistics support, safety, etc., the functional managers in DOD rightfully gave special emphasis to these areas. This, in turn, has resulted in the growth of specialist groups in both government and industry in these areas. New contract requirements have been established but, while not mutually exclusive with respect to one another, the technical efforts to satisfy these requirements are often managed separately and not as a part of the mainstream of engineering. There has been a natural tendency for each of these supporting activities to become an end unto itself, i.e., more and more we seem to get reliability for reliability's sake, etc. We often find that, in effect, the specialists themselves decide on the project effort in that area. This produces a built-in bias *for* complexity and *against* simplification. It is essential to recognize this aspect of the problem and the need for appropriate tailoring and timing of logistics efforts in the total system development effort.

Now, there is another reason for the sensible phasing of detailed and exhaustive planning *of any kind.* During the conceptual phase, prior to full-scale engineering development, we are normally in a competitive situation where at least two or three contractors are simultaneously expending research, development, test and evaluation (RDT&E) funds. Premature activity of *any* kind, therefore, may not only necessitate a 50 percent re-do on the part of the winning contractor but the costs associated with premature activity will be multiplied by the number of contractors who are actively engaged in the competition.

By simple arithmetic, if three competitors were accomplishing premature work, and the winning contractor's efforts were only 50 percent useable at a later date, we would reap one-sixth of the total work performed and paid for. I ask you: How meaningful is the detailed logistics plan for the paper avionics for a paper airplane?

Furthermore, because there are a number of people who take the results of premature work seriously, there is often substantial effort and cost to *undo* this work before the *re-do* can start. Is it necessary to add that *we cannot afford this?*

Let me now articulate my first challenge to you. Take a long, hard look at your total mission task. Decide very selectively what comprises the absolute minimum to be accomplished prior to full-scale engineering development and then prior to final production design. Don't feel you're alone in this matter; we in engineering are faced with doing exactly the same thing.

After you have accomplished this painful task, after you have defined that necessary minimum to be accomplished during the conceptual phase, you should then focus your attention and effort upon upgrading logistics design parameters to a degree commensurate with their importance. Herein lies my second challenge. Logistics system requirements must be clearly stated, and where possible quantified, in a "design to" fashion, lest we continue to experience deficiency and unnecessary compromise in supporting and maintaining the operational system.

I hasten to add that it is here that the system design and logistic support people must function together. If there is a single key to the solution of our total problem, it almost has to be the one I have just mentioned: a single-minded, problem-oriented, joint approach by engineers and logistics systems people. I believe we can help with your problem. I know you can help us with ours.

In summary, I would like to restate and emphasize the two challenges that I made earlier: first, that you clearly and distinctly define the two phases of your work, that which must be done *during* the conceptual, and that which can be done *afterwards;* and second, that you formulate the kind of definition of requirements which the designer can use to influence the hardware.

From my point of view, the design community at large must be convinced that no design is complete and that no system is adequate unless it is operationally effective and unless it is supportable in its ultimate environment. This turns my challenge into a *we* rather than *you* effort.

I hope that these thoughts will help to keynote this conference and possibly influence the thinking and discussion which will follow.

$$* \quad * \quad * \quad * \quad *$$

Logistic support planning including reliability and maintainability shall be consistent with the key program decisions and phases of activity

—*DOD Directive 5000.1,*
Major System Acquisitions

52

TRI-TAC: Architect and Planner for Joint Tactical Communications Equipment and Its Logistic Support*

Lieutenant Colonel Donald M. Keith
Charles A. McCarthy

In the present constrained resource arena, one of the most important but often misunderstood and misused buzz phrases is integrated logistic support (ILS). Some of the very real and extremely expensive areas of support that must be considered by DOD system acquisition program managers are:

- The maintenance plan
- Support and test equipment
- Supply support
- Transportation and handling
- Technical data
- Facilities
- Personnel and training
- Logistic support resource funds
- Logistic support management information.

*Extract from *Defense Management Journal*, October 1973, pp. 49–51.

TRI-TAC, an element of the Office of the Secretary of Defense under the staff supervision of the Office of the Assistant Secretary of Defense (Telecommunications), is the system architect and principal planner for joint tactical communications equipment and its requisite logistic support being developed for use by the military services and defense agencies.

Planning support for tactical communications equipment to be used by two or more military services or defense agencies gives an added dimension of complexity to the problems inherent in development and acquisition of military hardware. Conversely, it provides an opportunity for large scale economies.

Balanced Support Emphasis

TRI-TAC supplements basic ILS policy by providing an initial ILS plan, along with the system or equipment specification, to the acquiring DOD component which then prepares a more detailed plan. Because the equipment will be used by two or more services, the ILS plan must consider joint aspects of support and must be approved by TRI-TAC. The plan serves as the basis for inclusion of ILS requirements in specifications and other contractual documents.

The policy of TRI-TAC requires planning for logistic support to begin at the program initiation stage so support funding needs can be identified early in the program. It also requires the acquiring DOD component to issue a certificate to using commands attesting that ILS has been fully planned and acquired. Support costs must be clearly identified and any program changes, which cause a reduction or elimination of logistic support effort, must be documented, indicating the effect of the change on a system's operational capability and availability. Essentially, then, TRI-TAC seeks to assure a balanced emphasis between technical, operational and support requirements.

The purpose and objective of logistic support integration is to:
• Promote development of hardware which is technically excellent, cost effective, reliable and maintainable, and realistically supportable throughout its operational use.
• Attain operational readiness over a programmed life cycle.

Essential Requisites

It is essential that several significant requisites be met to successfully integrate logistic support into the design phase in both joint and independent DOD component system acquisition programs. These are:

• Top management must support integration of logistic requirements into the design process.

• The entire acquisition community must be made aware and convinced of the benefits of integrating requirements for logistic support with the design process.

• Logisticians must express support requirements explicitly for inclusion in specifications, requests for proposals and contracts.

• Equipment specifications must clearly state specific verifiable logistic requirements. Blue sky statements of "high reliability," "easy maintenance," etc., lead to confusion, misunderstanding, unenforceable requirements and unsupportable equipment.

• The specification for the contractor must contain only related equipment design and fabrication work tasks.

• Logistic planning must begin as soon as the conceptual need for the proposed acquisition is recognized.

• Qualified logistic managers cannot be created overnight by assignment to the job. Military departments and Defense agencies must train personnel, who are proficient in one or more areas of logistics, in the broader aspects of the logistic management career field.

• Interchange of information between various disciplines must be vigorously practiced by all specialists of the acquisition team.

Summary

Requirements for logistic support must be recognized and identified as early as possible in the acquisition cycle. The program manager must determine the what, when, who and how at the appropriate time and translate them into numerical requirements wherever possible and practical. Resources must then be programmed to meet approved requirements.

It is important for managers at all levels, especially at the top, to recognize that as the system development progresses through the acquisition cycle and funds are committed, available options for satisfying requirements for logistic support lessen.

Determining support needs concurrently with the design process should have the beneficial effect of achieving logistic readiness and supportable equipment at the least cost.

53

Reducing Risk Through Testing*

Rear Admiral L. S. Kollmorgen

Operational testing has a direct relationship to the military capabilities of operating forces. The greater the effort made to identify and correct any operational deficiencies discovered before the design of a system is frozen, the greater will be the capabilities of the operating forces when the new weapon system is deployed. Furthermore, significant cost and time benefits may be realized if major system deficiencies are found and corrected prior to either quantity production or operational deployment. Certainly it is less disruptive to such essential activities of operating forces as training, tactics development, and maintaining a high state of operational readiness if extensive in-service fault correction and retrofits can be avoided.

In effecting the testing policies set forth in DOD Directives 5000.1, "Acquisition of Defense Material," and 5000.3, "Test and Evaluation," it is sometimes difficult to reconcile the guidance that stems from different points of view. For example, concern has been expressed over the ponderous nature of the developmental process and the potential impact on the nation's military capability. Those voicing this concern view test and evaluation as a contributing factor to what they perceive as the excessive length of the acquisition process, and conclude that items needed in a hurry must be removed from the process in order to get the job done on time.

On the other hand, others feel that the process moves too fast and are disturbed by the pressure applied to get systems into production before development has been completed.

*Defense Management Journal, October 1977, pp. 2–9.

One of the more misinterpreted catchwords used in connection with test and evaluation is "fly before buy," which is often associated with the policies formulated by former Deputy Secretary of Defense David Packard. It has been variously interpreted, and is perhaps the cause of the more pejorative comments connected with operational test and evaluation. This results from the misperception of initial operational testing as a major hurdle to be overcome prior to receiving production approval. This is not and has never been the intention in requiring adequate OT&E before making the major production decision.

Reducing Risk

What Mr. Packard was advocating was sound program planning with the achievement of key development objectives validated through test and evaluation, and the provision of adequate time in the development and early production period to allow for the correction of deficiencies brought to light in developmental testing and OT&E. The intention was to reduce the risk of unpleasant surprises and costly corrections to deployed equipments through increased emphasis on adequate, as well as operationally relevant, testing.

A successful transition from development into production is not characterized by an abrupt termination of development followed by an immediate start of production. Rather, it is a gradual process by which the production effort is phased in as the development effort is phased down, but not necessarily out. Testing should be continued throughout this transition period to provide input to the production engineering effort and contribute to the maturing of the weapon system design.

The key is selecting the appropriate point to start the transition. Ideally this would be when a system's design and technology are well in hand and the government will benefit from the most advantageous application of investment dollars. In short, it requires an assessment of the risk involved in initiating production balanced against the need for acquiring the military capability. Of course, this implies the exercise of sound judgment.

Unsatisfactory Results

The policy contained in DOD 5000.3 has not been in existence long enough to have influenced a major weapon system throughout the acquisition cycle; that is, from initiation through production. It may be useful, however, to review some experiences that have been gained during the period the directive has been in effect.

For a variety of reasons, some programs have suffered severe delays or have produced results far short of the intended goals. The causes have ranged from insufficient testing, to testing which discovered deficiencies too late, to adequate testing which pointed out shortcomings but failed to influence decisions for adequate corrective action before production began.

For example, in the Encapsulated Torpedo (CAPTOR) program, an insufficient number of initial test articles prevented early determination, within acceptable probability bounds, of the causes of the inadequate performance observed in testing. The result was a deferral of the major production decision until follow-on T&E of pilot production items could be conducted. This is sometimes referred to as the T&E gap, which can be avoided by planning for sufficient test articles and adequate OT&E. Provision for such activity is necessary to bridge the transition from development to initial production. It also provides for a higher degree of assurance that lessons learned from the testing and incorporated into the early production items will preclude unpleasant surprises in production systems.

In the case of the Navy's HARPOON anti-ship missile, the engineering prototypes completed a successful developmental test program. However, operational tests of pilot production models disclosed failures in missile components which rendered reliability unacceptable. The failures developed when the transition was made from essentially handcrafting missiles to building them with production materials, tools, processes, and personnel. The initial, low-rate production was maintained until the problems were resolved and solutions verified by additional operational testing. This illustrates the desirability of early quality assurance tests, the need to be prepared to make required changes in materials and processes, and the value of a planned period of pilot production and testing to bridge the transition to full production.

After the POSEIDON missile was deployed in 1971, scheduled firings of operational missiles indicated that the missile was not maintaining the performance level demonstrated during developmental tests. Investigation determined that the degradations in performance were attributable primarily to the lack of adequate component testing and screening during production rather than to the missile design which had been verified in the developmental program. To correct this, the POSEIDON Modification Program was initiated at a cost of more than $200 million, and the subsequent performance of the missile improved as a result of changes made to production processes. This illustrates the validity of continued operational testing to ensure that no degradation in desired performance is induced by production methods or the operational environment.

When a program has provided for adequate testing in the appropriate environments and test results warn of problems, the warning must be heeded. In this way, situations similar to that of the Army's GAMA GOAT might be avoided. The GAMA GOAT is a 1-¼ ton truck designed to transport cargo, personnel, and weapons both on and off roads in military operations.

Even though prototype testing in 1966 indicated that the GAMA GOAT would not be suitable for military use until several modifications had been made and tested, the vehicle was approved for quantity production. Following 1967 tests in which reliability requirements were not met, a decision was made to procure more than 15,000 vehicles.

Testing in 1969 on preproduction vehicles revealed maintenance and durability problems, and in 1970 the first eleven production vehicles were rejected because of quality control defects. Production continued, however, and GAMA GOAT was deployed despite high maintenance requirements, poor durability, and indications that the Army did not have a satisfactory combat vehicle.

Early Correction

As mentioned previously, early detection and correction of deficiencies can result in more capability in the operating forces and less likelihood of costly retrofit programs.

A good example of a recent case where T&E revealed a system deficiency at an early stage was the crew-escape system designed for the B-1 bomber. Tests conducted with the B-1 crew-escape module at Holloman Air Force Base, New Mexico, demonstrated that the system's aerodynamic stability could not be assured at speeds above 300 knots per hour. Extensive redesign involving high risk and additional cost would have been necessary to provide that stability. Development of the module was therefore terminated, and an off-the-shelf ejection-seat system was modified to replace the crew-escape module.

In yet another example of the value of T&E in detecting system defects, the Navy discovered during tests of the prototype CH-53E helicopter that the main rotor shaft had a low fatigue life, requiring replacement after only 230 hours because the contractor had underestimated the dynamic flight loads the shaft would have to sustain. As a result of these tests, a redesigned main rotor shaft with a fatigue life of 11,000 hours was fabricated and will be fully tested and subsequently installed in the production aircraft.

During the early 1970's, emphasis was placed almost exclusively on conducting OT&E just prior to the major production decision, Defense Systems Acquisition Review Council Milestone III. This was because of the large procurement funding commitment usually implicit at Milestone III. Lately, however, it has been realized that earlier OT&E may be beneficial for four reasons:

• In considering system concepts during the early stages of a program, it is necessary to know not only whether they are technically feasible, but also whether they are operationally viable or tactically useful.

• To have any impact on the R&D phase of a program, OT&E must be conducted earlier than immediately prior to DSARC III, since by then the major portion of the research and development resources are usually expended.

• The earlier in the development cycle a deficiency is identified, the less will be the cost of corrective action.

• The successful completion of early and operationally valid testing reduces the risk in the long-lead release and limited production decisions.

Indications are that a better field product is resulting from emphasis on early operational testing. The early field demonstration of desired reliability goals in the UTTAS helicopter illustrates this. At program initiation, DOD placed strong emphasis on UTTAS reliability objectives by establishing realistic preliminary goals and rules for reliability measurements. These goals were met or exceeded during operational testing by Army troops, providing increased confidence that the production reliability goal would be achieved in the operational environment. Currently, DODD 5000.3 is being revised to reflect this emphasis on earlier operational testing.

Reliability

Another area in which T&E is now making a significant contribution is that of equipment reliability. This is not a new field of interest; the services have long concentrated on it and have given close attention to achieving improved reliability through proper design and quality control in the production process. T&E plays a major role in the measurement of reliability and isolation of failures. The actual correction of defects is accomplished for the most part by redesign of the equipment or improved quality control in its manufacture.

Laboratory and bench tests of components and assemblies are the mainstays of reliability testing by the contractor, and form the basis for proving that his equipment complies with specifications in his contract. What these tests do not do is expose the system to the full range of operational stresses, the harder handling of less-well-trained military operational and maintenance personnel, and the cumulative effects of harsh field conditions.

If these reliability weaknesses are to be discovered before they adversely affect a large number of deployed equipments, the equipment must be tested under typical operational conditions. Therefore, the services are now required to specify reliability requirements in operational terms, measurable under operational conditions.

A limiting factor in operational testing is that of obtaining a sufficient number of hours of system operation under relevant conditions; that is, full system operation in an actual field environment. These are costly hours. To augment them, it is necessary to ensure, to the greatest extent possible, that developmental testing of new systems is done under conditions sufficiently realistic that the failure data can be combined with the results of operational testing to give a comprehensive, yet more economical, method of evaluating weapon system reliability.

How Much Is Enough?

Although T&E makes a valuable contribution to the weapons acquisition process, it is important to ensure that testing is not conducted unnecessarily. There is obviously some point at which the incremental value of information obtained by additional testing is not worth the additional expense. The factors which influence the judgment about how much testing is needed vary from program to program.

The T&E policy changes emphasizing earlier operational testing, operationally valid reliability goals, and combined developmental and operational testing are expected to improve the efficiency of the acquisition process in general. Specifically, the greater emphasis on earlier operational exposure to systems under test should provide increased confidence that weapon systems so tested will have the desired operational characteristics upon deployment. In addition, the weapon design teams should profit from timely feedback of the results of operationally significant tests.

The requirement to set preliminary reliability goals specified in operationally relevant terms should go far toward producing equipment that meets the users' needs. Hopefully, reliance on statistical projections will be reduced.

A closer association of developmental and operational testing should provide for decreased costs of tests, schedule improvements, and more emphasis on operationally relevant testing. As a result, decision makers should have more and better information on which to base their judgments, and increased knowledge of any inherent risks.

Of course, these are the objectives desired. Only people can make things happen, and only through continued dialogue can we assure that the true intent and objectives of DOD policies are understood.

I submit overall cycle time could be decreased without sacrificing prototype testing. The method would be to schedule more elements of testing in parallel with the engineering development phase. In this way, necessary iterations and improvements could be made on a timely basis. The receipt of comments from the user regarding maintainability and human factors much earlier in the schedule would be helpful.

—Sam K. Smith, Texas Instruments, Inc.

54

Managing T&E Programs*

Dr. George J. Gleghorn

Specialized or custom design, low production rates, high reliability and other unique aspects of space vehicle programs impose requirements for significant management trade-off among cost, schedule and technical risk in the planning and implementation of test and evaluation programs. Although the test and evaluation experience gained over the past two decades now is reflected in a number of directives, standards, and specifications, there is a flexibility within this framework to custom design each test program, to make appropriate cost, schedule and risk trades to achieve maximum confidence that the design and workmanship will meet mission requirements.

Several significant considerations that can affect cost, schedule, or performance risk are discussed as examples of tradeoffs in the test program.

• To be effective in influencing design so that the vehicle can be adequately tested, and to reduce schedule, one should commit to and start implementation of a test philosophy and selection of test equipment very early in the program. However, the earlier the design of test equipment is begun, the more vulnerable it is to design changes imposed by changes in design of the vehicle. Cost and schedules are adversely impacted when these changes occur.

• The very low number of production articles in each program requires a different way of looking at how general purpose facilities, equipment, tooling, etc., will be supplied. Since each program is

*Extract from "Optimizing Space Vehicle Test Programs," *Defense Systems Management Review,* Vol. I, no. 5, Winter 1977, pp. 57–58.

specifically tailored to its unique mission, the amount of special purpose equipment and specialized computer software tends to be disproportionately high with respect to capital investment and as a percentage of total program costs. The challenge is to increase general purpose capability without jeopardizing the ability to accomplish specialized testing.

• Since test and evaluation starts at the piece part level and continues through component, subsystem and system level tests, cost and schedule can be reduced by the selective performance of environmental, burn-in, electrical compatibility and other types of tests only at one or two of the assembly stages, rather than at each of the four stages. Such cost and schedule reductions must be accomplished without adding significant risk.

• The constraints imposed by the space operating environment and the pressures to keep spacecraft weight down may result in a spacecraft that is relatively fragile, easily damaged, and difficult to maintain because of packing density. To reduce the possibility of damage, safety awareness programs and training need to be continuously worked, protective coverings and devices have to be used for sensitive components, and highly disciplined and procedural test operations are required. These requirements add schedule and cost constraints that must be traded off against potentially serious damage to the test article.

Although there are many considerations which are amenable to tradeoff, there is a significant body of experience that verifies standardization is a cost effective goal. Thus every test should be thoroughly planned in terms of objectives, data requirements, criteria for success, etc. Step-by-step procedures that call for quality assurance sign-off at all critical steps as the steps are performed are issued to test personnel well in advance of each test. Records are kept of all measurements and all anomalies or "out-of-spec" conditions. The data are evaluated by knowledgeable personnel for telltale trends after each major test or environmental exposure to determine any incipient failures that require repair or replacement of equipment prior to launch.

The overall management of test programs, especially for the larger and more complex systems, is enhanced by utilization of earned value and other advanced program management techniques that have been developed and proved over this past decade. The large investment represented by the test items, the many engineering internal and external interfaces involved, and above all the ever present requirement for long term, fault-free reliability demand that detailed cost effective management be exercised at all times. Nothing can be left to chance.

55

Production Design*

Elwood S. Buffa

The producibility and minimum possible production cost of a product originally are established by the product designer. The cleverest production engineer cannot change this situation, but can only work within the limitations of the product design. Therefore, the obvious time to start thinking about basic modes of production for products is while the products are still in the design stage. This conscious effort for producibility and low manufacturing cost is called production design, as distinguished from functional design. To be sure, the product designer's first responsibility is to create something that functionally meets requirements. However, once this has been accomplished, design alternatives ordinarily can be found. Which of these alternatives will minimize production costs? A well conceived design already has narrowed the available alternatives, and has specified, for example, a sand casting (if that is appropriate in view of both function and cost considerations).

Once the design has been chosen, process planning for manufacture must be carried out to specify, in careful detail, the processes required and their sequence. Production design first sets the minimum possible cost that can be achieved through the specifications of materials, tolerances, basic configurations, methods of joining parts, and so on. Final process planning then attempts to achieve that minimum by specifying the processes and their sequence to meet the exacting requirements of the design. Here, the process planner may work under the limitations of available equipment. But

*Extract from *Modern Production Management,* 5th ed. (New York: John Wiley & Sons, Inc., 1977), pp. 130–131. Copyright © 1977. Reproduced by permission of John Wiley & Sons, Inc.

if the volume is large, or the design stable, or both, the planner may be able to consider special-purpose equipment (including semiautomatic and automatic processes) and special-purpose layout. In performing these functions, the process planner is setting the basic design of the productive system.

The thesis of a production design philosophy is that design alternatives nearly always exist that still meet functional requirements. For the projected volume of the product, then, what differences in cost would result? Here, we must broaden our thinking, because there are likely to be more areas of cost that can be affected by design than we would imagine. There are the obvious cost components of direct labor and materials; but perhaps not so obvious are the effects on equipment costs, tooling costs, indirect labor costs, and the nonmanufacturing costs of engineering.

Indirect costs tend to be hidden, but suppose that one design required thirty different parts, while another required only fifteen (for example, the reciprocating automobile engine versus the rotary engine). There are differences in indirect costs due to greater paper work and the cost of ordering, storing, and controlling thirty parts instead of fifteen for each completed item. The indirect cost for each design is composed of those items that are necessary to process parts through the paper work system, and includes such items as: planning; tool ordering; material purchasing; shop and assembly order writing; storing materials; dispatching material, tools, and parts; order control; accounting, transportation, inspection; etc.

I conclude that industry can only play the game as defined by its customer, and a company which does a thorough and factual job of analyzing and pricing the risks attending its proposal may well find itself the loser to a more optimistic competitor.
—*Maj. Gen. Gerald F. Keeling, USAF, Ret.,*
Hughes Aircraft Company

Section 9—

THE DEFENSE/INDUSTRY INTERFACE

Introduction

Most Americans view defense contractors as depending almost entirely on defense business for their existence. This belief apparently sprang up during the Vietnam war when it was popular to attack the so-called military-industrial complex, usually with more prejudice than fact. The fact is that during the late 1960s defense business accounted for only 17 percent of the *largest* defense producers' revenues. Since then defense has fallen to 10 percent of their business, and only six of the 30 largest prime contractors depend on defense contracts for as much as half their revenue. Most of these companies are primarily involved in other than defense systems. Another fact is that no other industry in the free world lives with such constraints: a mound of acquisition regulations, the glare of publicity, and customers' representatives in their plants.

A problem facing the general manager of a systems-oriented company or division is how to strike a balance among business objectives, business opportunities, and organizational capabilities. These three factors each have multiple elements. They might be viewed as three-dimensional axes:

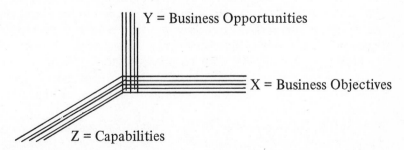

The intersection of these axes is where the general manager must make decisions between, for example, an objective such as developing a capability in a particular technology versus a current business opportunity; or going with a current lower profit project which may preclude his having resources available to commit to a higher profit one later. There is no substitute here for the business judgment and experience required.

The more direct knowledge an individual has of industry, the greater respect and appreciation he generally has for it and for its accomplishments. Former DARCOM Commander Gen. George Sammet observes:

> These people (officers sent to on-the-job training with industry) come back just loaded with ideas. They're impressed by industry's integrity, patriotism, energy and desire to do a good job. At the same time, they see that certain corporate aims are just different . . . seeing that the bottom line comes out black is what drives industry on a contract. In brief, the defense-industry team needs to be just that: a team.

Probably no single individual in industry has done more over the past three decades toward coming up with solutions to defense problems than Lockheed's famed Kelly Johnson. In the discussion with him contained in this section the importance of the systems generalist comes through. The points he makes, including goal-setting, motivating, and communicating, are the same themes presented in Chester A. Barnard's classic *Functions of the Executive.* As mentioned by Dr. John S. Foster, it would be difficult to identify successors to the handful of people having Mr. Johnson's total systems scope.

Boeing's Chairman T. A. Wilson presents an excellent summary of what makes a competitive industrial organization, including driving responsibility and authority *down* to the lowest practical levels. How often, in practice, one sees them go in the reverse direction, leaving too little capacity for planning at upper levels— and too little growth opportunity at lower ones!

Earl Molander hits on a classic problem in the defense business and many other businesses: the "system," the result of over-optimistic pricing. But what business can stay in business if it is pessimistic? How can it compete with companies more willing to take risks? To date there is no real answer to this problem, which stems from the perennial desire of the customer to get something at less than a realistic price.

Wayne Hinthorn's survey of industrial management of commercial programs versus management of defense systems confirms the observations of others who have made similar comparisons. A fact not mentioned is that industry personnel in systems management generally do very well promotion-wise, as do their counterparts in defense.

Mr. Hinthorn finds that although the PM in defense programs

has more authority in engineering design, the industrial PM has greater freedom to exercise initiative and ingenuity and to make trade-off decisions. Another key finding is the need for, but general absence of, specific training in *program management* in industry. The general approach is "throw 'em in the pool and see if they can swim," an approach the services have found to be too risky to programs' success, as well as to PMs' careers. An institution or graduate schooling comparable to the Defense Systems Management College appears to be needed for industrial managers.

The final selection, "Discussion With a Production Executive," is an interview with an individual who represents a company renowned for its expertise in efficient production. The care and logic with which he approaches the annual model year changeover could serve as a model in many types of hand-off from systems management to production.

$$\star \quad \star \quad \star \quad \star \quad \star$$

The program manager cannot disengage in any literal sense. He must manage contracted work in just the same sense as he manages all the other parts of his program. More precisely, in this case he manages contractor management of his program. It is not a question of *whether* he manages; it is only a question of *how* he manages—or mismanages.

Industry project managers and government program managers are agreed on this point:

> It seems clear that the government program manager must exercise rather tight control until such time as he is assured that the industrial project manager has the technical and managerial competence to perform as required. (Steiner and Ryan, *Industrial Project Management*)

The obverse is equally true, however: Once the government program manager has obtained the assurance he needs, he should relax his control and concede to his contractors a measure of freedom to exercise judgment and flexibility similar to that which he seeks for himself.

—*LMI Introduction to
Military Program Management*

The basic need of every company is to make a profit. Only then can it provide jobs and earnings for employees.

—*I. W. Abel,
United Steelworkers of America*

56

Impact of Defense Awards on Major Defense Contractors*

J. Stanley Baumgartner

Prime defense contracts constitute less than half the sales in 24 of the top 30 defense contractors, according to a comparison of figures released recently by the Defense Department and by *Fortune* Magazine. Only McDonnell Douglas, Grumman, Hughes, Northrop, Todd and Fairchild Industries have prime contracts that amount to as much as half their respective gross sales.

Collectively these thirty companies received contracts totaling $25.4 billion, or 50.1 percent of all prime contracts' value. Prime contracts awards and gross sales for these top thirty contractors are shown in the accompanying table.

Taken as a whole, defense work constitutes only 9.8 percent of the top companies' gross sales. When six heavily consumer-oriented companies are deleted, however (General Electric, Chrysler, IBM, AT&T, General Motors and Ford), defense awards constitute 28.0 percent of the remaining largest defense contractors. This still is contrary to the popular belief that major prime contractors could not survive without defense work.

Who needs whom more, as between the Defense Department and defense contractors, is a moot point. Competition between divisions of defense producers is often intense, because of such incentives as technology, cash flow and return on investment, among other reasons. But at the corporate level it is clear that defense has

Program Management Newsletter, May–June 1978, p. 25.

far less impact than is generally believed. And the in-house impact is even less, since a substantial part of these companies' business is subcontracted to smaller producers.

30 Largest Defense Contractors	Prime Contract Awards[1] (in millions)	Gross Sales[2] (in millions)	Defense Awards as % of Sales
1. McDonnell Douglas Corp.	$ 2,574.0	$ 3,544.8	72.6%
2. Lockheed Corp.	1,673.4	3,372.8	46.6
3. United Technologies	1,584.7	5,550.7	28.6
4. Boeing Co.	1,579.9	4,018.8	39.3
5. General Electric Co.	1,519.6	17,518.6	8.7
6. Rockwell International Corp.	1,479.8	5,858.7	25.3
7. Grumman Corp.	1,428.1	1,552.7	92.0
8. General Dynamics Corp.	1,371.5	2,901.2	47.3
9. Hughes Aircraft Co.	1,093.4	1,800.0[3]	60.7
10. Northrop Corp.	1,046.7	1,601.4	65.4
11. Raytheon Co.	1,040.9	2,818.3	36.9
12. Westinghouse Electric Corp.	802.1	6,137.7	13.1
13. Tenneco Inc.	744.9	7,440.3	10.0
14. Sperry Rand Corp.	651.5	3,270.0	19.9
15. Chrysler Corp.	619.9	16,708.3	3.7
16. Litton Industries, Inc.	609.3	3,440.5	17.7
17. International Business Machines	547.1	18,133.2	3.0
18. Todd Shipyards Corp.	468.4	213.2[4]	— [6]
19. American Telephone & Telegraph Co.	456.8	36,494.8[5]	
20. Honeywell Inc.	456.7	2,911.1	15.7
21. Textron Inc.	454.7	2,802.2	16.2
22. Fairchild Industries, Inc.	429.3	399.3	— [6]
23. Martin Marietta Corp.	426.4	1,439.8	29.6
24. General Motors Corp.	380.1	54,961.3	.7
25. RCA Corp.	364.0	5,880.9	6.2
26. TRW Inc.	361.3	3,263.9	11.1
27. Ford Motor Co.	351.9	37,841.5	.9
28. Singer Co.	350.1	2,294.3	15.3
29. Texas Instruments Inc.	324.1	2,046.5	15.8
30. Teledyne Inc.	304.8	2,209.7	13.8

[1]Source: News Release, Ofc of Asst. Sec Def (Public Affairs), March 28, 1978, "100 Largest Defense Contractors."

[2]Source: "The Fortune Directory of 500 Largest U.S. Industrial Corporations," *Fortune,* May 8, 1978, pp. 238–262.

[3]Estimate, privately-held company.

[4]Source: Moody's Industrials.

[5]Source: Moody's Public Utilities.

[6]Sales reported as lower than contract awards due to differences in report periods.

57

A Discussion With Kelly Johnson of Lockheed's Skunk Works

J. S. Baumgartner

Clarence L. "Kelly" Johnson is famous as one of the world's foremost designers and builders of advanced aircraft, including the F-80, U-2, F-104, and "others we can't talk about." The Skunk Works' YF-12 and SR-71 are the world's fastest operational aircraft, operating at more than mach 3. At the time of this discussion Mr. Johnson, now retired, was manager of Advanced Development Projects (ADP), better known as the Skunk Works, one of the best defense contracting operations in the nation.

Mr. Johnson discusses here the principles, many adopted by other organizations with varying success, that have enabled the Skunk Works to turn out this remarkable succession of outstanding aircraft.

Mr. Johnson, recently I saw these 14 "Basic Operating Rules" of the Skunk Works. Perhaps this gets to the guts of your philosophy in project management.

Actually there are 15; the last we put into effect is that you can't go skiing when we're in the middle of an important project.

Are these written up for internal use?

Yes. We've never published them because I want to be able to change them as we see fit. We started out on the F-80 in 1943 with nine rules, and they've now grown to 14. The 15th is merely a caution to my people, because I've had an average of three important people each winter who break their legs or sprain their ankles; and of course it has no authority whatsoever. But you don't change people's lives, just as I don't try to have people match my metabolism. I tend to get up early and I leave early. I claim that if you can't do it with brains, you can't do it with hours. But there are a lot of people around who like the hours. If they want to come in at 8:30 or 9 o'clock, I don't stare 'em down. How they do their work is their business, because they're here long after I leave.

You Can't Drive These People Away With a Sledge Hammer

I'm proud of our morale. You can't drive these people away from here with a sledge hammer. They don't want to get back in the other way of doing work. And yet we have dispersed some of them, because we've come down from our high peak. In 1967 we were the 237th largest corporation in the United States in terms of sales, just above Liggett and Myers. People don't think of the Skunk Works as doing this volume.

This is the volume of the Skunk Works alone?

This is just the Skunk Works, not Lockheed.

Most of us don't have any idea of the size of the Skunk Works, and feel this probably is an area we shouldn't probe into because of the classified nature of your projects.

Well, we've kept security on the thing. But I don't mind telling people that we can handle big projects and large volumes, as well as small volumes. We had a rate of production on the U-2 that is substantially greater than anybody would imagine.

So the Skunk Works is involved in both development and production; is that right?

We started out in 1943 building the F-80. At that time Lockheed California was building 17 P-38s a day, four B-17s, six Hudsons and Lodestars. We were building so damn many airplanes that when we finally got the go-ahead from the Air Force to produce a tactical jet, Mr. Robert Gross said, "Kelly, you've been pestering me for seven years to have an engineering experimental department. I don't think much will come of this because the range will be so short, but go ahead and try it."

You've Got to Communicate

And so we had to fit into a hell of a going outfit (Lockheed California). I took the wind tunnel model shop, a circus tent, and some Wright engine boxes and we built ourselves Skunk Works No.

1. This is Skunk Works No. 6 you're sitting in. We have grown from where initially we'd make two or three prototypes—F-80s, F-104s, and 19 different types to this point . . . that we can talk about. Also some we can't talk about. We've set up a completely independent organization, heavily oriented toward the engineering side of it, but not facing that problem that is so common where the engineers and the shop people fight. One of the basic concepts I've always had is that those who build it and those who design it had damn well better be within a few hundred feet of each other, and *talk*. The hardest thing in the world today is to get the designers and the tooling people and the planners and those who make it to *communicate*. It's a well-known thing that you've got to. When we started, the distance between the drawing board and the airplane was about 300 feet. And the shop people were perfectly free to come on into the engineer and say, "Damn it, this is stupid. Why don't you do it like that?" And so we built up a morale between the two and a mutual trust, which is the heart of our whole operation. And yet, when we get into a big program like the SR-71, I have 7 o'clock meetings right here each morning with the engineers, to see where they are on engineering problems. I have a 9 o'clock meeting with the shop people who are building it. No engineers can be in the shop meeting, and no shop people can be in the engineer meeting; because I find that if you intermingle them, they won't bring out the problems. Having two separate meetings, we take action. And no one knows who's squawking about the other, and we keep the personnel problems at a minimum and go for the facts. A fact is the hardest thing in the world to find. It still is.

There's No Place for Committee Action

A "fact" often is just an opinion or assumption or belief in disguise.

To recognize one is harder than hell. And so separating the meetings like we do works fine. I think we'd have a shambles if we got them together and the engineers started criticizing the people in the shop, and vice versa. If there are important decisions, I'll call in my shop superintendent and my project engineer, and we'll talk about it right here and settle it. But there's no place for committee action. If they can't come to a decision then I make it, right or wrong. Often it's better to make a decision, even if it's wrong, than not to make any at all.

What's an example of some of the toughest problems you've encountered?

One of the hardest problems we had was to teach people to use titanium. You take a good machinist, and we have lots of them, and you say, "From our research tests, this is the speed you use and the drill you use," and all the rest of it. You tell an old machinist to do this and, hell, he won't do it. So what I did was to make a research machine shop. I took the oldest and most skilled machinists and had them in there to run tests and develop data for six weeks. Then we put them back in the shop and developed our famous red book from their findings—we made it with plastic sheets, because if the man who's making a part has dirty hands, he won't want to open a clean book if it's paper. So they had the feeling they had developed this book as much as the engineers had; and we didn't have any problem with getting our own people, our machinists, to meet our goal that within six months we would double the rate of titanium removal, and within a year we would be up to 10 times the industry average. But you couldn't do it unless these fellows felt they had a part in it.

How did it work with your subcontractors?

We gave them the results, and they were free to see how we did it before submitting a price on this thing. It was fixed-price work. You carve this out, we said, and find out for yourself what a tough material this is. It wants to tear, it doesn't want to cut. Yet 40 percent of them lost money, and some went broke.

Why was that—they didn't take enough time or give enough attention to details on how to work with titanium?

They didn't have the equipment in certain cases; they didn't follow our book, which we distributed to anyone who wanted it. Our book is quite a classic thing, in terms of machining of titanium. When we started out on the YF-12, we had *10 years* of research on titanium. We *knew* what we were doing. And so I said, "Well, let's see if we do. Let's build the fuselage nose of it, the front end of it, because it has the thinnest gauges, double curvature, and is the hardest part of the airplane to build. Let's build that first." It has something like 6,900 parts in it; and 95 percent were failures. After 10 years of research! There's a hell of a gap between the research and its application.

Then you must have more than 20 years' experience with it.

We started in 1948 on titanium. But when you say titanium, it's like saying "animal"; there's all kinds of titanium. We bit off quite a chunk by using alloys that no one had ever used. We decided we weren't smart enough to go the stainless steel/honeycomb route the B-70 was going. And I went down to our Georgia plant where they were building a forward fuselage in a big pressurized tent in the middle of the shop, with people walking around with all their clean room clothing. And I said, "That's not for the Skunk Works.

We'll use a conventional type of construction with an unconventional material."

The Damnedest Paper Work System You Ever Saw

Then, for an outfit that doesn't like paper work at all, we put into effect the damnedest paper work system you ever saw. For every 10 parts we put through the various processes, we put in three test coupons subject to the same treatment. One of them we pulled to see how strong it was; one we put a ¼-in. cut in and then bent, to see to what radius you could bend it; and the third we kept in case we had to go back for more heat treatment. One month I found we were making nothing but test coupons; I thought we were going to go down the drain. But to this day, we can trace every part we have made of titanium back to the melt at the mill, what sheet it came out of, and what direction of the sheet it came out of. If we hadn't done this, we could never have built a titanium airplane.

How do you mesh technology that is in the initial stages of practical use with an emerging specific operational requirement?

If you've built 42 airplanes, you have some idea what the hell is coming. Titanium is very light, and yet it's stronger than steel. We faced some severe temperature problems—the ram air temperatures were well over 800 degrees Fahrenheit. Yet we had to cool the air down so it went into the cockpit at 32 degrees. And God knows we had electrical problems; we'd run into problems in electrical connectors in our control system, for instance. So everything about the airplane had to be invented and done over, and it was hard to get people to take these problems on, because the production run didn't promise to be long. And yet the technology that went with it was very advanced, and there were enough patriotic companies around that stepped up to it. Our relation with our vendors, the authority we delegated to them, was just unparalleled compared to any other program I've been on, or any I've seen.

You Have to Leave the State of the Art

So an advanced plane comes about partly based on need, as for materials that meet the tremendously high temperatures; and then it's a matter, I presume, of bird-dogging the state of the art. . . .

You have to *leave* the state of the art. The trouble with our present system of developing things is that we don't leave it. We left it when we built the YF-12, from the snoot, which carries the airspeed boom, right back to the tail. The problem is that often we don't take enough of a step. Take the B-1; here's an airplane of *aluminum* that will have to be fighting in the 1980–1990 period! And we see that in 1968 something like 19 percent of the titanium sponge used in the United States was brought here from Russia.

Bought from Russia?

Yes. They policy-priced it, and they lay it down 35 cents a pound cheaper than what we got the stuff for, on the YF-12, which has 35 percent duty on it. We found a warehouse full of it up in Oregon, when we went up to visit one of our vendors. It was laid down from a ship right out of Leningrad. And who the hell can afford to be in the titanium business and not save 35 cents a pound for the sponge? Now you go through 35 processes before you get an alloy, but that material price is still a big part of the whole thing. We have lots of ilmenite in this country, but it's not being developed because of the costs. The Russians are building titanium airplanes though. But the YF-12 is out of production; the United States, the greatest country in the world, can't afford to make these. And yet the cost, had they gone forward with the F-12B, would have been several million dollars cheaper than the F-14—each.

The YF-12 has a speed of mach 3 or more?

Or more. Whereas the F-14 is mach 2.2. Any time you say aluminum you're at 2.2.

The B-70 was . . .

Stainless steel; but at a fantastic cost. It hit mach 3 for a very few minutes. Every flight we make on this thing (SR-71) we put in three to five times as much time, at higher speed and higher altitudes, than the total time on two B-70s. Twenty-two minutes—hell, that doesn't mean anything. We fly round trips across the country every day in the SR-71.

The Russians Are Passing Us

In view of your own high security measures, is it feasible for companies with commercial products to set up similar measures to safeguard proprietary information?

Sure. In fact we did it on the JetStar. We had finished the U-2 and we built the prototype JetStars here. It came out in eight months and worked like it should. You can do it if you want to. Whether it's advisable may be another thing; what you're faced with is your sales campaign. You've got to tell your customer about it, and the customer talks. Also there may not be the need for security. But there sure is a need in the military field. And now that the Russians are passing us in all military fields, there's more requirement than ever that we have security; but we're not starting enough projects to put in your eye. They (Russians) average two or three prototype fighters per year and have for 10 years. It'll be 10 years between any prototype fighters in the United States. And long before then we will have published everything about it.

It's like when we put in that missileman site. We announced two years in advance where we were going to put them, in the best surveyed country in the world, and all a Russian had to do was go down to the county courthouse and find out where the nearest coast geodetic survey mark was; they don't need any satellites and things to find out where we are. Before the cement is ever poured, they know it to the foot. But we don't have that privilege over in Russia; we have to do it the hard way.

You mentioned before that you try to avoid paper work in the Skunk Works. How do you keep things as simple as possible without getting bogged down in administration?

Well, I think the best explanation and the most complimentary thing that has been said about us was said by Air Force Gen. Ben Bellis. He was sent out here by (General) Bernie Schriever to make a management survey. Before we got into the SR-71, Schriever and the Air Force wanted to know how can this little outfit go into production on a very sophisticated airplane and interface with SAC (Strategic Air Command)—the most sophisticated customer in the world, as far as I'm concerned. Well, he came out here with eight other people and I let them sit in on our morning meetings, gave them an office, and the run of the place. And here's what he concluded:

> "For those of us that had not previously been associated with the ADP program (that's the Skunk Works), this survey activity was indeed a revelation. The Skunk Works approach equals or exceeds the disciplines and detail required by the Air Force 375-series system management approach. In no place could we find where the Skunk Works operation had less centralized direction and detailed control. The thing missing is the requirement for detailed administrative and progress reporting, both in the program activity and financial expenditures."

You Can Put in a Billion Auditors

Now one of our rules guarantees to the government that it will get monthly both a progress report and a financial report, and it'll be honest and it'll be brief. Our financial report consists of a few sheets, the main one of which shows what we have spent, what we have committed, and what we think we're going to spend. We try to keep from surprising the customer, because we know it when we're going to run over. You can put in a billion auditors around here; they wouldn't know how it stands. We did something else. Early in the business we invited them to send an auditor here. We are the most audited outfit in the whole country, I'll bet. I'm audited by the Corporation; audited by Arthur Young, Inc.; and audited by a special auditor sent here by the Air Force. We invited them. Why? Because it's so damn much easier, when you see you're going to get in trouble, to call in Clarence Heckman—he's just a couple of offices away —and say, "Clarence, here's where we stand and we've got troubles. One of our vendors is going busted. We're going to overrun." It makes life so much easier and he knows how to plan and report, and he's accurate as hell. He has the run of the place, and he can see what's going on. But he can't tell how much is done; we have to do that. So we turn in a technical report.

But that Air Force report is an important statement on how we operate. They probably know more about our programs than they do with all their 375-series regulations, ASPRs (Armed Services Procurement Regulations), and everything else. We're as close as that green button (on the telephone); and we talk it over.

Another thing that's important is this: The Air Force has always given me a good, intelligent person to work with. Four have become full generals; the others have all wound up beyond brigadier general rank. But the thing that gets tricky is that they may change every two years; and if they do, you lose the continuity and trust that's built up. There have been plenty of times when we've had to teach the officers first assigned to us; they've had no experience building hardware, and we don't expect them to. But it isn't very long before every one of them has become technical enough to make an intelligent decision. I can't think of a single exception. But that's because you must have a competent guy with the authority delegated to him, on each side. Generally they do such a good job in the Air Force they get promoted and leave; I take it as a compliment when they get promoted. But by that time the project has jelled. You can't put a guy on a project and then, when it's through, just keep him there forever.

We Face the Facts

How do you get this open-mindedness, this willingness to learn, on both your side and the customer's side?

I guess fundamentally you have to have honest, interested people. This system wouldn't work worth a damn if we tried to trick anybody, and God knows we could. We're too stupid to tell lies; can't remember long enough. And if you tell the truth, it's so much easier. That doesn't mean we don't have our disagreements. But we face the facts and not the personalities.

How deeply do you get into details on a program?

You mean me personally?

Yes.

I guess I'm the highest paid project engineer in the country, and a member of the Board of Directors. Yet I spend 67 percent of my time on actual hardware. Because I like it.

And this is probably one reason you cut out a bunch of paper work?

Yes. Rule No. 7 is to keep reports to a minimum, but record important things thoroughly, like we did on titanium. We owed it to the country to have a damn good trail on how we handled these high alloys.

But we don't reinvent the wheel. For instance, the man I had who was the basic wing project engineer on the YF-12 designed the 22nd wing he had worked on that had flown. It was the 42nd airplane I had carried from an idea to fruition. There's no substitute for experience; I guess that's a big part of it.

And yet, you can take good kids out of other organizations— we have a rating system here where we rate them from one to five; one is top, and five is barely passable—and when they're here and know their responsibility, if they haven't upgraded two grades in three or four months, there's something wrong with us. They don't like all the damn paper work either. They like to see the hardware and see it work. They'll upgrade.

We Have Special Classifications Based on Achievement

This job satisfaction is probably more important than salary to many of them.

One of our 14 rules is that a man is not paid by the number of people he supervises. It took me a hell of a long time to get that one through. With unions and guilds and everything else, they tend to put people in groups such that generally the more people you have working for you, the more you get paid. I report directly to the

President of Lockheed actually; and I said, "This is no go. How can I keep a guy who can make a wing like that and has only 12 people, and pay him as if he had a normal number, 50 to 100?"

How do you do that?

We have special classifications.

So it's based on achievement then?

Achievement. That's why you can't drive 'em out of here. Good technical people don't necessarily want to go the administrative route. So I let them go the same route I do. I'm probably the world's worst staff person. . . .

Basic Operating Rules, ADP

1. The Skunk Works manager must be delegated practically complete control of his program in all aspects. He should report to a division president or higher.

2. Strong *but small* project offices must be provided both by the military and industry.

3. The number of people having any connection with the project must be restricted in an almost vicious manner. Use a small number of good people (10 to 25 percent compared to so-called normal systems).

4. A very simple drawing and drawing release system with great flexibility for making changes must be provided.

5. There must be a minimum number of reports required. But *important* work must be recorded thoroughly.

6. There must be a monthly cost review covering not only what has been spent and committed but also projected costs to the conclusion of the program. Don't have the books 90 days late and don't surprise the customer with sudden overruns.

7. The contractor must be delegated and must assume more than *normal* responsibility to get good vendor bids for subcontract work on the project. Commercial bid procedures are very often better than military ones.

8. The inspection system as currently used by ADP which has been approved by both the Air Force and Navy meets the intent of existing military requirements and should be used on new projects. Push more basic inspection responsibility back to subcontractors and vendors. Don't duplicate so much inspection.

9. The contractor *must* be delegated the authority to test his

final product in flight. He can and must test it in the initial stages. If he doesn't he rapidly loses his competency to design other vehicles.

10. The specifications applying to the hardware must be agreed to *in advance* of contracting. The ADP practice of having a specification section stating clearly which important military specification items will not knowingly be complied with and reasons therefore is highly recommended.

11. Funding on a program must be *timely* so that the contractor doesn't have to keep running to the bank to support government projects.

12. There must be mutual trust between the military project organization and the contractor, with very close cooperation and liaison on a day-to-day basis. This cuts down misunderstandings and correspondence to an absolute minimum.

13. Access by outsiders to the project and its personnel must be strictly controlled by appropriate security measures.

14. Because only a few people will be used in engineering and most other areas, ways must be provided to reward good performance by *pay not based on the number of personnel supervised.*

$$\star \quad \star \quad \star \quad \star \quad \star$$

One of my associates opines that we are lucky the airplane was invented back in 1903 and developed over the following years. In overstating his belief, he says we would probably be stopped from developing the aircraft in today's climate. The environmentalists would object to the noise. The consumerists would want them all recalled before they got out the factory door. The pacifists would complain that they could be used to carry troops. Preservationists would be afraid they would fly into City Hall. And 10 government study groups would prove that they definitely cause cancer.

—*Larry Kitchen*
President, Lockheed Corp.

For that matter, the most famous aviation expert in the United States, ten years after Kitty Hawk, was asked about the chances of flying across the Atlantic. The expert was dubious.

"It is a bare possibility," he explained, "that a one-man machine without a float and favored by a wind of, say, 15 miles an hour, might succeed in getting across the Atlantic. But such an attempt would be the height of folly. When one comes to increase the size of the craft, the possibility rapidly fades away. This is because of the difficulties of carrying sufficient fuel. It will readily be seen, therefore, why the Atlantic flight is out of the question." That clouded crystal ball was the property of none other than Orville Wright.

—*Robert J. Serling*

58

Reducing Costs Can Be Fun: Judgment, Flexibility Needed*

T. A. Wilson†

There are a number of companies which have done some excellent work in the design to cost field. I believe Boeing is one of these companies. The application of design to cost principles, which is a well established technique in high rate production industries, to the development of complex defense systems requires some fundamental changes in thinking as well as some imaginative work by a team of designers, manufacturing, quality, procurement and finance people. Before significant results can be expected, a cost and profit conscious environment must be developed throughout the entire organization. One program team cannot be expected to excel in cost performance if another team is allowed to retain its fat or use techniques which are archaic and inefficient. This applies at all levels of command, including corporate structures.

A very new organization, which has never built up the institutionalized hierarchies and functional checks and balances, will not achieve major improvements by belt-tightening or sharpening its management tools, or even inventing a new technique. These things, of course, must be accomplished well. However, when survival is the issue, fundamental changes in operating methods and elimination of functions must be considered. To do this intelligently, every manager needs complete visibility of his costs—an accounting system with maximum discreteness of both direct and

*Extract from *Defense Management Journal,* April 1973, pp. 60–64.
†Chairman of the Board and Chief Executive Officer, The Boeing Company.

indirect charges—and maximum authority to buy or reject the service being charged. The system must be real, with the benefits of a team's cost management skill passed on to its customer as a lower price or reflected in higher profits, or both. And last, but by no means least, a formal performance measurement system must be set up between a manager and his boss so that he knows the basis for his promotions. This can be a simple one-page contract of both quantitative and subjective items, but it helps to write it down and discuss the items before the fact and then reward commensurate with performance. Reducing costs can be fun. Once the designers and others realize this, they become highly motivated.

After responsibility and authority have been driven down to the lowest practical levels, the cost of every function challenged and functions that don't pay their way eliminated, the proper competitive environment necessary to achieve maximum benefit from a design to cost technology will probably have been created.

People in the organization should now be cost and profit oriented. They should have an accounting system that lets them understand their total costs. Now the engineering and manufacturing people have the tools to make the trades among various designs, various processes and the cost of labor versus capital required for automation. They can work with the quality and test people to discreetly trade the cost of disruptions for inspection or test versus the cost of buying or developing new equipment or techniques which will enable in-line inspection or test. They become very conscious of the cost of peaks and valleys of activity. They increase manpower at a slower rate and reduce it quickly, and vigorously work the problem of using the fewest possible high-skill/high-rate people. In developmental programs with reasonable schedule slack, each test is planned to get the most data for the lowest cost. In general, fewer tests will be called out; however, the team knows intimately what it costs to provide additional articles for schedule or mission confidence.

Data Deficiencies

The results of this approach are evident in current performance of both commercial and defense programs. However, there is a serious deficiency in our ability during the developmental phase to work life cycle costs. Our work in O&M (Operation and Maintenance) is for all practical purposes limited to specification compliance with reliability and maintainability requirements plus optimization of integrated logistics support specified requirements. I believe we have done as well as anyone in this but there is really not a good basis for working design to cost with a realistic consideration of life cycle influence. As I have heard so many government people deplore—the accounting system simply does not provide adequate data for this purpose.

My experience in dealing with government certainly indicates there is no shortage of accountants and although most of us in industry have gone through the process to make our cost management systems acceptable, I really don't expect those staffs to diminish. So there should be a surplus capability available to enable development of government accounting systems which would provide useful data for the life cycle parameters necessary to maximize design to cost benefits.

Change Military Service Concepts

I indicated earlier that, even with rapid development of effective design to cost techniques, it would be many years before substantial impacts were made upon the two greatest users of military funds—manpower and O&M. And the eventual total impact upon the big three spenders, which includes acquisition costs, will be inadequate to enable maintenance of the military posture which America will need for the price Americans will be willing to pay.

I believe this dichotomy can be resolved but it will take some radical revisions of military service concepts.

Manpower, O&M and acquisition are the 1-2-3 spenders. Yet our military services operate, in the broad context, essentially as they did before World War II when threats and responses were quite different, and when civilian interest and involvement were low. I'm not talking about strategy and tactics and weapons which *have* changed, but rather about the organic capability concepts which are so expensive to acquire and sustain and which, in many cases, are no longer required.

These concepts require a self-contained capability to operate and maintain a weapon system at all levels regardless of the basing and deployment plan—a complete and almost entirely separate logistics support system is acquired and sustained which duplicates the functions of the industrial team producing the weapon system. For example, an intercontinental ballistic missile system based in the United States obviously is not going to be redeployed. Really substantial savings could be made by never buying a "military specification" support system, by using contractor personnel for many of the operations and most of the maintenance functions, and by gross reduction of the subsidized infrastructure that doesn't show up in the accounting system in a fashion where it can be discreetly challenged.

The same is true for large portions of transport aircraft functions. In fact, if DOD is going to be able to operate effectively with future budgets, it will be necessary to make very serious studies of elimination of entire commands rather than the peanut butter reduction approach that can destroy everyone's effectiveness, while only saving a small percentage of dollars. An innovative concept could be worked with the airlines which would satisfy air transport functions efficiently at less than the present cost, assuming equitable accounting treatment, proper designation of training expenses, and elimination of passengers and cargo which are carried because "we are going anyway."

Changes Needed

If defense spending is going to provide a quality product, *national security,* for a price that is competitive with national social and economic needs, the defense establishment is going to have to go through the process many of our corporations have been going through. It must develop an accounting system that enables cost trades, examine the institutional hierarchies versus the necessity of their functions or the cost of reduced or increased activity, work the "make or buy" in the government on a real cost basis, drive management authority to the lowest possible levels, develop a performance measurement system for these managers that includes meaningful and understandable cost performance parameters and, by all means, continue the very productive efforts to improve cost management techniques in defense systems development.

These are very difficult political and institutional problems to deal with. It will take an enormous amount of courage but it may mean our survival. I believe Americans will support a strong America. We should, however, earn such support by vigorous effort to produce this strength within funding constraints which enable America to be as strong economically and socially as militarily. I believe we can achieve this balance.

✶ ✶ ✶ ✶ ✶

The successful conduct of a military campaign now depends upon industrial supremacy. As a consequence, the Armed Forces of a nation and its industrial power have become one and inseparable. The integration of the leadership of one into the leadership of the other is not only logical but inescapable.

—*General of the Army Douglas MacArthur*

59

Cost Overruns: The Defense Industry View*

Earl A. Molander

Probably more than any other single factor, cost overruns on major defense contracts have catalyzed the attack on the military-industrial complex and brought the American defense industry into the public eye. Dramatic overruns on the F-111, the C-5A, and the SRAM missile made headlines in the late 1960's just at the time when public concern over the political, social, and macroeconomic impacts of the military-industrial complex had begun to surface.[1]

In talking about cost overruns (or "cost growth," the preferred DOD term), one must begin with the strong cost-orientation of defense industry prices. This orientation owes much to the frequent use in defense contracting of cost-plus-fixed-fee contracts and renegotiation of price on firm-fixed-price and fixed-price incentive contracts. In renegotiation, the aim of both parties is generally toward full reimbursement for costs incurred plus a reasonable profit fee.[2] In effect, the producer's costs become the primary determinant of final price in a defense contract.

*Extract from *Perspectives in Defense Management,* Winter 1975–1976, pp. 98–104.

[1]F-111 costs increased by $3,300 million or 114 percent, C-5A costs by $1,630 million, or 61 percent, and SRAM costs $717 million or 193 percent. "Cost Overruns Bring on the SEC," *Business Week,* June 6, 1970, p. 31.

[2]When he testified before the Joint Economic Committee in the late 1960's, Robert H. Charles, Assistant Secretary of the Air Force for Installations and Logistics, was challenged by Senator Proxmire to name one big contractor who had ever lost money on a defense contract. At the time, he could name none. U.S. Congress, Joint Economic Committee, Subcommittee on Economy in Government, *Economics of Military Procurement,* Hearings, 90th Cong., 2d Sess., November 13, 1968 (Washington: GPO, 1968), Part 1, p. 317.

The Bidding Phase

In arguing the government's responsibility for cost overruns in the bidding phase, respondents cited three factors: "the system," the lack of well-defined technical baseline, and unrealistic technical requirements. The last two of these clearly are similar to the factors of engineering, support, and estimating changes cited by both Packard and the GAO. The most frequently cited factor in the survey, usually without elaboration, was "the system." As one North American Rockwell vice-president expressed it:

> People who complain in Congress have set the climate in which these things occur. Usually the low bidder takes it because Congressmen screech when other than low bid is taken and low bid is from their state.

The military also shares the blame, according to a Lockheed manager:

> A guy in DOD wants to get a program started. Realizing he can't sell it unless it costs less he will cut the estimate, sometimes unconsciously. The contractor does the same.

The other side of this coin, on the contractor side, was the "buying-in" factor or, as many respondents who objected to the overtone of dishonesty called it, "intentional optimism" or "underbidding." The program managers queried felt, in fact, that honest optimism often influenced bidding contractors. As another Lockheed manager responded:

> Underbidding; not knowingly, though. No one does that. As smart and senior as a guy is, he figures this is the sure fire way to do a job. There is an eternal optimism among the technical guys. But if you didn't have this, you might never start.

In an effort to probe further the thinking on these two aspects of the "buying-in" factor, respondents were asked whether it was prevalent. For some, undoubtedly "the system," which gives defense firms no choice but to "play the game," was a convenient rationalization justifying continued intentional underbidding on defense contracts. Underlying, however, was a more basic feeling that the contracting agency, DOD as a whole, the Congress, and the American public are all part of "the system"—all want to get a weapon system for less than it would cost a good contractor to produce it.

No respondents suggested any improvements in "the system." The implication was that the desire to get something "on the cheap" is inherent in human nature, nothing can be done to alter it, and the program manager must learn to live with abuse from an uncomprehending public. A Philco-Ford manager put it this way:

> The system encourages it (but I don't have a solution). The public doesn't understand our business. The government forces low estimates and price competition, e.g., we bid $1,000,000 on a contract for 8% fee—$80,000 profit; the government says "you can do it for $600,000," we say "O.K." to get the contract; it overruns to $1,000,000 and there's a public outcry, but that's what we bid! It's the government's fault.

Execution Phase

In the execution phase, many of the respondents cited customer initiated contract changes as the principal cost of cost overruns. "Once you start the program," complained one, "the customer just piles on the requirements." There are two reasons for this. First, the development process tends to be self-generating, creating new opportunities for improving the product which the military customer is reluctant to pass up. Second, requirements change because each government organization concerned wants something different from the program.

While prone to inject changes, the contracting agency is yet reluctant to give the contractor design freedom, insisting on rigid adherence to contract terms. One respondent asserted:

> There's too much technical concentration on the original specifications and not enough good common sense. When you're close to the design objectives you should weigh the costs to make them against the value of that increment of performance.

Running through both the bidding and execution phase is the inability to predict performance, cost and schedule when operating at the state-of-the-art. Although both parties to the contract share this inability, it is the contractor, responsible for program performance, who incurs most of the blame for cost overruns.

Program Management Responsibility

Finally, one-third of the respondents were prepared to accept "poor management" as a factor in cost overruns. One TRW manager expanded on the point:

> We can cost pretty well—within 10%. If overruns are greater than 10%, then it's bad management. But, if "unk-unks" come up, you

have a new program. From this new datum, if overruns are greater than 10%, it's bad management. It's too simplistic just to say "bad management."

Traditional business ideology holds that management must take the blame (and credit) for an organization's failures (and successes). The failure of most of the respondents to follow this precept presumably reflected their consciousness of the operation of numerous uncontrollable factors in defense contracting not present in other contractual situations. The respondents who did acknowledge management failures as a factor in cost overruns evidently bowed to the logic that if management wished to claim the credit for success, it should be equally prepared to accept responsibility for failure.

Respondents were also asked whether they felt it was possible to determine whether a cost overrun resulted from poor management. Fifty-two percent answered unequivocally that it was, the remainder expressing reservations, or strong doubts. The uncertain responses, interestingly enough, came mainly from the upper-level managers.

Summation

Program managers interrogated in this survey were both critical and cynical in their view of the role of price in the competition for defense contracts. Price, in their perception, has taken on artificial importance as a result of "the system" which forces contractors to bid lower than both they and the government know is realistic in order to win contracts, a practice known as "buying in." The respondents saw the practice as a basic cause of cost overruns. Implicit in the program managers' indictment of "the system" is the indictment of a client, the government, who demands a level of national security not achievable at the price he wishes to pay, and of a public ignorant of technical and economic uncertainties in "state-of-the-art" contracting.

A contractor's low bids are not always a conscious deception. Respondents held that there is a natural optimism, especially among technical personnel, that a system can be built cheaply and quickly. In the execution of contracts, frequent design changes dictated by the contracting agency commonly raise eventual program cost higher than anticipated by the contractor, but poor management, while difficult to detect in retrospect, also contributes significantly to cost overruns. Another factor, the survey indicated, is the difficulty of predicting program parameters inherent in state-of-the-art contracting.

This sampling of defense perceptions of the cost-overrun problem differs significantly from those of both defense critics and government spokesmen. The respondents' notion of an impersonal "system" which imposes certain patterns of behavior does not seem to be shared by the critics or the government, at least to the same degree. The managers interrogated did, however, recognize the practice of "buying in" to contracts cited by defense critics, although not all perceived it as based on conscious deception. They also were more inclined than government spokesmen to personalize responsibility for cost overruns, recognizing human errors and poor management as factors that tend to perpetuate "the system" and lead directly to cost overruns. On one major point the respondents agreed with official explanations of the cost overrun phenomenon, the difficulty of establishing a firm technical baseline and realistic requirements in this area of contracting.

$$\star \quad \star \quad \star \quad \star \quad \star$$

Part businessman, part scientist or engineer, part lawyer, the project manager is a versatile individual who is not easily found or developed. In every proposal it submits, however, the R&D organization states, in effect, to its owners, its customers, and itself, that it *does* have this kind of individual—and is willing to risk its profit and reputation on him.

—John Stanley Baumgartner

What the Industrial PM expects of his counterpart in the government: (1) Integrity (2) Firmness; firm guidance (3) Promptness—promptness in making decisions, and in taking actions that avoid unnecessary costs (4) Knowledge of the prime contractor's project team—personal rapport (5) Don't ask for personal favors (6) Clear understanding of the problem the system is expected to solve. *What the government PM expects from his industrial counterpart:* (1) Integrity; and, related to this, realism (2) Effective leadership over his team (3) Keeping project operations going according to plan (4) Effective management of subcontractors (5) Knowledge of the government PM's team—personal rapport (6) Clear understanding of the problem the system is expected to solve. *What's necessary on the part of both:* (1) Mutual confidence (2) Never losing sight of the program's technical, cost and schedule objectives (3) Frequent communications/personal liaison.

—Anonymous

60

An Industry View of Data on Major Systems Acquisitions*

J. Stanley Baumgartner

For at least two hundred years industry has held a unanimous view of defense data requirements: they are excessive and superfluous. And there is good reason for this viewpoint. A blue ribbon panel several years ago reported that the cost to the government for management systems applications and related reports was estimated to be $4.4 billion—in one fiscal year! Obviously the services could buy a tremendous amount of hardware instead of paper for this sum.

Industry is well aware of the rationale for data requirements, however, even though it does not agree with the extent. And the quality and meaningfulness of data has increased greatly in the past few years, as contractors' management control systems measure up to the criteria spelled out in the C/SCSC Joint Implementation Guide. More than a hundred industrial facilities have been validated as meeting these criteria. What then are industry's present concerns regarding data?

These concerns might be considered as falling in three categories: technical data, management data, and the Defense Department's use of data.

My contacts in AIA, the Aerospace Industries Association, cite these as being the foremost specific concerns regarding data:

*Extract from a presentation at the Airlie House Comptroller Conference, October 15, 1975.

- Providing computer software, including proprietary data
- The question of responsiveness to RFP's that require "all data will be furnished with unlimited rights"
- How to define manufacturing data packages so that all manufacturers, rather than one or two, can be reprocurement sources
- Continuing hearings on IRAD
- Interest in how MIL-D-1000, the date ordering document, will be revised.

Industry is also concerned that management systems may be proliferating again. In the past, the number of systems was reduced from more than 500 to about 170. A little over a year ago the GAO made a survey of reporting requirements and found that "reporting requirements are no longer burdensome." Nevertheless, AIA member companies currently believe that the NMARC, AMARC and ACE studies point to increased information and more systems.

There's another area though that affects every project and program office that gets data from industry. Industry has a lurking suspicion that much of the data provided *is never used.* And there is good reason for this suspicion, as exemplified recently on two major programs that got into trouble shortly after DSARC go-aheads. In one case cost performance reports were being received in the program office but were merely filed. In the other, the reports were received and apparently destroyed!

Why don't project offices make better use of data? And what effect does this apparent misuse have on the contractor? The answer to the first question is probably that many project offices do not know what value they can obtain from analysis of, for example, the cost performance report (CPR). As to the effect on the contractor, put yourself in the shoes of a PM in industry for a moment. If your customer never asks questions about the CPR, never challenges your facts, analyses or conclusions, how are you going to keep your people believing that the report is important? There's a morale and credibility factor here that has a great deal to do with whether a contractor continues to provide meaningful data or whether his reports degenerate to irrelevant formalities.

The quality of information the project office receives, and consequently the visibility derived from it, is directly proportional to the degree of effective use made of this information. The contractor will discover very quickly whether the project office sincerely expects good data, or whether it will settle for eyewash.

61

Industry Management of Commercial vs. Defense Systems Programs*

Wayne L. Hinthorn

Although there are a number of articles and books on the techniques of program management, little information on industry management of commercial vs. defense systems programs appears in the literature. Most of what has been written is concerned with teaching the specific tools of program management and their application to defense systems programs or military program management. The information presented here provides an interesting overview of the application of program management within industry, and definite indications of the differences in its application to commercial programs vs. defense systems programs.

Management Administrative Techniques

One of the management or administrative methods studied was the use of a formal program plan to describe in detail the scope of the program and the work required.

Formal work authorizations were used by all companies, both commercial and defense oriented, except in two cases where the particular administrative procedures used did not require such au-

*Extract from *Defense Systems Management Review,* Vol. I, No. 1, pp. 51–67.

thorization. In these cases, one commercial and one defense, sales orders took the place of the authorizations.

Schedule techniques vary considerably between companies and between commercial and defense systems programs. Somewhat surprisingly, PERT, CPM or critical path networking appears to be more widely used for commercial programs than for defense system programs. This may be indicative only of the fact that two large engineer construction firms were among the companies surveyed. In the case of these two companies, the complexity of their major construction programs in the power plant, mining and many other fields makes the use of techniques such as CPM or PERT networking mandatory. However, three other organizations engaged in commercial work also use PERT or CPM, whereas only three companies of those surveyed in the defense system field used PERT, CPM or other network techniques.

It is probable that the size of the programs in the defense systems field, which were generally small to medium size (5 to 85 million dollars), influenced the fact that networking techniques were not used more often. The attitude of many of the companies in the defense systems field is reflected by the statement of one program manager that PERT is generally considered a discredited technique. One company with a program in the 350 million dollar range uses milestone and Gantt charts. This is in comparison with the engineer construction firms where computerized critical path network scheduling is used for every program, and is apparently extremely useful both to the company and the client. See Table 1.

Table 1. Scheduling Techniques Used

				Defense Programs
Network	6	3		
Milestone		1	3	
Gantt			7	12
LOB	Commercial Programs		1	2

Cost control is an important requirement for both commercial and defense systems programs. Therefore, the type of cost control employed by the various companies and programs was of major interest. Nine of the twelve defense system oriented programs were using the DOD Cost/Schedule Control System Criteria (C/SCSC) approach to cost control. One additional program implemented a modified earned value type of system. This program probably would have implemented C/SCSC if not for the small size of the division and the implementation costs. See Table 2.

Table 2. Cost Control Methods and Techniques

Type program	Cost control methods			Are work packages used for cost control?		Are actual vs. planned costs compared?	
	Earned value	C/SCSC	Computed vs. actual				
Commercial	7	1	4	Yes	No	Yes	No
				7	5	12	0
Defense	2	9	1	11	1	12	0

Of perhaps greater significance is the fact that, of twelve commercial programs, one firm was using the C/SCSC system and three others used an earned value system not too different from the C/SCSC system.

Regardless of the techniques in use, the responses from program managers revealed that perhaps the dominant concern of all program managers was control of costs.

All of the defense systems programs were using the work package technique of breaking the work into small tasks. Half of the commercial programs were also applying this technique in one form or another. The concern for cost control and the particular techniques employed are discussed more fully later.

Program Manager Authority and Status

The major emphasis of this study was to see if there were interesting differences between the management of commercial programs as compared with defense systems programs. Many of the questions asked by interview or questionnaire were aimed at determining the value the organization places on the program manager as related to the success of the company.

The first question considered in this category was whether the program manager's name was placed in proposals for new work. This practice was found to be commonly used for both commercial and defense systems programs except where the product in the commercial field is a more or less standard product line and the identification of the program manager would have little meaning to the customer who is buying a known commodity.

The inclusion of the names of program team members in proposals for new work was found to occur with greater frequency in companies engaged in defense systems programs. This difference in emphasis may be because in commercial programs the client wants assurance that a program manager who is known to have successfully satisfied client requirements under past contracts, or has been recommended by other clients, will be assigned to the program. The commercial client already knows that the company is qualified in the field, and therefore has little interest in the program team members. By comparison, the customer for defense systems programs (usually the government) is very much interested in the team the contractor proposes to assign to the program. Knowledge of the team is a means of determining whether that team has the skills and experience to complete the program successfully.

The extent of participation of the program manager in the negotiation process with the proposed customer was also examined. It was apparent from the responses obtained that all of the companies with commercial *and* defense systems programs attach a rather high value to the participation of the program manager in the negotiation process. His participation usually takes two forms: one is as a background coordinator or policy maker; and the other is as a direct participant in the negotiations. In one case of a firm with a defense systems program, the chief negotiator was actually the program manager designee.

The use of a program plan was previously discussed. As would be expected, this plan was found to be the program manager's document, whether or not he actually signs the document, and it is used to establish the program goals and to define the specific tasks to be performed.

Since costs are of primary importance to the success of a program, the program manager's authority over initial budgets for both manhours and subcontract dollars was studied. The results indicate that the program managers of defense systems programs almost always have complete budget authority for their programs. However, it is not unusual for the program manager, in firms engaged in certain types of commercial programs, not to have control of one or more elements of the program budget. This was true, for example, in one company in the nuclear reactor field where engineering design costs for a more or less standard reactor product line are prorated to the various customers for that reactor and the engineering design budget is the responsibility of the engineering organization manager. Again, this difference between commercial and defense systems programs appears to be more the result of the special needs of a particular commercial product line than a significant difference between program management of commercial vs. defense systems programs.

The extent of the authority of the program manager over engineering design, subcontracts, and the quality and reliability of the product is discussed later in the analysis and evaluation of program manager techniques and methods. In these areas of responsibility the program manager's authority and influence differ widely from program to program and from company to company.

Another factor studied was the extent of program manager authority and degree of concern with the control of the "build cost" of the product. Build cost, simply defined, means "how much does the product cost to produce?" This implies that build cost must be controlled from the start of the design process to prevent development of a product that will be excessively costly to produce. The term also includes all of the other cost factors such as the cost of purchased parts and efficiency of the production process. The responses from program managers indicated that they were extremely concerned with the "build cost" and that they monitored this factor very closely. One program manager engaged in a commercial aerospace program defined a cradle to grave approach to monitoring "build cost" which is reviewed in the next part of this report.

Little difference was found between commercial programs and defense systems programs at the organizational level to which the program manager reports. The level varies from company to company ranging from the company president or division president down through the executive vice president, vice president, major department manager or manager of programs. Regardless of the title of the individual to whom the program manager reports, the level was seldom lower than the third layer from the top in the organizational hierarchy and in many companies it was higher. This would appear to indicate that in companies that have adopted the program management organization as generally understood, the program manager is considered to be an arm of the general manager (term used as descriptive of the top management level) for the program to which he is assigned.[1] See Table 3.

The number of people reporting to the program manager differs widely because of the organizational approaches of the different companies and divisions and the different types of programs. It is in this area that some of the key differences and similarities between commercial and defense systems program management were indicated. Most notably, there is no necessary correlation between the

[1]W. E. Diefenderfer, Vice President, United Aircraft Corp., "Application of Program Management in a Matrix Organization," lecture at Rensselaer Polytechnic Institute, Hartford, Conn., 16 Mar 1973 (ms), 1973, p. 7.

Table 3. Management Reporting Level

Commercial	Management Level	Defense
	Program Manager reports to	
1	President	1
4	Vice President	6
5	General Manager	5
2	Department Head	0

size of a program in dollars and the size of the permanent staff. See Table 4.

Job skills of personnel in the program organization follow what is probably a normal pattern ranging from engineers and other technical personnel through production, financial, budget, and schedules personnel.

The dollar value of the programs managed by the program managers surveyed varied from as low as $250,000 to hundreds of millions of dollars. Despite this wide variation, it was interesting to

Table 4. Program Costs Compared with Personnel Assigned

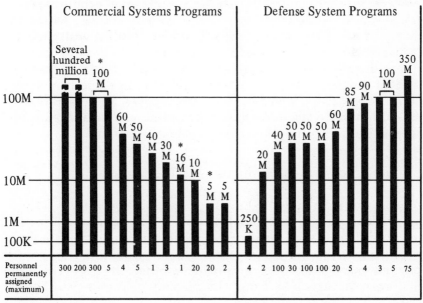

Notes: M = Million   K = Thousand

*Indicates annual rate,
all others show planned program costs

note that the spirit, enthusiasm, and determination which the various program managers displayed in their answers to questions regarding their programs differed little whether the program was of a large or small dollar value.

The question of specific program management training was explored because it might provide some indication of the significance of program management. This is true for the military program manager.

The Department of Defense, through the Defense Systems Management College at Fort Belvoir, Virginia, provides an extensive twenty week Program Management Course for military personnel, military department civilians, and some industry personnel. Although all of the companies represented in the sample provide various types of management training or make available such training outside the company, only three companies provided specific training in *program* management.

One of these companies is a large, technology-oriented organization with diverse programs and products in both the commercial and defense systems field. It provides specific program management training in a two week course conducted in conjunction with a major university. Whether or not this example and the example offered by the Defense Systems Management College point the way to future upgrading of the skills of program managers is unknown; however, this writer expects that the advantages of offering specific training in program management will become obvious within industry as industry comes more and more in contact with program managers who have received such training.

Although many other areas having significance to the management of programs could have been evaluated, the subjects reviewed above provided sufficient basis to form at least some preliminary conclusions as to the differences between industry management of commercial programs and defense systems programs.

Evaluation of Project Management Techniques

Several techniques and methods used by companies and program managers may be valuable in pointing the way toward better, more efficient management of programs. Particular approaches to management that have been found to be effective by individual program managers often are valuable to others. In a few cases, the findings indicate where changes in company policies may be beneficial.

Participation in Negotiations. The extent of the program manager's participation in the negotiation process for new business was of interest because it may indicate the importance of the program manager to the program and to the company. From the data obtained, there appears to be no significant difference between the extent of participation of program managers of commercial programs and managers of defense systems programs. In both cases, the degree of participation varied from that of a monitor, coordinator, or background strategist, to that of a direct participant in the negotiations in a supporting role, or as the negotiator. In a single instance, the program manager of a defense systems program was the chief negotiator, and it was he who received the support of marketing, pricing, and contract management.

From personal experience, the direct participation of the program manager at the negotiation table can be a significant factor in bringing a coordinated position to the table. This is particularly true in follow-on production type programs where the experience of the program manager with the overall program can definitely improve the calibre of the negotiating team. Without the support of skilled pricing personnel and contract management, the negotiating team cannot be effective.

As programs become more complex, as was the case in the single instance where the program manager was the chief negotiator, the possibility of the program manager designee being the chief negotiator will probably increase. This may be true also for commercial programs except where the contract is being negotiated for a more or less standard production item. This is indicated by one engineer construction firm where the program manager designee participates in negotiations to the maximum extent possible and may, on occasion, be the negotiator.

Authority for Engineering Design. Traditionally, in defense systems programs, it is common to assume that one of the key elements of program manager authority is that of control of the engineering design through definition of the requirements and design approval. The results of this study show that although this authority for engineering design still remains with the program manager of defense systems programs, the situation is quite different for commercial programs. In six of the twelve commercial programs, the program manager does not have design approval authority and has little influence over the engineering design except from the standpoint of cost. This is illustrated by one of the engineer construction firms that has developed an organizational structure that appears to be extremely effective. In this organization, the functional disciplines such as engineering have complete responsibility for maintaining the highest possible calibre of work in their particular discipline.

Even though the entire project team is collocated under the overall direction of the program manager, responsibility for the engineering design remains with the functional engineering manager.

Authority for Subcontract Management. Closely allied with the program manager's authority in the area of engineering design is his authority for subcontract management as reflected by whether he has technical authority in the subcontract area and whether he approves subcontracts and changes. Here too, the traditional view of program management is that authority for subcontract management is one of the major responsibilities of the program manager.[2]

As in the case of authority in the engineering design area, of those surveyed, fewer program managers of commercial projects had technical authority in the subcontract area than did defense systems program managers. As for approval of subcontracts, the results were almost identical for both commercial and defense systems programs with only fifty percent of the program managers having such approval authority. The question that may be asked is, without such authority, how can the program manager be held responsible for cost control? In the case of the engineer construction firm previously mentioned the organizational discipline and the program manager's influence, in the subcontract area where the cost is a consideration, may be sufficient. In another instance the program manager of a firm, high in the defense system aerospace field, stated frankly that the relationship of the program with the purchasing or procurement function was "strained." Other companies seem to have at least partially resolved this potential problem by having assigned a procurement representative as part of the program team even though this representative continued to report to the head of the functional procurement organization. Findings for another company, also in the aerospace field, indicated that the degree of authority remaining in the functional area is sufficiently great to result in the possibility of actions by the procurement organization which could be detrimental to the best interests of the program. This tends to be supported by the following finding of the Aerospace Industries Association, as cited in the *Harvard Business Review:*

> ". . . one survey of aerospace companies revealed that the inclusion of the procurement function in a program organization results in improved performance sufficient to offset the usual higher operating cost. . . ."[3]

[2]Steiner, George A., and William G. Ryan, *Industrial Project Management,* The Macmillan Company, New York, 1968, p. 53.
[3]C. J. Middleton, "How to Set Up a Project Organization," in "Managing Projects & Program Series," Reprint No. 21300, *Harvard Business Review.*

Authority in the Quality Assurance Area. Another area of program manager responsibility where there appears to be no clear definition nor understanding of the program manager's authority is the area of quality control and reliability. While some of the responses such as that from one company in the nuclear field are clear (responsibility for quality control in the nuclear field is carefully controlled by legal requirements), in many instances, the only authority of the program manager in the quality and reliability area is in terms of influence and the overall program requirements. A major reason for this in defense systems programs is probably the requirement for independence of the quality control function as expressed in military specifications such as MIL-Q-9858A.[4]

Some projects appear to have accommodated the need for program manager authority by assigning a quality control representative to the project team. The results of this study nevertheless indicate that this is potentially one of the major areas of weakness in program manager authority. Obviously if the quality of products is deficient or excessive quality control costs are incurred, these factors can have a detrimental effect on the success of the program and on the effectiveness of the program manager.

Build Cost. One of the more interesting findings of this study was the approach to controlling the "build cost" of a design as applied to one complex program in an extremely competitive commercial field. The program, involving major development work, was started by performing thorough, parametric cost estimates of all competing products. Then a determination was made as to what the cost of the proposed product had to be to be competitive. When this was completed, a detailed cost estimate was prepared by the responsible functional organizations in the company. The parametric cost estimate was then compared with the detailed cost estimate and where differences were found actions were taken to determine what the cost should be. Next, a fixed ceiling cost, not a target cost, was assigned to every part. In this way the program cost goal is maintained and absolute determination to meet these ceiling costs is required from every member of the program team. When a design that appears to exceed the cost ceiling is completed, the design, procurement, or manufacturing approach is reviewed to define the action necessary to bring the part cost within its ceiling.

This concept is closely allied to the current DOD concept of "design to cost." However, the program manager of this program expressed two perhaps significant reservations in regard to "design to cost." First, he expressed the opinion that "design to cost" will

[4]Dept. of Air Force, "Quality Program Requirements," military specification, MIL-Q-9858A, 16 Dec 63.

not be effective when the cost goal is imposed by an outside source. This occurs when a "design to cost" figure is imposed on a contractor. It was the program manager's opinion that for "design to cost" to work, the cost figure must be arrived at by the hardware developer. Secondly, this program manager stated that for "design to cost" to be effective, the cost figure assigned to each part must be a *ceiling* rather than a *target* cost.

Management Approval Requirements. The requirement for upper management approval of the program manager's actions was found to be generally the same for both commercial and defense systems programs. There did appear to be a slight difference of emphasis in the application of approval requirements. Program managers are usually required to obtain higher management approval of their actions by exception only. The exceptions cited were usually when the basic framework of the program plan or contract must be breached, such as for major changes in scope, schedule, or breaches of allowable budget authority. These requirements for upper management approval are outside the normal framework of weekly or monthly management reviews.

The findings for commercial programs indicated that the program managers were given slightly more latitude in directing the programs than were the managers of defense systems programs. This was found to be particularly true for one large, multiproduct organization where the program manager, who is called a venture manager, is given almost complete latitude to run his program within the limits of the business plan for the program and management reviews. This is particularly interesting since the type of programs in which the company is engaged may be several years long and involve very large expenditures.

Program Organizations. The organizational structure of the programs studied varied from the pure program or aggregate organization to the individual or staff program organization.[5] All four commonly seen types of program organizational approaches, i.e., individual, staff, intermix, and aggregate types, were represented. In addition, there were combinations of the above types of organizational approaches that appear to have been developed because of the particular needs of the project or because of company management philosophies or constraints. When an organizational structure other than the pure program organization was used the matrix principle, where specialized support is drawn from the functional organization, was generally used. Some significant variations in application of the matrix principle were noted. Interestingly, the use of the pure program or aggregate program organization for the programs

[5]Middleton, *op. cit.,* p. 21.

surveyed was restricted to programs in the commercial field. All defense systems programs that were surveyed could be generally characterized as using the matrix principle, although in one case the organization appeared to be moving toward an aggregate type.

The first interesting application of program management, from an organizational standpoint, is represented by the approach used in the engineer construction companies. An outstanding example of the use of the pure program organization is that of one of these firms that has developed and applied the matrix principle to the pure program organization. In this company the entire program organization is located in the same area. The personnel in the organization are individually selected for the program team from persons suggested by the functional organization managers. However, if the manager of the functional engineering or procurement organization, for example, suggests the assignment of individuals to the program who are unacceptable to the program manager, the program manager may veto the assignment. He may also request, although not always successfully, the assignment of particular individuals whom he believes to be best qualified for the program. Individuals assigned in this manner still report administratively to their functional organization manager and receive their performance reviews from the functional manager. This is similar to the collocated approach which is common to some military program organizations.[6]

In the particular engineer construction firm where this approach is used, two significant factors tend to counteract two major objections to pure program organizations. One objection is the supposed reduction in technical proficiency thought to occur when a specialized individual is located away from similar specialists in his functional organization. This objection is countered by making the functional manager of engineering, for example, responsible for assuring that the technical performance of the individuals assigned to the program meets all of the standards of that specialty as defined by the company.

The second often stated objection to pure program organization, that of diffused responsibility for individual personnel performance reviews, seems to be effectively countered by this firm. This is accomplished by leaving the responsibility for performance reviews with the manager of the functional specialty, but requiring that the program manager, who may be more familiar with the details of the individual's performance while he is assigned to the program, prepare an advisory performance review for the use of the functional manager.

The responsibilities of the functional organization managers in

[6]Logistics Management Institute, "The Program Manager Authority and Responsibilities," AD 748 622, Aug 72, p. 36.

relation to those of the program manager appear to be very clearly defined in this engineer construction firm. For example, the program managers understand that they are not responsible for the technical aspects of the design, nor for procurement, except as these matters affect the program cost and schedule. In these organizations, the program manager is responsible for the "what" and "when" part of the program with the "how" being left to the specialists in the functional areas.

This appears to work exceptionally well for this firm, which has a sales backlog of 2.5 to 3 billion dollars. The functional managers apparently understand that they must give the programs the best possible support. At the same time, the responsibilities of the program manager for meeting the requirements of the client and for making a profit for the company are well-defined and clearly understood within the company.

Client or customer satisfaction receives great emphasis in the engineer construction field. Second only to the program manager's responsibility for completing the program successfully, which means at a profit, is his responsibility to satisfy the client so that the firm can expect additional business from the customer. In a field involving major design and construction programs such as refineries, ore processing facilities or power plants, the life blood of the company is the next program the satisfied client will place with the firm.

Lastly, in the case of the engineer construction organizations discussed here, the philosophy of collocating the program team is followed whether the program team consists of three or three hundred people.

Where a matrix type program organization was used for both commercial and defense systems programs, the majority of the program organizations could be characterized as being staff program organizations with the number of personnel directly reporting to the program manager numbering from one to five. In most cases, however, this small number of direct reporting personnel is deceptive since many more personnel from the functional organization are directly assigned to the program and report to the program manager, although continuing to report administratively to the functional organization. This type of combined matrix type program organizational approach and pure program approach seems to have surmounted the common problem of the matrix organization, in which the allegiance of the personnel in the functional organization sometimes remains more with the functional organization than with the specific program.

In at least one instance, although the functional organization assigned a program representative to the program, the predominant allegiance of that individual appears to have been to the functional organization more than to the program, making this approach relatively ineffective. Significantly, in the instance noted, the number of people reporting directly to the program organization was large compared to the usual average, perhaps indicating the need to bring functions directly under the program manager for more effective control.

Where the program managers surveyed indicated a strong preference for the matrix type program organization, it was apparent that the individuals who were directly assigned to the program from the functional organizations understood their obligation to the program clearly, and were not affected by the split allegiance.

A third example of an organizational approach to program management which is somewhat unusual when compared with the customary defense industry approach is that used by a large, research oriented, multiproduct company operating solely in the commercial field. In this firm, the program manager, who is called a venture manager, is given a great deal of freedom within the confines of the business plan that establishes the program. The program manager is allowed to structure his organization in the way he considers suited to the program. This means that some ventures may operate with a very small program team while others may construct an organization that may closely resemble an intermix or aggregate type program organization. While the venture manager is encouraged to use the staff organizations, such as engineering, to perform the program work as in the usual matrix approach, he is free to incorporate the necessary skills within his own organization if he desires. A stated advantage to this approach is that it tends to keep the staff organizations responsive to the needs of the venture managers who usually come from the industrial departments (each responsible for a major product line) of the company. The success of this approach is indicated by the fact that the staff departments of the company have essentially no budgets of their own. Because a venture manager may choose to subcontract work, as opposed to having it performed by the staff department, the health of the staff departments in the company is probably indicative of the fact that they do a superior job of providing required services.

A further aspect of this company's approach is that the venture manager always has at least three key members on his team. These three members reflect the overall company approach based on the tripod of research, manufacturing, and marketing. The venture manager will begin the program with the support of a key man from the research or technical side, a similar individual from the production or manufacturing side, and another individual from the marketing side of the particular industrial department responsible for the program. This is similar to the matrix organizational approach used by the majority of the programs which were investigated, but the early inclusion of a production representative and a marketing representative is not typical of the program organizations for most defense systems programs.

Individual Program Manager Techniques. The question of individual program manager techniques was investigated. The fundamental question was, "What approaches work successfully for you as an individual program manager?" A summary of the data obtained is given in Table 5.

Most of the factors emphasized in program manager responses are well-known management principles such as effective communication, teamwork, qualified and dedicated personnel, and technical skill. Some of the points mentioned deserve further examination. Several comments received from companies with commercial programs may be significant.

Table 5. Major Factors Contributing to Program Manager Success

Factor	Times Mentioned
Technical competence and knowledge of the program	5
Communication and listening ability	14
Concentration on important details	2
Individual initiative, qualified people, aggressiveness	15
Timely decisions and early recognition of problems, visibility	6
Team cooperation, trust, morale	11
Minimum paperwork	3

One of the major engineer construction firms emphasized competence of the program manager in his application of sound management principles, attention to important details, and early recognition of potential problems. Also mentioned was the requirement for program manager knowledge of the resources available and the effective application of these resources.

Two firms with commercial programs stated that the most important ability of a program manager was that of satisfying the client.

An unusual organizational environment was indicated by a program manager in one company where a low key, low pressure approach to the job is apparently of major importance. In this organization, the program managers are making an effective contribution by getting people to work together. The absence of formal controls, a concept not usually associated with defense systems program management, was mentioned as a key contributor to success. A program manager in a different division of the same firm stated that his most important function is to bridge the gap between the line managers. This comment may be significant because the firm is using program management to increase the sales of a product line which was severely affected by recent business recession.

A company with many commercial product lines stated that program management success was a function of a small team approach, low overhead, strong dependence on individual initiative, and a minimum of checks and audits. This company believes that overcontrol is likely to result in lost time and profits.

Another company with extensive commercial product lines also described some unusual factors contributing to venture manager success. The venture manager in this company is given a new program with few rules to govern his actions, and a requirement for minimum paperwork. The venture managers are usually bright, young, aggressive individuals who haven't yet learned that "it can't be done." The keynote of the organization appears to be effective communications, with everyone including the first line supervisor having a clear understanding of his part in the program. Communications in this organization easily flow upward, downward, and horizontally. A participative management approach is used, and some programs have actually been successfully managed by a three man committee. The venture managers are given full responsibility and held accountable for the success of the programs.

One of the commercial program managers indicated that the most important factor contributing to success is mutual trust between the functional organization and the program manager. The same program manager mentioned the importance of program spirit and the selection of the right individuals in the functional organization to be program representatives. Other program managers in other divisions of the same company expressed the opinion that prompt attention to problems, program visibility, communicative ability, and the built-in checks and balances of the matrix organization are the keys to success.

Another program manager in the same company stated his belief that not getting lost in the details is an important factor. He believes that a program manager should not try to get perfect answers to every question, but should be satisfied with ninety-five percent correct answers. Time spent in trying to reach the perfect answer may actually be detrimental.

One program manager stated that people who are capable, hard-nosed, opinionated, self-starters are the most important requirement. He selects team members who are smarter than he is, and he will not tolerate "yes" men.

Another program manager who emphasized the need for the program manager to be a good listener also mentioned trust within the organization, technical competence of the program manager, motivation, and dedication.

Several managers stated that the presence of skilled people in the functional organizations is the most important requirement for success.

In another defense systems program, the program manager felt that welding the team through good communication was the key. He practices this to the extent that he holds periodic meetings with the secretaries to improve their understanding of the program goals.

Other program managers felt that appropriate delegation of authority, constant attention to the program, and management by objectives are most important.

Insistence on excellence of performance, personal initiative, minimum interference with the functional organization, avoidance of confrontation, and the ability to recognize when a decision must be made were also stated as being essential to program manager success.

Although none of the responses received were extreme or unusual, they reflect some refreshing approaches. The attitude of managers of commercial programs for the most part seems to indicate the presence of a more relaxed, generally less bureaucratic, and possibly more innovative approach than is usually the case in the management of defense systems programs. Whether this is a factor that should be considered by companies and program managers having defense systems programs is discussed in the conclusions and recommendations of this report.

Conclusions and Recommendations

What conclusions can be reached from this report? Are there lessons that may point the way to more effective program management within industry? Does the application of program management to commercial programs indicate ways to improve the management of defense systems programs?

Although sometimes subtle, differences between the management of commercial programs and the management of defense systems programs are evident. These differences may have application for commercial systems managers, for defense systems managers, and for military program managers.

Findings Applicable to Industry. Most of the conclusions of this study suggest approaches that may have application in the management of defense systems programs within industry. All of the findings need further consideration, yet, the conclusions suggested may point the way toward advances in the management of programs.

The major conclusions follow:

• An apparent disparity between commercial programs and defense systems programs in the use of networking techniques such as PERT and CPM is indicated.

The size of the defense systems programs surveyed may have unintentionally influenced the results obtained, and it is possible that networking is used for the very large defense systems programs in industry. However, the responses obtained from the defense systems program managers indicate that they see little value in such techniques. This attitude may be strongly influenced by the unsatisfactory experiences of individuals with the application of PERT in the mid 1960's. If so, it is possible that the defense systems program manager in industry should re-evaluate the use of networking, scaled to the size of the program, as a technique that could provide greater program control.

• While sweeping conclusions cannot be drawn from the findings of this study, it would appear that the role and function of the program manager in the contract negotiation process may need further evaluation in many companies. In summary, the question should be asked, "Should the program manager be the negotiator, or should he continue to play a background supporting role?"

• The results obtained indicate a wide disparity in the amount of authority held by individual program managers for engineering design, subcontract management, and quality control. It is not possible to state the single correct approach that should be used for every program. Obviously, the proper approach is the one which is most effective for the particular program.

The results may indicate that program management could be improved by greater program manager authority in the procurement and subcontract area. Perhaps the best way to obtain this improvement would be the assignment of a procurement representative to the program team.

Similarly, a change in the amount of program management authority in the area of quality control in defense systems programs might lead to greater success. Again, a firm conclusion is not offered, but the results do show that the program manager's influence is usually least in this area.

• The absence of formal program manager training in industry was one of the clear findings. The potential for such training is indicated by the emphasis it is receiving within the Department of Defense and by the three companies surveyed that are providing such training.

The success of such training will be determined in time. Meanwhile, the possibilities and advantages of such training should be investigated by the industrial community.

• The findings appear to indicate that improvements in the morale and dedication of the functional organizations in relation to the projects and programs are still needed in many companies having defense systems contracts.

How can the functional organizations be made to be more productive members of the program team? Do the functional organizations realize that their success is irrevocably linked with the success of the programs?

Here, the approach used by the engineer construction companies could be applied to obtain more responsiveness in the functional organizations.

The matrix organization, with assigned program team members in the functional organizations, has partially solved the problem. However, this is still a troublesome area in many companies. Only through an improved understanding of the importance of the program and continued improvement in organizational approach can there be greater program management success.

• The emphasis which many of the commercial organizations place on the program manager's function of satisfying the customer indicates an area of possible improvement in the management of defense systems programs.

Although the defense system program manager in industry is many times beset with the problems of technical requirements and cost control, he can never afford to ignore the need to satisfy the requirements of the customer. Perhaps many defense systems program managers should devote more attention to this important aspect of program management.

Customer satisfaction may be enhanced by increased training for both the industry program manager and the military program manager.

Findings Applicable to the Military.

• The concept of design to cost, which is receiving much emphasis within the Department of Defense, will probably be improved as more experience is gained. In applying this concept, a single finding of this study indicates that the Department of Defense should attempt to find out how industry applies this concept. If products cost too much to produce, they cannot be sold at a profit. Therefore, industry has always had to apply the principle of design to cost. These applications may hold the key to the success of the concept in weapons systems development.

• A possible solution to the often-repeated problem of the military program manager in obtaining the effective support of functional organizations within the military departments is suggested.

It may be possible for the military departments to apply two of the approaches used by one of the major engineer construction firms surveyed. These organizational methods are:

• Functional organization responsibility for the technical adequacy of the work performed by people assigned to the program, and
• elimination of the often-expressed fear that personnel located with the program organization may somehow lose their technical proficiency when located away from those with similar skills.

In practice, if the heads of the functional organizations are clearly aware of their responsibility to insure the technical adequacy of the work performed by their people who are assigned to the program manager, perhaps their support of programs will be more effective.

Findings Applicable to Industry and the Military. Perhaps most significant of all is the conclusion that the commercial program manager generally functions in an atmosphere of greater freedom than his counterparts in the defense systems and military program fields.

This was indicated by the results that showed the commercial program manager is generally subject to fewer rules, regulations, and administrative paperwork than is the defense program manager. The working environment of the commercial program manager evidently is more conducive to innovation and technical advance.

In contrast, the industry defense program manager usually works in an environment of closely controlled company policies, and the specifications, requirements, and restrictions of the contract. Regardless of how necessary these requirements may be, they do restrict the latitude of the program manager's freedom to develop innovative solutions to problems. Further these requirements absorb a great deal of time that might be more profitably spent on subjects critical to the success of the program.

Similarly, the military program manager works in the midst of a myriad of governmental rules, regulations, reporting requirements, and audits of his actions. Again, as necessary as all of these bureaucratic requirements may be, they must, of necessity, stifle innovation and retard progress.

A solution to the problem is not given here. The greater freedom of commercial program managers suggests that ways can be found to prevent the growing bureaucracy surrounding the weapons systems development field from counterbalancing the productivity of the military and defense systems program manager.

We've highlighted matrix organization . . . not because it's a bandwagon that we want you all to jump on, but rather that it's a complex, difficult and sometimes frustrating form of organization to live with. It's also, however, a bellwether of things to come.

> —*General Electric Company (internal)*
> *Organization Planning Bulletin, Sept. 1976*

As one program manager notes:

> You are deep in contractor problems from the beginning. If you are going to do your job right, you have to know your major contractors—their history, organization, people, and the way they do business. To understand a contractor, you have to know something about the industry he is a part of—its growth or decline, and its problems. And to understand the industry, you have to know something about what motivates business in general. Industry goes to great lengths to learn everything it can about its customer—the government. A program manager should do no less in learning about his major suppliers.
>
> —*LMI Introduction to*
> *Military Program Management*

62

Discussion With a Production Executive

J. S. Baumgartner

In his book, *My Years With General Motors,* the late Alfred P. Sloan says, "Annual car models are now such a natural and accepted part of American life that few persons, I would imagine, have thought about the vast effort of management that lies behind them."

The transition to production is in fact a project, one that requires a great deal of skill and attention to detail, although subsequent production is a functional process. An industry that does this particularly well is the automobile industry, with its annual model year changeover. At one plant the planning for phasing into production is so good that the production line downtime after changeover totaled less than 60 seconds in four years. The executive responsible for this annually recurring project describes how it takes place:

Actually, we know three years in advance when a particular model must start in production. In bringing out the 1980 models for instance (in the Fall of 1979), we knew the drop date three years before. This date, when the first body drops onto the first chassis, has never been extended, at least in my quarter-century experience.

What we're shooting for is to get up to line speed—48 cars per hour at this plant—in the minimum time, at the lowest possible cost and with the highest level of product quality. Now obviously we can't shut down the 1979 model at 48 jobs per hour and expect to go at this rate on the first day of the 1980s. We have a learning curve that allows time for getting up to speed; this past year it took 19 days.

The changeover involves three particularly critical things: the sequence of assembling the product, which is dictated by product buildability, specs, and safety features, among other things; the plant rearrangement required; and tooling. One of the worst things about this crazy business is that every year we stop the previous model, tear the plant apart, and start all over again.

Everything we do is aimed at the drop date, say August 2, 1979. The previous November I'll go to Detroit with several of our key planning people for our first brush with the new models. We see and hear what's new, from slides, photos, and oral means; and we bring back material to brief other people here at the plant. A couple of months later we go back to Detroit to see some hardware, mostly handmade mockups. Our purpose at this session is to determine the cars' buildability characteristics, and we watch while a mockup is assembled. This indicates to us the sequence of building the new models. Then in February we see complete handmade cars, one from each motor division. As a result of these three brushes with the new product, we have to know enough about it so that we can rearrange the plant facilities—we have to know exactly what we'll have to do physically to the plant.

In April I'll take about 20 men back to Detroit, three or four from each of our five major departments, for a workshop. This is a two-week program, with one week for each of our two shifts. We get a chance to take apart and put together the new models ourselves, and we "process the job." Each shift works out independently what it believes is the best way to do this. This gives us two separate approaches for doing the job, and we can compare them to determine the best way.

Shortly after this workshop the same cars are sent to our plant and we go through the disassembly and assembly with both salaried and hourly people working on them. We're building 1979s, for example, and here coming down the line is a 1980. We've briefed everyone ahead of time so they know that at 10:00 A.M., for instance, it'll be coming along. The hourly operators will have had several hours' training and orientation by then, and they'll have the necessary tools and components on hand. And the supervisors will have had training as well as experience at a Corporate assembly center. As it's being assembled all the "white shirts" watch what's happening, and anyone can write notes in a notebook attached to the vehicle. We get a tremendous amount of training out of this.

Then, two or three weeks before we "build out" the last of the old models, we have a pilot program where the new cars come down the line at regular speed, interspersed with the old ones. These are driveable cars, and we usually select ones we particularly want to get experience on—a station wagon, for example, that may have a new tail gate. Then, when the plant comes back from vacation, we can get up to line speed in about 15 days. Fifteen years ago, when the acceleration period used to be more than 40 days, you'd have been laughed out of your chair if you suggested doing it this fast. In the future we'll probably get up to line speed in 8 or 10 days.

One thing we're convinced of: In our planning efforts it isn't the big things that hurt us, but rather the accumulation of many small items that we may have missed, or that we didn't know about. We're perpetually planning, from the first day we get any information on a new model, and it pays off in getting up to speed sooner, which means more cars and better ones, and a better cost picture.

Incidentally, each of these new cars has to meet our quality standards. The first car is as good as the last one. What happens if something isn't right? We audit our cars all the time—take a car off the floor and give it a quality index rating and if it doesn't measure up, we work on it. Every job though has to meet the quality requirements.

Our method of organizing for this supercritical period has evolved mainly over the last several years. We used to have hook problems, for instance—maybe a hood would fall off a hook, or it wouldn't balance right; so we originated a hook committee five years ago, and our hook problems have disappeared. This committee is made up of people from each major department and they get the ideas from the people within their departments who'll be exposed to the hooks, so the guys who'll work with the hooks have an input to designing and planning them. Actually we have 22 of these subcommittees for plantwide matters, like hooks, parts identification, model mix, plant rearrangement, training, power tools, parts routing, and so forth. There are about 300 people on these subcommittees.

To coordinate this planning, we found there was no way I could handle it myself; so I have a planning committee, with a planning coordinator from each department who does nothing but plan for a 10-month period. These people always have about 50 questions in mind—like what are the special tooling requirements; what's the work content; what are the fixed stations on the line; will long-lead purchases be needed. They have to do this, because it would be disaster if you found out too late that you need a long-lead item, like a conveyor that may take 16 weeks to get. One of the most complex items is balancing the line—being careful not to go too fast in one area and too slow in another. In addition, we plan for surge banks of maybe 30 bodies; so if something unexpected happens in a particular area we can draw on these surge banks to keep from shutting down the whole plant.

We can no longer afford the luxury of changing operations after we start—the complexity of the job would start a chain reaction that couldn't be handled. Our processes and assembly techniques must be geared to meet split-second timing and full performance reliability, from the first moment on.

We don't know how much we can improve, actually, in getting up to line speed. But in 10 years, on a carry-over model and getting the line filled with the new model before the changeover layoff, we could conceivably get up to line speed after an acceleration of only one or two days. Planning, and experience in planning, has earned its way many times over.

✶ ✶ ✶ ✶ ✶

You don't fault the job to be done. You get the job done in spite of the obstacles. If you can't get the job done in spite of the obstacles, simply get a better player. You train him. You motivate him. You tell him what his responsibilities are. You tell him about the obstacles. You evaluate his performance, and if it doesn't measure up, you look for a better player. This is what project management is all about.

—*Mr. Barry J. Shillito,*
Teledyne Ryan Aeronautical Co.

Section 10 —

HIGHER LEVELS' GUIDANCE AND EXPECTATIONS

Introduction

Normally a program manager spends a substantial part of his time, 25 percent to 50 percent, in the sphere outside his project: higher command levels, congressional committees, the user of what he is developing, and people or organizations that can have an impact on his budget. Their guidance and expectations are a major influence in his life as a PM. It is necessary, therefore, to take a look at some of these influences and their perspective on the system management process.

Leading off, Senator Lawton Chiles discusses changes needed, including the need to give more decision-making responsibility to industry and the need for effective competition in design creativity. He comments also on the necessity of carefully establishing the need for a program in the first place. This theme is discussed in more depth by P. R. Calaway in his article on OMB Circular A-109, which requires a clearly established mission need before embarking on a program. The effectiveness with which this is being done in practice is indicated by the fact that only two of the first 14 programs' mission element needs statements (MENS) were approved. An Air Force officer, commenting on the multitude of small projects simmering at various levels of existence, says, "It's like feeding the animals at the zoo. They're there, and they get fed because they're there. But what is needed is someone to say which ones should continue to be fed and which ones shouldn't."

The congressional committee staffer is in a key role in the legislative process relative to defense programs. Maj. John Allsbrook gives an excellent summary of the steps in systems acceptance and approval and the role of the professional staffer. A key point: "In his contact with the staff, the program manager must assume that the staff is acting for the committee and with its full consent."

Dr. Al Dancy provides an outstanding and concise resumé of the impact of political and managerial conflicts between the executive branch and the legislature over money matters, the DOD budget, and, particularly, the vulnerability of Defense R&D, where most development programs live, in this conflict. The lesson to defense program managers is that Congress has a definite stake in the systems development process, and it has the ability to control this process through the annual funding appropriation. The key to successful R&D management, Dr. Dancy points out, is continued cooperation with Congress, rather than conflict.

Gen. William J. Evans, former Commander of the Air Force Systems Command, outlines higher levels' expectations of industry in a theme that recurs at regular intervals. Lt. Gen. Sammet then reviews the factors that lead to programs success, in a wide-ranging interview that spans a quarter century's involvement, in both industry and defense. Dr. Jack Bennett emphasizes the importance of life cycle costing, a top-level discussion of a topic presented from other perspectives in Sections 7 and 8.

The final selection is a threesome regarding the PM as a system advocate and his dealing with the press. The report of the Acquisition Cycle Task Force brings out the necessity for the PM's accepting this role. Dr. Ron Fox presents the who, what, when, and how of the PM as system advocate. And finally, in an interview loaded with potential pitfalls, Navy Capt. Glenn W. "Corky" Lenox illustrates how to step nimbly through a minefield.

$$\star \quad \star \quad \star \quad \star \quad \star$$

If a nation values anything more than freedom, it will lose its freedom; and the irony of it is, that if it is comfort or money that it values more, it will lose that too.
—*Somerset Maugham*

63

Changing Concepts of Responsibility for Federal Procurement*

Senator Lawton Chiles (D-Fla.)†

The problems, scandals and inefficiencies arising from major weapon system acquisition programs have been the subject of hundreds of separate studies and remedies, both proposed and applied, for twenty years.

In the main, however, each new symptom and each new cure receives isolated treatment, rarely going beyond defects in a particular contracting method, a particular organization, a particular policy. This band-aid approach to modernizing major weapon system acquisition can no longer suffice because it fails to cope with some underlying trends in shifting institutional roles and responsibilities which lie at the heart of acquisition difficulties and must themselves now be reversed if we are to see even symptomatic relief.

One cannot fully come to grips with the problems of weapon system acquisition unless all of the participants are considered: the program office, the military department, the Office of the Secretary of Defense and the Congress.

The military departments cannot pretend their acquisition problem would be solved if the Congress would step aside and change its ways in authorizing, appropriating and legislating.

*Extract from *Defense Management Journal,* January 1975, pp. 31–35.
†Chairman, Subcommittee on Federal Procurement, United States Senate.

And the Congress cannot pretend that if the military would do its job more correctly, the rash of defective programs and cost overruns would somehow disappear.

Responsibility and Accountability

What is needed is a comprehensive framework of decision-making, responsibility and public accountability. The main message in the Commission on Government Procurement's report on Major Systems Acquisition is that the decisions which have to be made during the course of any major program have become scattered across the Congress, the program office and everywhere in between. There is no clear understanding of what decisions should be reserved to each organization so it can do its job properly. As a result, responsibility and accountability have become diffused and scattered, both within the government and between the government and the private sector as well.

The problem or responsibility in procurement and systems acquisition has two dimensions; first, the broad problem of how to share responsibility between the public and private sectors, between government agencies and private contractors; and second, how the Congress and the executive agencies can reconcile their separate responsibilities.

The Modern Contract State

The first dimension of dividing public versus private responsibilities touches on a basic feature that distinguishes the American form of society; the idea that private firms can be depended upon to meet the public's needs through contracts.

Giving private contractors responsibility for meeting defense needs has produced a relatively new quasi-governmental sector in our economy about which little is known or understood in terms of the long range implications for the national economy or defense. The central question is: How can the government maintain the independence of the private sector to meet public needs and yet retain an adequate level of public accountability? The present situation is definitely unstable because, in the end, the military departments are going to be held responsible—and the defense mission degraded—when a contractor performs poorly.

The current make-shift solution is to levy what has become a hodgepodge of indirect government controls on industry in the form of regulations, specifications, mandatory management systems, cost accounting standards, audits, etc. These indirect regulatory controls to gain public accountability have disturbing ramifications. They set a different tone for business and blur the distinction between government and industry.

Regulatory Controls

Over the years, one effect is that the number and burden of these indirect controls have brought us close to the nationalization of some segments of our economy. The more regulatory controls are applied, the more firms lose their characteristic free enterprise traits. The effect of these controls is to teach companies to play a different kind of game. Not a game to take real risks to offer innovative products to meet a public need, but to promise the government what it wants more exactly than others and at a slightly lower price than they know is budgeted.

The weapon systems coming off the lines today are already as much a product of the bureaucracy and the military system commands as they are a result of private entrepreneurial design. The major systems that "win" today's competitions are basically the systems that went out in the Request for Proposals. A close look at the design decisions that are being made in the military system commands, as opposed to companies in free competition, will reveal a situation approaching Soviet design bureaus.

Private institutions need a genuine measure of independence to preserve their effectiveness. If the acts of the Congress, or the actions of agencies in the name of public accountability, unnecessarily intrude into the legitimate prerogatives of private sector institutions, we run a grave risk of converting segments of our economy into *de facto* operating extensions of our government bureaucracy.

There are no easy answers to strike the perfect balance between private sector independence and public accountability. Government arsenals and public enterprise are not the answer, but a cure that may be worse than the disease.

Independent Creativity

The key to forging a new equilibrium is to give back to private companies the responsibility for decisions they normally make in commercial competition—responsibility for decisions on what products they will create and offer. It now looks as though we can't trust private firms to innovate any more. We don't trust them to compete because it costs too much money. Independent creativity is the essence of the independence we need to preserve.

We must reinstitute effective competition which means giving contractors the chance to independently create new products and be responsible for their own business and technical judgments. We must challenge them to *demonstrate* they have the best product to meet a mission need.

One excellent example of this approach is the Navy's XFV-12A V/STOL fighter program. The Navy deserves much credit for pursuing a program that allowed contractors such a wide latitude in design responsibility. We need to set all our major programs on a course which so clearly defines design responsibility.

This Navy case also highlights the problems in the second dimension of responsibility of how the Congress and executive agencies share program responsibilities. The Navy had a great deal of difficulty getting funds for the fighter program because it was contrary to habitual Congressional demands for accountability. Because the Navy wanted to *explore* the best technical ideas that industry had to offer, it couldn't offer any pat answers to the usual program questions of how much will it weigh, how fast will it fly, how much will it cost and how does it compare with the F-4? Congressional committees found themselves face to face with a program in an early stage of evolution, but without the military standard claim of certainty that it was ready for large-scale commitments.

Shotgun Intervention

Congress has become used to dealing with the back-end of the acquisition process, trying to impose accountability after the fact, and trying to find someone responsible after the problems have finally come to light. As a result, Congress has engaged in a shotgun intervention into the program decisions that are more properly the responsibility of the executive agencies.

This has not been a successful approach. It is not enough for Congress to have an ex post facto revelation that five years and a billion dollars have been spent giving birth to another turkey. Accountability has to mean more than closing the barn door after the horse is gone, or even finding out who left the door open.

As more programs get into trouble, the response has been for Congress to become immersed in detailed decision-making trying to impose accountability. In other words, Congress is trying to perform a part of the executive branch operating role. Representative John

Rhodes, a member of three appropriations subcommittees, calls this kind of thing "stumbling over billions of dollars to pick up dimes," all in the name of trying to hold the agencies accountable.

Crucial Steps

What is needed to begin with is a basic framework of those key decisions which actually control program evolution and which can be used as benchmarks for allocating program responsibilities.

New programs to meet any need, civil or defense, don't spring full blown from executive agencies which may want to begin full-scale development or from legislation introduced by a senator to meet the needs of a particular constituency. As Elliott Richardson said when he was Secretary of the Department of Health, Education, and Welfare, "Pushing a button may pass a law but it won't necessarily solve a problem."

To solve a problem, to meet a mission need, there is a natural evolution of program steps which have to be performed. The need for a new program must be carefully established first along with program goals; then alternative approaches explored; a preferred approach chosen; and finally implementation. All of these steps are crucial to program success and accountability. If Congress cannot review and judge the first two, it is futile to try to control the last two. Only five percent of total program costs may be involved in the early steps but they will determine how effective the remaining ninety-five percent will be.

The most effective way to control program funds is to control the early steps which lock in the levels of spending that eventually will concern Congress. An improved framework for accountability will require that information come to the Congress at all steps of program development—from the time the goals are set and while alternative means of achieving those goals are being explored so that it can *restrain* itself from trying to second-guess and reverse detailed program decisions at later stages. Legislation to lay the groundwork for that kind of well-ordered program information was included in Title VI of the Congressional Budget and Impoundment Control Act of 1974. Over the next several years, hopefully, *all* major programs of *all* agencies can be exposed in such a regular, evolving fashion.

If we are going to have an improved allocation of responsibilities between Congress and the executive agencies, then both the military departments and the Congress need to understand what decisions *are* and are *not* theirs to make. Congress needs to bolster its involvement in the mission-related decisions that influence defense strategy, policy and overall budget priorities, the needs and goals for major programs. In exchange for this clear understanding and confirmation of goals and boundary conditions, Congress then must learn to further remove itself from the technical program decisions needed to find the best system and procure it.

To summarize, there seem to be two basic issues in reforming system acquisition program responsibilities. First, rebalancing responsibilities between the government and private sector by insisting that contractors take greater decision responsibility for defining their products in competition with others and thereby substituting effective competition for other regulatory-type controls to ensure public accountability. Second, rebalancing responsibilities between Congress and the agencies will require a common framework of program decision-making to permit program responsibilities to be more clearly separated.

The Program Manager

The person most often caught between the hell and high-water of both these conflicts is the program manager. In a real sense, the program manager is battered by both sides. He is caught up in the confused responsibilities of the Congress and the agencies, and also snared in the confusion of responsibilities between the agency and the private contractor doing the job.

The concept of project management was established, at least in part, to relieve the frustrations of Congress in finding a "person in charge" for major weapon system acquisitions; an individual in the bureaucratic labyrinth who could speak and take responsibility for a specific procurement of major dollar proportions. The concept was to bring a trained manager into a program very early in the acquisition process so he could act as the "general manager" for the project. The project manager was supposed to have a charter to confirm and protect his role and responsibilities. But, in practice, the program manager is most often brought aboard too late in the acquisition cycle so that he, like Congress, suffers from arriving on the scene too late, after key decisions have already set the shape and tone of the program. And, once assigned to the program, his theoretical decision responsibilities are preempted not only by Congressional intervention but also by the many layers of management review that sit on top of him in his service and in the Office of the Secretary of Defense.

Turning around, the program manager faces the dilemma of

shared responsibilities with the private sector. If he is involved with the program early, he is dependent upon the contractor's information which may be colored more to ensure a contract than a successful program. And if he is involved after the major award, the program manager may be more dependent on the contractor than the contractor is on the government.

Congress and Procurement

The Congress is in the process of training itself to better execute its responsibility for setting government-wide procurement policy. For years special attention has been focused on procurement in the House Government Operations Committee. Last year a new Subcommittee on Federal Procurement was created in the Senate. The creation of an Office of Federal Procurement Policy (OFPP) to provide government-wide direction of procurement was the Procurement Commission's paramount recommendation, and legislation to create the OFPP passed the Senate and became law August 30, 1974.

In addition, the subcommittee's agenda for procurement reform also includes: moving directly into reviewing major system acquisition; providing a new statutory basis for procurement; and examining the government's policy of reliance on the private sector.

Revising Concepts

These are beginning steps. There is much to be done and it will take time to do it, but the key point is that it is being attempted. But the most significant benefit will come from the highest order of responsibility that I haven't mentioned yet—the responsibility of the government to serve the American people and the ability of the people to hold their government accountable. That's what it's all about, in the end.

The contributions each of us can make in procurement and systems acquisition in revising our concepts of public and private responsibility are all to be measured by what they mean to the confidence that people have in the government.

We dare not tempt them with weakness. For only when our arms are sufficient beyond doubt can we be certain that they will never be employed.
—*President John F. Kennedy*

64

Role of Congressional Staffs in Weapon System Acquisition*

Major John W. Allsbrook

In recent years, the importance of the professional Congressional committee staff member has greatly increased in the weapon systems review and approval process. Committee staff members are involved heavily with both budgetary and technical details. The committee staffs work primarily for the committee chairmen and are in a position to exercise considerable influence on the decision process. They prepare committee members for hearings with briefings and documentation and at times become active participants during the hearings. The extent of staff influence depends upon the competence and initiative of the individual staffer. The confidence that the committee has in the staff is directly related to the quality of the information the staffer demands, and his ability to interpret such information and draw logical conclusions. A program manager should develop the staff's confidence through open, responsive, and forthright communication. A most critical aspect of the weapon system acquisition process is the budgeting activity that culminates in Congressional approval of program funds. A Congressional staff plays a very fundamental role during this decision-making process.

In order for a program to succeed, it must be accepted and approved by the Congress. This includes indorsement and support of the professional staffers and the Armed Services Appropriations Committee of both the House of Representatives and the Senate.

*Defense Systems Management Review, Vol. I, no. 2, pp. 34–41.

In the course of the program approval process, the program manager may have to appear as a witness before the committees in public or at closed hearings. Such appearances will, in most cases, be preceded by a session with one or more committee staffers. In other cases, a session with a committee staff may be the only opportunity the program manager has to defend his program to the Congress.

The Congressional Environment

Congressional authority over the DOD budget is rooted in the U.S. Constitution. Article I, Section 8, of the Constitution embodies in the Congress the power ". . . to raise and support Armies . . . ," ". . . to provide and maintain a Navy . . . ," ". . . to make rules for the government and regulation of the land and naval forces . . . ," and ". . . to make all laws which shall be necessary and proper for carrying into execution the foregoing powers."

One "rule" made to "regulate the land and naval forces" has been the establishment of a two-step process whereby military programs are first authorized by law and then, in a separate law, funds for carrying out the programs are appropriated. This process dates back to 1921 when the House of Representatives made a rule that appropriations could not be recommended by the Appropriations Committee for purposes not authorized by law. Similarly, another rule prohibited the substantive committees (e.g., Armed Services) from adding appropriations to the reported authorization bills.[1]

Appropriation. In 1959, the two-step process began to involve a detailed review of the total military budget. At this time the process was established in public law that provided:

> "That no funds may be appropriated after December 31, 1960 to or for use of any Armed Forces of the United States for the procurement of aircraft, missiles, or naval vessels unless the appropriation of such funds has been authorized by legislation enacted after such date."

Although this provision of the law dealt only with aircraft, missile and ship procurement, the Congress soon realized the desirability of expanding the requirement to other portions of the DOD budget. Consequently, there have been seven additional amendments to public law. A specific requirement now is that research, development, test and evaluation (RDT&E); tracked vehicles, personnel

[1]Dept. of Air Force, Comptroller of the Air Force, *The Air Force Budget,* Washington, D. C., 1976, p. 49.

strengths; and other weapons procurement (rifle, artillery, small arms, and torpedoes) be subjected to the annual authorization process prior to appropriation.[2]

Posture Hearings. How, within this two-step framework of authorization and appropriation, does the Congress meet its Constitutional obligation? The process begins in January of each year when the Congress begins its regular session. Before the detailed review of individual programs, the Armed Services Committee of both the House and Senate hold military posture hearings. The posture hearings usually cover only broad aspects of the military budget including force strength and overall weapon and personnel strength levels. Witnesses usually are service officials, including the Secretary of Defense and other top OSD representatives, the Service Secretaries and the military chiefs.

Authorization. Posture hearings are followed by the authorization hearings. The recent practice of the respective Armed Services Committees has been to hold separate hearings on procurement and Research, Development, Test and Evaluation (RDT&E). Although the principal witnesses at these hearings are normally Assistant Secretaries of the military departments and the military Deputy Chiefs of Staff, it is not unusual for a program manager to be called to testify, especially for designated major weapon systems. The primary responsibility of the witnesses is to defend and support specific programs outlined and the funds requested in the President's budget that are being considered by the committees.

Because of the shortage of time as well as the desire for independent analysis, authorization hearings are held simultaneously in the House and Senate. However, because of the statutory requirement that money bills originate in the House, the House Armed Services Committee is the first to complete its review and make any adjustments to the proposed budget. This process is referred to as bill "mark up." The marked up bill is then presented to the full House with a report containing the rationale for committee action. Without waiting for the Senate version, the House will vote on the bill after two or three days of floor debate. The Senate normally allows the DOD to submit a written appeal of the House action to include the adverse impact of any reductions imposed by the House. After considering the DOD appeal and its own analysis of the budget request, the Senate Armed Services Committee submits to the Senate its marked-up version of the bill and a report containing rationale for committee action. The full Senate, after floor debate, votes on this bill.

[2]Cecil W. Williams, "Annual Authorization Legislation," *United States Air Force JAG Law Review,* XIV: 103–108 (Spring 1972).

The result of separate House and Senate action is two different authorization bills. These differences are resolved in a conference committee made up of selected representatives from the respective Armed Services Committees. The conference committee may, during deliberation, consider only those matters that are in disagreement. The conference committee will not reconsider reductions agreed to by both Houses. During this process the DOD is once again permitted to submit a written appeal from actions under consideration. Once approved by both Houses, the authorization bill is forwarded to the President for signature.

The Two-Step Process. Meanwhile, the second half of the two-step process has already begun. The appropriations phase generally follows the sequence described for authorization but in different committees and with a whole new set of Congressional participants.[3]

Two general conclusions may be drawn from observing the legislative process. First, the process is long and involved and it may take from nine to twelve months to complete. Throughout the process a program manager may be called to explain his program many times. He may be required to testify as an expert witness, or he may be tasked (usually on very short notice) to provide written answers to questions posed by Congressmen, staffers, or other government witnesses.

The second general conclusion drawn from observing the legislative process is that the heart of the process is committee activity—and committee activity is the province of the professional staff.

Staff Organization and Background

The current concept of a professional committee staff was established in the Legislative Reorganization Act of 1946. Section 202(a) of the act provided for ". . . not more than four professional staff members . . ." on each standing committee except Appropriations Committees. Appropriations Committees, because of having the greater oversight responsibility, were permitted to hire as many persons as each respective chamber of Congress would permit.[4] Expansion of committee staffs was authorized by another reorganization in 1970. Today, the Senate Armed Services Committee has a total of twelve professional staff members, two counselors (lawyers), and a chief counsel who serves as staff director. The House

[3]Charles J. Zinn, *How Our Laws Are Made,* US Govt. Printing Office, Washington, D. C. 1974.

[4]Stephen Horn, *Unused Power: The Work of the Senate Committee on Appropriations,* The Brookings Institute, Washington, D. C. 1970, p. 63.

Armed Services Committee has eleven professional staff members and seven counselors, including the chief counsel. In the Appropriations Defense Subcommittees, the House has eight staff members assigned and the Senate has five.[5]

In general, committee staffs are appointed by committee chairmen. Although a staffer supports all members of the committee, primary loyalty is to the chairman. Rieselback, in his commentary on Congressional politics, observes:

> ". . . the committee staff is the creature of the chairman: he determines who will be hired, how much assistance will be provided for the minority side, what the majority staff will do, and often the vigor with which it carries out its assignments."[6]

The credentials and experience of professional staffers are varied, yet there are many similarities.

Many of the staffers have been recruited from the Executive Branch of the government, including the Department of Defense, ". . . thus securing the services of persons who are already well versed in the subject matter with which the committee deals."[7] A review of the background of those Armed Services and Appropriations Committee staffers who have provided a biography to the *Congressional Staff Directory* shows that the majority have at one time served on active duty with one of the military services. Some are retired military officers and at least one is currently a member of the U.S. Naval Reserve. Others have served on the civilian side of the DOD including one who served for seven years as a Deputy Director of Legislative Liaison.[8]

Budget experience in the Executive Branch is a highly desired qualification for staff members of the House Appropriations Committee.

Staff Roles and Influence

Staff members interviewed acknowledge that it is difficult to define their duties rigorously, however the performance of certain recurring tasks is expected of the staffer. The role of the House Appropriations Committee staffer, as described by Fenno, is typical of that of most committee staffers:

[5]Charles B. Brownson (ed), *Congressional Staff Directory,* 1975, Advanced Locator, Mt. Vernon, Va., 1975, p. 159.
[6]Leroy N. Rieselback, *Congressional Politics,* McGraw-Hill, New York, New York, 1973, p. 67.
[7]Joseph P. Harris, *Congress and the Legislative Process,* McGraw-Hill, New York, 1972, p. 115.
[8]Brownson, *op. cit.,* p. 585.

". . . For his subcommittee, each clerk is expected to schedule and oversee the routine of the hearings, suggest areas of inquiry for the hearing, make up specific questions for use in the hearings, prepare the transcript for publication, help prepare for the mark up session, oversee the routine of the mark up, help write the subcommittee report, and the subcommittee bill, participate in full Committee, sit with and advise subcommittee members during floor debates, help schedule and prepare for conference committee meetings, prepare materials for use by House conferees, participate in conference proceedings, receive and digest reports from the investigation staff, keep in constant communication, in season and out, with agency officials, and accompany committee members when they travel to visit agency installations. His role requires that he process all the committee's working documents and that he be present physically at every stage of decision-making. 'There may be some part of the process that I miss or don't know about.' said one staff man, 'but I doubt it.' "[9]

These responsibilities are inherent in behind-the-scenes activities that might be expected of a committee staffer. The role is important and certainly one that ensures the success of the legislative process.

Hearing Participation. The staffer also plays another, more visible, role that is not cited by Fenno. This is the role of questioner, along with the committee members, during hearings. This role appears to be more prevalent in the Armed Services Committees than in the Appropriations Committees. For example, a review of the published hearings on FY 77 authorization bill shows that almost half of the questions asked of the Office of the Secretary of Defense and service witnesses were asked by committee staffers.[10, 11]

Where the technology is advanced and the committee staff is competent, frequently the committee members assign to the staff the actual questioning of witnesses. The recent addition of two technically competent staff members to the House Armed Services Committee has permitted that committee to spend a greater portion of its hearing activity delving into technical issues.

Staff Influence. The activities of the committee staff, as previously discussed, strongly suggest that the staffers have an inherent potential to influence Congressional decisions on weapon systems acquisition. The exercise of influence varies, and for a number of reasons.

[9]Richard F. Fenno, Jr., *The Power of the Purse: Appropriation Politics in Congress,* Little Brown, Boston, 1966, p. 182.

[10]U.S. Congress, House Armed Services Committee (94th Congress, 2d Session), Hearings (Feb-Mar 76), "Military Posture and DOD Authorization for Appropriations for Fiscal Year 1977," H. Rept. 94-33, Parts II and V, US Govt Printing Office, Washington, D.C., 1976.

[11]US Congress, Senate Committee on Armed Services (94th Congress, 2d Session), Hearings (Mar 76), "Fiscal Year 1977 Authorization for Military Procurement, Research and Development, and Active Duty, Selected Reserve and Civilian Personnel Strengths," Part II, US Govt Printing Office, Washington, D.C., 1976.

Patterson notes:

">. . . Staff influence varies among Congressional committees as a result of differences in staff availability and competence, committee workload, and structural factors in committee organization. At the same time, the potential influence of committee staffs is considerable indeed."[12]

In the areas of committee workload and committee structure, staff influence is very much dependent on the personality and style of the committee chairman. Fenno, in his paper on the distribution of influence in the House of Representatives, states:

". . . Staff influence varies with the confidence which committee and subcommittee members, and especially their respective chairmen, place in staff abilities and staff judgment. Where the desire to use a staff and confidence exist, staff members constitute a linchpin to internal committee decision-making. When these conditions are not present, it does not make much difference what kind of staff a committee has. Such staff influence as does exist in the House exists here —in the committees."[13]

Similarly, Huitt comments regarding Senate staff:

". . . first rate professionals do more than carry out assignments. In the offices of individual senators they learn to think like the boss; they determine to some degree who sees him and what importunities reach him. In the committee rooms they identify the problems and provide the facts and questions. The product of the Senate is to some unmeasured and perhaps immeasurable degree their product. Their influence probably would be very easy to overstate, but it does exist . . ."[14]

The growing size of the DOD budget and the increasing complexity of modern technology make it more and more difficult for the individual Congressman or Senator to digest all information available. Rieselback observes,

". . . The more complex the issues, the greater the need of the lawmakers for technical expertise and the greater the opportunity for the staff to press its own views."[15]

A number of committee staff members have candidly commented on their ability to influence the legislative process:

[12]Samuel C. Patterson, "Congressional Committee Professional Staffing: Capabilities and Constraints," in Allen Kornberg and Lloyd D. Musolf (eds), *Legislatures in Developmental Perspective,* Duke University Press, Durham, N.C., 1970, p. 411.
[13]David Truman (ed), *The Congress and America's Future,* Prentice-Hall, Englewood Cliffs, N.J., 1973, p. 66.
[14]*Ibid.,* p. 113.
[15]Riesselback, *op. cit.,* p. 79.

". . . I like being close to the levers of power (said one staffer on a committee unrelated to DOD). My ideas have influence only to the extent that I can persuade the Senators that they are in the public interest. The staff man can have a lot of influence in these terms. If you know you can't persuade a member to your own policy position, you lay out the alternatives, and you've got to be as objective as you possibly can."[16]

Regardless of how staff influence is viewed, there can be little doubt that it exists—both in potential and in daily exercise. Nevertheless, such exercise of influence that does take place does so only to the extent that it is permitted by the committee members and especially by the chairman. The staff realizes this limitation and acts accordingly. In his contact with the staff, the program manager must assume that the staff is acting for the committee and with its full consent.

Information, A Source of Influence

The amount of influence possessed by a given staffer is measured to a great extent by the intelligence he is able to obtain. Information is his stock in trade.

What are the information sources of the staff? Much of the information gathered by the staff comes from the DOD itself in various forms. The Congressional inquiry is a popular channel for information flow. Such inquiry is treated by the DOD as a formal request for information and each request is treated with the same degree of importance, whether it comes from a Congressman needing information for either his own education or to reply to a constituent, or whether it comes from a committee staffer. Inquiries are normally handled through legislative liaison offices which have been established in the Pentagon by DOD and each of the military services. In addition, each service maintains a small detachment of liaison personnel located in the office buildings of both the House and the Senate. When a request for information is received (usually by telephone) it is relayed to the office having primary responsibility.

Usually the request is for written material—a position paper or a fact sheet. Occasionally, a briefing is requested and it will be conducted in the office of the staff member. This may involve having the program manager travel to Washington for the briefing.

An additional source of important program information is the justification material submitted to Congress with the President's

[16]Patterson, *op. cit.,* p. 411.

annual budget. This justification material is in the form of several volumes that contain thousands of pages of detailed program data. The data includes funding requirements, schedules, purchase quantities, technical performance parameters, and narrative discussions of requirements and planned activities. Detailed formats and instructions for this material are contained in the *DOD Budget Guidance Manual,* DOD 7110-1-M, published by the Office of the Assistant Secretary of Defense (Comptroller). The manual is revised periodically to reflect additional or changed requirements of the respective Congressional committees.

Witness statements and hearing transcripts also serve as information to committee staffers. Witness statements are required to be submitted several days in advance of hearings so that they may be analysed by the staff for issues to be raised during the hearings. Statements of service witnesses are reviewed and compared with previously received DOD policy statements. A comparison is made of the current position of witnesses with positions taken by the same witnesses in previous hearings. And finally, the statements are compared with other information gathered by the staff. Similarly, transcripts of hearings before other committees are reviewed.

Committee staffers occasionally take a request for information directly to the program manager. Certain staff members, for example, make annual trips to military installations for the purpose of gaining first hand information on major acquisition programs. In the course of these visits, the staff members expect to be briefed on program status, problem areas, and anticipated funding needs. Field trips are taken to contractors' plants where staff members receive program briefings, talk to engineers and technicians, see and touch the hardware, and witness tests and demonstrations.

Contractors recognize the potential benefits of such visits and actively court individual staff members. The preference of lobbyists for the attention of the staff instead of that of committee members is summed by one business representative who noted, "The members are busy. They usually don't have the time to listen to a sales pitch. And often it's the staff that really matters anyway."[17]

Other outside sources of information include the research services of the Library of Congress, reports of the Government Accounting Office, technical journals and trade magazines, newspaper stories, liaison with other committee staffs, and information from such private organizations as the Brookings Institute. In fact, the wide availability of information to committee staffs has brought about increasing suggestions that staffs be enlarged to handle all

[17]"Those Staffs on Capitol Hill: Power Behind the Scenes," *U.S. News and World Report,* 77 (1): (1974), p. 26.

data. A counter argument is that more staff would only create new, more complex problems to compete for the limited attention of the Congressmen and Senators. At the same time, there is always the danger of creating a legislative bureaucracy that will dilute and color the information gathered by the staff, thereby in effect making the committee a captive of the staff.

The fact that committee staffs have access to a wealth of data means that they must pick and choose the data that is passed on to busy committee members. This requirement for the staff to exercise judgment provides the greatest opportunity to influence, if not actually make, the ultimate Congressional decision affecting weapon system programs. Implications of this reality and the effects on program manager–Congressional staff relations are addressed in the following paragraphs.

Program Manager—Congressional Staff Relations

Clearly, the Congressional staffer can be an important force in determining the direction and funding level of a given weapon system program. Where the staff is not convinced of the value of the program, the chances are slim that the program will advance through the Congressional approval process without a reduction or redirection. Conversely, a program that makes sense to committee staff stands a good chance of approval. It is incumbent on the part of every program manager, when the opportunity arises, to ensure that he communicates total program understanding to the appropriate members of the committee staff.

In the process of budget formulation, individual program budgets may be reduced "inhouse" by the service headquarters, OSD, the Office of Management and Budget (OMB), or even the President, before the budget is submitted to Congress. The President's budget submission represents a balance in priorities of total demands on the nation's tax dollars. Therefore, all witnesses appearing at Congressional hearings are advised by OMB Circular A-10 that:

- Personal opinions will not be volunteered which reflect positions inconsistent with the program and appropriation requests the President has transmitted to the Congress.

Witnesses are permitted to respond to a direct request for personal opinion with the appropriate caveat:

- In expressing personal opinions relating to such program and appropriation requests in response to specific requests therefor, witnesses will refer to the extent, if any, and should make clear that the expression of the opinion is not a request for additional funds.

An attempt to lobby for additional funds with committee staff outside formal hearings would only create additional problems for the program concerned, and the budget as a whole. Issues created by an overzealous proponent might suggest that the budget as submitted does not reflect actual requirements. Such an indication could undermine the credibility of the entire budget.

Knowing the orientation and the needs of committee staff is the full time responsibility of legislative liaison personnel in the Pentagon, and the program manager should work through these channels. Liaison personnel maintain contact with committee staff on a daily basis and have established strong relations built on trust and mutual confidence. When information is sought by committee staff from the program manager, the request is usually directed through liaison personnel. On those occasions when urgency necessitates direct contact between a staffer and a program manager, liaison personnel should be notified as soon as possible to assure that appropriate service headquarters and DOD personnel are alerted to potential Congressional issues. Through frequent contact with committee staff, liaison personnel may be able to provide a measure of perspective as to what may be behind a specific request for information. This reduction of uncertainty offers greater opportunity for positive communication and less time is wasted on tangential issues.

One final comment is appropriate. Contact with a committee staffer sometimes places the program manager in a defensive role. He may find it necessary to justify his program to an individual who has an opposing view. In such situations, especially when the atmosphere is informal, extra attention must be given to maintaining high professional standards and to responding to disagreement in a reasonable, factual manner.

Summary

The professional staffer on those Congressional committees having oversight responsibility for military weapon system acquisition is a key element in the budget approval process. Staffs are increasing in technical competence and growing in size. The increased competence and numbers mean that probably they are going to exhibit more and more interest in technical and management decisions made by program managers.

The technical competence of committee staff combined with their knowledge of program information provide a unique opportunity to influence the budget decisions made by the Congress. Every program manager should work to earn the confidence and commitment of committee staffers just as he would work to earn the confidence of any military staff officer or other decision shaper.

We all know that appropriations are not interchangeable. Funds for RDT&E cannot be reprogrammed for O&M or Production. The same conditions generally hold for all combinations. This means that it is important to program the right types of money to support all aspects of a project—the aggregate amount of funds is of quite limited value unless the pieces fit the categories of work to be performed. There are some very narrow overlapping areas where some interchangeability may be accomplished, but they are quite limited.

—LMI Introduction to
Military Program Management

65

Effects of Congressional Funding Limitations on Development of Major Defense Systems*

Dr. Albert G. Dancy, Sr.

In the fiscal year 1972 Defense Authorization Bill,[1] the Senate imposed two restrictions on the funding for Defense Research and Development (R&D) that were to have extremely important consequences:

1. Funds appropriated by the Congress must be obligated not later than the end of the fiscal year following the year for which appropriated.

2. Research and development work to be accomplished by the services under contract or in-house must be programmed on an annual basis, and budgets submitted to the Congress must be in work increments designed to be accomplished within a twelve-month period. This period was generally to coincide with the annual budget cycle.

The first of these restrictions reduced Defense R&D funding from what was essentially a no-year cycle to a two-year cycle. It also required the immediate obligation of approximately one billion dollars in as-yet-unobligated funds appropriated in FY 1972 and preceding years. The second restriction required that the DOD in

*Armed Forces Comptroller, October 1976, pp. 24–27.
[1] U.S. Congress, Senate, Authorization for Appropriations for Fiscal Year 1972 for Military Procurement, Research and Development, and for Other Purposes, S. Rept. 92-359, 92nd Congress, 1st Sess. 1971.

the future ask Congress for only those funds necessary for utilization during the coming appropriation year. Through these restrictions Congress could better review past accomplishments on specific programs annually and provide for continued development of these programs through the following year. This would add impetus to the annual review cycle of defense research and development by Congress.

Although the above restrictions were not altogether inconsistent with previous Congressional requirements for R&D, they did represent a quantum jump in increased Congressional interest and control of defense spending. A study of the cause and effect of this legislation will thus enable a better insight into the problem for ever increasing Congressional financial control facing major defense system acquisition programs today. In the space below, answers to the following will be discussed:

1. What was the intent of Congress in imposing these increased restrictions on defense R&D spending?
2. Specifically, what were the immediate results of the FY 1972 restrictions on major systems development?
3. What are the long-term effects of those restrictions, and what reaction should DOD and the services take to increased Congressional control that will best serve the interests of national defense and the American public?

Interestingly enough, prior to World War I there was very little coordination within the executive branch of the Federal Government or conflict with Congress over money matters. During the early period of our history, there was no such thing as an "executive budget." The Congress was able to provide funds requested by the various Federal agencies, including the War and Navy departments, with very little difficulty. There was an abundance of Federal funds available largely through customs revenues, and "raids on the treasury" were not uncommon. Officials within the agencies merely made up their requirements for funds in the form of annual estimates of expenditures and went directly to the Congress for appropriations. Occasionally, when questions arose in Congress, it was not the funding that was in doubt, but whether the agency as part of Federal Government had the constitutional right to pursue a particular course of action. Later, to gain some semblance of order, these estimates were usually routed through a clerical office in the Treasury Department to form the Book of Estimates. It was not until the Budget and Accounting Act of 1921 and the subsequent consolidation of appropriation authority under a single committee of each house that real Congressional control began to take shape. By the beginning of World War I, the treasury surpluses that had persisted (except for the brief period of the Civil War) had been largely eliminated, and in going from a peacetime to a wartime basis, deficit spending was required. Despite these changes, budget review and decision-making within Congress was fragmented and uncoordinated. In describing Congressional control of appropriations as late as 1943, one historian concluded,

> It is not the Congress, not the House or Senate, nor even the Appropriation Committees as a whole . . . who make the decisions on agency requests. The reality is a handful of men from particular states or districts, working with a particular clerk on a magnitude of details.[2]

In contrast to our past history, today there is an intense interest by the Congress in agency funding and a very marked conflict with the Executive (including the various Executive agencies) over money matters.

This conflict has both political and managerial dimensions. It is *political* in that the President and Congress often disagree on what Federal programs are to be funded, on when these funds are to be provided, on which agencies or governmental entities can best administer the utilization of these funds, and, importantly, who should benefit from the expenditure of these funds. The President and Congress not only see Federal funding questions from different vantage points and sometimes differing party affiliations, but they also serve quite separate and distinct pressure groups. A president must view his obligations in terms of national business and industrial interests, the defense complex, the farm population, consumers, union workers, the urban poor, and others. He identifies these groups with the diverse yet overlapping bureaus and agencies of the Federal Government which serve their special interests. Members of Congress, alternatively, view their political obligations primarily in terms of the interests and aspirations of the special interest groups within the geographical bounds of their own particular constituency.

The *managerial* dimension of control of government expenditures also has two opposing sides. Congress needs to control how much funding is made available to the various Federal agencies annually. Despite the staggering amount of deficit spending by the Federal Government, national resources are not unlimited; there is always the immediate problem at a particular time to weigh spending in the public versus private sectors and to weigh funding for one purpose against another. The executive agencies, on the other hand,

[2]Arthur W. MacMahon, "Congressional Oversight of Administration," *Political Science Quarterly,* June 1973, p. 181.

need to know both the extent and timing of future funding to be available in order to undertake long-term program planning, to provide flexibility in scheduling in-house and contractual efforts in phasing research and development, and to coordinate the various resource inputs for procurement. Aside from the timing issue, agencies feel that because of their position at the working level, they can best exercise management authority over the operations of their respective agencies and best establish the extent and timing of financial resources.

In recent years the major battleground in control of Federal expenditures between the Executive and Congress has been the DOD budget. There are several reasons for this: the large proportion of overall annual Federal appropriations provided to the DOD, the extreme vulnerability of the defense budget as an expedient means of cutting Federal budget deficits, an increasing Congressional desire to use available funds for domestic social problems rather than military preparedness, and a pervasive dissatisfaction immediately following Vietnam over military involvement in international affairs to maintain peace and stability and to counter the spread of communism.

Within the defense budget, Congress has singled out research and development as a major category of DOD funding over which to exercise this increased control. The defense R&D budget is particularly vulnerable because of the large amount of money involved and the very unpredictable outcome of R&D expenditures. In addition, a successful end product is generally viewed as an increased potential and results in the need to spend even more before an advanced capability for defense is realized. This is in marked contrast to the more immediate and tangible results of the other expenditures for operating forces and new equipment and facilities. Hence, research and development is generally considered the most "postponable" of all DOD requirements.

The Intent of Congress in the FY 1972 Restrictions

With the above as background, and in order to pinpoint the specific intent of the FY 1972 restrictions, informal discussions were held with the senior staff members of the defense subcommittees of both the House and Senate Appropriations Committees and with the senior staff members of the House and Senate Armed Services (Authorization) Committees. Throughout these discussions, questioning went beyond the particular matter of the FY 1972 restrictions to the overall question of purpose and methodology of increased Congressional control over DOD financial management functions.

These discussions substantiated the political and managerial dimensions of the continuing conflict between the Executive and Congress and the extreme vulnerability of the Defense research and development budget to funding reductions. Discussions also provided the reasoning of the Congress in imposing specific restrictions in the FY 1972 Authorization Act. There can be no doubt but that the basic intent of Congress at this time was to gain better control over the acquisition process of major defense systems. It was on the larger programs—those included under the Systems Acquisition Report (SAR)—that Congress had focused its interest. Specifically, the stated purpose was to reduce major systems development costs by enhancing the annual Congressional review process on these systems and by requiring annual incremental budget submission.

Congress wanted to keep closer tabs on development progress and to cancel poorly achieving programs as early as possible in the development cycle: the providing of funds to DOD for these programs for use in future years and the build-up within DOD of appropriated yet unobligated funds precluded this control; hence, these practices had to be eliminated. Other purposes of apparent lesser importance were to reduce overall defense costs, to provide funds for the other more politically popular social programs, and to instill within the DOD, *and particularly the major program offices,* better financial accountability and responsibility. Going beyond these stated reasons was the inference that cost overruns and the general poor performance of some of the larger systems recently developed and still undergoing development raised considerable doubt that all was going well in the defense weapons systems acquisition process.

Results of the FY 1972 Restrictions

At the time of the FY 1972 restrictions, there were forty-five major defense development programs reported periodically under the SAR. Each of these had total cumulative RDT&E funding of fifty million dollars or more, or a cumulative procurement funding of two hundred million dollars or more. Reports on 39 of these were routinely forwarded to the Senate Armed Services Committee. The focus of management within DOD for major systems development centers in the System Program Offices (SPO's) of the three services. Discussions were held with key personnel in nine of these SPO's to determine the immediate effects of these restrictions. Personnel contacted were the program managers, financial and budget officers, program administrators, and the various management personnel for development testing, systems engineering, maintenance engineering, logistics, product assurance, and others. In addition to discussions with those within the SPO's, various personnel within the Army and Navy Materiel Commands and the Air Force Systems Command were also interviewed.

The immediate effect on these SPO's of the FY 1972 restrictions was the elimination of the backlog of prior year funds and initiation of procedures to insure future compliance with the two-year obligation cycle. The changes were met with some degree of initial confusion, a considerable amount of detailed work, a relatively small amount of lost funding, and a general restructuring of fiscal responsibility and authority upward in the chain of command. In general, the immediate reaction to the new two-year obligation cycle within the SPO's was mixed. Compliance was accompanied by tighter financial controls throughout DOD and the services and by considerably more dependence on the Congress for annual funding requirements.

Immediate reaction to the second restriction—the decision of Congress to refuse to provide R&D funds for use beyond the appropriation fiscal year—was quite different. There was general surprise and confusion within DOD, the services, and the SPO's by the severity of this restriction and extent of applicability which resulted in additional workload, and delayed and hindered compliance. One distrubing question in the submission of annual budgets—which still has not been fully resolved—is a working definition of just what constitutes "work increments designed to be accomplished within a twelve-month cycle." However, in general, the newer and more currently funded programs were able to meet these restrictions with less difficulty than the older and generally the larger programs, some of which had at their disposal considerable amounts of unobligated funds.

As to the long-term effects of these restrictions, there is no assurance that they will have in the future either a beneficial or a harmful effect within the DOD in terms of planning for future research and development or in actual program development operations. It would appear from the opinions expressed during discussions that the flexibility of planning and operations might, in fact, over the long run be somewhat enhanced within the services. This would be especially true of the newer programs where funding was on a more current basis at the time of these restrictions. In the higher echelons of R&D management and control within the services and at the DOD level, flexibility of planning and operations over the long run will be somewhat lessened. This results primarily because the Congress by these restrictions has taken over a considerable amount of top-level managerial responsibility previously held at these higher levels.

There is also the problem facing DOD in coordinating the annual program review cycle required by Congress, and the program milestone accomplishment review required by the Defense Systems Acquisition Review Council (DSARC). These two reviews do not come at the same time nor do they cover the same aspects of program progress, yet continued program development depends on their close coordination.

Conclusions Drawn From the FY 1972 Restrictions

Of primary importance to an understanding of these restrictions is that the Congress has once again demonstrated its ability to control a particular segment within the DOD. Since the period following World War II, there has been a definite trend toward tighter Congressional control of the various functions of the defense establishment. The recent financial restrictions originating with the FY 1972 R&D budget hearings, although representing a large increase in control of major systems acquisitions, were but a part of this overall evolutionary trend. Of equal importance, by imposing these restrictions, Congress served notice that it was dissatisfied with the R&D of major defense systems—despite whatever efforts had been made in the recent past in improvement—and that, henceforth, a closer control would be exercised.

Also significant is that this control by the Congress was exercised through what has aptly been described as the "power of the purse"—generally considered the most potent weapon for Congressional control of the Federal agencies. Congress did not legislate reduced costs and better technical performance of systems development (which were its primary concerns) or specifically command adherence to accomplishment of specific lesser objectives: Congress, by setting up new criteria under which R&D funds would be appropriated, established the conditions within DOD in which progress toward these goals would be assured.

It is also highly significant that at no time did DOD seriously question the right of the Congress to exercise this control. Steps were taken immediately within DOD and the services to assure compliance. It must be noted, however, that the degree of this compliance depended largely on the interpretation placed on each restriction. Where limitations were unambiguous—as in the two-year obligational cycle and the requirement to obligate FY 1971 and prior year funds by the end of FY 1972—compliance was immediate and complete. Where the limitation was subject to alternate interpretations—as in the precise definition of what constitutes "work increments designed to be accomplished within a twelve-month cycle"—compliance within DOD was, on the whole, less satisfactory to the Congress.

Of final importance was the resiliency of the DOD in coping with these restrictions. At no time was adherence considered unobtainable and at no time were operations completely disrupted during the initial periods of compliance.

The lessons to defense systems acquisition managers of the FY 1972 Congressional restrictions are clear. Congress has a definite stake in the systems development process and has the ability to control this process through annual funding appropriations. Defense managers must recognize these facts. Secondly, the fundamental problem involved in control of this process is that of balancing the Congressional need to exercise a proper degree of management and authority of the defense acquisition process to satisfy their interests and the equally valid need of defense managers to exercise the proper degree of flexibility in both the planning and operations of these programs which their expertise warrants.

The hurdle of the FY 1972 Authorization Act restrictions has now largely been overcome. There will be more. To best serve the interests of national defense and the American public, defense systems acquisition managers must recognize the needs and prerogatives of Congress and must learn to live within new Congressional controls in the future as they have in the past. The key to successful defense R&D management is continued cooperation with Congress, not conflict.

✷ ✷ ✷ ✷ ✷

Notwithstanding his best efforts, it is a rare and fortunate program manager who does not have to absorb reductions in funds or reprogramming of funds to later fiscal years. Advance planning for these contingencies is recommended strongly. Higher authority is likely to want to know the impact of funding changes on ridiculously short notice and some advance planning reduces the turmoil of responding. In addition, an inadequately supported response is detrimental to maintaining one's image as a manager who is on top of his program.

—LMI Introduction to
Military Program Management

But certain realities cannot be ignored. The military trend lines for the Soviet Union and their allies appear to be moving sharply upward in many critical areas. Their force improvements are steady, deliberate and impressive.

—Gen. George S. Brown, USAF

66

Modernizing and Cutting Costs*

General William J. Evans

Immodest as it may sound, I think the commander of the Air Force Systems Command has one of the most challenging jobs in the Air Force, especially in peacetime. The challenge is to modernize our weapon systems through advanced technology and to do it with about a quarter of the Air Force annual budget. That's a tall order, especially considering the price of sophisticated military hardware in today's market.

Individual systems are so expensive that we have to select very carefully those we pursue into advanced development and production. And because of their cost, there's a limit on the number of copies we can afford to buy. This implies the need for some sort of trade-off—some reasonable balance—between the quality or effectiveness of individual systems and the quantities we procure.

Assessing Power Balance

In a sense, of course, the United States can afford whatever is needed to keep it secure. It cannot afford to be so weak that either its own independence or its position of leadership in the Free World is lost. But the question of exactly what is needed for that kind of strength is a subject of continuing debate. How much is enough? And how much should "enough" cost? There are no easy answers to those questions.

We know our own strength—at least in terms of numbers and

*Remarks by General William J. Evans, Commander, Air Force Systems Command, at the National Security Industrial Association luncheon, Los Angeles, Calif., July 23, 1976.

quantities. We know the capabilities of our weapons and our defenses. We have a pretty good idea of the strength and nature of foreign forces. So we can make comparisons and arrive at a fairly accurate idea of how well the power is balanced . . . who has an advantage, if any . . . and in what areas.

Soviet Build-Up

We know, for example, the Soviet Union caught up with and passed the United States in numbers of land-based missiles. While we concentrated on improving accuracy rather than increasing size, the Soviets built bigger and bigger boosters that could carry heavier and heavier payloads or give their ICBM's longer and longer range.

And we know that with the same kind of concentrated effort, they succeeded in building a blue-water navy that outnumbers ours in surface ships and submarines. They developed the most extensive ground-to-air defenses in the world. Their manpower grew to twice the number we have under arms. They forged ahead by at least 25 percent in tactical fighter-attack aircraft. And to top it off, they have increased military expenditures by such an extent that in both total military investment and military RDT&E they lead the world.

Maintaining a Stable Balance

So—knowing these facts—even allowing for the margin of error that must be considered in any calculation of manpower and weapons in a closed society—we realize that there exists today something of a "rough equivalence" in strategic power between the United States and the Soviet Union. Russia's continuing growth suggests that this "rough equivalence" could tip more and more in her favor unless the United States continues its emphasis on quality, on effectiveness, on superior performance in its weapons.

As long as we do not match the Soviets man for man, tank for tank, ship for ship, missile for missile, we have to outmatch them in the capability and reliability of our weapon systems if we are to maintain the equivalence needed for a stable balance of deterrent power. The Air Force Systems Command contributes to that balance, through its management of aerospace weapon systems research and development.

Our planners are constantly working and reviewing the threat and proposing new systems to counter this threat for the next five, ten, and fifteen years. Since we do not have a corner on the brainpower, we look to you representing American industry to help us in this search for new ideas and systems to counter this threat.

Funding Problems

Funding, as you have probably guessed, is one of our most critical problems. It has always been a critical problem, but it has taken on added importance because of the inflation we have experienced over the past few years and because of the inversion that has taken place in that portion of the Federal budget devoted to defense and the portion that goes to other federally supported programs.

Since fiscal year 1964, defense spending has dropped from 43 percent of the Federal budget to about 25 percent. It has declined from more than eight percent of the gross national product to less than six percent. And although the dollars have doubled, the buying power today is less than it was twelve years ago.

Expenditures for social and economic programs, on the other hand, have risen 116 percent in the last five years, 96 percent in the five-year period before that, and are now two and one-half times the size of defense outlays.

I'll be among the first to acknowledge the benefits of Medicare, Social Security, environmental protection, and other health and welfare programs. But I would also like to point out that these and other social and economic programs are only possible because of the substratum of freedom and independence sustained by our national defense posture.

Modernization Trends

Our defenses need to grow with the times too—just like other programs. Operations in Southeast Asia took their toll in weapons and warning systems. Our bombers are aging. Our fighter forces are thin. Our radar coverage has to be improved. In terms of people, air bases, and aircraft, we have the smallest Air Force since the beginning of the Korean War.

In an effort to reverse this trend, the Air Force is now in the midst of probably the greatest modernization period of its short history. We have in operation or under development the most advanced aerospace weapon systems this world has ever seen: the F-15 and F-16 supersonic fighters; the YC-14 and -15 tactical transports; the A-10 close support aircraft; the E-3 Airborne Warning and Control System; the E-4 Airborne Command Post; not to mention the munitions, avionics, and communications gear they carry and the effective combination of land-based terminals and spaceborne satellites that provide attack warning, weather data, communication links, and positioning and navigation information for American forces wherever they may be. If we don't develop and deploy these systems according to plan and within budget constraints constantly placed upon us, it is clear to see the disturbing impact this can have on our national security.

Program Management

We assign each development program to a manager—military or civilian—whose responsibility it is to see that each program comes in on schedule, satisfies the performance requirements, and is worth every penny spent on it.

We select System Program Managers carefully on the basis of their education, experience, managerial qualifications, and, most importantly, past performance. Although they have a great deal of autonomy, they are expected to keep their commanders informed of their progress and any problems they face.

For our dozen or more top priority programs, there are monthly reviews at my headquarters. The program manager personally attends that review at least every third month to report his accomplishments. From my headquarters, these quarterly reports go to the Secretary of the Air Force and, ultimately, to the Office of the Secretary of Defense.

If there is a glitch—any significant problem that threatens the program goal—we want to know about it early enough to take some corrective action and hold the turbulence to a minimum. Toward that end I expect the contractors to surface any problem areas as well as my program directors.

We question anything that doesn't satisfy sound management principles and come down hard on anything that looks as though it's costing more than it should. We solicit industry's help, as well, in keeping our costs down and quality up.

Reducing Total Costs

In addition to subjecting requirements to increasingly critical analysis, we have been taking a front-end look at downstream costs —operation and maintenance costs—to see if we can't reduce those as another effort to reduce the total cost of developing, buying, and supporting a system throughout its existence. Sometimes we find that through trade-off analysis of technical requirements, we can reduce the development cost by ten or fifteen percent or more. At other times, we may add to the development cost (through competitive prototypes, for example) to get a more reliable system and wind up paying less in the long run for the total cost of ownership.

We're gaining valuable experience in estimating those downstream costs and factoring them into our design. As time goes on, I think we will get better and better at designing our systems to meet a cost goal. But we need help from industry. We need help in making accurate estimates and living up to them.

Help From Industry

We expect our contractors to do their utmost to develop weapons within the limitations prescribed. We expect them to tell us of cost-effective trade-offs between range and speed, reliability and maintainability, performance and schedule, or other variables. Innovative contractors who will streamline their operations, cut their overhead, and pass some of the savings on to the government serve both themselves and the nation. When you consider the impact of such actions on increased quantities and greater program stability, the bottom line is that they simply make good business sense.

Other Cost Reduction Efforts

To help lower costs further, the Air Force Systems Command has turned to what we call Business Strategy Panels. Composed of experienced procurement personnel, logistics personnel, legal and technical personnel from our own command, from the Air Force Logistics Command, and from the Air Staff, these panels explore such areas as technical and economic risk, sourcing, and types of contracts. Their purpose is to find the business strategy that best fits program needs and to apply lessons learned from previous experience to the current situation so that we don't repeat mistakes or overlook opportunities for improved efficiency and economy.

We're emphasizing closer reviews of our requests for proposals (RFP) and more critical analysis of contract provisions. We have what we call a "Murder Board"—a Procurement Evaluation Panel —composed of interested experts in our own command, who review our major RFP's before they are released to industry. The idea is to get on the street with the clearest, most concise, and easiest-to-answer RFP it's possible to produce. In addition, the Murder Board attempts to optimize incentive arrangements and encourage competition among the potential contractors.

One of the newer actions is giving potential contractors an opportunity to comment on draft requests for proposal before we formally issue them. We want contractors to go over the provisions, point out any ambiguities, and suggest ways of cutting costs without diluting essential reliability and performance.

Contract Management

In the area of contract management, we have put a Contract Management System Evaluation Program into effect. CMSEP, as it's called, has been greeted with less than open arms by some in industry. It's undergoing some growing pains. But it has been a conscious effort by the Air Force Systems Command's Contract Management Division to prevent defects rather than try to eliminate them after the fact or try to "inspect" quality into hardware.

For those of you not familiar with CMSEP, the evaluation is based on a series of questions posed by the cognizant Air Force plant representative. If the answers reveal a potential or existing problem somewhere in the contractor's management system, he is advised in writing. The plant representative meets with company executives to discuss the significant problems and assure corrective action.

We think the Contractor Management Systems Evaluation Program is benefiting our contractors as well as the Air Force. To date, CMSEP has permitted us to eliminate numerous costly surveys which were disruptive on your operations. Among these are contractor purchasing system surveys, management system surveys, engineering surveys, property surveys, and transportation and packaging surveys. CMSEP has excellent potential for improving the quality and effectiveness of pre-award surveys, production readiness reviews and should-cost studies. We're also looking into the possible use of CMSEP in the source selection process as an aid to management evaluation in lieu of a documented management proposal. Recently I've met with various industry associations and representatives regarding possible abuses of CMSEP. Most objections have been over potential for things that might occur rather than specific problems. I've asked them, and I'm asking you, for specifics—but to date I haven't received any.

Its goal is to foster problem prevention and to stop costly, nonproductive "after-the-fact" surveys and reviews. Ultimately, CMSEP could lead to reduced government presence in-plant with improved visibility and greater reliance on contractor management systems.

Need for Aerospace Industry Efficiency

As I said, AFSC is continuing to attack the cost problems related to weapons acquisition. I think we're doing a good job. But we need the full support of all levels of our contractor organizations. From the executive suite to the machine shop, cost-consciousness must be emphasized. New ways of doing business that are rewarding to the contractor and help save taxpayer dollars must be actively solicited and implemented.

The aerospace industry is a Twentieth Century phenomenon. Throughout the world, it is considered evidence of America's engineering expertise. In the United States, it's a leader in the exportation of technology and the envy of other nations. However, the lack of new capital investment by the aerospace industry in modern equipment and efficient manufacturing processes is quickly becoming the industry's "Achilles' heel." Industry can do better. Modernizing aerospace manufacturing operations will result in superior aircraft and weapon systems at reduced cost. I think there is a tremendous opportunity to take advantage of the computer, for example, to assist in design, engineering and manufacturing operations. As we continue initiatives to improving profits in aerospace business, we expect increased capital investment. Firms that fail to replace obsolescence and inefficiencies are going to feel the results because we are going to find better and better ways of buying efficiency.

Capital Investment Incentives

I recognize the problems associated with the uncertainties of the defense business and the cost of capital in today's economy. We have been assiduously working this problem in the past year by developing incentives to assist you in making positive capital expenditure decisions. The ten percent tax credit is still available and we're willing to explore application of other provisions such as termination protection, guaranteed amortization, interest credits, increased profits, and possibly entering into sharing agreements along the lines of value engineering clauses. I trust that these initiatives will soon result in the flow of modern, more efficient equipment into our defense contractor plants. The possibilities for using technology and innovation to create more advanced technology and to lower life cycle costs in the process are limited only by the extent of our imagination and creativity.

Production Problems

It's ironic that here we are building the most modern Air Force the world has ever known, and we're doing it, in many cases, with inefficient equipment that would be at home in a museum. More time and money may be wasted on old tools and techniques than it would take to replace them.

Another thing. We have increased emphasis on operational testing in the Air Force, mainly because over and over again we have been given assurances of reliable performance and even empirical evidence of test accomplishments, only to have the equipment fail to live up to promise in operational environment. Contractor testing has frequently not been realistic. Maybe the government is at fault for not spelling out the requirements in greater detail. Yet one of industry's favorite complaints is that rigid government specifications too often leave insufficient room for judicious interpretation.

The Best Insurance

Somewhere there's a happy medium. And I believe we can find it if we work together for better quality and lower cost in our weapon systems. Only with a proper balance of quantity and quality can we have the strength required for deterrence. And only with the help of industry and the continued backing of the American public will we be able to support it.

Now is the time to be building our strength for the future, while we are not under the burdens of war, while our economy is climbing, and while we can also afford to care for our domestic ills. Deterrent defenses are the best insurance the United States can buy in a troubled world. And as with any insurance, better to have it and not need it than to need it and not have it.

$$\star \quad \star \quad \star \quad \star \quad \star$$

"A Soviet leader, steeped in a history of invasions from the East and West, exposed to German invasion in two world wars, has a visceral feeling about defense needs," says Hardt. "Talk about improving housing or building automobiles seems pretty trivial by comparison."

—Fortune, *Aug. 1, 1969, p. 126, quoting*
John Hardt, Research Analysis Corporation

We make no secret of the fact that we see detente as the way to create more favorable conditions for Communist construction.

—*Leonid Brezhnev*

67

OMB Circular A-109: How It Affects R&D and IR&D*

P. R. Calaway

What is the Department of Defense doing to implement Office of Budget and Management Circular A-109? How will A-109 affect Defense-related Research and Development (R&D) and Independent Research and Development (IR&D)? Before I get into the specifics, let's take a quick look at what A-109 is all about.

There seems to be some question about what it says, and there seems to be some doubt about our support for or commitment to implementing A-109 and its precepts. Let me deal with the second of these first by saying that as far as we in the Department of Defense (DOD) are concerned, A-109 is here to stay. We agree with its principles, and we support it. Why? Because we think it makes sense, and because we think it has the potential to help us shorten the acquisition cycle and get us more capability for our dollar.

The key provisions of A-109 call for formalizing the front-end of the acquisition process, getting high-level affirmation of our mission-oriented needs early on, tapping a wide variety of sources to competitively derive system designs, maintaining the integrity of competing design concepts, and extending competition as long as possible through the process. We are attuned to trying to streamline and simplify the process, but we recognize that there is a possibility of messing it up if we do not implement the provisions of A-109 properly. So, let's take a look at what we are doing to try to avoid

*Extract from *Program Managers Newsletter,* May–June 1978, pp. 9–11. Based on a speech by Mr. Calaway to the National Security Industrial Association.

making the process too bureaucratic and to focus on getting the most from our scarce resources within the required time constraints.

Department of Defense Directives 5000.1 and 5000.2 describe the basic policy and process for major system acquisitions within DOD. These directives were revised in January 1977 to incorporate the provisions of A-109. Since then our progress has been slower than we had hoped, but we think we are moving in the right direction and we are getting better.

Much of the improvement in the acquisition process will have the objective of improving the stature of DOD as a stable and reliable customer. Program stretch-outs, abortive program starts and costly contract cancellations undermine public and Congressional confidence. They also are disruptive to the government-contractor relationship. To remedy these problems it is important that the acquisition process be started off properly. We must first be sure of the validity and priority of the mission task we want to perform and equally important, determine whether we can afford it.

Particular attention has been paid to strengthening the first phase or the front-end of the acquisition process, so that proper management attention and visibility are focused on a new program before it starts. A program "go" decision will be given when the Secretary of Defense approves a mission need document termed "Mission Element Need Statement" (MENS). The MENS will form the basis for advising industry and the academia of our mission deficiencies and requesting their alternative proposals for solution in a wide latitude of conceptual approaches.

We have been conducting concept formulation and mission need determinations in the DOD for some time. The MENS approach formalizes the process so that program initiation, operational need date and affordability are highlighted. In a program's early phase, alternate conceptual solutions will be identified. The most promising ones will be competitively selected and then evaluated. Our new front-end policy will require, among other things, a very careful assessment of design and manufacturing technologies, logistics factors, and an early, aggressive pursuit of program voids and deficiencies.

Another aspect of the new policy is focused at getting at the affordability issue of our acquisition programs. We must start facing up to this problem as early as possible, and one of the elements in the MENS is aimed squarely at affordability. We are also coupling a tentative decision to produce and deploy with the decision to enter full-scale development. Since full-scale development entails a major expense, we should explicitly consider the follow-on affordability issue at the same time. Hopefully, the affordability issue will be faced early enough to prevent the government and industry from committing resources to the full-scale development of a system that will never be produced.

As I have said, the biggest change has been right at the front-end. Here, the basic requirement for performing vigorous mission area analyses to define our mission needs forces us to think in terms of the missions we have to satisfy. All these activities are closely related to another recent, significant change—mission budgeting as specified in the 1974 Congressional Budget Act.

Mission budgeting is simply a requirement to present our annual budget in a mission-oriented structure—in effect to justify our resource requirements on the basis of the end-purposes that our acquisitions are to satisfy. Circular A-109 and our implementing DOD Directives require that we justify our major system acquisition on the basis of the end-purposes and levels of effort that they are to satisfy.

Both these requirements stemmed from growing concern for the magnitude and purpose of the Federal Budget. Our current presentation of the budget does not really show why an item is needed, and there is no apparent relationship between the various procurement/development items in the budget. In short, it lacks focus. The same could be said of the acquisition process itself. Individual acquisition programs often proceeded without considering other developments which could contribute to satisfying the same needs.

When we began to realize that better focus was needed, the Director of Defense Research and Engineering (DDR&E) Mission Area structure was established. A major deficiency was that it was a DDR&E view of the R&D world and the Services generally developed their programs using their own structures. For example, the Army developed a detailed structure based on Army capability categories, and the Air Force developed a structure for their own requirements. These had to be translated into DDR&E language during program objective memorandum (POM) reviews, and they had to be translated further in trying to provide the Senate Appropriations Committee with a missionized budget. With the emphasis on the front-end required by our new procedures, we needed to develop a common structure to be used by DOD and the Services. We needed a structure that would eliminate the need to translate from one system to another, that could be used for the POM and budget preparation, and that would help us make better decisions on the basis of the missions and jobs that we need to accomplish.

The benefits of these efforts include a focusing on basic policies and assumptions as well as missions and specific needs.

Improved mission area definitions and mission area analyses are intended to result in a better understanding of our mission deficiencies. This is just the basis for initiating an acquisition program. If it is a major effort, DOD Directives 5000.1 and 5000.2 apply and the component identifying the deficiency is expected to develop a Mission Element Need Statement and forward it to the Secretary of Defense for approval . . . a Milestone 0 decision. If he approves of the need, he authorizes that component to begin looking at various alternatives to satisfying the need. Although 5000.1 and 5000.2 are applicable specifically to major programs, we expect the same principles to be used as a guide for all acquisition programs.

The implication of our front-end changes is that we are going to have to place greater emphasis on maintaining a viable technology base. We have to reverse the trend of serious erosion that our Science and Technology program has suffered over the last ten to fifteen years. Because the keystone of our investment strategy is to build on our technological lead, we must continue to increase our efforts for basic technology.

We want to avoid diluting our technology base activities, because we want to preclude foreclosing on our options in searching for alternative solutions. Consequently, we plan to emphasize maintaining a sufficient separation between technology base R&D and the R&D that is devoted to developing solutions to specific mission needs. By definition, technology base R&D activities are those supported by 6.1 (research), 6.2 (exploratory) and 6.3A (advanced technology) development categories of dollars. The same emphasis also applies to separation of IR&D activity from solution-oriented activity.

Consequently, when one asks what the impact of A-109 will be on IR&D, the correct answer is that there should not be any impact on genuine IR&D activities. By definition, IR&D is contractor initiated and performed, product-oriented research and development that is not sponsored by contract. It is not required in the performance of a contract or grant and is not required for the preparation of a specific bid or proposal. Independent Research and Development has been, and continues to be, a major source of support for building the technological strength, breadth, and depth of DOD industrial contractors. The DOD has profited from this effort by obtaining original technical approaches, concepts, and inventories that are applicable to our needs. DOD engineering, development and production contracts have benefitted from IR&D through its exploration of difficult technical problems. Recent contributions include the development of laser gyroscopes and charge-coupled devices which have become the basis for solutions to specific mission needs. In view of these kinds of contributions, it is easy to see why we want to ensure that IR&D, as well as the rest of the technology base effort, maintains its own identity. Fortunately, there are several facets of our current policies which should help us out:

For example, a by-product of our mission area analyses should be a focusing of attention on long-range technology deficiencies. With these deficiencies defined, IR&D activities should become more effectively aligned in the areas where they will help most. Mission Element Need Statements could be used as another source of technology deficiencies, particularly before acquisition programs are initiated in response to the MENS.

A second consideration is the impact of our goal to increase the funding for the front-end of our acquisition programs. Increased funding of R&D contracts for the exploration of alternative design concepts should reduce the need and temptation to guide IR&D efforts toward specific near-term mission problems and solutions.

A third consideration is that now we expect to have a clearly defined starting point for an acquisition program, so that we should have a better audit trail to help us maintain the integrity of our S&T program. For example, it should be easier to tell if an IR&D program was truly IR&D or if it should have been done under contract.

In summary, the features of A-109 and our resulting policies should not have any negative impact on our basic R&D and IR&D activities. On the other hand there are positive pressures for ensuring that these activities are pursued for the intended reason, that is, to ensure that we maintain a viable technology base that will be the source for the best possible solutions to our needs. Because the keystone of our investments strategy is to build on our technology lead, it is vital for us to avoid focusing our activities on near-term solutions to our needs, and that is the way we are headed.

$$\ast \quad \ast \quad \ast \quad \ast \quad \ast$$

The biggest difference in whether a program is a success is the front end of the program—how it's planned, how structured, how funded, what the expectations are.

—*Hon. Malcolm Currie, Deputy Secretary of Defense (Research and Engineering)*

68

"Up Front Is Where Dollars Are Most Important . . ."*

Interview With LTG George Sammet, USA, Ret.

LTG Sammet, who retired in 1977 as Deputy Commanding General for Materiel Development, HQ DARCOM, had extensive experience in the Army's materiel acquisition business. He joined the R&D community as lieutenant colonel in the old OCRD staff agency, in charge of cannon artillery programs in 1959. He served in virtually every capacity, from an action officer, division chief, executive officer, director, and deputy, under every Chief of R&D from that time until he joined DARCOM in 1973.

Known for his forthright manner and his vast institutional memory bank of management know-how in the acquisition business, Gen. Sammet is now a Director of Materiel in industry.

General Sammet, during your distinguished Army career you came to be regarded as one of the Army's foremost experts on managing research and development. What were the areas where you saw the greatest change between the time you first entered the R&D field and the time you retired from active duty?

I think there are two changes in the last twenty years that really make a difference today. The first is the coming of age of the Army's acquisition people. When I first became involved back in the days of General Trudeau, there were very few "Green Suiters," especially combat arms types, who truly understood how to acquire materiel. Thus, I think the most important change was the development of

*Army Research, Development & Acquisition Magazine, Sept.-Oct. 1978, pp. 2–4.

the Army Project Management System. The Army was not the first service to have project managers. The Navy and the Air Force both started out way ahead of the Army but in my opinion today the Army's project management system is at least equal and probably excels the other services.

The other big difference between today and twenty years ago is the involvement of Congress. Twenty years ago we used to go over and "visit with" Congress. They would ask general questions and they got general answers. Later on that evening we'd get the transcript and if our boss had made a mistake we could adjust the transcript and that was it.

Today the Congressional committees have staffs far larger than they had twenty years ago, and they are far better informed. In fact, in many cases staff members know at least as much about the problems as do the Army's witnesses.

Over the 25-odd years of your R&D experience you certainly saw a number of highly successful development programs. Do you recall any one as being of particular note?

If you'll allow me, I'd rather pick out three of them. I say three because they were successful for different reasons.

I think one of the most successful was the Pershing program. Pershing was a success maybe by accident; the accident being that there weren't enough people who knew what was going on to bother those who were doing the program. Secondly, Pershing, being one of the first missile programs, was adequately funded from the start. It amazes me how in the 1960's, when there was no base of technology, no precedent for that kind of a system, industry could develop a Pershing system and field it in less than four years. Today the Army is developing Pershing II, and it is taking twice as long. I attribute that to inadequate funding and a necessity to prove everything to the nth degree before flying. Both of those faults can be found in many programs today. There was a time when we understood "Advanced Development" to mean proving of components. Today "Advanced Development" is a first generation "Engineering Development." ED then becomes a second generation ED. Pershing is also a good example of the proper use of product improvement obviating the unnecessary expenditure of large sums of money for a new development program.

The next program which I think was a very successful one was UTTAS, or as it is now called—Black Hawk. I'm fully aware that just recently there was an accident with a Black Hawk utility helicopter, but that doesn't detract from the success of the program. I think two things contributed to the UTTAS success. The first was the very deliberate development of an engine prior to the time the Army started the system development. Secondly, the project manager was given a reasonable dollar reserve which enabled him to make timely management decisions. If you don't have that reserve there is no way but to miss some management decisions. It takes time to get money. It may even mean going to the next year's appropriation, and that may take as long as a year.

The third successful program is really a group of programs, one which I personally advocate very strongly, and that is the "Skunk Works" variety. The Army has two that are coming to fruition right now. One is the chain gun where the Army competitively selected a contractor to deliver a gun for a shoot-off competition in 24 months. The other project is the improved TOW vehicle, for which DARCOM was given the mission of developing competitively and then producing this item all in less than 24 months. The only way the job could have been done was by a "Skunk Works" program wherein DARCOM provided very clear guidelines to three contractors and then let them do their thing.

Both the chain gun and the improved TOW vehicle were delivered within the time frame specified and are now under test.

The new Air Defense Gun Program is also a skunk-like program, but this one will be more difficult to keep in that context because of its greater cost and complexity. What you're seeing, however, is the Army using the "Skunk Works" approach for programs ever increasing in size and cost. The approach is doing fine.

Does industry like the "Skunk Works" approach?

One knowledgeable manufacturing official told me he could reduce his budget by 60 percent if he were allowed to just go and do the job without all of the government procedures. Skunk Works programs allow him to do just that.

What other reasons were there that lead you to believe were the reasons behind the success of these programs?

I'll add one more. As in any activity, success is often equal to the amount of non-interference by people who contribute nothing to the product. Too many people want to be policemen, but have absolutely no responsibility or accountability for the item itself. Along with that is the fact that there are still some people in the acquisition business who like having their hands held. They like operating on a committee basis. If it goes wrong, blame the committee. In a "Skunk Works" program, nobody is allowed to even visit the contractor unless invited by the contractor himself. That scares some people who worry about supervision. First of all you pick a proven contractor, secondly you give him a fixed price contract, and thirdly his carrot is a follow-on production contract if he is success-ful. You would be amazed at how much more successful that ap-proach is over detailed supervision.

The R&D story obviously had its unfortunate episodes as well. Do you recall any of these that were worthy of note—from the lessons-to-be-learned point of view? Perhaps the Mauler program is an example.

You thought I'd say Mauler? Its only fault was it was too far ahead of its time. The Army was not ready for it, either in its sophistication or its cost. Mauler was cancelled because it appeared to be too expensive and would prove difficult to maintain in the field. What was expensive then? Mauler was to have cost $100,000 per firing unit. When it was killed it appeared the cost would be more like $1.1 M. Compare that cost today with Patriot or even Roland. For what we were asking Mauler to do, that was not exorbi-tant—but the Army wasn't ready for it. The Army wasn't ready for that level of cost or that level of complexity at the time. With 20–20 hindsight, I believe killing Mauler set back Army air defense twenty years.

Now to answer your real question, I have to say that generi-cally, those programs which are joint programs are the most difficult to run. Mallard and the present TRITAC series of equipment are good examples. I'm a firm believer that if you want a joint program, do not give it to one service to be the executive agent to perform the program. Instead, establish a project manager in OSD to run it. Here's why. The initial funding for the program is accommodated by OSD and given to a service. But in future years, when an overrun occurs, the dollars came out of the hide of the service which is the executive agent, and this creates an environment which is difficult to accommodate. Some would say well, you managed the program, therefore, the overrun is your problem. However, this is not always valid as many of the overruns are because of new requirements. Then, too, these are cost plus R&D programs which by their very nature will generate some overruns. If they aren't expected to be difficult they should have been fixed price in the first place.

Are there any common threads that exist in all of the other than successful development programs?

I'd say the lack of a firm requirement—lack of total acceptance of a requirement—and lack of total dedication or support by the branch concerned. Advocates of certain proposals seem to have difficulty accepting a "final" decision if it is not in line with their thinking. I suppose this is human nature, but development pro-grams would have more success if a proposal, once everyone has had his say and a final decision made, was backed 100 percent by all concerned.

During your long service in the R&D community you saw a number of reorganizations. Did any of these, in your opinion, assist in solving R&D management problems?

I think every reorganization solves problems. Reorganizations elevate what the commander or somebody sees is a problem. And that's what reorganizations are designed to do—solve the problem. What did AMARC see as the problem? They saw the acquisition of materiel subordinated to the maintenance of materiel in the field. Now they did not mean to denigrate the importance of readiness. The reorganization elevated acquisition to a level equal with maintenance and readiness. That's what AMARC recommended and that's what the recent DARCOM reorganization did. As we all know, any organization will work if the people want it to work.

Have you been able to notice any trends in the types of people, both military and civilian, that are choosing to enter the R&D field?

Today there is more "Green Suit" involvement than there was years ago. I recall when the first project manager board met in 1974, we had fewer than 100 candidates to select from, and frankly most of those 100 were not qualified. By last summer, just before I retired, the number of candidates for the board which met in July 1977 had grown to 250, all fully qualified. I have since been advised that the PM board which met on 1 May 1978 had 612 fully qualified candidates to select from.

This tells me that the Army recognizes the importance of the acquisition business, and that involvement in the acquisition business is no longer a dead-end job.

Even with the three wars we have had since 1941, an Army officer today is in combat maybe only 10 to 15 percent of his career, three years or so out of thirty. But project managers are in combat every day. There is no peacetime for a project manager. He never gets the chance to go out in the woods on a practice maneuver. His battles are for real, every day of the year.

Now that you have had some time with private industry, what are the major differences you see in the ways that industry runs its R&D programs and the way government handles theirs?

Well, the first thing is that in industry if they need specific types of people they can go out and hire them right away. It still takes time, but industry can do it quicker.

The second difference is that industry recognizes that up front is where dollars are the most important. You can't start slow and catch up later, or start, then slow down, and then restart. Industry has learned that there is only one way to shorten a program schedule —put bucks up front—accept and understand the risks you are taking. One of the reasons that GSRS and ARTADS are taking so long to develop is that neither of these programs was funded properly at the start. Too often the government would like to see a riskless program, but that animal doesn't exist.

But don't let me mislead you. Industry, too, has difficulty in starting up an internal program because it takes time to get the funding squared away and find sufficient engineers. But here industry does have some advantage. When additional dollars are needed, it's usually within the corporate capability to add them immediately without waiting until the next budget cycle. There are normally "new business" dollars available for this purpose.

A problem faced by both industry and the Army is that industry project managers are just as optimistic as Army project managers. They, too, are reluctant to tell the bad news. But it is like a cockroach nest—you had better get at problems early, for problems beget other problems.

Over the years of your senior level involvement in R&D, what changes did you see occur in the ways that the Services dealt with Congress?

There are two major changes that have occurred during the period of LTG Trudeau (1957–1961) to LTG Keith (1977–   ). I had the privilege of serving under six Chiefs of R&D—Trudeau, Beach, Dick, Betts, Gribble, and Deane. Year by year the changes appeared slight, but when you compare 1959 to 1977, the change is precipitous.

In 1959 we dealt in broad statements and generalities—laced with high hopes—like our 1959 thoughts on air cushion vehicles. There was little fact but great faith! And there still aren't many ground effects vehicles.

Then, too, as I said earlier, by 1977 Congressional staffs had grown tremendously, in size and in expertise. Maybe one doesn't always agree with the views of a particular staffer, but one has to admit that he is usually highly knowledgeable and his questions usually cogent.

The second change has been the role of the Assistant Secretary of the Army (R&D), now the ASA (RD&A). It used to be that he never became involved in the hearings. Not so today. This change has been a good one. I worked with every ASA (R&D) the Army had, and each had his strong points. We "Green Suit" guys had never built a thing. The Secretaries were visible evidence to the Congress of proven real-world experience. Participation by the ASA adds credibility to the Green-Suiter requests. Today the Assistant Secretary is a key figure at hearings and I personally believe he brings a lot to the party.

As you are aware, there is now a major effort to increase standardization and interoperability between US and NATO forces. From your position or advantage of seeing both industry's and the government's views, what do you feel about this effort?

Interoperability is an absolute necessity. It is a good objective and not too hard to reach. I had the opportunity way back in 1961 to work with the British in standardizing our 155mm cannon chambers so that we could shoot each other's ammunition. That standardization spread to the other NATO nations. So it can be done.

It's absolutely mandatory that the US-produced Rolands be able to fire European missiles and vice versa.

As for total standardization, I don't believe it is necessary, nor do I believe we can afford it or even will achieve it. It would be too expensive. We ought to first restrict ourselves to the so-called expendables—fuel, ammunition, and food—and communications. Standardize on the interoperability of those and the battle is really won.

More important is industry's attitude toward production in another country. How do you divide the profit pie? Some corporations may take a dim view of giving away technology and business. However, they must realize that industries outside the US are rapidly increasing their capabilities because their governments are collaborating to fund them.

The subject is beset with not only military difficulties, but economic and political issues—not the least of which is potential third country sales.

When you were a senior military R&D manager, how did you evaluate programs; how did you determine what programs were doing well and those you felt were bad programs, for whatever reasons?

First off, I never permitted a rubber baseline. Measure a program constantly against what was originally proposed. If the baseline is allowed to change, due to such things as added requirements or alternative approaches, overruns are rationalized and you have destroyed any measurement system you ever had. Even potentially good changes are hazardous until the baseline system has been fielded.

Another signal is that bad programs always have the same symptoms—overruns, schedule slips, and technical problems. Very seldom does one of these occur singly. One is always a precursor of the others.

One can get a quick handle by looking at a trend. Then find out what is causing the variation. There are people who know those answers, but they often do not understand the importance of carrying the news to the top. Frequently, if top management knows about a problem area early, it can be corrected—at a minimum cost.

At my former level in the Army there was no way that I could, or for that matter should, be intimately familiar with every one of the several hundred ongoing programs. That is the project manager/project officer's job. In the Army I was forced to manage by trend indicators. One can chart a spending plan very easily. Any significant variation from that spending plan is cause for eyebrow raising and an ensuing investigation. One can do the same thing in the functional areas: if one has a continual increase in inventory, increase in number of line stoppers, sudden increase in materiel costs, it's time to re-evaluate. These things have to tell you something, or at least should make one curious enough to ask questions. The surprising thing is that no matter what questions one asks, they always elicit answers to questions which weren't asked but should have been. Very often this unsolicited information becomes more significant than that which was solicited.

What determination or measurement process does industry use to evaluate its independent R&D programs?

There is no simple answer to that. One obvious measurement is return on investment. Profit is often, but not always, the bottom line. Industry usually conducts quarterly reviews of every program. Each will be evaluated in terms of its goal versus reality to include where does it stand on the profit line.

Another measurement used by industry is overhead. Staff is overhead. Overhead is the worst word in industry's management vocabulary. There is no intermediate layering as with government —it can't be tolerated. Even vice presidents frequently have no personal staff. If they need a study done, they have to pull people off other jobs or do the work themselves.

But I want to make it clear that companies are just as interested in delivering good equipment to the Army as the Army is in receiving it—or they won't be in the defense industry structure very long. There are even times when an industrial firm will not bid on a job if its management believes it is wrong for the Army.

Another measurement is, "is there competition?" Industry would be the first to tell you that without it you will never get the lowest price or the best product. Without it, innovation would cease.

69

Comment*

Dr. John J. Bennett†

Over the past decade the annual unit cost to operate and support ships and aircraft systems has increased severalfold. Even adjusting for inflation, there are still major augmentations which can be ascribed to greater weapons complexity and higher personnel and fuel costs. The effects of poor field reliability and expensive-to-maintain designs must also be acknowledged. Finally, some recent operating and support (O&S) budget increases have been needed to maintain readiness at acceptable levels.

These problems are taken very seriously by the services as well as the Office of the Secretary of Defense (OSD). As such, some fundamental examinations of the traditional methods and concepts of support are now taking place. For example, expensive periodic overhaul activities are being questioned and supplanted by other means; personnel specialties and manning are being re-examined; and concurrent with reducing the costs to maintain current weapons, there is a major initiative to control anticipated costs for those weapons now in development.

Relating DTC and LCC

DOD is not lessening its emphasis on design to unit costs in favor of life cycle costs; but it is considering the impact of operation and support costs in choosing a unit cost goal and is assessing these tradeoffs throughout the development process.

*Defense Management Journal, January 1976, pp. 1–4.
†Acting Assistant Secretary of Defense (Installations and Logistics).

There are two significant documents which amplify the basic acquisition strategy outlined in DOD Directive (DODD) 5000.1. The first of these, DOD Instruction 5000.2, particularly emphasizes that proposed new systems be economic to operate and support. The second, DODD 5000.28, explicitly emphasizes management of weapon systems to ensure establishment of "costs as a parameter equal in importance with technical requirement and schedules." This is the first official policy statement relating design to cost (DTC) and life cycle costs (LCC); it defines DTC as a philosophy and a goal. As a philosophy, DTC means the control of system acquisition, operating and support costs, e.g., managing the life cycle cost. As a quantitative contractual goal, DTC in general practice is defined as the average unit flyaway cost with visibility maintained in parallel with the total LCC.

There are three major points in implementation of DODD 5000.28 which should be emphasized. First, unit acquisition cost as well as O&S cost goals should be specified, preferably by Defense Systems Acquisition Review Council (DSARC) I and not later than DSARC II. There will necessarily be tradeoffs to establish the best balance between acquisition and support to minimize life cycle costs. Second, specific measurable quantities such as meantime between failures and numbers of personnel should be established contractually and as Defense Concept Paper thresholds. These parameters, directly related to O&S costs, will be measured during test and evaluation and in operation. Third, incentives to reduce life cycle costs should be established.

Higher O&S costs generally result from systems with higher unit costs. In the past, higher unit costs generally reflected higher performance rather than higher reliability levels. This added complexity tended to reduce reliability, thus increasing O&S costs. A preferred approach to reduce O&S costs for new systems would be to iterate the design to simplify the end product, where schedules permit. An alternative would be to spend proportionately more on quality rather than complexity, where availability needs and future cost reductions clearly warrant the investment.

Problems and Actions

There are several reasons why DOD has more experience in controlling production costs than O&S costs: The production cost aspect is initiated earlier, O&S costs are more complex and insufficiently understood, and the O&S cost data base is just now being developed. Thus, three needs must be realized:

- Consider O&S in the design process.
- Generate management awareness and visibility.
- Implement O&S in the contract.

O&S Cost in Design

Much of the O&S cost problem can be attributed to the lack of emphasis on the downstream operating costs of weapons during their development. The greatest payoff, of course, comes when supportability considerations are built in early in the design process, so that design considerations can impact O&S costs. For example, the T-700 engine for Utility Tactical Transport Aircraft System has a modular design and can be broken into four sections in the field. In case of failure, only the defective section is shipped to the depot. Spares costs are lower since modules rather than entire engines are stocked. This type of savings can only be realized through intentional effort in design.

The Navy's DTC electronic weapon project determined that a high contributor to equipment O&S costs was the shipboard manpower needed to operate and maintain the equipment. Contractors were told to design equipment that minimized shipboard manpower requirements. Thus, the electronic warfare equipment was designed with a high degree of automation for both operation and maintenance. This is expected to result in as much as a 100 percent savings in the number of operating and maintenance personnel required for the new system.

O&S cost improvements can even be obtained after the equipment has reached an approved production configuration at DSARC III. This may be contrary to standard opinions that 96 percent of the O&S cost is determined by DSARC III. This is generally true since requirements and design drive a large part of the LCC. But cost reduction does not totally cease when design is completed. For example, engines for the A-10 aircraft are a redesign of the S-3A engines. The A-10 engines have 88 percent commonality, weigh only 35 pounds more, and cost 20 percent less than the S-3A model.

There is no question that design influences O&S costs. But the awareness and importance of this is just now becoming apparent to the design community.

Awareness and Visibility

The need for management awareness and visibility in the LCC area is well known. Yet, there is a particular need to define what management objectives are being sought in this area and provide the technical tools, such as definitions and cost models, to accomplish the specified tasks.

Progress is being made, as witnessed by the recently revised Office of the Assistant Secretary of Defense (Installations and Logistics) (OASD I&L) charter emphasizing I&L participation in DSARC I and II. This charter, as envisioned by former Assistant Secretary Mendolia, would have the I&L staff become "involved in the weapon systems acquisition process right from the start, coordinating with ASD (Comptroller) and the Director, Defense Research and Engineering, to ensure that proper financial, design, production, and support are considered in all phases of the acquisition process."[1]

Thus, at an appropriate phase in the development of each new weapon system, there will be a review of the following points:

- The estimated O&S cost of the proposed system as compared to current systems and possible improvements on them.
- The approach to field reliability as differentiated from paper or laboratory reliability, including the adequacy of the planned test program.
- Management approach to reducing LCC, including source selection, contract, and incentives.
- Design tradeoffs to reduce LCC.
- Logistic support alternatives considered and their cost impact.

Management awareness within DOD and the services of the life cycle and O&S cost problem has manifested itself in many ways. The individual services are making LCC a prime criterion in the source selection process. The use of reliability improvement warranties has been encouraged, and a tri-service warranty data bank and educational program are being established. To improve electronic field reliability, a working group chartered by the Joint Logistics Commanders is recommending specific implementary changes to test specifications, standards, and data collection methods. The services are also examining the field reliability of existing equipment and are budgeting funds to improve this reliability.

Historically, visibility has not been maintained on the cost to operate and support weapons by the system supported. Without such data, there is no reference point to identify the high cost subsystem or verify the cost estimates of the new systems. However, a major effort is underway with the services to obtain O&S

[1]See Arthur I. Mendolia, "ASD for Installations and Logistics Establishes New Charter," *Defense Management Journal,* July 1975, pp. 41–43.

cost data on current weapons. By the third quarter of calendar year 1976, a management information system to get aircraft data should exist in all three services. Systems to compile data for other weapon classes will follow.

DOD-Industry Interface

There must be a strong interface between DOD and industry in the LCC and O&S cost areas. This must involve free and open discussion on the real incentives to motivate designs with adequate reliability and to have low O&S costs. Some actions that will strengthen this interface are:

• DOD must provide contractors greater visibility into the O&S cost structure. LCC and O&S cost estimates must reflect mission requirements. If LCC and O&S cost models are to be used properly, the procuring agency must specify them and the appropriate operational factors.

• DOD must provide high quality, baseline O&S concepts to contractors very early in each program so that contractors can generate consistent LCC estimates and make meaningful LCC tradeoff studies.

• DOD must occasionally be willing to revise DTC production cost goals when LCC benefits are possible.

• Early in the design process industry must provide designers with an understanding of LCC implications of their designs. Designers must be knowledgeable of service problems in the field, and all participants in the acquisition process must be reoriented away from nonessential design attributes.

• With current emphasis on O&S contractual incentives such as reliability improvement warranties, industry may have to reorient its profit-making strategy from a current profit emphasis to a consideration of future profit opportunities.

• Finally, both DOD and industry must start an educational program to provide those involved in the design and development process with an understanding of the LCC area.

An Effective Approach

Industry and organizations such as the National Security Industrial Association (NSIA) can help DOD evolve an effective approach to managing the acquisition of more economical systems. Clearly industry must better understand DOD problems and be motivated to produce systems designed with inherently lower support costs as well as more efficient support facilities. But this is a long-term problem and one-shot efforts won't suffice.

In 1974 an ad hoc NSIA task force[2] on LCC was enjoined to come up with specific recommendations for improvement to the acquisition process to make LCC—the operating and support cost as well as acquisition cost—an equal partner with performance in the source selection, contractual commitment and incentives process.[3] The study effort was organized into five major types of equipment: aircraft, ships, vehicles, weapons, and electronics.

The results of the effort are in the process of final review and compilation preparatory to their publication in a study report. The preliminary results, however, recommend a "go slow and steady" approach which includes the following specifics:

• The current work breakdown structure is inadequate. To handle the intent of LCC requires a major overhaul, perhaps incorporating a cost breakdown structure.

• Management cost centers should be established for measuring and controlling costs; this implies improved internal data reporting and management systems.

• Reliability Improvement Warranties cannot be used as a club; however, they can be useful if both the producer and user are directly involved in the cost reduction process.

• The capability to correlate logistic support costs into the DTC affordability limit must be developed.

• LCC should be used as a source selection criteria subject to the resolution of standard model criteria, data validity and responsibility, and reasonable weighting factors.

• The current LCC estimate differences between the source selection and evaluation board, the contractor, and the independent cost estimator must be reconciled.

• LCC considerations should be a factor in every design and management decision.

• Costing methods must be tailored to the specific acquisition and type of hardware.

• LCC should be in current dollars and be a line item in each contract.

• A refinement of terms, conditions, requirements, and data validity and availability is badly needed.

---

[2]The select team of industry personnel was managed by the NSIA Logistics Management Advisory Committee under the direction of Mr. Donald R. Earles of the Raytheon Company.

[3]It was noted by the task force that in excess of 50 acquisitions have had LCC imposed in some degree and in excess of 30 items of hardware are presently being acquired by some type of LCC procurement. While the task force considered this indicative of the importance placed upon LCC in the procurement process, industry is still concerned about "too much too soon" and the potentially inordinate management risks to be assumed.

• LCC should be made an allowable independent research and data project, and the mock-up and simulation of resource consumption should be encouraged.

• The current emphasis on reliability growth implies a concomitant improvement in reliability prediction and testing.

From the work of this task force, it is apparent that specific viable improvements are possible, particularly in the areas of providing more uniform and complete data on the mission support concept and costs on both current and new systems.

Ultimately, however, DOD must go beyond these recommendations and obtain more specifics in the form of examples and cases to effectively manage the acquisition of new weapon systems.

✶　✶　✶　✶　✶

Costs of acquisition and ownership shall be established as separate cost elements and translated into firm design-to-cost and life cycle cost requirements for the system selected for full-scale engineering development.

—DOD Directive 5000.2,
Major System Acquisition Process

Over the past ten years, social and economic spending in this country has grown about five times faster than defense spending. If the effects of inflation are taken into account, defense spending has declined by 23 percent over this period while social and economic spending has increased by over 100 percent. Though this period compares defense from the peak levels during the conflict in Southeast Asia, it still appears that many people do not realize how sharp the decline in public resources allocated to defense has been since that time.

—Harold Brown, Secretary of Defense

70

The Program Manager as an Advocate

Program Advocacy*

Acquisition Cycle Task Force

In examining the history and outcome of various major system acquisitions, the Task Force found that there was a common thread relating to the matter of program advocates and advocacy. It was clear that development programs which lacked strong advocacy were much more likely to be cancelled than those which had energetic and dedicated advocates. The Condor program is a typical example of an effort which ultimately was cancelled because the system simply lacked strong advocates for the particular operational capability which it was intended to provide. In a more recent case, the B-1 program, which had clear-cut advocacy for much of its life, eventually lost the most influential of its advocates in the Executive Branch following the change of Administration and was cancelled by Presidential order.

On the other hand, there are numerous examples of programs which appear to be continually in trouble for one reason or another —TOW, SAM-D, F-111, etc.—which are carried on year after year because they have the support of active and vocal advocates, either in the sponsoring Service, in OSD, in the Congress, or elsewhere. Without passing judgment on the specific programs mentioned, it

*Extract from *Report of the Acquisition Cycle Task Force* to the Defense Science Board, March 15, 1978, pp. 45, 46.

seemed clear to the Task Force that, without advocacy, the chances of a program proceeding through its complete acquisition cycle into production and deployment are significantly diminished, while with strong advocates, certain programs may be continued in existence long after they should have been terminated for technical problems, inadequate capability, cost or schedule overruns, or similar reasons.

Thus, program advocacy may be either good or bad in terms of system acquisition. It is often a necessary ingredient if a program is to be continued through to completion; and a lack of advocates can spell serious danger to even a "good" program. In other cases, strong advocacy may result in the continuation of programs which would otherwise be terminated. Such advocacy covers the entire range of possibilities: it may be political, it may be mission-related, it may be extremely parochial, it is often misdirected and misused, and it is frequently needed.

The government procurement system is filled with seven to eight levels of management (above a program), all of whom (two to three times a year) feel *obliged* to requestion the program's continued existence. Without a really strong advocate, these drops wear away armor. If the MENS concept of A-109 is fully implemented as intended, the Secretary of Defense in effect becomes the advocate for the *need,* and the Program Manager can concentrate on his job of advocating the optimum *solution.*

Systems Advocacy and Interaction of the Program Manager With Higher Levels*

Dr. J. Ronald Fox

First, I'd like to discuss systems advocacy with you: what it is, what it is *not,* when the program manager is a program advocate, and who the recipients of systems advocacy are. Related to these aspects of systems management is the interaction of the PM and higher levels in the Department of Defense and in Congress. I want to touch on these relationships in the second part of this discussion.

*Extract from a presentation by Dr. Fox at the Defense Systems Management College, February 23, 1972.

Systems Advocacy

Systems advocacy includes several actions on the part of the program manager. One of these is presenting the advantages and strongpoints of his program in a persuasive manner. He may need to do this to obtain funding, for example. Particularly important is the need to describe his system in such a way as to create confidence, a key attribute of successful program managers. Related to this point is the need to operate a program office that can maintain strong governmental control. By this I do not mean doing the contractor's job, or extending the functions of the government program office beyond its charter and capabilities. I do mean vigorous actions and timely decision-making in the responsibilities that are properly the program office's.

At this point it is important to note several things that systems advocacy does *not* mean. It does not include concealment of problem areas and risks. It does not mean acting as a spokesman for the prime contractor without an independent analysis. And it does not mean understating the cost of a project.

There are five occasions, in my opinion, when the PM has the role of program advocate:

1. Formulation of the budget involving his program.
2. In responding to threats to the program, which may come from other programs.
3. At the time of technical failures in the program.
4. During visits by government officials to the contractor or to the program office.
5. During higher level reviews, such as DSARC reviews.

Two groups of individuals often act as program advocates. One, of course, is the program management office, who is naturally interested in the success of the program and in defending against attacks on it. The other is the user organizations, such as SAC and Army helicopter pilots. The users may view their particular role as the most important. But they don't have OSD responsibility for balance among programs and capabilities.

Who then are the recipients of systems advocacy, and what are their objectives?

Higher levels of the buying command are one type of recipients. What they are seeking is to avoid surprises, and to have the program meet its cost, schedule and performance goals. They are also trying to establish the best balance of funds for programs within the buying command. And they are seeking a greater portion of the service budget for development and production programs.

The Office of the Secretary of Defense has some key objectives. Like the buying command, it seeks to avoid surprises, and to have programs meet their cost, schedule and performance objectives. It also is seeking the best balance of capabilities among the four military services, however. And it seeks to advance the technical state of the art.

A third recipient of advocacy is the General Accounting Office. One of GAO's objectives is to identify deficiencies in Defense activities. Another, often not recognized, is to develop an in-depth understanding of Defense activities, including systems acquisition and the manner in which programs are being managed.

Fourth, Congress may be a recipient. Its objectives are similar to those of higher Defense levels and the GAO. In addition, however, some members of Congress may be looking for deficiencies which can attract public attention.

Finally, the press may be a recipient. Bear in mind that the press is seeking dramatic stories; dramatic success or failures. Routine good news simply doesn't sell newspapers.

In his role as systems advocate, the PM may encounter some basic conflicts. For example, the PM and the contractor may from time to time find themselves on the opposite sides of an adversary relationship—for instance regarding changes or relaxing specifications. It is important in this type situation that he keep his immediate superior fully and frankly informed, and that he be as objective with him as possible.

The PM has two roles: Mr. Inside and Mr. Outside. Inside, he's a judge, a controller, a questioner. But when he is facing outside he may have to wear his advocate hat. Often where a PM gets in trouble is wearing the wrong hat at the wrong time.

Interaction of the PM and Higher Levels

Let's turn now to dealing with higher levels in DOD and in Congress.

Here are several suggestions in dealing with aggressive questions in Congressional committee appearances:

- Deal with the questions and questioners and make answers in a calm way. A witness' credibility goes way down if he becomes excited or emotionally disturbed.
- Do your homework; be prepared.
- Read samples of testimony previously made to the committee beforehand as part of your homework.
- Don't be arrogant or talk down. Recognize that Senators and

Congressmen may have strong egos, and don't cause them to lose face.

- Answer in a forthright way, and be concise. Don't enlarge in answering. This invites probing into possible loopholes.
- Don't assume your audience knows the meaning of abbreviations and Service-peculiar terms.
- Congressmen generally don't have an understanding-in-depth of a program. They have limited manpower and limited time.
- An aggressive line of questioning may be a cover for lack of preparation. Recognize this, and answer coolly.

In replying to questions, both from Congressional and press sources, it is important to listen to the question asked. Might an answer be true in some circumstances and not in others? If so, address both aspects in the answer. If there's a complex question or one requiring a complex answer, don't hesitate to request permission to enter a full answer later in the record. And then prepare the answer carefully in writing.

A witness should not *assume* that the purpose of a line of questions is to find answers. It may simply be a way for the questioner to prove a point. The witness may be able to detect this by looking at other committee members' reactions, to determine who is interested and who is not. In connection with this, the witness should find out the concerns of, and talk with, staffers and GAO personnel.

Under all circumstances, it is essential that the witness remain calm. The key to this is preparation. One way of preparing is to have another person serve as devil's advocate, and have him be merciless in questions. Another way is to sit in on similar types of hearings.

In dealing with the press, there often are two problems. First, an interview may not be for fact-finding, but for substantiating a particular point of view, for or against. And second, your entire statement may be only partially used. A conclusion that can be drawn here is not to talk to an individual from the press unless you know him and his point of view. Let the professionals (PIO) talk with him.

And finally, in dealing with Congress *do* use the Office of Legislative Liaison. It can assist you in planning your appearance; can provide background briefing and previous testimony; and has good liaison with staffers.

An Interview With the F-18 Program Manager*

Aerospace Daily

Asked how he felt about the drumfire of criticism leveled at the F-18, some of it from Navy officials, Lenox (Captain Glen W. Lenox, F-18 Program Manager) paused and picked his words carefully.

"I guess I feel that there are a number of people in various walks of life who have their own advocacy and they are going to press for what would be beneficial to them for whatever reason. And in some of those cases, it becomes convenient to criticize the F-18 program."

The question was put to Lenox as to whether he thought the Hornet would ever live down the reputation of being a political plane forced on the Navy as a White House accommodation to House Speaker Thomas "Tip" O'Neill (D), in whose home state of Massachusetts the F404 engines are made.

Lenox understandably was reluctant to get into a discussion of the motives of high-level officials but did respond this way:

"Within the Navy, I don't think there is now that opinion.

"I have now detected that wherever I go, talking to Naval personnel in the fleet, I find a very high level of excitement about the 18. Both fighter and attack communities are looking forward to the 18."

Lenox was asked if the tests last year (DAILY, July 13) of performance and air combat maneuverability weren't rigged in the sense that, as one of the pilots pointed out, the F-14 was used outside its element and was not in a position to use the AWG-9 radar.

Lenox candidly responded that, of course, any plane can be made to look better than another one "if you let me select the ground rules and the assumptions."

He said the pilot who noted the F-14 was being used outside of its normal environment was trying to be fair in pointing out that there are a number of ways an aircraft can be assessed in different operational areas.

In the ACM area, the F-18 prototype with its high thrust to weight radio was clearly superior. He said there were other F-18 advantages in reliability and maintainability.

*Extract from *Aerospace Daily*, August 2, 1978, p. 137.

And, in an obvious reference to the high cost F-14, which the Navy has never been able to afford in the numbers that it wanted, he added:

"If you have a greater number of aircraft you have a distinct advantage in many ways. . . ."

$$\star \quad \star \quad \star \quad \star \quad \star$$

If I were to stress any advice to PMs, it's this: don't oversell, and don't underprice. In the advocacy stages of your project, *understate,* don't overstate.
—*Gen. George S. Brown, USAF*

What the program manager has a right to expect and what in fact he will be offered are often quite different. Experienced program managers would remind the new program manager that often he must struggle to obtain the management flexibility he is supposed to be given. Higher authorities, and especially their staff organizations, tend to standardize their requirements and to insist on the use of familiar techniques and methods. Their initial disposition is to avoid changes and exceptions to the general rule. Requests for deviations are rarely conceded without being pushed and sold.

—*LMI Introduction to
Military Program Management*

Glossary

ACO—Administrative Contracting Officer.

ACWP—Actual Cost for Work Performed.

Advanced Development—The period in which the major program characteristics (technical, logistics, cost and schedule), through extensive analysis and hardware developments, are validated, primarily by the contractor(s) who will do full scale development.

AFLC—Air Force Logistics Command.

AFPRO—Air Force Plant Representative's Office.

AFSC—Air Force Systems Command.

Allocation—An authorization by a designated official of a component of the Department of Defense making funds available within a prescribed amount to an operating agency for the purpose of making allotments, i.e., the first subdivision of an apportionment.

Allotment—The authority, expressed in terms of a specific amount of funds, granted by competent authority to commit, obligate, and expend funds for a particular purpose. Obligation and expenditure of the funds may not exceed the amount specified in the allotment, and the purpose for which the authorization is made must be adhered to. Allotments are granted for all appropriations except the operating accounts, such as O&M and RDT&E, which use operating budgets. All allotments must be accounted for until the appropriation lapses or until all obligations are liquidated, whichever occurs first.

APP—Advanced Procurement Plan.

Apportionment—A determination made by the Office of Management and Budget which limits the amount of obligations or expenditures which may be incurred during a specified time period. An apportionment may limit all obligations to be incurred during the specified period or it may limit obligations to be incurred for a specific activity, function, project, object, or a combination thereof.

Appropriation limitation—An amount fixed by Congress within an appropriation which cannot be exceeded.

Armed Services Procurement Regulation (ASPR)—A comprehensive document that spells out the many details of contracting. (See ASPR.)

ASA—Assistant Secretary of the Army.

ASAF—Assistant Secretary of the Air Force.

ASBCA—Armed Services Board of Contract Appeals.

ASD—Assistant Secretary of Defense.

ASD(C)—Assistant Secretary of Defense (Comptroller).

ASD(C³I)—Assistant Secretary of Defense (Command, Control, Communications & Intelligence). Also principal Deputy Under Secretary Defense (R&E).

ASD(MRA&L)—Assistant Secretary of Defense (Manpower, Reserve Affairs & Logistics).

ASD(PA&E)—Assistant Secretary of Defense (Program Analysis & Evaluation).

ASN—Assistant Secretary of the Navy.

ASPR—Armed Services Procurement Regulation (being replaced by DAR-Defense Acquisition Regulation–per DODD 5000.35).

Baseline—See Performance Measurement Baseline.

Boondoggle—A trip of minimum usefulness, taken under the guise of official duties.

BCWP—Budgeted Cost for Work Performed.

BCWS—Budgeted Cost for Work Scheduled.

Budget Authority—Authority provided by law to enter into obligations which generally result in immediate or future outlays of Government funds. The basic forms of budget authority are: appropriations, contract authority, and borrowing authority.

Buy-In—Submission of a bid more optimistic than anticipated cost with expectation of subsequent resource add-ons.

CCB—Configuration Control Board.

CFSR—Contract Funds Status Report.

CIA—Central Intelligence Agency.

CNM—Chief of Naval Material.

CNO—Chief of Naval Operations.

compt—Comptroller (pronounced "controller").

Contract Administration Office (CAO)—The activity identified in the DOD Directory of Contract Administration Service Components (DOD 4105-59-H) assigned to perform the contract administration responsibilities listed in ASPR. It is a general term and includes AFPROs, NAVPROs, SUPSHIPs, Army plant representatives, and DCAS field officers.

Contract Work Breakdown Structure (CWBS)—The complete WBS for a contract, developed and used by a contractor within the guidelines of MIL-STD 881A, and in accordance with the contract work statement.

Contracting Officer—Any officer or civilian designated with authority to enter into and administer contracts for the service.

Contractor—An entity in private industry which enters into contracts with the Government. In this book, the word also applies to Government-operated activities which perform work on major defense programs. KR is the commonly used abbreviation.

Cost/Schedule Control Systems Criteria (C/SCSC)—Criteria used to evaluate the effectiveness of contractors' internal systems. The C/SCSC do not require any data to be reported to the Government, but do provide for access to data needed to evaluate the system and monitor the operation during the life of the contract.

CPAF—Cost-Plus-Award Fee.

CPIF—Cost-Plus-Incentive Fee.

CPFF—Cost-Plus-Fixed-Fee.

CPM—Critical Path Method; Contractor Performance Measurement.

CPR—Cost Performance Report.

C/SCSC—Cost/Schedule Control Systems Criteria.

C/SSR—Cost/Schedule Status Report.

CWBS—Contract Work Breakdown Structure.

DAR—Defense Acquisition Regulation (replaces ASPR per DODD 5000.35).

DARCOM—U.S. Army Materiel Development and Readiness Command.

DCAA—Defense Contract Audit Agency.

DCAS—Defense Contract Administration Services.

DCASO—Defense Contract Administration Service Office.

DCP—Decision Coordinating Paper; Development Concept Paper.

DCS—Deputy Chief of Staff.

Decision Coordinating Paper (DCP)—The principal document to record essential system program information for use in support of the Secretary of Defense decision-making process at Milestones I, II, and III.

Defense Acquisition Executive—The principal advisor and staff assistant to the Secretary of Defense and the focal point in OSD for system acquisitions.

Defense System Acquisition Review Council (DSARC)—An advisory body to the Secretary of Defense on major system acquisitions. The council members are the OSD staff principals.

DEPSECDEF—Deputy Secretary of Defense.

Design to Cost (DTC)—Management concept wherein rigorous cost goals are established during development and the control of systems costs (acquisition, operating, and support) to these goals is achieved by practical tradeoffs between operational capability, performance, cost, and schedule. Cost, as a key design parameter, is addressed on a continuing basis and as an inherent part of the development and production process.

Development Test I (DT I)—Test conducted early in the development cycle, normally during the validation phase. Components, subsystems, or the entire system are examined to determine whether the system is ready for full-scale development. State-of-the-art technology is addressed in DT I.

Development Test II (DT II)—Test providing the technical data necessary to assess whether the system is ready for low-rate initial or full-scale production. It measures the technical performance and safety characteristics of the item and evaluates its associated tools, test equipment, training package, and maintenance test package as described in the development plan. DT II addresses accomplishment of engineer design goals.

DLA—Defense Logistics Agency.

DOD—Department of Defense.

DODD—DOD Directive.

Dog and Pony Show—A briefing which uses a number of viewgraph slides, flip charts, or other training aids. Sometimes this term is used to simply indicate that someone is to be briefed.

DODI—DOD Instruction.

DSARC—Defense Systems Acquisition Review Council.

DSARC Milestone 0—Program Initiation.

DSARC Milestone 1—Demonstration and Validation.

DSARC Milestone 2—Full Scale Engineering Development.

DSARC Milestone 3—Production and Deployment.

DSMC—Defense Systems Management College.

DT—Development Testing.

DT&E—Development Testing and Evaluation.

DTLCC—Design to Life-Cycle-Cost.

DT/OT—Development Testing/Operational Testing.

DTUPC—Design to Unit Production Cost.

EAC—Estimated Cost at Completion.

ECP—Engineering Change Proposal.

Engineering Change Proposal—A proposal to the responsible authority recommending that a change to an original item of equipment be considered; and the design or engineering change be incorporated into the article to modify, add to, delete, or supersede original parts.

Estimated Cost At Completion (EAC)—Actual direct costs, plus indirect costs allocable to the contract, plus the estimate of costs (direct and indirect) for authorized work remaining.

FAR—Federal Acquisition Regulations (to replace Federal Procurement Regulations).

FFP—Firm-Fixed Price.

File 13—The wastebasket.

Flaky—Refers to a staff paper that contains conclusions and recommendations that will not hold up under analysis.

Fly—Means action will be approved. More commonly used in a negative sense, as in "it won't fly."

FMS—Foreign Military Sales.

FP (E)—Fixed-Price (Escalation).

FPIF—Fixed-Price Incentive Fee.

FPR—Federal Procurement Regulations (to be replaced by FAR).

FY—Fiscal Year.

FYDP—Five-Year Defense Program.

G&A—General and Administrative Expense.

Gameplan—Refers to plan of attack (e.g., how to monitor an ongoing program).

GAO—General Accounting Office.

GFE—Government Furnished Equipment.

GFP—Government Furnished Property.

GOCO—Government-Owned, Contractor-Operated.

Government Furnished Equipment (GFE)—Items in the possession of, or acquired by, the Government and delivered to or otherwise made available to the contractor.

Grease—Refers to preliminary effort or lobbying in support of a position or paper. Sometimes referred to as "greasing the skids."

Gross National Product (GNP)—The final value of all goods and services produced in the U.S. economy in one year. This is equal to the sum of personal consumption, gross private investment, and Government expenditures on goods and services.

GSE—Ground Support Equipment.

HAC—House Appropriations Committee.

HASC—House Armed Services Committee.

I&L—Installations & Logistics.

IFB—Invitation to Bid.

ILS—Integrated Logistics Support.

Indirect Cost Pool—A grouping of incurred costs identified with two or more cost objectives but not specifically identified with any final cost objective.

Integrated Logistic Support (ILS)—A composite of all the support considerations necessary to assure the effective and economic support of a system for its life cycle. The principal elements of ILS related to the overall system include: (1) Maintenance Plan, (2) Support and Test Equipment, (3) Supply Support, (4) Transportation and Handling, (5) Technical Data, (6) Facilities, (7) Personnel and Training, (8) Logistics Support Resource Funds, (9) Logistics Support Management Information.

IOC—Initial Operational Capability.

IR&D—Independent Research & Development.

JCS—Joint Chiefs of Staff.

JSOP—Joint Strategic Objectives Plan.

LCC—Life Cycle Cost.

Learning/Improvement Curve—A mathematical way to explain and measure the rate of change of cost (in hours or dollars) as a function of quantity.

Life Cycle Cost (LCC)—The total cost to the Government of a system over its full life. It includes the cost of development, acquisition, operation, support, and, where applicable, disposal.

Life Cycle of a Weapon System—All phases of the development cycle plus the in-service phase including the phasing out of the system.

LOA—Letter of Agreement (Army); Letter of Offer and Acceptance; Letter of Authorization.

Logistics—The science of planning and carrying out the movement and maintenance of forces. In its most comprehensive sense, those aspects of military operations which deal with: (a) design and development, acquisition, storage, movement, distribution, maintenance, evacuation, and disposition of materials; (b) movement, evacuation, and hospitalization of personnel; (c) acquisition or construction, maintenance, operation, and disposition of facilities; (d) acquisition or furnishing of services.

Long-Lead Items—Those components of a system or piece of equipment for which the times to design and fabricate are the longest, and, therefore, to which an early commitment of funds may be desirable.

Major System Acquisition—A system acquisition program designated by the Secretary of Defense to be of such importance and priority as to require special management attention.

Management Reserve—An amount of the total allocated budget withheld for management control purposes, rather than designated for the accomplishment of a specific task or set of tasks.

Memorandum of Agreement (MOA)—An agreement between a program manager and a Contract Administration Office (CAO), establishing the scope of responsibility of the CAO.

Memorandum of Understanding (MOU)—An agreement between a contractor and a cognizant DOD Administrative Contracting Officer.

MENS—Mission Element Need Statement.

Mission Element Need Statement (MENS)—A statement prepared by a DOD component to identify and support the need for a new or improved mission capability. The mission need may be the result of a projected deficiency or obsolescence in existing systems, a technological opportunity, or an opportunity to reduce operating cost. The MENS is submitted to the Secretary of Defense for a Milestone 0 decision. (Reference DOD Directive 5000.2.)

MOA—Memorandum of Agreement.

MOU—Memorandum of Understanding.

MTBF—Mean Time Between Failure.

MTTR—Mean Time to Repair.

NAVPRO—Naval Plant Representative's Office.

NAVAIR—Naval Air Systems Command.

NAVMAT—Naval Material Command.

NAVSEA—Naval Sea Systems Command.

NMC—Navy Material Command.

O&M—Operations and Maintenance.

O&S—Operating and Support (costs).

Obligational Authority—(1) An authorization by Act of Congress to procure goods and services within a specified amount by appropriation or other authorization. (2) The administrative extension of such authority, as by apportionment or funding. (3) The amount of authority so granted.

OFPP—Office Federal Procurement Policy.

OMB—Office of Management and Budget.

Operating and Support Cost (O&S)—Those resources required to operate and support a system, subsystem, or a major component during its useful life in the operational inventory.

Operational Effectiveness—The overall degree of mission accomplishment of a system used by representative troops in the context of the organization, doctrine, tactical threat, and environment in the planned operational employment of the system.

Operational Test 1 (OT I)—Test of a hardware configuration of a system, or components thereof, to provide an indication of military utility and worth to the user. Testing should refine identified critical issues, report areas that should be addressed in future OT, and identify new ones for subsequent testing. OT I is accomplished during the Validation Phase on brassboard configuration, experimental prototypes to provide data leading to the decision to enter Full-Scale Engineering Development.

Operational Test II (OT II)—Test of engineering development prototype equipment prior to the initial production decision. Its goal is to estimate an item's military utility, operational effectiveness, and operational suitability in as realistic an operational environment as possible. Test objectives are based on the critical issues which are best examined by using elements of/or complete TOE troop units in controlled field exercises.

Operational Test and Evaluation—Test and evaluation conducted to estimate a system's operational effectiveness and operational suitability, as well as the need for any modification.

OSD—Office of the Secretary of Defense.

OT—Operational Testing.

OT&E—Operational Test and Evaluation.

Parametric Cost Estimate—A cost estimating methodology using statistical relationships between historical costs and other program variables such as system physical or performance characteristics, contractor output measures, manpower loading, etc. Also referred to as a top-down approach.

PCO—Procuring Contracting Officer.

Performance Measurement Baseline—The time-phased budget plan against which contract performance is measured.

PERT—Program Evaluation Review Technique.

PM—Program Manager/Project Manager; Program Memorandum.
PMD—Program Management Directive.
PMO—Program Management Office.
PPBS—Planning, Programming, Budgeting System.
Procuring Activity—The command in which the Procuring Contracting Office (PCO) is located. It may include the program office, related functional support offices, and procurement offices.
Procuring Contracting Officer—The Contracting Officer at the purchasing office which awards or executes a contract for supplies or services on behalf of the Government.
Program Evaluation Review Technique (PERT)—A technique for management of a program by constructing a network model of integrated activities and events and periodically evaluating the time/cost implications of progress.
Program Manager—The individual in the DOD chartered to manage a major system acquisition program.
Program Manager Charter—A document stating the program manager's responsibility, authority, and accountability in the management of a major system acquisition program.
Program Objectives—The capability, cost, and schedule goals being sought by the system acquisition program in response to a mission need.
Project Summary Work Breakdown Structure—A summary WBS tailored to a specific defense materiel item by selecting applicable elements from one or more summary WBSs or by adding equivalent elements unique to the project (MIL-STD-881A).

RAM—Reliability, Availability, Maintainability.
R&D—Research and Development.
RDT&E—Research, Development, Test and Evaluation.
Request for Proposal (RFP)—The solicited document between the Government and contractor on a contemplated procurement.
RFP—Request for Proposal.
RFQ—Request for Quotation.
RIW—Reliability Improvement Warranties.
ROC—Required Operational Capability.
ROI—Return on Investment.

SAF—Secretary of the Air Force.
SAR—Selected Acquisition Report (DOD).
SASC—Senate Armed Services Committee.
SECDEF—Secretary of Defense.
SEMP—System Engineering Management Plan.
SOW—Statement of Work.
SPO—System Program Officer (Air Force).
(S)SARC—(Service) Systems Acquisition Review Council.
System—Interacting or interrelated elements forming a collective entity.

System Acquisition Process—The sequence of acquisition activities starting from the agency's reconciliation of its mission needs, with its capabilities, priorities, and resources, and extending through the introduction of a system into operational use or the otherwise successful achievement of program objectives.

System Program Office—The office of the program manager and the single point of contact with industry, Government agencies, and other activities participating in the system acquisition process.

Thresholds—Monetary, time, or resource limitations placed on a program to be used as guides as the program progresses, and the breaching of which is cause for careful review of at least some aspects of the program.

USD(R&E)—Under Secretary of Defense for Research and Engineering (formerly Director of Defense Research and Engineering).

WBS—Work Breakdown Structure.

Work Breakdown Structure—A product-oriented family tree division of hardware, software, services, and other work tasks which organizes, defines, and graphically displays the product to be produced, as well as the work to be accomplished to achieve the specified product.